Reforming the International Financial System for Development

Initiative for Policy Dialogue at Columbia

Initiative for Policy Dialogue at Columbia

José Antonio Ocampo and Joseph E. Stiglitz, series editors

Reforming the International Financial System for Development

Edited by

Jomo Kwame Sundaram

Columbia University Press
New York
2010

Initiative for Policy Dialogue at Columbia
José Antonio Ocampo and Joseph E. Stiglitz, series editors

The Initiative for Policy Dialogue (IPD) at Columbia University brings together academics, policy makers, and practitioners from developed and developing countries to address the most pressing issues in economic policy today. IPD is an important part of Columbia's broad program on development and globalization. The Initiative for Policy Dialogue at Columbia: Challenges in Development and Globalization presents the latest academic thinking on a wide range of development topics and lays out alternative policy options and tradeoffs. Written in a language accessible to policymakers and students alike, this series is unique in that it both shapes the academic research agenda and furthers the economic policy debate, facilitating a more democratic discussion of development policies.

For more information about IPD and its upcoming books, visit www. policydialogue.org.

Columbia University Press
Publishers Since 1893
New York   Chichester, West Sussex
Copyright © 2011 Columbia University Press
All rights reserved
Additional permissions appear in the back of this book.

Library of Congress Cataloging-in-Publication Data
Reforming the international financial system for development / edited by Jomo
Kwame Sundaram.
        p. cm. — (The initiative for policy dialogue at Columbia)
    Includes bibliographical references and index.
    ISBN 978-0-231-15764-3 (cloth : alk. paper)—ISBN 978-0-231-52727-9
    (ebook)
    1. International finance—Government policy. 2. Economic development—
Developing countries. 3. Financial crises—Prevention. I. Jomo K. S. (Jomo
Kwame Sundaram) II. Title. III. Series.

    HG3881.R36165 2011
    332.1'53—dc22

                                    2010017182

∞
Columbia University Press books are printed on permanent and durable acid-free
paper.
This book is printed on paper with recycled content.
Printed in the United States of America

c 10 9 8 7 6 5 4 3 2 1

References to Internet Web sites (URLs) were accurate at the time of writing.
Neither the editor nor Columbia University Press is responsible for URLs that may
have expired or changed since the manuscript was prepared.

A pre-publication limited edition of this book was printed in Istanbul for the G24
ministerial meeting at the October 2009 IMF–World Bank meeting.

Contents

List of Tables

List of Figures

Acknowledgements

I wish to thank the various Chairs and Bureaux of the Intergovernmental Group of Twenty-Four on International Monetary Affairs and Development (G-24) who have consistently supported various initiatives and efforts of the G-24 Research Program since I was appointed Research Coordinator in December 2006. In particular, I wish to acknowledge the leadership of Syrian Central Bank Governor Adib Mayaleh who was chair of the bureau leading up to the G24 ministerial meeting in Istanbul in early October 2009. I also want to thank Amar Bhattacharya for his unstinting support and cooperation. The staff of the G24 Secretariat, Ndzouli Menzouga and Laura Dosreis, as well as Rudiger von Arnim, Sheba Tejani, Sara Burke, Suzette Limchoc and Meriam Gueziel have also been reliable in their support.

Ivan Foo helped in the final copyediting and attended to the typesetting as well as the extensive revisions speedily. Dominik Zotti and Orient Blackswan have helped with copyediting and proofreading.

I thank them all, but implicate none for any remaining shortcomings.

Many of the chapters in this volume are abridged from papers originally commissioned for the G24 research program. Many were presented at technical group meetings in March and September 2009 preceding the spring and annual meetings of the International Monetary Fund and the World Bank.

The chapter by Yılmaz Akyuz was originally written for the South Centre and is published here with its permission, while the chapter by Andrew Cornford was originally written for the DITC in Geneva and will be published under Selected Issues in International Trade, Assuring Development Gains as document UNCTAD/DITC/TNCD/2009/1. The chapter by Jayati Ghosh and the banking chapter by C.P. Chandrasekhar were previously presented at an IDEAs seminar in Beijing in April 2009. Michael Lennard helped prepare David Spencer's chapter for inclusion in this volume.

Jan Kregel kindly prepared an additional chapter at very short notice. I am also indebted to my colleagues Anis Chowdhury, Rob Vos, Pingfan Hong and their colleagues in the Development Policy Analysis Division of the United Nations Department of Economic and Social Affairs for allowing me to draw on material previously prepared for other purposes for the other additional chapter.

Jomo Kwame Sundaram

Contributors

Yılmaz Akyüz is Special Economic Advisor, South Centre, Geneva, and was Director, Division on Globalization and Development Strategies, United Nations Conference on Trade and Development (UNCTAD), Geneva.

C.P. Chandrasekhar is currently Professor and Chair at the Centre for Economic Studies and Planning, Jawaharlal Nehru University, New Delhi, India. He has published widely in India and abroad. He is the co-author of *Crisis as Conquest: Learning from East Asia*, *The Market that Failed: Neo-Liberal Economic Reforms in India* and *Promoting ICT for Human Development: India*. He is a regular columnist for *Frontline* (titled *Economic Perspectives*) and *Business Line* (titled *Macroscan*). Chandrasekhar is a member of the Executive Committee of International Development Economics Associates (IDEAS), an international network of heterodox development economists (www.networkideas.org)

Andrew Cornford is with the Observatoire de Finance, Geneva. He was previously with the Division on Globalization and Development Strategies, United Nations Conference on Trade and Development (UNCTAD), Geneva.

Jane D'Arista is a Research Associate at the Political Economy Research Institute (PERI) at the University of Massachusetts, Amherst, and at the Economic Policy Institute (EPI), Washington, DC. She served as a staff economist for the Banking and Commerce Committees of the U.S. House of Representatives and as a principal analyst in the international division of the Congressional Budget Office. She has lectured in graduate programs at the Boston University School of Law, the University of Massachusetts at Amherst, the University of Utah and the New School University. Her publications include *The Evolution of U.S. Finance*, a two-volume history of U.S. monetary policy and financial regulation. Jane is co-founder of SAFER, an Economists' Committee for Stable, Accountable, Fair and Efficient Financial Reform (www.peri.umass.edu/safer/).

Gerald Epstein is Professor of Economics and Co-Director of the Political Economy Research Institute (PERI), University of Massachusetts, Amherst. His research focuses on topics in international finance and monetary and financial policy. He has consulted for the G24, ILO, UNDP and

UNCTAD, is the author of numerous articles in journals and edited volumes, and is the (co) editor or author of nine books.

Jayati Ghosh is Professor, Centre for Economic Studies and Planning, School of Social Sciences, Jawaharlal Nehru University, New Delhi. She has published widely in India and abroad, and is co-author (with C.P. Chandrasekhar) of *Crisis as Conquest: Learning from East Asia* and *The Market that Failed: Neo-Liberal Economic Reforms in India*. She is a regular columnist for *Frontline* and is Executive Secretary of International Development Economics Associates (IDEAS), an international network of heterodox development economists (www.networkideas.org)

Stephany Griffith-Jones is Head of Research on Financial Programs at the Initiative for Policy Dialogue at Columbia University and was Professorial Fellow at the Institute of Development Studies, University of Sussex. She is author or editor of eighteen books and numerous articles. She has worked for the Central Bank of Chile, the Commonwealth Secretariat, UN ECLAC and UN DESA, and has been consultant for numerous international institutions, such as G24, UNDP, UNCTAD, European Commission and World Bank, as well as several governments.

Eric Helleiner holds the CIGI Chair in International Political Economy at the Balsillie School of International Affairs, University of Waterloo, Canada, and is also Professor in the Department of Political Science, University of Waterloo. He obtained his Ph.D. from the London School of Economics in International Relations in 1991.

Jan Kregel is Rapporteur of the Commission of Experts of the President of the UN General Assembly on Reform of the International Monetary and Financial System, a Program Director at the Levy Economics Institute of Bard College, Distinguished Research Professor at the Center for Full Employment and Price Stability of the University of Missouri–Kansas City and Professor of Development Finance at Tallinn Technological University. He was formerly Chief of the Policy Analysis and Development Branch of the United Nations Financing for Development Office, professor of economics in the Università degli Studi di Bologna, as well as professor of international economics at the Johns Hopkins University's Paul Nitze School of Advanced International Studies.

Jomo Kwame Sundaram is United Nations Assistant Secretary General for Economic Development, Research Coordinator for the G24 Inter-governmental Group on International Monetary Affairs and Development, and a member of the [Stiglitz] Commission of Experts of the President of the United Nations General Assembly on Reforms of the International Monetary and Financial System.

José Antonio Ocampo is Professor of Practice and Co-President of the Initiative for Policy Dialogue at Columbia University, and a member of the [Stiglitz] Commission of Experts of the President of the United Nations General Assembly on Reforms of the International Monetary and Financial System. He was United Nations Under Secretary General for Economic and Social Affairs, Executive Secretary of the Economic Commission for Latin America and the Caribbean (ECLAC) and Finance Minister of Colombia.

Chakravarthi Raghavan is Editor Emeritus, South-North Development Monitor *SUNS*. He is the author of *Recolonization: GATT, the Uruguay Round & the Third World*, Third World Network, Penang, and Zed Books, London, 1990, and *Developing Countries and Services Trade: Chasing a black cat in a dark room, blindfolded*, Third World Network, Penang, 2002.

David Spencer is an attorney in New York, specializing in banking law and taxation. He is Senior Adviser to the Tax Justice Network.

Foreword

The current financial and economic crisis came as no surprise to those who had been warning of the likely repercussions for international finance and the world economy of the bursting of the US housing market bubble and the unsustainability of the massive global imbalances of recent times. In a world of weakly regulated, but closely interconnected financial markets and persistent global macroeconomic imbalances, the resulting adjustments have undermined growth, and continue to damage development prospects in the world economy, especially in developing countries and transition economies which have all become much more integrated into the world economy.

The US current account deficit has been the most widely discussed indicator of the global imbalances. Growing reliance on the greenback as the world's reserve currency is one reason for these imbalances. For the five years preceding the crisis, the US was absorbing more than two billion dollars of other countries' savings daily. The growing US deficits were financed by increasing trade surpluses—in China and other developing countries besides countries like Japan and Germany—used to buy dollar-denominated assets including US Treasury bonds.

The Crisis and the Developing World

Before the current crisis, the world economy had boomed on the basis of strong consumer demand in the US, stimulated by easy credit and soaring house prices, especially on the coasts. In aggregate, US households were spending more than they were earning, made possible by the easy availability of domestic credit on an unprecedented scale. Such borrowing was especially attractive as asset (house and equity) prices kept rising, interest rates remained low, and each new generation of financial innovators persuaded investors that they had mastered risk and overcome the laws of financial gravity. Thus, further lending, even against already over-valued collateral, was successfully presented as signaling more good times ahead.

Warnings about irrational exuberance were largely ignored, especially as US consumer spending helped fuel strong growth performances across the global economy. Robust exports from Japan and Europe supported economic recovery and steadied investor confidence, providing, in turn, further export opportunities for newly industrializing countries, most notably China, as well as primary commodity, especially mineral, exporters.

Meanwhile, greater international competition helped contain inflation, while interest rates remained low, further boosting consumer spending as part of what seemed like a virtuous circle of sustainable growth. At long last, many of the poorest countries seemed to be benefiting, achieving strong growth with rising mineral prices, more foreign mining investments and rising fiscal revenues.

Increasing financial deregulation made it easy to move capital around the world and helped keep the cost of borrowing low. Strong economic performance during the middle of the decade diverted attention away from the unsustainable bases of the seemingly widespread growth. The growing need to correct the global imbalances was ignored by influential market pundits and policy makers who ignored the need to reconsider what seemed to be a winning formula.

Meanwhile, of course, a financial crisis of unprecedented proportions was unfolding. Since late 2007, several major financial institutions in the United States and Europe have failed, as stock market and commodity prices became highly volatile before collapsing. Although far less involved than the mature economies in the most vulnerable financial institutions and instruments, emerging markets have been hit much harder in general, as stock markets and commodity prices collapsed much more than economic growth or even international trade. Not surprisingly, the most financially integrated of the emerging markets, often the transition economies which opted for shock transitions, have been hit hardest. Most businesses, of various sizes and in different activities, have found it much more difficult and costly to obtain credit as banks and other financial institutions became much more reluctant to lend.

All recent forecasts predict a significant slowdown in world economic growth during 2009 while opinions about the future continue to remain sharply divided. Sharp downturns in the United States, Europe and Japan have already slowed growth in developing countries and transition economies. This comes on top of the high food and energy prices from which billions, especially the poorest amongst them, suffered in early and mid-2008 as speculation shifted from stock to mercantile exchanges and Western bio-fuel incentives raised staple food prices. Slower growth, lower commodity prices, reduced employment, higher food prices and other adverse consequences of the crises will undoubtedly set back efforts to achieve the internationally agreed development goals, including the Millennium Development Goals.

The fate of the world—especially of those in developing countries, which have become much more open and economically integrated internationally—clearly depends on international responses to the financial instability and the still spreading economic crisis. The collapse of both property and stock markets has already dampened US household borrowing and demand, triggering a downward spiral well beyond its borders. And if trade protectionism continues to spread, then, the knock-on effects could have even more devastating consequences for all. Other forms of protectionism, affecting international finance as well as migration, are also exacerbating problems, especially in developing countries.

While the ongoing global financial and economic crisis unquestionably has its origins in the West, its consequences have undoubtedly been no less severe for the rest of the world. Discussions of "decoupling" or "de-linking"—so popular in some large developing country capitals during much of 2008—have been relegated to the dustbin of history, even in the economies seemingly least adversely affected by the crisis. Economies in transition, which hastily liberalized their financial systems in the 1990s, have been among the worst hit by the crisis. Many emerging market economies, especially those most financially integrated with the rest of the world, have also been hard hit. Many other developing countries not sufficiently integrated into international financial markets have not been much hit directly by the financial crisis, but most, if not all, have been very adversely affected by the general economic crisis it has precipitated.

Stock markets in emerging market economies plunged by about 50 percent on average, some by more than 60 percent (China and Russia, for example)—much more than the average drop of about 30 percent in rich countries. With the global financial crisis and uncertainty, international investors (pension funds, mutual funds, hedge funds, etc.) became much more risk averse, reducing their exposure to emerging markets, considered riskier than other investments. Some international institutional investors were forced to withdraw by "margin calls" at home, as their losses in developed country markets forced them to withdraw some of their investments from emerging markets. Also, the global financial crisis has seriously weakened growth worldwide, including in emerging markets. As a consequence, earnings in emerging markets will fall, further reducing investor interest in emerging market stock.

FDI inflows to emerging markets were expected to be more stable than short-term equity investments and other portfolio flows. Nonetheless, the global financial crisis has also affected FDI inflows negatively. With total funding available in developed countries tightening, financial crisis and global recession has reduced investments, including investments abroad. To make matters worse, there is considerable evidence of excess economic capacity, exacerbated by the earlier easy availability of cheap credit. With the slowdown, FDI will slow further in 2009, and investment recovery, like job recovery, is expected to lag considerably behind, even after output recovery takes place, owing to the huge overhang of underutilized capacity.

Shrinking economies, especially falling consumption in the United States and other rich countries, have already reduced export opportunities for developing countries, also undermining the strategies favored by conventional wisdom and promoted by the major international financial institutions. Fifty percent of US imports are from developing countries. So, shrinking demand in rich countries will adversely impact developing countries' exports, and consequently, growth prospects. The slowdown in exports of developing countries adversely affects industrial production and overall output growth, especially in the major export-oriented newly industrializing countries, particularly in Asia. In Latin America and Africa, export growth, mainly driven by primary commodities, has also been adversely affected, after half a decade of growth propelled by higher raw material, especially mineral prices.[1] These high commodity prices began to fall sharply from the second half of 2008.

In the short run, developing countries should stimulate domestic demand, so as to offset weakening foreign demand, as China has been doing. But for the poorer countries, the scope for doing so is more limited; they typically need more foreign aid to cope with the drops in export earnings because of weakening commodity prices. In the long run, however, they need to engage in active investment and technology policies to diversify their economies and to reduce their dependence on a few primary commodity exports.

Immediate policy responses are needed to stabilize financial markets and international capital flows, halt economic decline and initiate as well as sustain recovery. Many emerging market economies have also adopted measures to ease credit conditions and stimulate private spending to counter the deflationary impact of the crisis. However, most developing countries face resource constraints in mounting countercyclical policies. More effective policy responses depend critically on adequate international liquidity on appropriate terms and conditions through multilateral financial institutions.

To be sure, finance ministers and central bankers have already injected trillions of dollars into the financial system, lowered interest rates at which they lend to private banks, and embarked on some reflationary policies despite ominous inflationary warnings, especially by market fundamentalists. But while such actions have undoubtedly helped to stabilize financial markets, at least temporarily, they certainly will not be enough to redress the more fundamental problems giving rise to the recent financial turmoil and the ongoing global spread of recession. In today's interdependent world, a coordinated strategy is needed to check and reverse this recessionary dive, to restore lasting stability to financial markets and to create conditions for sustainable development.

Various national rescue packages have sought to calm financial markets and to induce banks to start lending again. Governments have also bailed out several major financial institutions, while new liquidity injections have sought to resume short-term lending to stave off more bank and even corporate failures as well as economic recession. Most measures taken to date have sought to keep international finance—and presumably, the world economy—afloat. The failure of the international community to contain the economic fallout from the financial crisis highlights the lack of real progress since the Asian crisis over a decade ago despite the promise then of a new international financial architecture.

Instead, as the late Robert Triffin observed in the 1970s, since the end of the Bretton Woods system in 1971, we have had a "non-system" instead. Various financial innovations and financial market liberalization, especially across borders, have combined with inadequate and inappropriate financial regulation, including the fiction of self-regulation, to enhance financial rents in recent decades. Financial lobbies have successfully promoted national and international reforms to this end, with national regulation in such circumstances opening new opportunities for regulatory and other arbitrage. Monetary and financial stability have been the victim, with the frequency and severity of financial crises growing in the wake of financial liberalization and globalization.

Developing Countries and the Post-Crisis Reform Agenda

The crisis has also broadened support for fundamental reform of the international financial system to ensure greater stability and to prevent disruptive crises with global ramifications, though it is unclear whether this will result in the kind of changes needed. Developing countries have a much greater stake in such reform due to the much greater damage caused to them by international financial instability. For developing countries, the reforms must address IMF governance and operations, while ensuring adequate policy space in managing the financial system, financial globalization as well as exchange rates.

It is now time to search for solutions, and this obviously requires an understanding of the deeper causes of the present crisis, due to global imbalances and financial deregulation carried too far. While there has been some modest progress on harmonizing standards and extending surveillance, there has been little attention to systemic problems related to unregulated private capital flows. As the problems are global and systemic, the solutions should be likewise to be effective. The present system of global economic governance has proven inadequate to prevent financial instability precipitating the current crisis. In this crisis, as with others in recent decades, there has been little else but *ad hoc* fixes, instead of developing a truly multilateral system for policy coordination and reserve management.

Efforts to safeguard global economic stability have been undermined by the vastly greater resources of private finance little constrained by national boundaries, uncoordinated national and regional policy responses, as well as the domination of multilateral financial institutions by the rich and powerful. The marginalization of the Bretton Woods institutions in run up to the current crisis has been further aggravated by their reduced legitimacy due, in part, to their biased governance arrangements, lending conditionalities and policy advice.

With global recession in 2009, global imbalances are declining for the wrong reasons, with the collapse of international trade. With the urgent need for stronger, multilaterally coordinated reflationary measures, austerity measures should not be recommended at this time to correct global imbalances. Rather, the US needs to export much more in order to achieve balance, while surplus countries should have less reason to accumulate reserves. Also, more productive investments are needed in most developing countries, especially the poorest countries, to resume economic development. Policy makers need the required policy—especially fiscal and monetary—space to move in this direction. Institutionalizing inclusive international economic surveillance and policy coordination will be important in the longer-term, but much more needs to be done soon to rebalance global demand and improve exchange rate management.

A well coordinated response will need to address immediate short-term problems and develop medium-term solutions while accelerating recovery from the world economic recession. Only appropriate financial system reforms can provide a lasting solution to the global imbalances and address the threats posed by unfettered international finance. Making progress will require all governments to act through inclusive multilateral organizations and arrangements. Despite the IMF's skewed governance and policy record, which has undermined its legitimacy and credibility in the developing world, there is no other inclusive multilateral monetary and financial organization available for the time being. Strengthening IMF resources, without reforming the institution adequately, risks exacerbating the inequities of the international monetary and financial system, and its limited existing multilateral governance arrangements.

The international monetary and financial system was reformed at Bretton Woods in 1944 due to a series of deliberate political decisions. After all, with its entry into the war, the US economy had surged very strongly from a decade of uncertainty; the recovery following President Franklin Delano Roosevelt's New Deal during his first term (1933-1937) had given way to pressures to balance the budget which, in turn, undermined the recovery of the mid-1930s. The need to reform the international monetary system was hardly a compelling priority in the middle of the war while the UK, under Churchill, preferred a bilateral agreement with the US without involving the rest of the world.

Although the United Nations Organization only formally came into being in San Francisco in 1945, the United Nations Conference on Monetary and Financial Affairs was held for almost a month at the foot of Mount Washington in New Hampshire in the preceding year. Forty four countries were represented, including 28, mainly from Latin America, which would be deemed developing countries today. The Bretton Woods conference envisaged a system of post-war international economic governance as part of the nascent post-war United Nations system of inclusive multilateralism involving a post-colonial world. Besides seeking to ensure international monetary and financial stability, post-war international economic governance would also seek to ensure the conditions for sustained economic growth and employment generation as well as post-war reconstruction and post-colonial economic development. All these systemic reform objectives continue to remain relevant six and a half decades later, not only for developing countries, but also in the interests of maintaining the conditions for sustainable development, global justice, world peace and inclusive multilateral cooperation on a variety of fronts such as climate change.

This Book: The Crisis, Developing Countries and Reform Priorities

This volume has been prepared by the G24 research program in order to enhance common understanding of the origins, consequences and policy implications of the ongoing global financial and economic crisis from the perspectives of the broad range of developing countries. As important as they are, it does not seek to directly address the current debates on the origins of the financial crisis in the rich western economies as well as the appropriate policy responses except in so far as these have a direct bearing on the broad range of developing countries.

Hence, for instance, it is important to favorably consider the significance of the United Nations' (2009) plea for global macroeconomic policy coordination, especially in so far as available simulations suggest that all economies—developed and developing, economies in transition as well as the least developed countries—will be better off with such a coordinated response. A well coordinated multilateral response promises to yield more than the mere sum of its parts in the form of uncoordinated national responses. The case for multilateral macroeconomic coordination also serves as a compelling argument against "beggar thy neighbor", "go it alone" protectionist policies likely to further proliferate as the crisis becomes more protracted.

As the world experiences its worst financial crisis since the 1930s, policy makers are increasingly calling for a new Bretton Woods conference. To claim the mantle of the historic 1944 conference, Eric Helleiner's opening chapter argues for more creative and ambitious thinking about international financial reform than has been the case so far. The global financial crisis of the early 1930s generated bold thinking about the need to assert more public authority in international finance. Thus, Bretton Woods involved genuine innovations in global financial governance designed to better regulate international financial markets, address global imbalances, and promote international development. Policy makers today should minimally address all the major issues identified at Bretton Woods, but the reform agenda put forward so far by the G20 leaders has fallen well short of the Bretton Woods precedent. Helleiner reminds us that some long-forgotten proposals from the Bretton Woods negotiations—such as those relating to debt restructuring, heterodox financial and macroeconomic policy advice for developing countries, and the role of international cooperation in controlling capital movements—should also be revisited.

New reforms, more appropriate to contemporary circumstances, should also be considered. A contemporary agenda to regulate international financial markets must, of course, assess new mechanisms and address a broader range of topics than in 1944. The management of global imbalances needs to address the reserve currency status of the greenback as well as regional cooperation options. The requirements of sustainable development must also consider contemporary international prudential regulatory initiatives. A broader governance agenda should also seek to make international financial institutions—including, but not only the

Bretton Woods institutions—more inclusive and open to the principles of subsidiarity and regionalism.

C.P. Chandrasekhar reviews some implications of recent trends in global liquidity and financial flows to emerging markets before the current financial and economic crisis in the second chapter, emphasizing the robust revival in capital flows to developing countries after the slump following the 1997-1998 East Asian financial crisis. He argues that following financial liberalization, supply-side factors better explain the resurgence in cross-border flows, rather than the financing requirements of recipient countries. Increasingly, the investment decisions of key individuals in a few major financial institutions determine the exposure and vulnerability of the global financial system as cross-border capital flows are largely intermediated by these institutions. This has exacerbated the concentration of risk and vulnerability to financial crisis in markets to which these flows gravitate.

Chapter three reviews the origins and impact of the worst world recession since the 1930s, due to an unsustainable growth pattern, related global imbalances as well as weaknesses in the global financial and economic system. Despite some signs of recovery, its strength and sustainability remain in doubt. The crisis did not originate in developing countries, which have nevertheless been severely hit by commodity price collapses, tighter global credit conditions, lower remittances and new forms of protectionism. Poverty and hunger are increasing, and major reversals in hard-won progress towards the internationally agreed development goals, including the Millennium Development Goals (MDGs) are likely. Many of the most vulnerable have been hit hardest, while there is increased risk of accelerated environmental degradation and greater social tensions. The severity and extent of the crisis also provides an opportunity to respond by ambitiously reforming the international financial and economic system, including international economic governance, in order to address the crisis in an integrated fashion by creating the international institutional arrangements conducive to equitable and sustainable development.

In chapter four, Jayati Ghosh explains the dramatic world food price spikes in 2007-2008 as largely due to greater speculative activity in global commodity markets, enabled by earlier financial deregulation and the flight of capital from Wall Street following the bursting of the housing bubble with the sub-prime mortgage market crisis. Despite the subsequent fall in agricultural prices, food prices remain higher than before 2007, and remain volatile in many developing countries. Of course, the neglect of public investments in food agriculture since the 1980s with the abandonment of food security commitments as well as the recent advent of Western bio-fuel subsidies have also exacerbated the situation. Meanwhile, the financial crisis has worsened food insecurity by constraining public investment in agriculture, limiting food imports in balance of payments constrained developing countries, causing exchange rate devaluation due to the reversal of capital inflows, and adversely affecting employment and incomes, thereby reducing the ability to buy food.

Yılmaz Akyüz reviews major immediate and medium term proposals for policy responses to the global financial crisis by developing countries in chapter five. He discusses deficiencies in the global institutional arrangements for crisis management as well as the international initiatives undertaken thus far. Akyüz critically assesses the constraints developing countries face in trying to respond more adequately and appropriately to the crisis. This is followed by a discussion of crisis prevention as well as crisis management, before reviewing other significant reform and major policy proposals from the perspective of developing countries.

Jane D'Arista and Stephany Griffith-Jones suggest, in chapter six, that the agenda and criteria for financial regulatory reform has to be carefully considered in view of the differing circumstances, experiences, capacities and capabilities of various economies in the global financial system. They argue that liberalization of financial markets, not accompanied by appropriate regulation, has been a major cause of costly crises, especially in the last two decades. In recent decades, a shadow banking system has emerged, which remains opaque and unregulated. D'Arista and Griffith-Jones argue that regulatory reform needs to be comprehensive in order to avoid regulatory arbitrage. Such reform should also strive to be countercyclical to try to compensate for the inherently pro-cyclical behavior of financial markets. Their chapter proposes some key criteria for financial regulatory reform involving capital provisions and liquidity requirements, bearing in mind the perspectives and needs of developing countries.

In chapter seven, Andrew Cornford examines the ongoing revisions to Basel II, the international standards for bank regulation developed by the Basel Committee on Banking Supervision (BCBS) to replace the 1988 Basel Capital Accord (Basel I). The 2006 text of Basel II, following a protracted drafting process, had been considered closed before the current crisis began in mid-2007. The crisis has shown up major shortcomings in the regulatory framework for financial institutions now also the subject of wide-ranging reform efforts. The ongoing emphasis on capital adequacy actually shaped the crisis by encouraging regulatory arbitrage The introduction of Basel II is already proceeding, or about to proceed, in a large number of emerging-market and other developing countries. Cornford argues that the Basel II rules may engender new problems in the future. In the absence of appropriate controls, banks may be exposed to risks associated with cross-border asset-backed investments as well as investments linked to operations in their own financial markets.

As the international financial crisis spread, most governments began searching for means to protect themselves, with some resorting to "unconventional tools" of monetary and financial policy, alongside more "conventional" ones. In chapter eight, Gerald Epstein argues that policies to better manage international capital flows should be part of the government "toolkits" in facing these difficult challenges. After describing the economic arguments for and against using capital controls, prudential regulations and other "capital management techniques" to manage international financial flows, he reviews empirical evidence on their impacts and the variety of policies countries have successfully implemented to achieve macroeconomic and financial stability, enhance policy space, and achieve other national development goals.

In chapter nine, Chakravarthi Raghavan examines the critical role of the World Trade Organization (WTO) in promoting the liberalization and globalization of financial services, and considers its implications for global financial reform efforts. A reformed global financial regime will not be compatible with further liberalization of the trade in financial services and capital movements. However, the ongoing global financial crisis and the systemic reform processes being initiated in various forums seem likely to lead to some governance reforms, better regulation and stricter enforcement in the public interest. However, these are unlikely to succeed unless they consider and involve the WTO and its ongoing Doha Round, and its negotiations for the further liberalization of services, particularly the "trade in financial services". Raghavan also shows that these trade negotiations have not been informed by reliable data.

David Spencer makes the case, in chapter ten, for significantly enhanced international tax cooperation, not only to enhance economic justice, but also to enhance fiscal space, especially in developing countries. Developments contributing to cross-border tax evasion are reviewed, set within a broader discussion of the need for more effective supervisory and regulatory regimes. He notes the systemic risks posed by regulatory arbitrage, including encouraging tax evasion, and emphasizes the need for cooperation among a larger group of countries in crafting a new Bretton Woods-type agreement to address such issues. A discernible change in public attitudes to tax evasion has become more apparent recently. Spencer concludes by calling for the automatic exchange of tax information.

In another chapter, C.P. Chandrasekhar argues that the crisis is encouraging serious consideration of a new global banking model as banking crises cannot be resolved without sufficient capital infusions tantamount to nationalization. Deregulation had been brought about by earlier regulation which did not adequately compensate the private owners of finance. But deregulation also triggered processes leading to crisis which, in turn, require nationalization as the solution. Chandrasekhar's chapter eleven urges developing countries to *reverse* the movement from public to private ownership of banks, and to consider the advantages of public ownership, especially to ensure more equitable and broad-based growth. Public ownership would also allow bank profits to be low in order to be able to direct credit to sectors and groups at "subsidized" interest rates in order to garner higher social returns from more equitable, inclusive and sustainable development supported by appropriate financial, investment, technology and employment policies.

In chapter twelve, Jan Kregel provides the economic rationale for the proposals to reform the international monetary and financial system made by the United Nations 63rd President of the General Assembly's Commission of Experts chaired by Joseph Stiglitz. Divided into six chapters, its final report considers both macroeconomic and financial regulatory failures leading to the global financial and economic crisis as well as challenges of international economic governance and systemic reforms. Clarifying the rationale for the reform proposals facilitates understanding the systemic reasons for the report's seeming recommendation of institutional proliferation. In the spirit of Bretton Woods, the proposals are not only concerned with macro-financial reforms for greater financial risk mitigation and monetary stability, but also with creating the conditions for more equitable and sustainable development in light of contemporary conditions.

Finally, in chapter thirteen, José Antonio Ocampo urges reforming the global reserve system in light of three fundamental problems of the *status quo*. First, it has a deflationary bias as the burden of adjustment falls on deficit countries. Second, it has inherent sources of instability associated with the use of a national currency as the major reserve asset and the high demand for foreign exchange reserves by developing countries, due to the pro-cyclical nature of cross-border capital flows and the inadequate availability of "collective insurance". Third, it exacerbates inequities by transferring resources to reserve currency issuing countries. Instead, Ocampo argues for a system based on the countercyclical issue of Special Drawing Rights (SDRs) to finance IMF facilities, and suggests the "development" potential of SDR allocations. For Ocampo, the dollar fiduciary standard overcame Keynes' deflationary dilemma, but like Akyuz, he favours a non-national fiduciary standard, seeing no need for a commodity reserve alternative.

Note

1. Various issues of the United Nations' *World Economic and Social Survey* and *World Economic Situation and Prospects* as well as UNCTAD's *Trade and Development Report* have reiterated the risks of heavy dependence on primary commodity exports which do not have strong linkages with the domestic economy. Such economies tend to be very vulnerable to external shocks.

Reforming the
International Financial System for Development

1

Contemporary Reform of Global Financial Governance: Implications of and lessons from the past

Eric Helleiner

As the world experiences its worst financial crisis since the 1930s, there is a widespread sentiment that bold innovations in global financial governance are needed. Reflecting this mood, many analysts have begun to call for a Bretton Woods II, invoking the 1944 conference that established the post-war international financial order. Even some leaders took up the banner during the lead-up to the first G20 leaders' summit in November 2008 that was called to draw lessons from the crisis and set an agenda for global financial reform. The global financial reforms endorsed by the G20 process so far, however, have not matched these ambitions. If they are to claim the mantle of Bretton Woods, policy makers will need to think more creatively.

This chapter suggests that there are, in fact, important lessons to be learned from the Bretton Woods experience for those searching for a more ambitious vision. The contemporary relevance of the Bretton Woods conference is that policy makers then were driven by a similar goal as those today: the *desire to assert public authority in the realm of international finance in the wake of a major international financial meltdown.* This overall goal culminated in three sets of proposals at Bretton Woods which were genuine innovations in global financial governance: 1) those designed to regulate international financial markets more tightly, 2) those aimed at addressing global economic imbalances, and 3) those promoting international development. For policy makers seeking to move beyond the G20 reform agenda, this chapter suggests that the three innovations could provide some inspiration at this moment. Even a number of the detailed—and often long-forgotten—mechanisms to achieve these goals may deserve revisiting today. At the same time, given how the world has changed, a Bretton Woods II must tackle these issues in some ways that are different from Bretton Woods I. It must also embrace a broader governance agenda of making international financial institutions—including, but not restricted to, the Bretton Woods institutions—more inclusive as well as more open to the principles of subsidiarity and regionalism.

The Bretton Woods Precedent

The international financial crisis that began in 2007 is generating a significant backlash against the lack of accountability of many private actors in international financial markets. Left to their own devices, global markets have created a mess. After the liberalizing and deregulatory trends of the past few decades, many analysts and policy makers are calling for public authority to be reasserted in the international financial arena.

The architects of Bretton Woods drew a similar lesson from the momentous international financial crisis of the early 1930s. Before that crisis, the world of international finance had been dominated by private international financiers as well as central banks, most of which were still privately owned at that time. Those groups favored a *laissez faire* order in which financial capital moved freely across borders and international payments imbalances were corrected by the automatic mechanism of the international gold standard. When the system came crashing down in the early 1930s, that liberal vision and its supporters lost their privileged position in international financial politics. If a multilateral financial order was to be rebuilt, it was clear that it would need to be one in which governments played a more active role.

This view was held particularly strongly by the New Dealers from the US who played the lead role in the Bretton Woods negotiations. They had blamed the financial crisis and Great Depression on the recklessness of private bankers, especially the internationally-oriented New York financial community. The first years of the New Deal were spent asserting greater public control over the US financial system by creating new regulations over the markets as well as by bringing the Federal Reserve System under tighter public control. When wartime pressures encouraged ambitious thinking about the post-war world order, New Deal policy makers began also to consider the possibility of creating what Treasury Secretary Henry Morgenthau called a "New Deal in international economics" (quoted in Van Dormael, 1978: 52).

With their country likely to emerge from the war as the dominant economic power, US policy makers were determined to play a leadership role in rebuilding a multilateral international economic order. The closed economic blocs and economic instability of the 1930s were believed to have contributed to the Great Depression and World War II. But US policy makers did not want to see a return to the classical liberal international economic order of the pre-1930s' era. Instead, they sought to reconcile liberal multilateralism with the new interventionist economic policies that had been pioneered in the New Deal and elsewhere. This objective was shared by John Maynard Keynes who had emerged as lead policy maker in charge of British planning for the post-war world economy during the early 1940s. Both Keynes and his American counterpart, Harry Dexter White, saw the goal of bringing international finance under greater public control as a central objective of their blueprints. To achieve this goal, they advanced three sets of proposals, each of which signaled a major innovation in global financial governance. Not every specific idea put forward within each of the three categories ended up in the final Agreements. But some of those that were discarded deserve mention, not just to highlight the bold vision of the negotiators, but also because they may be useful for ambitious reformers today to revisit.

International Financial Regulation

The most dramatic departure from pre-1930s norms concerned the treatment of cross-border movements of private financial capital. Although countries agreed to make their currencies convertible for current account transactions under the Articles of Agreement of the newly created International Monetary Fund (IMF), they were given the right to control all capital movements under Article VI. Capital controls were also encouraged by the fact that IMF resources could not be used to cover "large or sustained outflows of capital" (quoted in Helleiner, 1994: 49). The contrast with post-World War I thinking could not have been more dramatic. The Brussels International Financial Conference of 1920 had passed a resolution condemning all barriers to the international movement of capital (League of Nations, 1920: 9). Now, an international agreement endorsed the use of capital controls in a comprehensive and unambiguous manner. As John Maynard Keynes put it: "What used to be a heresy is now endorsed as orthodox" (quoted in Helleiner, 1994: 25).

The Bretton Woods architects were under no illusions about the difficulties involved in controlling financial flows given the fungibility and mobility of money. But the seriousness of their commitment was made clear in two ways in the IMF charter. First, to curtail capital movements, governments were entitled to use comprehensive exchange controls in which all transactions—capital account *and* current account—could be scrutinized for illegal financial flows (as long as payments for current account transactions were not restricted). Second, the negotiators also endorsed the idea that each government might help to enforce the capital controls of other governments. During the lead up to the 1944 conference, Keynes and White had discussed how this kind of cooperation might involve governments sharing information about financial holdings within their countries that contravened other countries' controls, or helping foreign efforts to repatriate capital through regulations or the taxing of foreigners' holdings. At one point, White even suggested that governments could be asked to stop inflows of capital that were considered illegal in the sending country (Helleiner, 1994: ch. 2).

These ambitious plans were not designed to stop all private financial flows. In fact, the Bretton Woods architects strongly welcomed "equilibrating" private international financial flows and those designed for "productive" investment (Helleiner, 1994: 36). Indeed, they hoped that their overall effort to re-establish international currency stability would revive these kinds of private flows. But by explicitly permitting governments to control *all* financial movements, the IMF's Articles of Agreements were written to give states the maximum freedom to decide which financial movements were desirable and which were not.

The Bretton Woods architects were particularly concerned about speculative and "disequilibrating" capital movements. There was widespread agreement that these movements had severely disrupted efforts to stabilize exchange rates in the interwar period. Many also feared that their volatility could undermine efforts to foster the expansion of international trade after the war. Even more important was the concern that these cross-border financial flows would undermine the policy autonomy of government to pursue macroeconomic planning. In addition, policy makers sought to protect governments from having their policy agendas thwarted by capital flight motivated by "political reasons" or the desire to evade domestic taxes or "the burdens of social legislation" (quoted in Helleiner, 1994: 34).

Public Management of Global Imbalances

The Bretton Woods architects also sought to assign public authorities a more conscious and active role in the management of international economic imbalances. The international gold standard had been idealized by classical economic liberals because it promised an automatically self-correcting international monetary order. In theory (although not in actual practice), international imbalances under the gold standard were corrected promptly and efficiently by market forces, rather than the discretionary behavior of governments. By requiring all countries to fix their currencies' value to the dollar, which in turn was convertible into gold, the Bretton Woods conference appeared to re-establish an international gold standard—or to be more precise, a "gold exchange" standard or "gold-dollar" standard. But several other features of the agreements made it clear that this was to be an international monetary order in which public authorities played a much more central role.

To begin with, governments were allowed to adjust the par value of their currency whenever their country was in "fundamental disequilibrium". Second, the IMF would provide short-term loans to help countries finance their temporary balance of payments deficits, thereby soften the kind of external discipline that private speculative financial flows and the gold standard had imposed. The IMF was also given the broader task of promoting global monetary and financial cooperation among governments. The most important part of this mandate involved encouraging countries to change policies that might be generating large international economic imbalances. Its lending capacity gave it some potential influence over deficit countries. But another clause in its charter—the scarce currency clause—also provided a means for official pressure to come to bear on surplus countries. If the Fund's resources were drawn upon so extensively by deficit countries that its ability to supply a surplus country's currency was threatened, the IMF could declare that currency "scarce". Member governments would then be permitted to impose temporary restrictions on trade with that country.

These various provisions gave public authorities a much more active role in the management of international economic imbalances. It was not just that national governments were assigned this role, but also that an international public authority, the IMF, had been created to look out for the global public interest. The only existing international financial institution at the time was the Bank for International Settlements, created in 1930, whose principle mandate had been that of addressing war debt and reparations issues and whose members were central banks. The IMF, by contrast, had a much broader mandate and its members were politically-accountable government officials.

The New International Development Vision

The third major innovation embodied in the Bretton Woods Agreements was the creation, *for the first time*, of an official international commitment to promote the "development" of poorer member countries through mechanisms of international finance. This commitment was outlined most clearly in the creation of an international public institution with this goal as one of its two central purposes: the International Bank for Reconstruction *and Development* (IBRD). The conventional view is that the Bank's development mandate "arrived almost by accident and played a bit role at Bretton Woods" (Kapur, Lewis and Webb, 1997: 68). More generally, it is widely assumed today that the Bretton Woods architects had little interest in development issues and the concerns of poorer countries. This conventional wisdom understates the interest in international development issues at the time, and has led scholars to overlook a number of innovative proposals put forward during the Bretton Woods negotiations to make the international financial system serve poor countries more effectively (Helleiner, 2006, 2009c).

To understand the innovative nature of Bretton Woods thinking in this area, it is important first to locate the negotiations within the context of broader post-war planning. This planning process was launched by Roosevelt's and Churchill's 1941 Atlantic Charter which set out very broad aspirations for all the world's peoples, aspirations that Roosevelt compared to those of the US constitution and the British Magna Carta. One of the central commitments in the Atlantic Charter was an "assurance that all the men in all the lands may live out their lives in freedom from fear and want" (quoted in Borgwardt, 2005: 304). The concept of guaranteeing "freedom from want" had been developed earlier that year by Roosevelt and reflected his belief that the promotion of the economic security of individuals throughout the world would provide a crucial foundation for post-war political stability, domestically and internationally. In this way, he and other US policy makers sought to make the promotion of development in poorer countries an international responsibility for the first time (Borgwardt, 2005; see also Staples, 2006).

The earliest phases of US planning for Bretton Woods were strongly influenced by this sentiment. In his first draft for the World Bank in 1942, White suggested that all members should have to "subscribe publicly to a 'Magna Carta of the United Nations'" which would constitute "a bill of rights of the peoples of the United Nations" (quoted in Oliver, 1975: 319). White and other US officials had, in fact, already endorsed the creation of an international institution to promote development in Latin American countries in 1939-40. This "Inter-American Bank" (IAB) initiative was part of the broader New Deal "Good Neighbor" policy towards the region at the time and its goal was to provide public capital that would support the development goals of national governments. Although opposition from isolationists and conservatives in the US Congress as well as New York financial interests prevented the IAB from being established, the first US drafts of the IMF and IBRD in early 1942 drew very heavily on the IAB precedent and inherited its commitment to promoting development goals (Helleiner, 2006, 2009c).

The most obvious continuity in this respect was the commitment to provide international public funds via the IBRD to support the economic development of poorer countries. Far from being an accident, the Bank's mandate to promote development was strongly endorsed at the time. The commitment to large-scale public international development lending was widely shared in US policymaking circles during the war, and reflected a deep distrust of the ability of private markets to serve the new development agenda that the Roosevelt administration had committed to (Helleiner, 2009c). These sentiments were strongly supported by many other delegations to Bretton Woods, particularly those from poorer countries. It is often forgotten that well over half the countries attending Bretton Woods were from non-industrialized regions. Latin America was particularly well represented with 19 of the total 44 delegations at the conference.[1] When the USSR suggested that the IBRD focus on reconstruction loans for war-devastated areas, the Latin American delegations mobilized successfully to insist that the Bank's development mandate have at least equal standing (Oliver, 1975: 184, 188). The delegates representing still-colonized India (who were both Indian nationals and British citizens) also strongly backed the Bank's development function and even pressed for the IMF to focus more explicitly on distinct development priorities of poorer countries (Kapur, Lewis and Webb, 1997: 60; Gold, 1971: 270-276). Strong support for the development function of the Bank also came from the Chinese delegation (Eckes, 1975: 91).

There were three other ways in which US policy makers attempted to integrate development goals into the post-war international financial architecture, each of which has been largely overlooked by scholars of Bretton Woods despite their contemporary relevance. The first relates to the problem of capital flight from poor countries. This issue had interested US officials during the IAB discussions because Latin American capital flight to New York had increased considerably during the 1930s. To recycle this capital, US policy makers had suggested that the Bank be allowed to accept private deposits and issue bonds directly to Latin American citizens, and then lend the funds back to the region for developmental purposes in ways that would "assure to each country the availability of the savings of its citizens" (quoted in Helleiner, 2009c). In his first drafts on the Bretton Woods institutions, Harry Dexter White abandoned that specific proposal since it had been strongly opposed by New York banks. In place of recycling the funds via an international public institution, he chose instead to recommend the control of flight capital, noting that the Fund's endorsement of capital controls would be particularly useful to poorer countries for this reason (Horsefield, 1969: 67).

US policy makers also sought to address the question of restructuring the debts of poorer countries. The issue had been controversial in US-Latin American relations in the wake of widespread Latin American defaults on external debt in the early 1930s. As far back as 1933, some Latin American governments had proposed the creation of an international institution that could renegotiate these debts in a manner that avoided the kind of heavy-handed creditor interference of the past. This issue reappeared in the late 1930s when US financial assistance to the region was opposed by financial interests who felt it should not go to countries that had not settled their debts with US private lenders. Frustration with this opposition prompted some in the US Treasury to suggest that the proposed IAB could appoint independent arbiters to force settlements of outstanding debts.

White's first drafts of the Fund and IBRD picked up on this proposal. He gave the Fund the ability to engage in "compulsory arbitration" by including a rule that member governments could not default on external loans "without the approval of the Fund" (Horsefield, 1969: 44, 71). In the case of the Bank, early drafts prevented it from lending to governments in default on a foreign loan, but an exception was made if the government "has agreed to renew service of the defaulted debt on a basis worked out by a special committee appointed by the Bank for that purpose" (quoted in Oliver, 1975: 292). The idea that new post-war international financial institutions could assist in debt restructuring, found support in the US State Department and elsewhere. Ultimately, however, it was withdrawn from negotiations, partly because of concerns that it might encourage more defaults and partly because of Morgenthau's longstanding opposition to US government involvement in any debt-collecting arrangements (Helleiner, 2008).

The final way that US policy makers attempted to bring development concerns into the realm of international finance also did not find its way in any formal sense into the final Bretton Woods Agreements, but it was influential and widely welcomed across Latin America. Beginning in the early 1940s, the US Federal Reserve launched a set of financial advisory missions to the region explicitly intended to signal the new US interest in supporting Latin American development objectives. Instead of prescribing orthodox gold standard policies as US "money doctors" had in the 1920s, the new US advisors explicitly sought to boost the ability of Latin American governments to build more diversified, industrialized and inward-focused national economies by endorsing the use of capital controls, activist monetary policy aimed at domestic goals, adjustable exchange rate pegs and government-controlled central banks. This "heterodox" advice was in keeping with the overall Bretton Woods vision, and the officials involved in these missions initially saw their advisory work as an activity that the post-war international institutions could soon take over. While the advice of US money doctors in the 1920s had been almost identical in every country, US officials also now insisted on adapting their advice to the distinctiveness of each country's circumstances and needs. They also gave very high priority to learning from Latin American expert views as well as including country officials in the process of developing the reform proposals and encouraging intra-Latin American expert exchanges (Helleiner, 2009a).

What Relevance Today?

In what ways, if any, is this history of the Bretton Woods experience relevant to the contemporary context? As we experience the worst global financial crisis since the early 1930s, it is perhaps not surprising that some similar political reactions are emerging. Bankers find themselves under attack, and governments everywhere are being called upon to reassert their authority in global finance. Responding to this mood, US President Bush convened the G20 leaders' summit in November 2008 with the goal of setting an agenda for global financial reform. Analysts, and even some leaders, raised expectations that the summit would be a kind of sequel to Bretton Woods. This section compares the agenda for reform endorsed by the G20 leaders so far to that of Bretton Woods across the three areas outlined above. The comparison reveals how cautious the G20 agenda has been to date. But it also provides a framework for thinking about how the agenda could be made more ambitious, if leaders so wished. This is not to suggest that all the specific proposals discussed at Bretton Woods deserve revisiting. Different circumstances today require that policy makers think through problems considered at Bretton Woods in new ways.

Widening the Agenda of International Regulation

The G20 reform agenda has focused heavily on the question of the regulation of international financial markets. But the meaning has been quite different than at Bretton Woods. Instead of discussing capital controls, they have focused primarily on the task of strengthening various provisions of an international prudential regulatory regime that governments have constructed in a piece-meal fashion since the mid-1970s and which sets common standards for national regulators to follow. The G20 leaders have outlined a number of initiatives that will fill holes in the existing international regulatory framework relating to a wide range of issues involving banks, credit rating agencies, derivatives markets, hedge funds, and accounting practices. They have also committed to move beyond the usual calls for improved transparency and risk management to address the pro-cyclicality of existing regulatory frameworks.

Because the Bretton Woods architects did not anticipate the re-emergence of highly integrated global financial markets, they devoted no attention to the need for this kind of international prudential regulation. The G20 initiatives are important in filling this gap. At the same time, however, the G20 have devoted much less attention to the kinds of regulations on cross-border flows that occupied the Bretton Woods architects. Rodrik and Subramanian (2008) question this neglect. They note that the recent financial bubble experienced by the US was exacerbated by large-scale capital inflows in a similar way that earlier crises in developing countries—such as the debt crisis of the early 1980s and the 1997-1998 crises—were preceded by massive inflows of capital which generated bubbles in those countries (see also Reinhart and Rogoff, 2008; Wolf, 2008). Given these experiences, they argue that an agenda of reducing capital mobility could play a role in minimizing future international financial crises. Indeed, they go further to suggest that this agenda may be more important than efforts to strengthen international prudential regulation since the latter will never be able to keep up with financial innovation. As they put it, "if the risk-taking behavior of financial intermediaries cannot be regulated perfectly, we need to find ways of reducing the volume of transactions…. What this means is that financial capital should be flowing across borders in smaller quantities, so that finance is 'primarily national', as John Maynard Keynes advised" (Rodrik and Subramanian, 2008).

In specific terms, Rodrik (2009) has recommended that developing countries strengthen their "counter-cyclical capital-account management"; that is, they restrict excessive foreign borrowing in good times and control capital flight during crises. Although these policies are already permitted under the IMF's Articles of Agreement, Rodrik suggests that the IMF should be more active in advising on their national implementation (see also South Centre, 2008). Rodrik also backs two international regulatory proposals. The first was also endorsed by the Bretton Woods architects: the sharing of information about financial holdings that may contravene other countries' tax laws. Rodrik is particularly concerned about how developing country governments have trouble gaining accurate information on the deposits of their wealthy citizens abroad, but the problem also affects developed countries, especially *vis-à-vis* tax havens. A number of international initiatives have been launched in recent years to address this issue and this is one area where the G20 leaders have taken some important new initiatives to strengthen compliance with tax information sharing agreements.

The G20 did not, however, endorse the other initiative supported by Rodrik: the Tobin tax. First put forward in the 1970s by Nobel laureate James Tobin, the initiative would introduce a very small transaction tax (Rodrik suggests 0.25 percent) on all foreign exchange transactions. Tobin's (1978) case for the tax paralleled the arguments of the Bretton Woods architects: it would discourage short-term, speculative cross-border financial movements that are causing socially-disruptive adjustments to trade patterns, exchange rates and governments' policy autonomy. At the same time, the tax would not interfere with more desirable and more productive long-term financial movements since its level would be quite insignificant as a cost item. Given the widespread criticism of international financiers at the moment, the tax might be seen by the general public as an appropriate discipline to apply against their past behavior. Support for the tax may also be generated by the fact that it would provide considerable revenue—as much as several hundred billions of dollars each year—which could be used for a variety of public purposes, including not just the funding of fiscal deficits at the national level, but also international initiatives to address development or global environmental issues. Although some dismiss the Tobin tax on the grounds that it would require the cooperation of every country in the world, others have highlighted that the coordination problems are grossly exaggerated (e.g. Cooper, 1994: 141; Ul Haq, Grunberg and Kaul, 1996).

Managing Global Imbalances in New Ways

The recent crisis has also raised the question of whether public authorities need to take a more active role in the management of global imbalances. Many analysts argue that the crisis was caused at least partly by large imbalances that had emerged in recent years, with the US running enormous current account deficits funded by capital from surplus countries, particularly oil exporters and the most successful East Asian exporters. The G20 leaders have largely ignored this issue, in part because major deficit and surplus countries blame each other for the problem. To move this debate forward, it may be useful to reiterate the Bretton Woods principle that both surplus and deficit countries should share responsibility for addressing global imbalances.

The specific international public mechanisms needed to foster this goal, however, will be very different from those put forward at Bretton Woods (BW). The BW architects hoped that the IMF could play the key role in prompting both deficit and surplus countries to undertake adjustments by virtue of its central position in the international monetary system. But the IMF has little influence in this situation today because the surplus countries' currencies are not becoming "scarce" in the Fund and because the major deficit country, the US, has no intention of borrowing from the institution. In this context, the IMF's recent efforts to encourage cooperation by strengthening the multilateral surveillance process are laudable, but unlikely to have significant impact.

Other international mechanisms deserve consideration. Looking first at the United States, the international policy problem is the opposite of the one that Keynes faced at Bretton Woods. Keynes had worried about the traditional asymmetry between deficit and surplus countries, where the latter faced less immediate market pressures to adjust than the former. Today, we are faced with a situation that he did not anticipate: the most important deficit country faces few constraints. The dollar's role as world currency has enabled the US to delay adjustments as foreigners finance its current account deficits with dollar holdings. It is for this reason that a number of analysts and policy makers have been discussing the possibility of scaling back the dollar's international role as part of the international reform agenda.

The agenda has been given a further push because of fears of a collapse of confidence in the dollar, given the US's financial difficulties and the emergence of alternative international currencies such as the euro. International currencies are sustained in part by a kind of inertia; people continue to use a specific currency because other people use it. If there was a sudden change of expectations, a "tipping point" could be reached where foreign support for the dollar's international role could diminish quite quickly. Dollar crises in the past—recall 1971, 1978-79, and 1987—have been associated with worldwide instability. To minimize this risk, it would be helpful if a mechanism could be developed to enable those governments wishing to diversify their reserves away from dollars to do so without generating a major dollar crisis.

Precisely such a mechanism was negotiated during 1978-80 by the top G5 policy makers, with the strong support of US and IMF officials (Gowa, 1984). Under this proposal, foreign governments would have been allowed to deposit dollars in a special "substitution account" at the IMF and be credited in certificates denominated in the IMF's currency: Special Drawing Rights (SDRs). Because this exchange was off-market, foreign governments would have been able to diversify their assets without undermining the value of the US dollar. Of course, there would have been some costs. Assets denominated in SDRs are less liquid than those in dollars. The IMF account also risked losing money if the dollar fell, since its liabilities were denominated in SDRs whereas its assets were dollar-denominated US Treasury bills. Efforts to shift this exchange rate risk to the IMF—by asking the Fund to back the account with its gold holdings—ultimately complicated the negotiations. When the dollar rose sharply after US monetary policy tightened dramatically in 1979, the issue left the global public policy agenda.

Proposals for a substitution account deserve to be considered again today. Prominent US economists such as Fred Bergsten (2007, 2009)— who was involved in the 1978-80 discussions—have raised the idea and Chinese officials have expressed interest in it (Zhou, 2009). By boosting the role of the SDR, the initiative would work towards Keynes's goal—laid out in his initial Bretton Woods drafts—of centering the international monetary system more firmly on a supranational form of money. If this multilateral solution proved too difficult to negotiate, Peter Kenen (2005) has also suggested that the European Central Bank (ECB) could create a special facility that bought dollars from other central banks in exchange for newly-issued, off-market, *euro* instruments. This proposal would enable the ECB to minimize the risk of a dollar sell-off that would generate a further appreciation of the euro. US and European officials could even share the exchange rate risk if the Europeans were to exchange some portion of the US Treasury bills they purchase for special euro-denominated US T-bills.

What about surplus countries? As Martin Wolf (2008) has recently noted, a key reason many developing countries have been accumulating such large foreign exchange reserves is their fear of financial crises; more specifically, they seek to insulate themselves against a repetition of the kinds of financial crises experienced in the 1980s and 1990s. If developing countries could be persuaded to pool their reserves with the IMF and draw on them when needed with minimal conditionality, Wolf notes that they would feel less compelled to hold such large reserves (at considerable financial cost to themselves). This solution would have sounded very familiar to the Bretton Woods architects. Unfortunately, however, the IMF's recent record has undermined trust in it among potential borrowers. Policy makers in many developing countries have preferred costly self-insurance against balance of payments crises rather than reliance on an institution whose recommendations in the recent past have been seen as unhelpful, too intrusive, and/or overly influenced by US and European goals.

An important step on the road to reducing global imbalances is thus to reform the IMF in a more serious manner to regain the trust of developing countries. The G20 leaders have committed to advance the reform of the Bretton Woods institutions to give emerging and developing economies greater voice and representation. Alongside this reform, there needs to be a shift in the style and content of the IMF's advice. In this context, Triffin's money-doctoring missions could act as a possible model for rebuilding trust in the institution among developing countries. These missions were welcomed across Latin America because they took seriously the concept of "country ownership" and showed openness to a diversity of policy approaches (including the kinds of capital controls recommended by Rodrik).

If surplus countries continued to have misgivings about the IMF, it may be that other international institutions—particularly those at a more regional level—could be useful. Already, East Asian countries have been expanding regional cooperation of this kind through the Chiang Mai Initiative. With the largest reserves in the world, the countries in this region have the capacity to create a regional reserve pooling arrangement that could dwarf the size of the IMF. European Union countries are also being called upon to take a large role in crisis-lending to Eastern European countries. In Latin America, initiatives to expand the regional provision of balance of payments finance are also being considered. If meaningful IMF reform continues to prove politically difficult, these regional arrangements are likely to become more important.

This regionalization trend would allow for greater pluralism in international financial governance. The existence of regional development banks has long enabled quite regionally distinct approaches to development lending. Mistry (1999) argues that the case for pluralism may even be stronger in the area of balance of payments financing given some of the problems that have been associated with the IMF's monopoly in the past. Some might object that this trend will undermine the Bretton Woods commitment to multilateralism. But it is important to remember that the European Payments Union ended up playing a very constructive and complementary reserve-sharing role in the early years of the Bretton Woods system. Some supporters of regional institutions, such as the South Centre, have even suggested that the IMF could emerge in the future "as the apex of a network of regional reserve funds—that is, a system closer in design to the European Central Bank or the Federal Reserve System than to the unique global institution it currently is…. A denser network of institutions seems better adapted to a heterogeneous international community, and it is likely to provide better services and give stronger voice to smaller countries" (South Centre, 2008: 4).

Strengthening Development Priorities in International Finance

Finally, what has been the place of development issues in the international reform agenda? The widening of the G7 to the G20 at the leaders level was intended to provide key developing countries with a voice in setting the agenda. One would then expect development issues to assume a more prominent place. At the first summit, the G20 communiqué did reaffirm commitments to the Millennium Development Goals and the principles of the 2002 UN Conference on Financing for Development in Monterrey, including that of "country ownership and mobilizing all sources of finance for development" (G20, 2008). In addition to the IMF and World Bank governance issues already mentioned, the G20 leaders also encouraged international financial institutions and aid donors to maintain and enhance financial support for developing countries. These points reiterate some principles embodied in the original Bretton Woods development agenda.

On the international regulatory reform agenda, the G20 also declared its support for "capacity-building programs" relating to "the formulation and the implementation of new major regulations" (G20, 2008). The more dramatic goal, however, is that of expanding the membership of the Financial Stability Forum (FSF)—which has played a lead role in coordinating the international regulatory response to the crisis—and other major standard setting bodies to include more developing countries. These bodies have been dominated by industrialized countries in the past. At the April 2009 G20 summit, the FSF was transformed into a stronger Financial Stability Board (FSB) whose membership was expanded to include all G20 countries. Other narrowly constituted standard setting bodies also invited key developing countries as new members in 2009, such as the Basel Committee on Banking Supervision, the Technical Committee of the

International Organization of Securities Commissions, and the Committee on Payment and Settlement Systems. These efforts to make international regulatory bodies more inclusive still leave many developing countries outside the decision making process. But they will provide at least some developing countries with more opportunities to inject "development" content into the international regulatory reform agenda.

So far the development content of this reform agenda has not been prominent beyond the governance question just mentioned. To be sure, some parts of this agenda involve issues that have been of great importance to developing countries in the past, such as sharing tax information, the content of Basel II or the regulation of hedge funds. But the distinct contributions of developing countries to debates on these issues do not appear to have been prominent so far. Other parts of the regulatory reform agenda may raise opportunities to explore links between financial regulation and development problems that have not received much attention before. For example, the initiative to bring greater order and regulation to derivatives markets may provide a chance for developing countries to raise questions about the relationship between speculation in commodities futures markets and the recent food crisis (IATP, 2009).

Are there other international regulatory issues that have not been raised at all by the G20 leaders that could be put on the agenda? The Tobin tax has been mentioned above and it might be particularly attractive for developing countries if the revenue it raised could be used for international development assistance. Another initiative might be Rodrik's proposal for the IMF to take a more active role in encouraging counter-cyclical capital account management. The Bretton Woods negotiations suggest two additional regulatory issues that might be of special interest to developing countries—the regulation of debt restructuring and capital flight.

The case for creating an orderly multilateral mechanism for facilitating debt restructuring parallels that for domestic bankruptcy rules. Because sovereign debt crises can be caused, or at least exacerbated, by "rushes to the exit" in the form of capital flight, the international legitimization of a standstill on payments in these circumstances would be helpful to sovereign debtors *and* private creditors alike. Once crises have broken out, the resolution of sovereign debt crises has also often been a messy and time-consuming affair that has been damaging to the interests of both private creditors and sovereign debtors. In that context, all can benefit from a clear set of international rules and procedures that force holdout creditors to accept the terms of debt restructuring, impose stays on litigation during restructuring negotiations, and perhaps outline provisions for the extension of new credits during restructuring exercises. Of course, debtors can *unilaterally* prevent rushes to the exit by introducing exchange controls and can set the terms of debt restructuring through *unilateral* debt write-downs. But the experiences of the 1930s and more recently of Argentina show that debtors undertaking these actions on their own face the threat of creditor retaliation and litigation, as well as damage to their reputation as a borrower. An international mechanism that legitimizes and supports these actions will minimize these risks (Helleiner, 2008).

These kinds of arguments have generated support for some kind of international bankruptcy mechanism, not just in the early 1940s, but also during 1980s' debt crisis and, more recently, with the very detailed IMF proposals during 2001-2003 for a "sovereign debt restructuring mechanism" (SDRM) (Rogoff and Zettlemeyer, 2002). As the IMF's then senior Deputy Managing Director Anne Krueger (2001) put it in 2001, the absence of such a mechanism is a "gaping hole" in the governance of international finance. Although her proposed SDRM failed to gain enough support, it helped generate momentum for two more limited initiatives to address this issue after 2003. The first was the inclusion in all new international bond issues of collective action clauses (CACs) which allow for such provisions as altering repayment terms by a super majority of bondholders and restrictions on individual creditors from disrupting restructuring processes.

The second was the creation of a set of voluntary international "principles" in 2004 to govern the behavior of both debtor governments and private creditors relating to issues such as information sharing, transparency, commitments to dialogue and cooperation, good faith actions in debt restructurings, and equal treatment of all investors in cases of default (Helleiner, 2009b). These "Principles for Stable Capital Flows and Fair Debt Restructuring in Emerging Markets" were the product of negotiations between a small group of developing countries (Brazil, Mexico, Turkey and South Korea) and private international financial interests, most notably the Institute of International Finance (IIF) which represents the world's major international banks. They were welcomed by the G20 finance ministers and central bank governors at the time. The IIF subsequently established a "Group of Trustees" to review the implementation and further development of the Principles which includes senior representatives of the private international financial sector as well as prominent officials and ex-officials from industrialized and emerging market countries. That Group provides guidance to a twenty-three member "Principles Consultative Group" (PCG) made up of senior private financial sector members and emerging market government officials (with the former in the majority), which evaluates individual country situations and provides advice to private creditors and governments about compliance with the Principles and any possible amendments to them. The PCG receives technical support from the IIF and includes, as observers, a representative of the Federal Reserve Bank of New York and IMF staff (Principles Consultative Group, 2008).

These initiatives represent an advance in the international regime for debt restructuring, but their limitations are likely to be exposed during the current crisis. Most CACs do not include aggregation provisions for the terms of a country's debt restructuring to be extended across all categories of bonds. CACs also do not usually endorse standstill provisions, but rather are designed primarily only to facilitate the restructuring of sovereign debts *after* a crisis had broken out. In addition, CACs leave many of the key decisions concerning debt restructuring in the hands of private creditors, rather than allocating them to an independent arbiter or sharing power more equally with sovereign debtors in a formal institutional setting. The dominant role of the private sector in the governance of the Principles is also open to criticism, as is their voluntary nature and ambiguous content in many areas (Herman, 2008). Finally, neither CACs nor the Principles include commitments of the kind recently endorsed in the December 2008 Doha Declaration from the follow-up conference to the 2002 Monterrey summit. The declaration stated that the objectives of debt resolution must include "furthering development" and "taking into account debtors' national policies and strategies linked to attaining the internationally agreed development goals, including the Millennium Development Goals" (UN, 2008). The current moment offers an opportunity to try to address these various issues (see also Herman, 2008).

The other development issue raised during the Bretton Woods preparations that deserves more attention today is the regulation of capital flight. Estimates of the size of capital flight from developing countries vary considerably, but for many of the poorest debtor countries, the private assets of their wealthy citizens abroad surpass the size of their official debt. In other words, these countries are often creditors to the world at the very time that they are experiencing debt crises (e.g. Ndikumana and Boyce, 2008). If this private capital could be brought home—or discouraged from leaving in the first place—the development prospects of these countries would be enormously improved. Some argue that flight capital can only be stopped by changing the afflicted countries' economic policies such as overvalued exchange rates or inflationary monetary policies. This view ignores the extent to which capital flight may be related to other factors such as tax evasion, political instability or corruption. For these reasons, many analysts argue that capital controls have a role to play—usually alongside various economic stabilization measures—in stemming capital flight.

In many poor countries, however, the capacity of the state to enforce capital controls effectively is not very high. Here is where the ideas of Keynes and White about the role of international cooperation in boosting the effectiveness of capital controls may be relevant. They noted how capital controls can be enforced more easily if recipient countries help by sharing information about foreign holdings, by directly assisting efforts to repatriate funds or even by blocking capital inflows in the first place. It is often forgotten that international cooperation of this kind was implemented in a very modest way during the Marshall Plan when the US assisted some European efforts to track flight capital in the US by sharing information about these assets. The issue was also debated during the Latin American debt crisis of the 1980s when a number of observers suggested that US banks should be prompted to share information with Latin American governments about the assets of Latin America citizens they held as well as to refrain from soliciting flight capital from Latin America (Helleiner, 1995, 2001).

This "Bretton Woods moment" may be the time to consider whether some kind of international cooperation stemming capital flight could be embedded permanently within the international financial architecture. In their initial drafts, both Keynes and White had, in fact, intended international cooperation to control capital movements to be mandatory (Helleiner, 1994: ch. 2). Today, this could easily be accomplished by simply widening the definition of money laundering activities used by the international community—and for which extensive arrangements do not exist for international information sharing—to include capital flight (e.g. Sherman, 1993: 13; Lissakers, 1991: 158). A limited move in this direction has come with the World Bank-UN Stolen Asset Recovery Initiative—an initiative which the G20 leaders endorsed at their November 2008 summit. But the assets it targets make up only a small portion of flight capital. A more wide-ranging initiative would be in keeping with the initial ideas of Keynes and White. In this context, it is encouraging that the recent Doha follow-up conference to Monterrey called for strengthening multilateral efforts to address capital flight (UN, 2008).

If wider initiatives involving permanent mandatory cooperation were too ambitious, the idea could be implemented on a more temporary basis in the context of financial crisis management. When a crisis breaks out, the IMF could be empowered to require foreign governments to share information about capital flight from the crisis-hit country. This might appeal to developed countries if it reduced the potential costs of financial bailouts by slowing capital flight and by enabling the mobilization of existing flight capital. During the Marshall Plan era, a number of interesting proposals of this latter kind were considered by the US government, including one IBRD proposal that would have seen a portion of the European flight capital invested in either US or IBRD bonds with the proceeds used for aid or loans to European governments. During the 1980s' debt crisis, proposals were also made to tax the interest income earned by the US deposits of Latin American citizens and to give the proceeds to the Inter-American Development Bank (Helleiner, 1995; Williamson and Lessard, 1987). These efforts to recycle flight capital back to the original capital via international public lending echo the ideas that US Treasury officials pioneered in the late 1930s in developing the IAB initiative.

In addition to boosting resources available to debtor countries, this proposal might also have two other benefits. First, it would help spread the distribution of the adjustment burden within the country experiencing a financial crisis in a more equitable fashion. When international creditors pressure debtor governments to assume the private foreign debt of their citizens as part of crisis-management procedures, the burden of adjustment to private borrowing behavior—usually that of more wealthy citizens—is shifted to the country as a whole. By mobilizing flight capital in crisis moments to help service the external debt of the country, the international community would ensure that wealthier citizens contributed more to the resolution of the crisis as well. Second, the existence of this kind of procedure at the international level might also discourage flight capital in the future. At the moment, there are strong incentives for wealthy domestic asset holders in poorer countries to engage in capital flight at the first sign of an impending crisis. Not only do they protect their money from a potential devaluation or imposition of capital controls in this way, but they also have the prospect of "round-tripping" the money after a devaluation to buy up domestic assets at bargain prices. If domestic asset holders were aware that their foreign assets might be mobilized for public purposes as part of a financial rescue plan, they might be less inclined to flee so quickly.

Conclusion

The G20 leaders' summit in November 2008 invariably invited comparisons with Bretton Woods. At both meetings there was a shared desire to assert public authority more centrally into the international financial system in the wake of a devastating international financial crisis. But the G20 leaders have so far been much more cautious than their Bretton Woods predecessors in laying out an agenda to achieve this goal. This chapter has suggested that the three broad innovations in global financial governance outlined at Bretton Woods may serve as useful road map if policy makers want to set their sights higher: the regulation of international financial markets, the management of global imbalances, and the promotion of international development.

Some of the specific long-forgotten proposals the Bretton Woods architects put forward in each of these three categories also deserve reconsideration today, such as those relating to debt restructuring, heterodox financial advice for developing countries, and the role of international cooperation in efforts to control capital movements. This is not to suggest that history should simply repeat itself. If the Bretton Woods objectives are to be met in the contemporary context, a number of the proposals they discussed would need to be adjusted to the new economic and political circumstances. Efforts to regulate international financial markets today must go far beyond the border control issues addressed at Bretton Woods to strengthen international prudential rules. For those wanting to curtail speculative international financial flows, the Tobin tax provides a new approach not considered at Bretton Woods. With respect to the management of global imbalances, the Bretton Woods principle that both surplus and deficit countries have shared responsibilities needs to be reinforced via new mechanisms such as an international substitution account and reformed reserve pooling arrangements at the global and regional levels. The promotion of international development must also be extended to cover the new international prudential regulations being developed.

Important to all these areas is also the need for governance reform to adjust international financial institutions to today's more decentralized international political environment. At the Bretton Woods conference, US leadership within the multilateral Bretton Woods institutions was simply assumed. Today, the world is changing in ways that make governance questions a much more important part of the agenda of global financial reform. It is not just a question of giving developing countries more say in the Bretton Woods institutions as well as in the FSB and other standard-setting bodies. Also significant is the need to consider decentralizing international financial governance by assigning more tasks to the regional level. At the same time, greater resort to a principle of subsidiarity via regional arrangements in international financial governance must be grounded within the broad multilateral framework set not just by the Bretton Woods institutions, but also the United Nations system more generally.

This last point deserves special emphasis for those seeking to build a new Bretton Woods. As we have seen, from the very start, US policy makers in the early 1940s intended the planning for the post-war international financial order to be situated within the larger process of creating the UN system. It is no coincidence that the formal title of the Bretton Woods meeting was the "United Nations Conference on Monetary and Financial Affairs". In the lead-up to the conference, British policy makers had pressed at various moments for bilateral negotiations, but US policy makers insisted on a more inclusive multilateral meeting which included not just smaller industrialized countries, but also countries from the non-industrialized world (Helleiner, 2006). In the contemporary period, the US decision to create a summit of the G20 leaders for the first time in November 2008 marked an important effort to be more inclusive of emerging powers in discussions of global financial reform. If the goal is to build a new Bretton Woods order, however, the process will need to be embedded within a more representative, inclusive and universal political framework.

Note

1. Beyond Latin America, other non-industrialized countries from outside Europe that were represented at the conference included China, Egypt, Ethiopia, India, Iran, Iraq, Liberia, Philippines and South Africa.

References

Bergsten, Fred (2007). How to solve the problem of the dollar. *Financial Times*, 11 December.

Bergsten, Fred (2009). We should listen to Beijing's currency idea. *Financial Times*, 9 April.

Borgwardt, Elizabeth (2005). *A New Deal for the World*. Harvard University Press, Cambridge, MA.

Cooper, Richard (1994). What future for the International Monetary System? In Siklos Pierre (ed.). *Varieties of Monetary Reforms*. Kluwer Academic Publishers, London.

Eckes, Alfred (1975). *A Search for Solvency: Bretton Woods and the International Monetary System, 1941-1971*. University of Texas Press, Austin.

G20 (2008). *Declaration of the Summit on Financial Markets and the World Economy*, Washington, DC, 15 November. Available at http://www.whitehouse.gov/infocus/financialmarkets/

Gold, Joseph (1971). 'To contribute thereby to…development…': Aspects of the relations of the International Monetary Fund with its developing members. *Columbia Journal of Transnational Law*, 10 (2): 267-302.

Gowa, Joanne (1984). Hegemons, international organizations, and markets: The case of the substitution account. *International Organization*, 38 (4): 661-683.

Helleiner, Eric (1994). *States and the Reemergence of Global Finance*. Cornell University Press, Ithaca.

Helleiner, Eric (1995). Handling 'hot money': US policy towards Latin American capital flight in historical perspective. *Alternatives*, 20: 81-110.

Helleiner, Eric (2001). Regulating capital flight. *Challenge*, 44 (1): 19-34.

Helleiner, Eric (2006). Reinterpreting Bretton Woods: International development and the neglected origins of embedded liberalism. *Development and Change*, 37 (5): 943-967.

Helleiner, Eric (2008). The mystery of the missing sovereign debt restructuring mechanism. *Contributions to Political Economy*, 27 (1): 91-113.

Helleiner, Eric (2009a). Central bankers as good neighbors: US money doctors in Latin America during the 1940s. *Financial History Review*, 16 (1): 1-21.

Helleiner, Eric (2009b). Filling a hole in global financial governance? The politics of regulating sovereign bond restructuring. In Walter Mattli and Ngaire Woods (eds). *The Politics of Global Regulation*. Princeton University Press, Princeton.

Helleiner, Eric (2009c). The development mandate of international institutions: Where did it come from? *Studies in Comparative and International Development*, 44 (3): 189-211.

Herman, Barry (2008). Why the code of conduct for resolving debt crises falls short. Working Paper Series, February, Initiative for Policy Dialogue, Columbia University, New York.

Horsefield, John (1969). *The International Monetary Fund 1945-1965: Twenty Years of International Monetary Cooperation – Volume 1*. International Monetary Fund, Washington, DC.

Institute for Agriculture and Trade Policy (IATP) (2009). Betting against food security. January. http://www.iatp.org/iatp/publications.cfm?refid=105065

Kapur, Devesh, John Lewis and Richard Webb (1997). *The World Bank: Its First Half Century*. Brookings, Washington, DC.

Kenen, Peter (2005). Stabilizing the international monetary system. *Journal of Policy Modeling*, 27: 487-493.

Krueger, Anne (2001). International financial architecture for 2002: A new approach to sovereign debt restructuring. Address given at the National Economists' Club Annual Members' Dinner, 26 November, American Enterprise Institute, Washington, DC. Available at: http://www.imf.org/external/np/speeches/2001/112601.htm

League of Nations (1920). *International Financial Conference, 1920, Vol. 1*. The Dewarichet, Brussels.

Lissakers, Karin (1991). *Banks, Borrowers and the Establishment*. Basic Books, New York.

Mistry, Percy (1999). Coping with financial crises: Are regional arrangements the missing link? In UNCTAD. *International Monetary and Financial Issues for the 1990s*. United Nations, New York.

Ndikumana, Leonce, and James Boyce (2008). Capital flight from Sub-Saharan Africa. *Tax Justice Focus*, 4 (1): 5-6.

Oliver, Robert (1975). *International Economic Co-operation and the World Bank*. Macmillan, London.

Principles Consultative Group (2008). Report on implementation by the Principles Consultative Group. October, Institute of International Finance, Washington, DC.

Reinhart, Carmen, and Kenneth Rogoff (2008). Is the 2007 US financial crisis so different? An international historical comparison. *American Economic Review*, 98 (2): 339-344.

Rodrik, Dani (2009). Let developing nations rule. *Vox*, 28 January. http://www.voxeu.org/index.php?q=node/2885

Rodrik, Dani, and Arvind Subramanian (2008). Why we need to curb global flows of capital. *Financial Times*, 26 February.

Rogoff, Kenneth, and Jeromin Zettelmeyer (2002). Bankruptcy procedures for sovereigns: A history of ideas, 1976-2001. *IMF Staff Papers*, 49 (3): 470-507.

Sherman, Tom (1993). International efforts to combat money laundering: The role of the Financial Action Task Force. In David Hume Institute. *Money Laundering*. Edinburgh University Press, Edinburgh.

South Centre, Statement by Board Members of (2008). South Centre calls for revamping the global financial architecture. 29 October, South Centre, Geneva. http://www.southcentre.org/index.php?option=com_content&task=view&id=871&Itemid=1

Staples, Amy (2006). *The Birth of Development*. Kent State University Press, Kent, OH.

Tobin, James (1978). A proposal for international monetary reform. *Eastern Economic Journal*, 4: 153-159.

Ul Haq, Mahbub, Isabelle Grunberg and Inge Kaul (eds) (1996). *The Tobin Tax*. Oxford University Press, New York.

UN (2008). *Doha Declaration on Financing for Development*. 2 December. United Nations, New York.

Van Dormael, Armand (1978). *Bretton Woods: Birth of a Monetary System*. Macmillan, London.

Williamson, John, and Donald Lessard (eds) (1987). *Capital Flight and Third World Debt*. Institute for International Economics, Washington, DC.

Wolf, Martin (2008). *Fixing Global Finance*. Johns Hopkins University Press, Baltimore.

Zhou Xiaochuan (2009). Reform the international monetary system. March 24, People's Bank of China, Beijing. http://www.pbc.gov.cn/english/detail.asp?col=6500&id=178

2

Global Liquidity and Financial Flows to Developing Countries: New trends in emerging markets and their implications[1]

C.P. Chandrasekhar

After a slump in cross-border flows of capital in the years following the East Asian financial crisis, international financial flows have seen a robust revival in recent years. The magnitude of cross-border transactions has grown exponentially during the current decade. Further, qualitative changes that accompanied this quantitative expansion have transformed the nature of the financial integration of developing countries with their developed country counterparts.

This chapter examines: (i) the factors responsible for this surge in capital flows into developing countries; (ii) the qualitative changes in financial integration accompanying this surge; and (iii) the impact that this surge is having on financial volatility and vulnerability, macroeconomic management and growth, in countries that have been "successful" in attracting such flows. Besides data from developing countries as a group, evidence from one country that epitomizes the effects of the recent surge in capital flows, viz. India, is used to illustrate the effects that recent trends have on macroeconomic policy and growth.

Measuring the absolute size of globally dispersed finance capital is indeed a difficult proposition. Given the diversity of agents, instruments and markets and the lack of transparency in certain over-the-counter markets, it is extremely difficult to gauge the size of the corpus that functions as international finance. Nevertheless, available figures do point to galloping growth in the global operations of financial firms.

One obvious form this has taken since the international lending boom of the late 1970s is the expansion of operations of international banks in less developed countries, especially the so-called "emerging markets". The net result has been an increase in the international assets of the big banks of the developed world. This trend has only gained strength in recent years. At the time of the East Asian crisis (mid-1997), the international asset position of banks resident in 23 countries reporting to the Bank of International Settlements stood at US$9.95 trillion, involving US$8.6 trillion in external assets after adjusting for local assets in international currencies (BIS, 1997). By June 2007, when 40 countries were reporting, this had risen to US$33.71 trillion, with external assets totaling US$29.98 trillion (BIS, 2007). This expansion in international assets was not only the result of the increase in the number of reporting countries.[2] The trend was visible in countries that reported on both dates as well. For example, the international assets of UK-based banks had increased from US$1.5 trillion to US$6.1 trillion, and that of US banks from US$0.74 trillion to US$2.8 trillion.

But this was not all. Increasingly non-bank financial firms—pension funds, insurance companies and mutual funds—have emerged as important intermediaries between savers and investors. According to a Bank of International Settlements study (Committee on the Global Financial System, 2007: 5), the total financial assets of institutional investors stood at US$46 trillion in 2005. Of this, insurance firms accounted for close to US$17 trillion, pension funds for US$12.8 trillion and mutual funds for US$16.2 trillion. The United States dominated, accounting for as much as US$21.8 trillion of institutional investors' assets, while the United Kingdom was far behind at just US$4 trillion. Here too, growth has been rapid with total assets more than doubling between 1995 and 2005 from US$10.5 trillion in the US and US$1.8 trillion in the UK. The assets of autonomous pension funds in the US, for example, rose from US$786 billion in 1980 to US$1.8 trillion in 1985, US$2.7 trillion in 1990, US$4.8 trillion in 1995, US$7.4 trillion in 2000 and US$8 trillion in 2004 (OECD, 2001, 2003)

Besides these institutions there are other less regulated and opaque institutions, particularly highly leveraged institutions like hedge funds and private equity firms, which directly manage financial assets for high net worth individuals, besides the institutional investors themselves. Assets managed by around 9000 surviving hedge funds are now placed at around US$1.6 trillion (Financial Stability Forum, 2007). And, according to one study, private equity assets under management were nearing US$400 billion

Table 2.1 Developing countries and other emerging markets: External financing, 1997-2006 (US$ bn)

	1997	1998	1999	2000	2001	2002	2003	2004	2005	2006
Balance on Current Account	-85.6	-113.4	-21.2	85.8	39.4	77.3	147.6	212.6	428.0	544.2
Net external financing	360.1	265.9	230.7	240.3	182.2	173.5	311.0	479.6	607.0	785.5
Non-debt-creating flows	197.7	185.7	184.8	202.1	171.4	151.3	190.0	283.6	371.1	491.0
Capital transfers	19.8	6.4	9.5	21.0	1.9	-2.5	7.7	8.3	5.6	44.2
FDI and equity security liabilities	177.9	179.3	175.3	181.1	169.5	153.8	182.3	275.2	365.5	446.7
Net external borrowing	162.4	50.2	45.9	38.2	10.9	22.2	121.0	196.0	235.9	294.5
Borrowing from official creditors, of which:	13.0	42.7	34.5	-8.1	24.1	10.6	0.7	-6.4	-50.9	-64.5
– credit and IMF loans	3.3	14.0	-2.4	-10.9	19.0	13.4	1.7	-14.9	-39.9	-30.1
– borrowing from banks	9.6	9.4	-13.0	-10.9	-12.5	-18.0	13.8	30.8	40.1	57.8
– borrowing from other private creditors	139.9	28.1	24.3	57.2	-0.8	29.6	106.4	171.6	246.6	301.2

Note: External financing is defined as the sum of — with opposite sign — the goods and services balance, net income and current transfers, direct investment abroad, the change in reserve assets, the net acquisition of other assets (such as recorded private portfolio assets, export credit, and the collateral for debt-reduction operations), and the net errors and omissions. Thus, net external financing, according to the definition adopted by the IMF, measures the total amount required to finance the current account, direct investment outflows, net reserve transactions (often at the discretion of the monetary authorities), the net acquisition of non-reserve external assets, and the net transactions underlying the errors and omissions (not infrequently reflecting capital flight).

Sources: International Monetary Fund. *World Economic Outlook*. Biannual, Statistical Appendices, various issues.

in the United States and just under US$200 billion in Europe. Private equity expansion is also reportedly strong, with aggregate deal value growing at 51 percent annually from 2001 to 2005 in North America (Bloomberg and Schumer, 2006).

Flows to Developing Countries

This massive expansion of finance capital has been accompanied by a substantial increase in capital flows to developing countries. Net external financing flows which had fallen from US$360.1 billion in 1997 to US$173.5 billion in 2002, have since risen sharply to US$785.5 billion in 2006. While foreign direct and portfolio investment increased from US$153.8 billion in 2002 to US$446.7 billion in 2006, net external borrowing rose from US$10.9 billion in 2001 to US$294.5 billion in 2006. Thus, underlying the surge was an expansion in both investment and debt flows to developing countries.

Do Developing Countries Need this Capital?

While the search for higher interest rates and larger capital gains underlies the surge in capital flows, these flows are not required by most developing countries for balance of payments financing purposes. Between 2002 and 2006, when external financing to developing countries and emerging markets (as defined by the IMF) rose from US$174 billion to US$786 billion, developing countries and emerging markets as a group (as defined by the IMF) recorded consistent current account surpluses, with the surplus rising from US$77.3 billion to US$544 billion. What is more, a few developing countries recording either small deficits or large surpluses on their current account received the major share of external financing.

The argument that still sounds credible is that such flows help finance the investment boom that underlies the acceleration of growth in developing countries. If the evidence from a successful emerging market like India is any indication, there does seem to be some basis for this argument. Between 2003-2004 and 2006-2007, which was a period when foreign institutional investor (FII) inflows rose significantly and stock markets were buoyant most of the time, equity capital mobilized by the Indian corporate sector rose from Rs676.22 billion to Rs1,771.7 billion (Figure 2.1).

Not all of this was raised through equity issued in the stock market. In fact, a predominant and rapidly growing share, amounting to a huge Rs1,455.71 billion in 2006-2007 was raised in the private placement

Figure 2.1 Mobilization of capital through equity issues

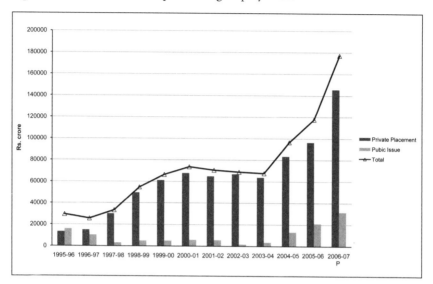

Source: Reserve Bank of India. *Handbook of Statistics on Indian Economy, 2007.*
Tables 77 and 82. Available at http://rbidocs.rbi.org.in/rdocs/Publications/
DOCs/80257.xls and http://rbidocs.rbi.org.in/rdocs/Publications/
DOCs/80262.xls. Accessed 2 January 2008.

market, involving negotiated sales of chunks of new equity in firms not
listed in the stock market to financial investors of various kinds such as
merchant banks, hedge funds and private equity firms. While not directly
part of the stock market boom, such sales were encouraged by the high
valuations generated by that boom and were, as in the case of stock markets,
made substantially to foreign financial investors.

However, these trends notwithstanding, foreign equity does not
account for a significant share of total corporate finance in the country. In
fact, internal sources, such as retained profits and depreciation reserves, have
accounted for a much higher share of corporate finance during the equity
boom of the first half of this decade. According to Reserve Bank of India
(RBI) figures (Figure 2.2), internal sources of finance, which accounted
for about 30 percent of total corporate financing during the second half
of the 1980s and the first half of the 1990s, rose to 37 percent during the
second half of the 1990s and to a record 61 percent during 2000-2001
to 2004-2005. Although that figure fell during 2005-2006, the last year
for which RBI studies of company finances are currently available, it still

Figure 2.2 Sources of funds for Indian corporates

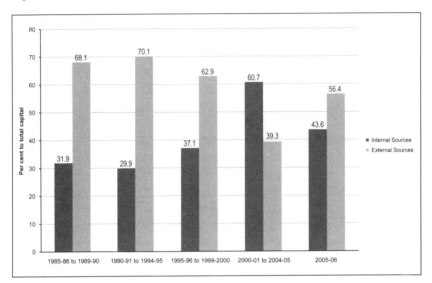

Source: Reserve Bank of India. *Report on Currency and Finance, 2006-2007*. Reserve
    Bank of India, Mumbai, Chapter 7, Table 7.5, p. 268.

stood at a relatively high 56 percent. Overall, internal resources and bank
finance dominate corporate financing, and not equity, which receives all the
attention because of the surge in foreign institutional investment and the
media's obsession with stock market buoyancy.

Thus, the surge in foreign financial investment, while important
because of the impact that it has on the pattern of corporate sector
ownership, is of much less significance as a source of corporate finance.
This challenges the defence of the open door policy to foreign financial
investment on the grounds that it helps mobilize resources for investment.

Supply-side Influences

If the needs or requirements of developing countries are not responsible
for the surge in capital inflows, what are the determining influences? There
is reason to believe that the capital flows to developing countries (before
netting out the investment of their large reserves in external markets) were
driven more by supply-side push factors, rather than developing country
demand. It is undoubtedly true that this capital could not have crossed
borders without relaxed regulations regarding the inflow of foreign equity

and debt in the developing countries. But liberalization has not ensured large inflows either in all countries or at all times. It appears that an expansion of liquidity in the international financial system has driven funds into emerging markets, as it did before the debt crisis in the early 1980s and the East Asian crisis in 1997.

Markets are liquid when those who hold assets can sell them at prices that do not involve significant losses, so as to access the finance they need to meet other commitments. Given its definition, measuring liquidity is near impossible. But, as is well recognized, a market is more liquid when there are more investors active in that market. So the volume of transactions occurring in markets is an indicator of the extent of liquidity in the system. Despite the diversified and complex nature of financial markets today, the banking sector sits at the center of the financial system, mobilizing and allocating much of the capital that goes to determine the overall state of liquidity. Based on that perception, researchers have used changes in the external or international exposure of banks in different reporting countries as indicators of trends in global liquidity (Fornari and Levy, 2000). Since the debt crisis, the Bank of International Settlements has encouraged banks located in different countries to report their international exposure through an official system, with institutions from 40 countries currently reporting. As noted earlier, the number of reporting countries has increased over time making the absolute figures incomparable. However, continuous figures are available from 1994 for 23 reporting countries.

When we examine these figures it becomes clear that there has been a sharp increase in global liquidity (as proxied by the international exposure of banks) in the period after 2002 (Figure 2.3). Having touched a low of US$716 billion that year, the exchange rate-adjusted changes in the external asset positions of banks in these 23 countries registered a more than five-fold nominal increase to reach US$3.6 trillion in 2006. This compares with a previous peak of US$1.3 trillion recorded in 1997, at the time of the East Asian financial crisis. Obviously, with global liquidity increasing at this rate, liquidity in the countries in which these banks are located rose as well. They are not merely recipients of flows from banks located elsewhere, but the domestic exposure of banks tends to rise with their international exposure, even if the rise in cross-border inter-bank flows results in a higher ratio of such flows relative to the corresponding measure of domestic liquidity.

Experience from previous crises, especially the East Asian crisis of 1997, suggests that a rapid expansion of international liquidity results in an increase in the proportion of speculative positions taken by market participants and a decline in credit quality. In particular, increased cross-

Figure 2.3 Exchange rate adjusted changes of external positions of banks in
              23 countries

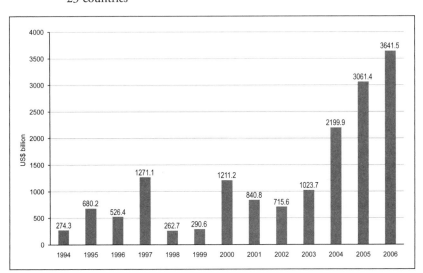

Sources: Bank of International Settlements, BIS reporting banks: Summary of
international positions. *BIS Quarterly Review: International Banking and
Financial Market Developments*, various issues. Available at http://www.
bis.org/publ/quarterly.htm

border flows can be accompanied by complex carry trades, with money
flowing from locations, markets and instruments where returns are low to
targets offering high returns. This can lead to speculative bubbles in one
or more locations. In addition, cross-border flows increase the potential
for "contagion"—the international transmission of the effects of financial
instability.

For example, apropos 1997, a Bank of Italy study found: "In the
period between 1995 and 1997, global inter-bank activity expanded
rapidly, characterized... by net outflows from Japan. During this period, the
banking system of the industrial countries (excluding Japan) played the role
of intermediary in the reallocation of flows, having made loans to offshore
centers that were nearly equal to fund-raising from Japan (US$50 billion).
The flows to emerging economies were enormous: US$150 billion to
banks and US$130 billion to non-bank agents. Large capital flows (around
US$100 billion) were recorded in favour of non-bank agents located in
offshore centers, among which some non-bank financial intermediaries such
as hedge funds are also probably included" (Fornari and Levy, 2000: 2).

There is reason to believe that similar developments occurred in the course of the more recent liquidity surge. Between June 2003 and June 2007, total foreign claims of banks in all reporting countries increased by 112 percent with respect to developed countries, 102 percent with respect to offshore centers and 163 percent with respect to developing countries (Table 2.2). There is a high degree of concentration of flows to emerging markets in Europe and Asia-Pacific. Flows to offshore centers and developing countries from different developed country locations increased by between 100 and 240 percent over this four year period. This implies that though instability currently characterizes the market for mortgage loans and mortgage-backed securities, the problems created by excessive liquidity expansion affects all favoured investment locations including developing countries in Europe and Asia.

Not surprisingly, in the recent surge of capital flows to developing countries, almost all emerging markets, especially those in Europe and Asia have experienced increased inflows, with attendant buoyancy in their stock and real estate markets. These inflows have implied the accumulation of larger speculative positions by many investors, including highly leveraged ones. One possible indicator of that tendency is that, while the outstanding

Table 2.2 Percentage increase in exposure to different locations by
          nationality of banks, 2003-2007

Claims vis-à-vis	Total foreign claims	Japan	UK	US	Other
All countries	115.5	65.9	122.1	118.1	119.8
Developed countries	112.0	54.8	122.0	116.0	116.4
Offshore centers	102.2	105.4	69.8	150.0	110.1
Developing countries	163.2	118.7	240.5	114.0	165.1
Africa & Middle East	154.6	88.5	399.7	164.0	98.1
Asia & Pacific	181.2	111.2	244.2	204.4	169.6
Europe	267.9	392.4	251.3	192.8	271.9
Latin America/Caribbean	74.0	74.9	108.6	39.1	82.3
International organizations	-13.7	...	-71.7	...	42.3
Unallocated	-61.0	...	-70.1	...	-60.9

Sources: Computed from data available in Bank of International Settlements, BIS reporting banks: Summary of international positions. *BIS Quarterly Review: International Banking and Financial Market Developments*, various issues. Available at http://www.bis.org/publ/quarterly.htm

Table 2.3 Changes in outstanding positions for key international financial assets
(US$ billion)

	June 2007	*June 2003*
Total external asset positions of banks	29980.5	14853.8
Claims on banks	19094.6	9663.6
Claims on non banks	10886.0	5190.2
External Loans	21920.0	11130.7
International debt securities	20878.3	10268.7
International money market instruments	1114.3	519.3
International bonds and notes	19764.0	9749.5
OTC derivatives (notional value)	513407	169678
Exchange-traded derivatives		
Futures	31676.9	13930.5
Options	65006.7	24286.6

Sources: Bank of International Settlements, BIS reporting banks: Summary of
international positions. *BIS Quarterly Review: International Banking
and Financial Market Developments*, December 2003; December 2007.
Available at http://www.bis.org/publ/quarterly.htm

values of all kinds of international assets held by banks doubled during the
recent surge (2003-2007), derivative contracts, especially over the counter,
have increased by much more (Table 2.3).

What this suggests is that the problems arising from the sub-prime
mortgage crisis and the collateralized debt obligations associated with
sub-prime loans reflects the unravelling of only one set of problems
created by the liquidity spiral of recent years. Another, which could have
unravelled and can still unravel, is the excessive exposure, encouraged by
excess liquidity, of international investors and lenders in a few developing
countries and the securitized assets built on that exposure. That is, a supply-
side push of capital into the stock, credit and real estate markets in emerging
market economies could have created a second source of fragility in the
international financial system besides the US sub-prime mortgage market.

This is of significance because the lesson from the sub-prime loan crisis
is that when suspect loans result in payments defaults, those loan assets and
the securitized obligations that have been built on them become suspect as
well, resulting in a drying up of demand for such assets. Holders of such
assets who want to sell, even if at a loss, to meet commitments that fall
due, find there are no takers, so that a financial world, that was till recently
awash with liquidity suddenly turns illiquid. This has happened with only

one segment of the market experiencing a doubtful loan or investment problem. If the build-up of speculative positions in other markets associated with the recent surge in liquidity generates new problem loans and investments, the transformation from liquidity excess to liquidity squeeze may be far too severe for central bankers and governments to resolve without much damage.

Determinants of Liquidity Movements

What needs investigating, therefore, is the set of factors that led to the liquidity build up in the first place. One factor is, of course a sudden accumulation of foreign exchange surpluses within a few countries and firms, resulting from the increase in oil prices, for example. With these oil surpluses looking for investment opportunities finding their way to financial markets, an excess liquidity syndrome may result. In fact, there is a close association between oil price movements and the build-up of global liquidity in recent years (Figure 2.4). But this is only one fortuitous development contributing to liquidity. Moreover, since speculation touches commodities as well, the direction of causation also moves from liquidity to oil prices, as it does the other way around.

Figure 2.4 Global liquidity and oil prices

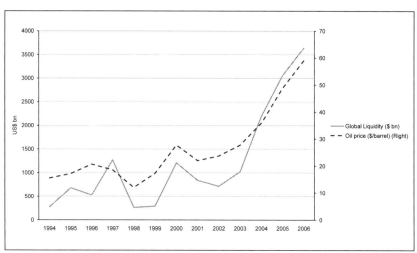

Sources: Global liquidity figures from source quoted in Figure 2.3. Oil prices from
US Energy Information Administration. Available at http://tonto.eia.doe.
gov/dnav/pet/hist/r1300____3a.htm. Accessed 20 December 2007.

There are three other factors that could have played a role in influencing the level of liquidity. The first is the long term tendency inherent in the dynamic of the contemporary global system for an increase in liquidity. The liquidity that drives the supply-side push of capital to emerging markets originates in the transformation of capitalism that has occurred under the tutelage of neoconservative ideologies. The growing inequality characterizing an unregulated capitalism, in which wages stagnate while productivity and profits rise, has resulted in the accumulation of vast sums of capital in the hands of a few investors in the metropolitan centers of global capitalism.[3] These gains are lightly taxed by governments that are not committed to appropriating a part of the surpluses of the rich to improve the welfare of the poor. Lower down the ladder, investment capital accumulates with mutual and pension funds in which less protected populations deposit the savings they put aside to insure their future. The decline of state-funded welfare in today's more liberalized and open capitalism is forcing the middle classes in the developed countries to save by subscribing to these funds that have become important sources of financial capital. Financial firms in developed countries leverage capital from these sources by borrowing huge sums to invest, increasingly in high-risk, high-return speculative investments.

A second reason for the liquidity build-up noted by many observers is a tendency in recent years for developed country central banks to adopt an easy money policy, aimed at encouraging credit-financed spending in housing and consumer goods markets, that keeps consumer demand buoyant and GDP growth at "acceptable" levels. Considering the US, which is at the center of the global financial system, while the relationship between formal measures of US money supply (M3 to GDP ratio) and the global liquidity index is not perfect, there does appear to be a significantly strong positive relation between US domestic monetary conditions and global liquidity in recent years (Figure 2.5).

Third, developing countries adversely affected or threatened by the financial crises of 1997-1998 have since been more cautious about the use of foreign exchange. In most cases, this has involved maintaining investment rates below domestic savings rates to generate current account surpluses in the balance of payments, or, in the face of current account deficits, making sure that not all net capital inflows were exhausted through current or capital expenditures. The result has been a huge build up in foreign exchange surpluses in developing countries which, in myriad ways, find their way to financial centers in the developed countries, only to partly return as investments in emerging markets. That is, the crisis generated by

Figure 2.5 Global liquidity and ratio of M3 to GDP in the US

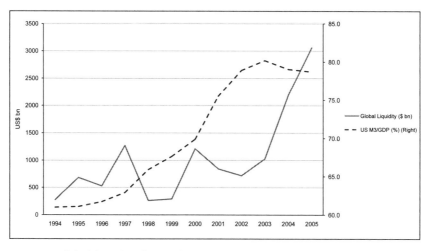

Sources: Global liquidity figures from source quoted in Figure 2.3. US monetary aggregate M3 from US Federal Reserve Board. Available at http://www.federalreserve.gov/releases/h6/HIST/h6hista.pdf. Accessed 20 December 2007. (The Federal Reserve discontinued issue of M3 figures as of 23 March 2006.)

Figure 2.6 Global reserves and global liquidity

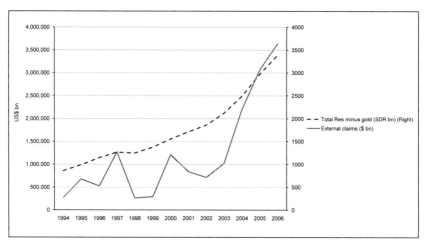

Sources: Global liquidity figures from source quoted in Figure 2.3. Global reserves (excluding gold) figures from IMF, International Financial Statistics Online.

excess liquidity in the past results in an environment that contributes to a new round of liquidity accumulation. Figure 2.6 tracks the relationship between global reserves and global liquidity, and shows a strong relationship between the two.

This reverse flow of capital essentially means that excess savings in emerging markets are being "recycled" in ways that puts the responsibility of allocating that capital in the hands of a few financial decision makers at the apex of a concentrated global financial system. For example, according to reports, in the wake of China's decision to invest part of its foreign exchange surpluses in funds managed by the Blackstone (private equity) group, much of this capital flowed back as investment into firms located in China itself, feeding a spiral that leaves the problem of large surpluses unresolved. More recently, much has been made of the rise of sovereign wealth funds in developing countries, epitomized by the China Investment Corporation (CIC), that are seen as a challenge to financial institutions from the developed countries, especially the US and UK, which have traditionally dominated global finance. However, a significant part of the investments by these sovereign wealth funds is in global financial intermediaries or the funds they manage.

Consequences of Supply-side Capital Flow Pressures

When liquidity accumulates in the international financial system, financial firms are not only under pressure to keep money moving to earn returns from spreads, but also to "innovate" in order to profit from the situation of excess liquidity in the more liberalized financial environment of today. One consequence of the desire to keep money moving is that, at different points in time, one or another group of developing countries is discovered as a "favorable" destination for foreign financial investors. Increased competition and falling returns in the developed countries are also encouraging financial firms to seek out new opportunities in emerging markets. This supply side push translates into an actual flow only when developing countries as a group, including the "emerging markets" among them, relax controls on inflows of capital and the repatriation of profits and investments as well as liberalize their financial systems to attract international players and accommodate their operating strategies. In practice, despite the East Asian crisis and similar crises in other parts of the world, and the evidence that these crises resulted from more open capital accounts, developing countries have competed with one another to attract such inflows by opting for international financial liberalization.

New Trends in Capital Flows to Developing Countries

Overall, the willingness to accommodate supply-side pressures has had rather dramatic implications for capital flows to developing countries. The first of these is an acceleration of financial flows to developing countries precisely during the years when as a group they have been characterized by rising current account surpluses. Total flows reached a record US$571 billion in 2006, having risen by 19 percent after an average growth of 40 percent during the previous three years. Relative to the GDP of these countries, total flows, at 5.1 percent, are at levels reached at the time of the East Asian financial crisis in 1997-1998 (figures in this section are from World Bank, 2007).

A second feature is the acceleration of the long term tendency for private flows to dominate official (bilateral and multilateral) flows. Private debt and equity inflows, which had risen by 50 percent annually over the three years ending 2005, increased a further 17 percent in 2006 to reach a record US$647 billion. On the other hand, net official lending has, in fact, declined over the last two years, partly because some developing countries have chosen to make advance repayments of debt owed to official creditors, especially the IMF and the World Bank. Once flows between private lenders and borrowers or private investors and firms dominate, the implicit sovereign guarantees associated with lending to governments or providing government guaranteed credits no longer exist, increasing the probability of default.

Third, after a period following the 1997-1998 crisis when debt flows almost dried up, both equity and debt flows to developing countries have risen rapidly in recent years. Net private debt and equity flows to developing countries have risen from a little less than US$170 billion in 2002 to close to US$647 billion in 2006, an almost four-fold increase over a four-year period. While net private equity flows, which rose from US$163 billion to US$419 billion, dominated the surge, net private debt flows also increased rapidly. Bond issues rose from US$10.4 billion to US$49.3 billion, and borrowing from international banks from US$2.3 billion to a huge US$112.2 billion. What is more, net short-term debt, outflows of which tend to trigger financial crises, rose from around half a billion in 2002 to US$72 billion in 2006. According to BIS statistics, syndicated loan agreements signed by developing country borrowers rose after the immediate post-1997 slump, from US$6.9 billion in 2002 to US$237.9 billion in 2006, which compares with the previous peak of US$129.2 billion in 1997.

The fourth feature, a corollary of these developments, is the high degree of concentration of flows to developing countries, implying excessive exposure in a few countries. Ten countries (out of 135) accounted for 60 percent of all borrowing during 2002-2004, and that proportion has risen subsequently to three-quarters in 2006. In the portfolio equity market, flows to developing countries were directed at acquiring a share in equity either through the secondary market or by buying into initial public offers (IPOs). IPOs dominated in 2006, accounting for US$53 billion of the US$96 billion in inflows. But here too, there were signs of concentration. Four of the 10 largest IPOs were by Chinese companies, accounting for two-thirds of total IPO value. Another 3 of the 10 were by Russian companies, accounting for an additional 22 percent of total IPO value.

Finally, despite this rapid rise in developing country exposure, with the exposure highly concentrated in a few countries, the market is still overtly optimistic. Ratings upgrades dominate downgrades in the bond market. And bond market spreads are at unusual lows. This optimism indicates that risk assessments are pro-cyclical, underestimating risk when investments are booming, and exaggerating risks when markets turn downwards. But two consequences are the herd behaviour of investors in developing country markets and their willingness to invest a larger volume of money in risky, unrated instruments.

In sum, we are now witnessing a return to a period when large and rising inflows, herd behaviour and over exposure have come to characterize capital flows from the North to the South. Is there reason to believe that—unlike in 1997, say—this time around, these developments are benign, or even positive, from the point of view of the developing countries, as some would suggest? Besides the many crises that have occurred across the developing world, including in Argentina and Turkey, during the decade since 1997, structural changes in the global financial system suggest that risk, including systemic risk, has only increased. And the experience with the sub-prime mortgage crisis suggests that even in developed countries, the regulatory framework has not evolved to match the complexity of markets, institutions and instruments that characterize today's financial systems, and prudential regulation, new disclosure norms and changed accounting practices have not been successful in identifying fragility before it is too late.

Structural Transformation of Global Finance

This experience matters because of evidence that the rapid rise of capital flows to developing countries has been associated with the increasing dominance of the global financial architecture by a few institutions, which are present in almost all countries. During the 1990s, the three-decade long process of proliferation and rise to dominance of finance in the global economy reached a new phase. Financial consolidation saw greater concentration of financial activity and decision making in a few organizations. And financial integration joined hitherto demarcated areas of financial activity that had been dissociated from each other to ensure transparency, check conflicts of interest and discourage unsound financial practices.

A study (Group of 10, 2001) of financial consolidation commissioned by finance ministers and central bank governors of the Group of 10 found, as expected, a high level of merger and acquisition (M&A) activity in the study countries during the 1990s, with an acceleration of such activity in the last three years of that decade. The number of acquisitions by financial firms from the survey countries increased from around 337 in 1990 to between 900 and 1000 by the end of the decade. Further, the average value of each of these acquisitions increased from US$224 million in 1990 to US$649 million in 1999. Clearly, M&As in the financial sector were creating large and complex financial organizations in the international financial system.

Further, over the 1990s as a whole, the evidence seems to be that M&A activity was largely industry-specific, with banking firms tending to merge dominantly with other banks. However, the pattern was changing over time. While in 1994, there was one instance of cross-industry M&A for every five instances of intra-industry mergers, the ratio had come down to one in every three by 1999. The mergers and acquisitions drive within the financial sector was not merely creating large and powerful organizations, but firms that increasingly straddled the financial sector. Exploiting the process of financial liberalization, these firms were breaking down the Chinese walls that had been built between different segments of the financial sector.

With growing financial liberalization in the developing world, it was inevitable that this process would affect developing countries as well. According to a study by the Committee on the Global Financial System (CGFS), (2004), there has been a surge in foreign direct investment in the financial sectors of developing countries. The study, by using cross-border M&As targeting banks in emerging market economies (EMEs), found that cross-border deals involving financial institutions from EMEs as targets, which accounted for 18 percent of such M&A deals worldwide during 1990-1996, rose to 30 percent during 1997-2000. The value of financial sector FDI rose from about US$6 billion during 1990-1996 to US$50

Table 2.4 Ownership structure in the banking systems of emerging market economies[1]

Country	1990			2002[2]		
	Domestic		Foreign	Domestic		Foreign
	Private[3]	Government		Private	Government	
Asia						
China	0	100	0	98	2[4]	
Hong Kong SAR	11	0	89	28		72
Indonesia	...	...	4	37	51	13
India	4	91	5	12	80	8
Korea	75	21	4	62	30	8
Malaysia	...	...	...	72	18	
Philippines	84	7	9	70	12	18
Singapore	11	0	89	24	0	76
Thailand	82	13	5	51	31	18
Latin America						
Argentina	...	36[5]	10[6]	19	33	48
Brazil	30	64	6	27	46	27
Chile	62	19	19	46	13	42
Mexico	1	97	2	18	0	82
Peru	41	55	4	43	11	46
Venezuela	93	6	1[7]	39	27	34

Table 2.4 (continued)

Country	1990 Domestic		1990	2002[2] Domestic		2002[2]
	Private[3]	Government	Foreign	Private	Government	Foreign
Central & Eastern Europe						
Bulgaria	…	…	0	20	13	67
Czech Republic	12[5]	78[5]	10[5]	14	4	82
Estonia	…	…	…	1	0	99
Hungary	9	81	10	11	27	62
Poland	17[7]	80[7]	3[7]	10	17	63
Russia	…	…	6	23	68	9
Slovakia	…	…	0	9	5	85

Notes: [1] Percentage share of total bank assets. 2002 figures for central and eastern Europe: percentage share of regulatory capital. [2] Data are shown for the latest year available, which is mainly 2002. [3] Calculated as residual. [4] 1999. [5] 1994. [6] Average of 1988-93. [7] 1993.

Source: Committee on the Global Financial System (2004, Table 1, p. 9).

billion during the next four years. Such FDI peaked at US$20 billion in 2001, declined sharply in 2002, but stabilized in 2003. The net result is a clear shift in the ownership of the financial sector (Table 2.4). Anecdotal evidence indicates that this figure has risen sharply since.

Thus, the global financial system is clearly characterized by a high degree of centralization. With US financial institutions intermediating global capital flows, the investment decisions of a few individuals in a few institutions virtually determines the nature of the "exposure" of the global financial system. The growing presence of a few consolidated global players in the developing countries has implications for the accumulation of risk in markets where agents tend to herd. Unfortunately, unregulated entities making huge profits on highly speculative investments are at the core of that system.

Transformation of the Financial Sector

The increased foreign presence in the financial sector in developing countries has meant that capital flows are accompanied by the movement of firms and institutions from developed to developing countries. Countries wanting to attract financial investments have to accommodate financial investors as well. Further, when these entities are permitted to enter developing country markets, they would want to replicate their business practices in the new environment. Policies of financial liberalization are, *inter alia*, meant to meet these requirements of finance capital in countries seeking to attract financial investments. Financial liberalization therefore: (i) opens the country to new forms and larger volumes of international financial flows; (ii) allows entry of foreign financial entities, varying from banks to private equity firms, into the country; and (iii) dilutes or dismantles regulations and controls the operations of financial entities and the pursuit of their preferred practices. A consequence of such liberalization is financial consolidation and the proliferation of new institutions and instruments. It has been argued for some time now, especially since the East Asian crisis, that financial liberalization, involving liberalization of controls on inflows and outflows of capital respectively, has increased financial fragility in developing countries, making them more vulnerable to periodic financial and currency crises.

Analyses of individual instances of crises have tended to conclude that the nature and timing of these crises have had much to do with the shift to a more liberal and open financial regime. What is less emphasized is the vulnerability that stems from the proliferation of new kinds of foreign institutions, new instruments and new business practices in the wake of liberalization. The increased extent of liberalization over the last decade has not only led to the surge in capital flows in recent years, but also encouraged the entry of speculative investors adopting unusual lending and investment practices in environments even less regulated than the US. This would, therefore, have substantially increased, rather than reduced, financial vulnerability over the last decade.

Lessons from the US Sub-prime Crisis

The US sub-prime mortgage crisis illustrates how underlying such vulnerability is the financial entanglement which results from the layered financial structure, "innovative" financial products and inadequate financial regulation associated with the increasingly liberalized and globalized financial system in most countries. Few would deny that the source of the crisis in the sub-prime housing loan market in the US—consisting of loans to borrowers with a poor credit record—is the way in which the preceding housing market and consumption booms were triggered and sustained. Housing demand grew rapidly because of easy access to credit, with credit extended to borrowers considered less than creditworthy. These sub-prime borrowers were offered credit at higher rates of interest, made attractive by special offers and unusual financing arrangements—with little documentation or self-certification of income, little or no down payment, extended repayment periods and structured payment schedules involving low interest rates in the initial phases which were "adjustable" and moved sharply upwards when "reset" to reflect premiums on market interest rates. All this encouraged high-risk borrowers to take on loans they could ill understand, let alone afford, either because they did not fully understand the payment burdens they were taking on, expected to profit from the booming property market, or expected their incomes to rise sufficiently to cope with their new debt burden.

Clearly, the problem is largely a supply-side creation driven by factors such as easy liquidity, low interest rates and "debt-pushing" efforts by lending institutions competing for new business. In these circumstances, mortgage brokers attracted clients by relaxing income documentation requirements or offering early grace periods with low or no payments, after which higher rates would kick in. As a result, the share of such sub-prime loans in all mortgages rose sharply. Estimates vary, but according to Inside Mortgage Finance, quoted by the *New York Times* (Creswell and Bajaj, 2007), sub-prime loans reached US$600 billion in 2006, or 20 percent of the mortgage loan total as compared with just 5 percent in 2001.

The increase in this type of credit occurred because of the complex nature of current-day finance that allows an array of agents to earn lucrative returns, even while transferring the risk associated with the investments that offer these returns. Mortgage brokers seek out and find willing borrowers for a fee, taking on excessive risk while in search of volume. Mortgage lenders finance these mortgages, not with the intention of actually garnering the interest and amortization flows associated with such lending, but in order to sell on these mortgages to Wall Street banks and other investors in collateralized securities. The Wall Street banks buy these mortgages because they can bundle assets with varying returns to create securities or collateralized debt obligations, involving tranches with differing probabilities of default and differential protection against losses. They charge hefty fees for structuring these products and having them rated with complex mathematical models, before selling them to a range of investors such as banks, mutual funds, pension funds and insurance companies. These entities in turn, can then create a portfolio involving varying degrees of risk and different streams of future cash flows linked to the original mortgages. Firms like the unregulated hedge funds make speculative investments in derivatives of various kinds in search of high returns for their high net worth investors. Needless to say, institutions at every level are not fully devoid of risk, but these risks are shared and rest in large measure with the final investors in the chain.

This structure is relatively stable so long as defaults are a small proportion of the total. But if the proportion of defaults increases, as the share of sub-prime mortgages in the total rises, the bottom of the barrel gives, and all assets become less liquid. Rising foreclosures adversely affect property prices and saleability as foreclosed assets are put up for sale as credit is squeezed because lenders turn wary. And securities built on these mortgages turn illiquid because there are few buyers for assets whose values are opaque since there is no ready market for them.

Entanglement also makes nonsense of the theory that a complex financial system with multiple institutions, securitization, proliferating instruments and global reach is safer because it spreads risk. Banks wanting to reduce the risk they carry resort to securitization to transfer this risk. But institutions created by the banks themselves, linked to them in today's more universalized banking system or leveraged with bank finance, often buy the very instruments created to transfer risk. In the event, as *The Economist* ("Prime Movers", 11 August 2007) put it, "banks (that) have shown risk out of the front door by selling loans, only… let it return through the back door." This, it notes, is exactly what transpired in the relationship between the three major Wall Street firms—Goldman Sachs, Morgan Stanley and Bear Stearns—that offered prime broking services, including loans, to highly leveraged institutions like hedge funds. The bail-out of Long Term Capital Management (LTCM) in 1998 was necessitated because of such entanglement involving all the leading merchant (investment) banks.

There are many lessons being driven home by the sub-prime mortgage crisis of particular significance for developing countries rapidly liberalizing their financial systems. First, easy liquidity in a loosely controlled financial system, which encourages the flow of capital to developing countries, facilitates speculative and unsound financial practices that increase fragility. Second, such practices are encouraged by the "financial innovation" that liberalization encourages, which often increases the layers of intermediation and allows firms to transfer risk. As a result, those who create risky "products" in the first instance are less exposed to or worried about the risk involved than they should be. Third, as the product moves up the financial chain, investors are less sure about the risk and value of these products than they should be, rendering even low risk, first-stage tranches prone to value loss. Fourth, this inadequate knowledge appears to be true even of the rating agencies on whose ratings investors rely, resulting in misleading and pro-cyclical ratings and belated adjustments. This implies that as and when a rating downgrade does occur, the asset becomes worth much less, since nobody is willing to buy the asset without large discounts. Fifth, new forms of self-regulation appear to be poor substitutes for more rigorous control, since the current crisis originates in a country whose financial sector is considered the most sophisticated, well regulated and transparent and serves as a model for others reforming their financial sectors. And finally, financial globalization and entanglement imply that countries that have more open and integrated financial systems are more prone to contagion effects, even if the virus originates in remote locations and markets. These are lessons that must inform policy in these so-called emerging markets.

Signs of Vulnerability

If a supply-side driven surge in liquidity increased vulnerability in the US, it would be much more difficult for developing countries with even poorer regulatory systems seeking to emulate the Anglo-Saxon financial model not to be vulnerable. One obvious indicator of such an increase in vulnerability is the massive "boom" in their stock markets that emerging markets across the Asian region have been experiencing. Market observers, the financial media and a range of analysts agree that foreign investments have been an important force, even if not always the only one, driving markets to unprecedented heights.

There are a number of reasons why this trend exacerbates vulnerability. To start with, the spike in stock prices is usually sharp, i.e. very temporary. Second, this boom is generalized and occurs independently of the relative economic performance of the country concerned. This not only implies that fundamentals do not have the prime role in determining the behavior of markets, but also means that the danger of contagion is real. Third, this occurs both in countries where investors have burnt their fingers in 1997-1998 and in those where they did not.

A second indicator of vulnerability is the revival of the credit spiral, which underlay the East Asian crisis. It was undoubtedly true that in the years immediately following the crisis, the flow of private non-guaranteed debt to developing countries as a group fell until 2000 and registered a marginal decline in the subsequent two years to 2002 (Table 2.5). With governments wanting to discourage debt-dependence, and creditors wary of lending any further, even public and publicly guaranteed debt from private creditors sharply declined during those years. But matters seem to have changed dramatically over the last four years. The flow of non-guaranteed debt from private sources to developing countries increased by 250 percent during 2003-2006. Simultaneously, governments too seem to have overcome their fear of debt with public or publicly guaranteed debt from private creditors having risen by more than 150 percent. In sum, creditors appear willing to lend, and debtors willing to borrow, resulting in an aggregate scenario that spells debt dependence of a much larger magnitude than before the 1997 crisis.

Table 2.5 Private credit to developing countries, 1998-2006 (US$ bn)

	Bonds	Banks	Others	Short-term	Total
1998	38.8	49.4	-5.3	-65.3	17.6
1999	30.1	-5.3	-1.5	-17.3	6.0
2000	20.9	-3.8	-3.7	-6.3	7.1
2001	10.3	7.8	-6.5	-23.7	-12.1
2002	10.4	2.3	-6.9	0.5	6.3
2003	24.7	14.5	-4.4	55.0	89.8
2004	39.8	50.6	-4.0	68.4	154.8
2005	55.1	86.0	-4.9	67.7	203.9
2006	49.3	112.2	-5.5	72.0	228.0

Source: World Bank (2007).

There has been some change in composition by source as well. While in the immediate aftermath of the 1997-1998 crisis, the relatively small inflow of debt was due to bond issues by developing countries, with bank credit contracting, in more recent years there has been a revival of bank credit. The corporate share of external debt has risen from less than one-fifth of the total in the late 1990s to more than half in 2006.

What is disturbing is the extreme concentration of these flows, with a growing and now substantial share of it flowing to Europe and Central Asia. In 2006, 57 percent of flows of private non-guaranteed debt went to this region, while East Asia and the Pacific received 14 percent, and Latin America and the Caribbean 19 percent. Just 10 countries accounted for three-quarters of all borrowing in 2006, a sharp increase from the already high 60 percent average during 2002-04. What is more, the evidence points to a growing share of lending to banks in developing countries, interested in exploiting the lower interest rates in international—as opposed to domestic—markets. Loan commitments to the banking sector totaled US\$32 billion in 2006, which exceeded commitments to the oil and gas sector, a traditional leader.

Finally, the World Bank *Global Development Finance 2007* noted a decline in credit quality accompanying these developments. To quote: "As private debt flows swell, riskier borrowers may be taking a larger share of the market. The share of bonds issued by unrated (sovereign and corporate) borrowers rose from 10 percent in 2000 to 37 percent in 2006, and the share of unsecured loans in total bank lending rose from 50 percent in 2002 to almost 80 percent in 2006" (World Bank 2007: 47).

However, despite these disconcerting trends, creditor confidence is at a high. The average spread between interest rates charged on developing country loan commitments and the benchmark LIBOR fell from more than 200 basis points in 2002 to 125 in 2006, as average loan maturities have become longer.

The inevitable conclusion from this evidence that needs explaining is that creditors are not pricing risk adequately and taking it into account when determining exposure. One explanation could be that creditor profiles have changed significantly, with the entry of intermediaries, such as hedge funds and other less risk-averse entities, into the credit market. The other could be the growing role of credit derivatives, which allows for risk pooling and the transfer of risk to entities less capable of assessing them.

These two aspects are indeed related. The emergence of credit derivatives has rendered credit assets tradable, attracting those looking for quick or early profits. But even here, financial innovation has played a role. Until recently, other than banks, the major players in the credit business were pension funds and insurers. But with equities proving to be inadequately remunerative investments, banks increasingly geared to creating new instruments based on debt, and credit derivatives offering liquid credit instruments, new players—hedge funds and pension funds—have emerged as investors, and new operators—specialized credit funds and managers of collateralized debt obligations—have emerged as providers of instruments.

In sum, a decade after the 1997-98 crisis we are witnessing trends which imply an increase in financial fragility that can lead to further financial crises, with adverse implications for growth, stability, employment and social welfare. This is the element of continuity in a world that is seen as having changed substantially. Self-regulation clearly does not help. New measures to govern finance and financial flows are needed.

Macroeconomic Fall-out of the Capital Surge

Besides increasing fragility and vulnerability, the surge in capital flows to developing countries is making the macroeconomic management of these economies increasingly difficult, with potentially adverse implications for development. The growing presence of foreign capital is disconcerting, not just because such flows are in the nature of "hot money" which renders the financial sector fragile, but because efforts to attract such flows and accommodate surges in such flows have macroeconomic implications.

To start with, inasmuch as financial liberalization leads to financial growth and deepening and increases the presence and role of financial agents in the economy, it forces the state to adopt a deflationary stance to appease financial interests. Deflation follows because financial interests favor tax cuts, but oppose deficit financing for a number of reasons. First, deficit financing is said to increase the liquidity overhang in the system, and therefore as being potentially inflationary. Inflation is anathema to finance since it erodes the real value of financial assets. Second, since government spending is "autonomous" in character, the use of debt to finance such autonomous spending is seen as introducing into financial markets an arbitrary player not driven by the profit motive, whose activities can render interest rate differentials—that determine financial profits—more unpredictable. Third, if deficit spending leads to a substantial build-up of the state's debt and interest burden, it may intervene in financial markets to lower interest rates, with implications for financial returns. Financial interests wanting to guard against that possibility tend to oppose deficit spending. Finally, the use of deficits to finance autonomous expenditures by the state amounts to an implicit legitimization of a proactive and interventionist state and a de-legitimization of the market. Since finance generally seeks to de-legitimize the state and legitimize the market, it strongly opposes deficit-financed, autonomous state spending.

Efforts to curb the deficit under a lenient tax regime obviously result in a contraction of public expenditure, especially state investment, which adversely affects growth and employment; curtails social sector expenditures that sets back the battle against deprivation; impacts adversely on food and other subsidies that benefit the poor; and sets off a scramble to privatize profit-earning public assets, which render the self-imposed fiscal strait-jacket self-perpetuating. All the more so since the finance-induced pressure to limit deficit spending is institutionalized through legislation which constitutionally binds the state to eliminating revenue deficits and limiting fiscal deficits to low, pre-specified levels.

Implications of Curbing the Monetized Deficit

This macroeconomic fall-out and its effects are aggravated by the perception that accompanies the financial reform that macroeconomic regulation should rely on monetary policy pursued by an "independent" central bank rather than on fiscal policy. The immediate consequence of this perception is the tendency to follow the principle that even the limited deficits should not be "monetized". Fiscal reform was not only concerned with reducing the size of the deficit, but also with the manner in which any given deficit should be financed. In this regard, fiscal reform involved a sharp reduction of the "monetized deficit" of the government and its subsequent elimination. In many countries, this shift away from low-interest borrowing from the central bank has resulted in a sharp rise in the average interest rate for government borrowing, worsening the fiscal problem. This shift, it is argued, is essential for giving the central bank a degree of autonomy, and monetary policy a greater role in the economy. This understanding, in turn, stems from the premise that monetary policy should have a greater role than fiscal maneuverability in macroeconomic management.

The question that remains, therefore, is whether this "abolition" of the monetized deficit in order to appease financial capital actually results in central bank independence. It does not if the country is successful in attracting capital leading to a rapid increase in the level of its foreign exchange reserves. Reserve accumulation is the result of pressure on the central bank to purchase foreign currency to shore up demand for and dampen the effects on the domestic currency of excess supplies of foreign currency.

In India's liberalized foreign exchange markets, for example, excess supply leads to an appreciation of the rupee, which in turn undermines the competitiveness of India's exports. Since improved export competitiveness and increased exports are leading objectives of economic liberalization, the persistence of a tendency towards rupee appreciation implies that the reform process is inherently contradictory. Not surprisingly, the central bank and the government have been keen to dampen, if not stall, appreciation. Thus, the Reserve Bank of India's (RBI's) holding of foreign currency reserves has been rising with the surge in capital inflows.

Unfortunately, the RBI's ability to persist with this policy without eroding its ability to control domestic money supply is increasingly under threat. Increases in the foreign exchange assets of the central bank amount to an increase in reserve money, and therefore in money supply, unless the RBI manages to neutralize increased reserve holding by retrenching other assets. If that does not happen, the overhang of liquidity in the system increases substantially, affecting the RBI's ability to pursue its monetary policy objectives. Till recently, the RBI has been avoiding this problem through its sterilization policy, which involves the sale of its holdings of central government securities to match increases in its foreign exchange assets. But even this option has now more or less run out. Net Reserve Bank Credit to the government, reflecting the RBI's holding of government securities, fell from Rs1,673.08 billion at the end of May 2001 to Rs46.26 billion by 10 December 2004. With its stock of government securities deteriorating, there was little by way of sterilization instruments available with the RBI.

There are two important consequences of these developments. First, the monetary policy of the central bank de-linked from the fiscal policy initiatives of the state is no more independent. More or less autonomous capital flows influence the reserves position of the central bank and therefore the level of money supply, unless the central bank chooses to leave the exchange rate unmanaged, which it cannot. This implies that the central bank is not in a position to use the monetary lever to influence domestic economic variables, however effective those levers may be. Secondly, the country is subject to a drain of foreign exchange inasmuch as there is a substantial difference between the repatriable returns earned by foreign investors and the foreign exchange returns earned by the RBI from the investment of its reserves in relatively liquid assets. While partial solutions to this problem can be sought in mechanisms like the Market Stabilization Scheme adopted in India, it is now increasingly clear that the real option in the current situation is to either curb inflows of foreign capital or encourage outflows of foreign exchange. As the RBI's survey of monetary management techniques in emerging market economies—reported in its *Survey of Currency and Finance 2003-2004*—makes clear, countries have chosen to use stringent capital control measures or market-based measures, such as differential reserve requirements and Tobin-type taxes to restrict capital inflows.

Conclusion

To conclude, the evidence is strong that the surge in capital flows to developing countries in recent years is supply-driven and not warranted by the financing needs in these countries. This supply-side driven surge of capital has three kinds of effects: (i) it results in a situation where financial decisions in these countries are increasingly made by international firms seeking environments and pursuing strategies similar to that in their countries of origin, necessitating fundamental changes in financial policies and regulatory structures; (ii) it increases financial vulnerability in these countries resulting in periodic crisis that can have damaging effects on the real economy; and (iii) it leads to macroeconomic adjustments that reduce the fiscal and monetary autonomy of the governments and the central banks in these countries, with potentially adverse consequences for economic growth. If developing countries want to avoid such outcomes in the current environment, the only option they have is that of adopting domestic policies that restrict the volume and the nature of capital inflows into their economies.

Notes

1. This is a slightly abridged version of G-24 Discussion Paper Number 53 published by UNCTAD and available at http://www.unctad.org/Templates/ Download.asp?docid=11278&lang=1&intItemID=2103. Comments on earlier versions of that paper from Jomo K.S., Jayati Ghosh and Prabhat Patnaik are gratefully acknowledged.
2. Very often, countries not reporting have been characterized by small or negligible international exposure of banks operating from within their borders. There have been exceptions, such as the Republic of Korea which joined the countries reporting to the BIS in 2005.
3. For example, the wealthiest one percent of Americans reportedly earned 21.2 percent of all income in 2005, according to data from the Internal Revenue Service. This was an increase in share relative to the 19.0 percent recorded in 2004, and exceeded the previous high of 20.8 percent in 2000, at the peak

of the previous bull market in stocks. Compared with this, the bottom 50 percent earned 12.8 percent of all income in 2005, which was less than the 13.4 percent and 13.0 percent in 2004 and 2000 respectively (Ip, 2007).

References

BIS (1997). BIS reporting banks: Summary of international positions. *BIS Quarterly Review: International Banking and Financial Market Developments*. Monetary and Economic Department, Bank of International Settlements, Basel, pp. A1-A2.

BIS (2007). BIS reporting banks: Summary of international positions. *BIS Quarterly Review: International Banking and Financial Market Developments*. Bank of International Settlements, Basel, pp. A7-A8.

Bloomberg, M.R., and C.E. Schumer (2006). *Sustaining New York's and the US' Global Financial Services Leadership*. Office of the Mayor, City of New York and United States Senate, New York.

Committee on the Global Financial System (2004). *Foreign Direct Investment in the Financial Sector of Emerging Market Economies*. Bank for International Settlements, Basel.

Committee on the Global Financial System (2007). *Institutional Investors, Global Savings and Asset Allocations: Report Submitted by Working Group*. Bank of International Settlements, Basel.

Creswell, J., and V. Bajaj (2007). A mortgage crisis begins to spiral, and the casualties mount. *The New York Times*, 5 March.

Financial Stability Forum (2007). *Update of the FSF's 2000 Report on Highly Leveraged Institutions*, 18 May. http://www.fsforum.org/publications/HLI Update-finalwithoutembargo19May07.pdf (accessed 15 June 2007).

Fornari, Fabio, and Aviram Levy (2000). Global liquidity in the 1990s: Geographical allocation and long-run determinants. BIS Conference on International Financial Markets and the Implications for Monetary and Financial Stability, BIS Conference Papers No. 8. Available at http://www.bis.org/publ/confer08a.pdf (accessed 20 December 2007).

Group of 10 (2001). *Report on Consolidation in the Financial Sector*. Group of 10, January. http://www.imf.org/external/np/g10/2001/01/Eng/index.htm (accessed 15 May 2002)

Ip, G. (2007). Income inequality widens. *The Wall Street Journal*, 12 October.

OECD (2001). *Institutional Investors Statistical Year Book*. Organization for Economic Cooperation and Development, Paris.

OECD (2003). *Institutional Investors Statistical Year Book 1992-2001*. Organization for Economic Cooperation and Development, Paris.

World Bank (2007). *Global Development Finance 2007: The Globalization of Corporate Finance in Developing Countries*. World Bank, Washington, DC.

3

The Global Financial and Economic Crisis and Its Impact on Development

Jomo Kwame Sundaram

The world was plunged from late 2008 into its worst recession since the 1930s. The global financial and economic crisis has severely disrupted economic growth worldwide, and it is feared that much of the progress towards the achievement of development goals is being reversed. The United Nations' (UN) late 2009 global forecast estimates that world income per capita could drop by 2.2 percent in 2009.[1] Although there are some signs of recovery, thanks to fiscal, monetary, financial and regulatory measures taken by some major economies, significant uncertainty remains regarding its sustainability and robustness. There is also the risk of premature and uncoordinated termination of stimulus packages as pressure mounts in some quarters due to rising government debt and the threat of inflation. Even if the world economy recovers, unemployment rates are expected to continue to rise and remain at double digits in many developed countries for a considerable period of time. Besides tens of millions becoming unemployed, hundreds of millions are expected to join the ranks of the working poor globally, if effective policies to redress the situation are not implemented in time.

Causes and Nature of the Crisis

The crisis has its roots in the large asymmetries caused by an unsustainable pattern of development since the early 1980s. This has seen rising inequality within and probably among countries. In 2000, the richest 10 percent of adults accounted for 85 percent of total world assets; in contrast, the bottom half of the world's adult population owned barely one percent of global wealth. More than 80 percent of the world's population lives in countries where income differentials are widening. The poorest 40 percent of the world's population accounts for only 5 percent of global income, while the richest 20 percent account for 75 percent of world income.[2]

Thus, this latest crisis emerged against the background of an unsustainable global growth pattern characterized by strong consumer demand in the United States, funded by easy credit and a housing market bubble. Far-reaching financial deregulation had facilitated unfettered expansion of new financial instruments, such as highly-rated sub-prime mortgage securities, sold on financial markets worldwide. This growth pattern saw strong expansion of trade and high commodity prices benefiting many developing countries, but also led to mounting global financial imbalances and overleveraged financial institutions, businesses and households. In the context of a highly integrated global economy without adequate regulation and global governance, breakdown in a central part of the system reverberated throughout.

This crisis is considered systemic because its origins lie in the workings of financial markets. The painful lessons of the 1930s had led to some progress in the quarter century from the mid-1940s to create conditions more favorable to sustained economic growth, employment and development. Many of these conditions were undermined over the last three decades with economic deregulation and economic policies favoring the private sector, following the more general de-legitimization of the role of government. Globalization or greater international economic integration during this period was actively promoted by the institutions responsible for international economic governance, sometimes contrary to their own mandates. Financial deregulation and globalization thus replaced national financial arrangements, institutions and policies for sustained growth and employment, investment and technology promotion as well as inclusion and equity at the national or regional level.

These trends were hardly weakened by growing evidence that the ostensible benefits of the new policies and institutions were actually greatly wanting. For example, there has long been strong evidence that capital account liberalization had led to new capital flows from the capital-poor to the capital-rich, raised financial sector profitability at the expense of the real economy and economic growth, and exacerbated financial volatility and instability. Thus, the financial system and the real economy became increasingly pro-cyclical, more volatile, less developmental and less inclusive. Instead of providing adequate checks and balances, many government and inter-governmental institutions accelerated this process due to policy and regulatory capture and other influences on governance and reform.

Not surprisingly then, the recent crisis has affected all financial institutions and national economies, reducing the supply and raising the cost of credit, with devastating effects for the real economy. Credit is an essential part of any economy where decisions take time to come to fruition, and managing credit risk is necessary in a healthy economy. However, the greater the intermediation between those who borrow and those holding the risk, the more likely the number and diversity of creditors for any individual borrower will increase. Also, the greater the capacity to actively trade credit risk, the greater the danger that risks will go undetected or be under-priced. The interconnectedness of excessive risk-taking in financial markets with the problem of the global imbalances, vast dollar reserve accumulation (especially in parts of the developing world), volatile commodity prices and declining productive investments helps explain why this crisis is systemic and synchronous worldwide.[3]

Policymakers initially responded in a piecemeal fashion to the turmoil, failing to see the systemic risk and its global ramifications, with the symptoms already apparent in 2007. The initial approach included massive liquidity injections into the financial system and bailouts of some major financial institutions. As the crisis intensified, crisis management became more comprehensive from September 2008. The measures taken have reshaped the previously deregulated financial landscape. Massive public funding (amounting to US$18 trillion or almost 30 percent of world output)[4] has been made available to recapitalize banks, taking partial or full government ownership of ailing financial institutions, and providing guarantees for bank deposits and other financial assets. Recognizing that monetary and financial measures will not be enough to halt the slide into deeper recession, many countries—mostly developed but also some developing—have introduced fiscal stimulus plans amounting to (by April 2009) about US$2.7 trillion (about 4 percent of world output) to be spent over 2009-2011 (Ghosh, 2009).

Still, the problems have not gone away. Although the bold policy responses seem to have halted the slide, the risk of a prolonged global recession still remains, as problems in the financial and corporate sectors in the major economies persist, protectionist tendencies are on the rise, and business and consumer confidence remain low in most economies. The risk of the world economy sliding back into recession remains particularly high if there is uncoordinated and premature abandonment of recovery packages.

Indications of recovery have also weakened the momentum for regulation of the financial sector and reform of the international financial architecture.

Developing countries are particularly adversely affected by the turmoil and the ensuing financial downturn, but most are constrained from responding with robust countercyclical measures. Generally, poor countries are less resilient and thus more vulnerable to fluctuations in world markets. With less foreign exchange reserves, fiscal resources and policy space, they are typically forced to pursue pro-cyclical monetary and fiscal policies, leading to greater variability in economic performance and thus adversely affecting long-term growth.

The G20 Summit in London on 2 April 2009 pledged to restore confidence, growth, and jobs; repair the financial system to restore lending; strengthen financial regulation to rebuild trust; fund and reform the international financial institutions to overcome the crisis and prevent future ones; promote global trade and investment and reject protectionism; and ensure an inclusive, green and sustainable recovery. They announced US$1.1 trillion in international financial support, including a quadrupling of IMF resources to US$750 billion (including a new SDR allocation of US$250 billion), additional lending by multilateral development banks of at least US$100 billion, and greater support for trade finance, though much of this was neither truly additional nor intended for developing countries. At the same time, they pledged to reform and modernize international financial institutions to strengthen their longer term relevance, effectiveness and legitimacy, without specifying the nature of governance reforms envisaged. The G20 also reaffirmed all existing commitments to provide more aid and debt relief to the poorest countries, including US$50 billion to support social protection, boost trade and safeguard development in low-income countries.

While these measures were significant, much more needs to be done, not only to avoid this crisis from becoming a humanitarian disaster, but also to address systemic biases and flaws in the international financial architecture and global governance, as well as to steer the global economy in a more equitable and sustainable direction.

Impact of the Crisis on Development

Impact of Declining Trade, Finance and Remittances

Many developing countries, especially the poorer ones, were not very directly exposed to financial globalization, and hence, to the recent financial turmoil, capital flow reversals and higher costs of borrowing. Yet, they have been adversely affected through a variety of other channels, including reduced trade and commodity prices, declining remittance incomes and strains on official development assistance. As the crisis has had uneven effects, countries are hurt in different ways and to differing extents, depending on their economic structures and vulnerability.

The impact of the crisis has also been shaped by government capacities to contain and counter its consequences. Much depends on the counter-cyclical macroeconomic policy mechanisms and the robustness of their regulatory governance frameworks, social protection and political stability. Such influences shape how various social groups are affected. Generally, being more dependent on external finance (including aid), narrowly based foreign trade, and foreign-exchange earnings (e.g. workers' remittances or international tourism), the poorest countries have been much more vulnerable to global economic vicissitudes. Many have weak social protection arrangements while most smaller developing countries rely on only a few commodities.

External financing for developing countries has declined and become more expensive as needs have risen with the collapse of export and commodity prices. Private capital flows to developing countries have dropped sharply or even been reversed, accompanied by sharp rises in risk premiums and external financing costs. According to the Institute of International Finance report of October 2009, after peaking at about US$1.2 trillion in 2007 before the crisis, the inflows halved in 2008, fell further in 2009 to an estimated US$350 billion, and are expected to recover to about US$650 billion in 2010.[5] The transition economies of Eastern Europe and the former Soviet Union experienced the most substantial fall. While relatively small in global terms, Africa too has become increasingly reliant on private capital inflows. There were no international bond issues by African countries in 2008, while Kenya, Nigeria, Tanzania and Uganda had to cancel plans to raise funds in international capital markets for infra-structure projects.

External financing costs for emerging markets surged, but have since receded, albeit not yet to pre-crisis levels. Even small declines in such flows significantly impact securities' prices, given the small size of most domestic capital markets. Risk premiums on foreign lending more than tripled on average, from 250 to 800 basis points, in a few weeks in the third quarter of 2008. Unlike in past crises, when spreads varied significantly across regions and countries, reflecting investor discrimination of country-specific risks, the recent rise has been more uniform, reflecting contagion in global financial markets. Although spreads declined to 500 basis points by April 2009 and further since then, they remain much higher than before the turmoil.

The sharp reduction of affordable finance has adversely affected infrastructure investments, critical for long-term growth. Both public and private infrastructure investments in Latin America and sub-Saharan Africa fell significantly after various crises and fiscal adjustments in the 1980s and 1990s, as in East Asia after the financial crisis of the late 1990s, and still had not recovered to pre-crisis levels by 2007.[6] Constructing, maintaining and rehabilitating needed infrastructure are critical for sustained development, usually influencing the location of new private investments and other initiatives.

The increasing costs of foreign borrowing—especially debt servicing—have also affected debt sustainability. Over US$1 trillion in external corporate debt and some US$3 trillion of foreign debt for transition economies and developing countries matured in 2009, of which much has been "rolled over" at much higher cost. Thus, debt sustainability will be adversely affected by much lower growth rates and export earnings. As external debt is usually denominated in the major currencies, the debt-servicing capacity is highly sensitive to exchange-rate shifts. Deteriorating external conditions have generally weakened the exchange rates of most developing countries. Many low and middle income countries have experienced currency depreciations since late 2008 by as much as half. Currency depreciations make external debt servicing more burdensome in the face of lower export earnings and weaker budget positions.

Thus, debt has become less sustainable in many developing countries. Many low income countries are more vulnerable, including those that have benefited from substantial debt relief under the heavily-indebted poor countries (HIPC) initiative. Only eight HIPCs had low risk of debt distress in 2008. According to the IMF and World Bank, 31 countries face moderate to high risk, including 10 already debt distressed.[7] About a third of low and middle-income countries in sub-Saharan Africa are vulnerable to external shocks and at risk of debt distress with external debt-to-GNP ratios of more than half, and debt service-to-GNP ratios of more than 2 percent. Recent efforts to make the debt sustainability framework more flexible will allow countries to taken on even more debt, probably leading to a new round of debt problems.

The fall in international trade is also hurting developing countries much more. Trade flows were falling sharply in most economies in late 2008 and early 2009, with the more export-oriented Asian economies experiencing the sharpest declines. 2009 will witness a drop in the volume of world merchandise trade by about a tenth, the largest such decline since the 1930s,[8] due to falling demand as well as scarcer and costlier trade credit. Although seemingly less integrated into the world economy, many poor countries have been hard hit by heavy dependence on a few exports, which have become important sources of foreign exchange and government revenue. International tourist arrivals have dropped with the economic crisis, cutting foreign exchange earnings for many developing countries, especially small island developing states. The costs of dealing with recent global public health threats (e.g. H1N1 influenza or "swine flu") have not helped.

Commodity price collapses have made things worse, especially for developing economies highly reliant on primary exports. From 2002 to 2008, many developing countries gained from the rising prices of primary, especially mineral commodities. The adverse impact of the global financial crisis on the real economy after mid-2008 sharply reversed this trend. Oil and metal prices collapsed from their peaks in mid-2008. Agricultural prices, especially food prices, also declined sharply after the price hikes in early 2008. No significant rebound is expected in the outlook, continuing to depress export earnings and government revenues in many developing countries. Food and energy-importing countries are consequently better off, although this must be compared to the lower export earnings, remittances and government revenue, and rising borrowing costs.

Remittances to developing countries have also moderated significantly.[9] Worth more than US$300 billion in 2008—almost thrice the official development assistance (ODA) to developing countries, and many times more than actual net aid transfers (minus interest payments)—remittances have provided important income support to sustain family consumption and investment finance in many developing countries.[10] Total income from remittances in sub-Saharan Africa was US$20 billion in 2008, more than either ODA or foreign direct investment receipts. Remittance flows are especially important for several countries, accounting for over a fifth of national income in some cases.

The World Bank estimates that remittance flows to developing countries will fall to US$317 billion in 2009, representing a decline of 6.1 percent, although measuring the decline in depreciated US dollars understates the fall.[11] Remittances to Latin America and the Caribbean started to decline from mid-2008 with job losses in the United States, the source of four-fifths of its remittances. The transition economies of Eastern Europe and Central Asia also saw reduced remittance inflows as the Russian ruble depreciated. Slower growth in the Middle East in 2009 has reduced migrants' remittances, especially to South and Southeast Asia. Remittances to developing countries could drop by between 25 and 67 billion dollars in

2009; the countries most adversely affected get relatively more remittances from the high income countries more negatively hit by the crisis.[12]

Remittances have been reduced by growing migration barriers, job losses, forced repatriations and other factors reducing incomes for immigrant workers.[13] Many host countries of immigrant workers have restricted immigration and tightened requirements for visas, residence or work permits for immigrant workers. Immigrant workers are often the last to be hired and the first to lose their jobs. These have become attractive policy options for host countries in this crisis, but reduce remittances to home countries which have helped cushion the impact of previous crises. Nevertheless, remittances may still be more resilient than other sources of foreign incomes, but are no substitute for more adequate social protection.

With declining national income and larger fiscal deficits in donor countries, aid flows are expected to decline even though current levels are less than half the 0.7 percent commitment of the last four decades. As the aid discourse measures ODA as a share of national income, aid is expected to fall with national income even if shares do not decline, especially if the current crisis becomes protracted. In past crises, humanitarian and social disasters were often avoided by increased donor funding. Financing humanitarian and social spending is usually politically easier for donors. Besides their volatility, aid flows are likely to fall when major donor countries are experiencing recessions. However, as with remittances, reporting such flows in weakened US dollars has under-stated the depth of the decline.

Already unreliable, official aid flows can also become even more volatile. Before the crisis, low-income countries saw large fluctuations in aid flows equivalent to 2-3 percent of their GDP. Most low-income countries have few alternatives to ODA in the face of drops in export and fiscal revenues. Therefore, uncertainty about net aid inflows constrains responding to the crisis. Meanwhile, IMF credit needed to meet external payments obligations typically require tighter monetary and fiscal policies, thus further constraining governments' fiscal space needed for counter-cyclical and other recovery efforts.

Most developing countries are experiencing serious balance-of-payment problems due to the crisis. The World Bank estimates that 98 of 104 developing countries will not be able to cover their external financing needs; this could get worse with further declines in private capital inflows and increased capital flight. The IMF estimates that the balance-of-payments shock to low-income countries alone could be around US$140 billion in 2009. While some developing countries have huge foreign reserves, these are very unequally distributed; most developing countries do not have sufficient reserves to cope with the external shocks caused by the crisis. A growing number of mainly low-income countries do not have adequate reserves to cover three months of imports, while many emerging market economies have seen sharp declines in their foreign reserves, putting further pressure on their currencies to depreciate. More countries will have no choice but to turn to the IMF for emergency financing, which, in turn, constrains their fiscal and policy space, albeit not as restrictively in the short-term as before.[14]

Implications for Growth and Employment

On average, per capita incomes in developing countries are likely to stagnate in 2009 as growth decelerates significantly from 5.4 percent in 2008 and almost 5.7 percent annually during 2004-2007 (Table 3.1). Per capita incomes in 60 developing countries were expected to shrink in 2009. These

Table 3.1 Per capita GDP growth by main country groups, 2007-2010[+] (percent)

	Per capita GDP growth rate			*Change in growth rate*	
	2004-07	*2008*	*2009*	*2009–2008*	*2009–2004-7*
World	**2.6**	**1.9**	**-2.2**	-4.1	-4.8
Developed economies	**2.1**	**0.5**	**-3.5**	-4.0	-5.6
USA	1.6	0.4	-2.5	-2.9	-4.1
Japan	2.1	-0.7	-5.6	-4.9	-7.7
European Union (EU27)	2.4	0.9	-4.1	-5.0	-6.5
Economies in transition	**7.7**	**5.5**	**-6.4**	-11.9	-14.1
Developing economies	**5.7**	**5.4**	**1.9**	-3.5	-3.8
Africa	3.4	5.6	1.6	-4.0	-1.8
North Africa	3.6	3.8	3.5	-0.3	-0.1
Sub-Saharan Africa	3.6	6.4	-2.3	-8.7	-5.9
East and South Asia	7.3	6.1	4.3	-1.8	-3.0
Western Asia	3.7	4.5	-1.2	-5.7	-4.9
Latin America and the Caribbean	4.0	5.4	-2.2	-7.6	-6.2

Source: UN/DESA, LINK Global Economic Outlook, October 2009.
Note: [+] Data for 2009 are pre-meeting forecasts.

setbacks are widespread, but greatest in Sub-Saharan Africa, Latin America and the Caribbean. The least developed countries (LDCs) will also be severely affected, with growth dropping by five percentage points from the robust growth of the last half decade.

Very limited or no stimulus measures in most developing countries will only delay recovery. Delays in initiating recovery measures will also slow recovery as impact lags generally increase with the delays; furthermore, the weaknesses of the subsequent recoveries are likely to be exacerbated by under-resourcing.[15] Private investments have been discouraged by excess capacity due to over-investments, thanks to easy credit availability before the crisis. Also, the job recovery lag is expected to be much greater than output recovery for related reasons.[16] Furthermore, as the experiences of previous crises shows, the labor share of national income lags behind the pre-crisis level for a considerable period of time, exacerbating inequality.

According to ILO estimates in early 2009, based on IMF forecasts in late 2008, over 50 million more people worldwide could become un-employed and over two hundred million may join the ranks of the working poor due to the crisis. People who lose jobs in developing countries try to survive by doing some other work, especially in the low-productivity, low-wage informal or rural sector, as there is little or no social protection or security to fall back on. Thus, the published unemployment figure may not reflect the extent of the problem as well as the number of working poor. Hence, the adverse effects of the crisis will be lasting, causing significant hardship as the economy performs sub-optimally.

As Ghosh's chapter shows, the financial crisis contributed to and exacer-bated the 2008 food price spikes with the exodus from financial asset markets to commodity markets. According to the FAO, higher food prices pushed an estimated 115 million people into hunger in 2007 and 2008, raising the number of hungry to 1.02 billion people, or nearly one in seven. The FAO estimates that the global financial crisis has added at least 100 million people to the ranks of the hungry by reducing their means to buy enough food.[17]

Before the current crisis, two billion people suffered from nutritional deficiencies. Even though food prices have declined significantly from peaks in early 2008, they still remain above the preceding levels. Also, recent exchange-rate depreciations have increased the domestic prices of imported food in many developing countries. The FAO food price index in January 2009, for example, was 27 percent above the 2005 level, and 64 percent above the 2000 level. Various factors have conspired to raise food prices, including reduced food stocks and agricultural land, low agricultural productivity growth, climate change and the related increased demand for bio-fuels. Food prices in the next ten years should be significantly higher than the low levels earlier this decade.

Reduced employment and income opportunities due to the crisis will undoubtedly generate further setbacks in poverty and hunger reduction. Lower per capita incomes in 2009 will almost surely reverse progress in poverty reduction significantly, especially in South Asia. In China alone, 20 million workers had lost their jobs by the end of 2008. Existing projections may underestimate the poverty impact of the crisis as distributional consequences have not been adequately factored in. These trends are likely to jeopardize poverty reduction as it will take time before workers regain jobs with better remuneration.

Global Responses to the Crisis

Recognizing the limited potential of further monetary easing, some major economies, including some developing countries, have undertaken massive fiscal stimulus efforts. The stimulus plans so far are worth about US$2.7 trillion to be spent over 2-3 years; the annual fiscal injections will be less than 2 percent of annual world output, and fall short of the amount required to make up for the contraction in global aggregate demand.[18] At the London G20 Summit of 2 April 2009, leaders promised to enhance the total fiscal effort to US$5 trillion by the end of 2010, though actual plans to do so have not been forthcoming.

As Table 3.2 shows, the amount per country varies considerably. While the response so far has been unprecedented, even more is needed, including improving financial sector balance sheets; better coordinated macroeconomic stimuli; more development financing, especially for the poorest countries; countering protectionist temptations; and sustained investments in a more sustainable and equitable future.

Coordinating Macroeconomic Recovery Efforts

The crisis has challenged multilateralism and existing international governance arrangements, as it has hit the whole world, demanding more international cooperation. UN economic recovery scenarios for 2009-2015 with coordinated and uncoordinated global stimuli suggest that better international macroeconomic coordination with adequate resources for fiscally constrained developing countries, particularly the LDCs, would have a win-win outcome, with stronger recoveries for all—developed, transition and developing countries, especially the LDCs[19]. Inadequate international

Table 3.2 Fiscal stimulus to address the global financial and economic crisis[#]

	Share of GDP (%)	Fiscal stimulus (US$ billion)		Share of GDP (%)	Fiscal stimulus (US$ billion)
Argentina	1.2	3.9	Lithuania	1.9	0.9
Australia	4.7	47.0	Luxembourg	3.6	2.0
Austria	4.5	18.8	Malaysia	5.5	12.1
Bangladesh	0.6	0.5	Mexico	2.1	22.7
Belgium	1.0	4.9	Netherlands	1.0	8.4
Brazil	0.2	3.6	New Zealand	4.2	5.4
Canada	2.8	42.2	Nigeria	0.7	1.6
Chile	2.4	4.0	Norway	0.6	2.9
China	13.3	585.3	Peru	2.6	3.3
Czech Republic	1.8	3.9	Philippines	4.1	7.0
Denmark	2.5	8.7	Poland	2.0	10.6
Egypt	1.7	2.7	Portugal	1.2	3.0
Finland	3.5	9.5	Russia	1.2	20.0
France	1.3	36.2	Saudi Arabia	12.5	60.0
Georgia	10.3	1.3	Singapore	5.8	10.6
Germany	2.2	80.5	Slovenia	1.0	0.5
Greece	0.0	0.0	South Africa	1.5	4.2
Honduras	10.6	1.5	Spain	0.9	15.3
Hong Kong SAR	5.2	11.3	Sri Lanka	0.2	0.1
Hungary	10.9	17.0	Sweden	2.8	13.4
Iceland	0.0	0.0	Switzerland	0.5	2.5
India	3.2	38.4	Taiwan Pr. of China	3.9	15.3
Indonesia	1.4	7.1			
Israel	1.4	2.8	Tanzania	6.4	1.3
Italy	0.7	16.8	Thailand	14.3	39.0
Japan	6.0	297.5	Turkey	5.2	38.0
Kazakhstan	13.8	18.2	United Kingdom	1.4	38.0
Kenya	0.9	0.3	United States	6.8	969.0
Korea	5.6	53.4	Vietnam	9.4	8.4
			All countries above	**4.7**	**2,633**
			All countries	**4.3**	

Note: [#] This list of countries is not necessarily exhaustive.

Source: UN-DESA, based on information from IMF (2009), OECD (2009), Credit Suisse (2009) and Zhang, Thelen *et al.* (2009). Note that the definition and contents of the policy measures vary from country to country and that the size of these packages may not be comparable across countries.

coordination has not only weakened economic recovery, but has ominous implications for other challenges requiring greater international cooperation such as climate change.

More adequate crisis responses require addressing its systemic causes and the development emergency it has caused, and should therefore consider:

- the global imbalances;
- constraints imposed on developing countries in undertaking needed counter cyclical policy interventions and social protection; and
- systemic flaws in global finance exacerbating its fragility.

Thus, actions are needed for:

- *Coordination and financing macroeconomic stimulus measures.* Lack of coordination, in terms of size and timing, have limited the multiplier effects of fiscal stimulus measures, reducing their potential impact on economic growth and employment. More than four-fifths of the fiscal resources are being expended by the major developed countries. This will not reduce imbalances in the global economy as much of the stimulus is by the major deficit countries. Like them, most developing countries lack fiscal resources, but are also prevented by IMF policy conditions and the fear of inflation and market punishment from undertaking needed countercyclical measures.
- *Cleaning financial sector balance sheets.* Effective actions are required to restore the financial health of banks with adequate recapitalization to resume lending. Comprehensive macro-prudential regulatory reforms and improved oversight of the entire financial sector is also needed to restore confidence and to keep the system solvent. Borrowing costs must be kept down to ensure adequate liquidity for early and sustained recovery. Developing countries will also need to reconsider current policies regarding capital account and financial liberalization, and to adopt active capital account management measures.
- *Preventing possible adverse long-term effects.* Macroeconomic stimuli should be coordinated within a medium-term financing framework to reduce the undesirable effects of financing the fiscal stimuli, such as destabilizing exchange-rate movements, inflation, unsustainable public debt accumulation, and renewed widening of the global imbalances.[20] It should also broaden support for international coordination.

Concerns over possible adverse repercussions from greater fiscal deficits and public debts continue to deter stronger fiscal responses. Despite uncertainty about the sustainability and strength of the recovery so far, there are already calls to abandon fiscal stimulus measures. If these calls are heeded, recovery will be undermined, resulting in protracted recession; and when exit becomes necessary, it should be orderly and coordinated. The severity of the crisis calls for policy responses adequate to the scale of the problem, and should thus be considered on an extraordinary basis. If they effectively reduce the depth and duration of the economic downturn and save jobs, incomes and domestic demand, the employment costs of widening fiscal deficits due to stimulus packages, could well be smaller than the costs of a deep and protracted recession. Both financial rescues and fiscal stimulus packages demand much from current and future taxpayers, with significant redistributive implications. The medium-term framework should also consider the inter-generational, international and social class distributional consequences of financing fiscal stimuli.

Successful economic recovery should not lead back to the *status quo ante* with its unsustainable growth pattern, but should instead ensure sustainable development including job creation and poverty reduction. Without this, the development emergency will worsen, with further setbacks in achieving development goals. Declining government revenues will provide governments with fewer resources to meet increased social needs due to greater unemployment and poverty caused by the crisis. If governments cut back on social expenditures, this will have lasting effects on the education and health of their people, especially the young. If they are forced to cut back or delay essential investments in infrastructure and sustainable development, there will be long-term implications for poverty reduction, food security as well as climate change mitigation and adaptation.

Additional Finance to Address the Development Emergency

More resources are needed to finance adequate responses by developing countries, especially the most vulnerable countries. The G20's US$1.1 trillion package, mainly strengthening the IMF without requiring its reform, and reiterated ODA donor commitments are significant, but much more is needed to address the development emergency caused by the global crisis:

- *Greater and easier access to unconditional emergency financing for low-income countries is urgently needed.* Additional SDR allocations to increase the IMF lending capacity will boost the reserves of IMF members in line with their existing quotas rather than their financing needs. A mechanism of ex-post reallocation should enhance lending capacity to developing countries, especially to the poorest with the smallest quotas, supplementing the doubling of access limits on IMF concessional lending to low-income countries, to provide more easily accessible low-cost emergency financing to the most needy. Regional efforts to augment international liquidity provisioning (e.g. through the Latin American Reserve Fund, the Chiang Mai and other regional initiatives) should also be supported.

- *Reform of the IMF financing framework for developing countries is needed* to support countercyclical responses and to more flexibly respond to country needs. Further steps towards greater flexibility in IMF lending are needed as restrictive, pro-cyclical monetary and fiscal policy conditions are still being required for IMF emergency credit support to emerging markets and other developing countries.

- *More long-term development lending and ODA are needed* for enhanced long-term official financing to fund external finance gaps and to provide developing countries with the required fiscal space to finance fiscal stimulus packages and infrastructure spending.[21] Some US$250 billion could be mobilized for long-term financing by the multilateral development banks. The World Bank Group is already committed to increase IBRD lending capacity by at least US$100 billion, while the regional development banks could expand development lending by about US$150 billion. To meet the needs of the most vulnerable low-income countries, especially in Africa, ODA would need to be raised very significantly. About US$50 billion could be mobilized by front-loading resources in the already replenished International Development Association (IDA) window of the World Bank and those in the concessional windows of the regional development banks.[22] Much more could come by accelerating delivery on long-standing ODA commitments.[23]

- *Development financing will need to become more reliable.*[24] To reduce the volatility in official financing and sustain long-term investments in developing countries, development financing should become more predictable through multi-annual agreements between donor and recipient countries in line with the Paris Declaration[25] and the 2008 Accra Agenda for Action for improving aid effectiveness.

Minimizing Protectionist Responses and Unfair Trading Practices

Crisis responses should avoid protectionist urges. After the G-20 leaders pledged in November 2008 to avoid protectionist measures, 17 G20 countries implemented 47 measures restricting trade at the expense of other countries. Commitments to refrain from new trade barriers and "financial protectionism" should be adhered to and measures already taken should be rectified. In this regard, financial rescue packages are especially problematic in the face of commitments to preserve "level playing fields".

Early conclusion of a truly developmental Doha Round of trade negotiations has probably been made impossible by the crisis. As noted earlier, the WTO's strong rules-based multilateral trading system has not been effective in stemming the growing trade protectionism since late 2008. As Raghavan's chapter shows, the WTO's Financial Services Agreement (FSA) under the General Agreement on Trade in Services (GATS) may have contributed to the crisis by enhancing financial globalization. Developed countries should immediately grant 100 percent or full market access to all LDC exports, including cotton, and eliminate all production and export subsidies for their own agriculture besides significantly enhancing trade finance and facilitation for all developing country exports.

The international community should ensure the crisis does not penalize migrants in receiving countries. Their countries of origin have already been harmed due to migrants' disproportionately higher job and income losses, and hence, by lower remittances. Although migrant remittances in recent crises have been counter-cyclical, rising as home country conditions deteriorated, in the current synchronous global recession, remittances are less likely to increase owing to the job and income losses of the emigrants.

Towards Fairer and More Sustainable Development

The crisis response should support long-term investments in sustainable development. The fiscal stimulus should seek to revive economic activity and employment, and to ensure social provisioning, but also to invest in human development and "green" growth. The UN has proposed a Global Green New Deal to ensure that the stimulus is used for investments and technology sharing to greatly expand decent work opportunities and sustainable development, including climate change mitigation and adaptation. This would include investments in "climate-proof" infrastructure, technology development, renewable energy generation and energy efficiency to slow down and adapt to climate change. Such investments would yield significant employment benefits while also reducing energy consumption and greenhouse gas emissions. For example, renewable energy investments are expected to generate five times as many jobs as conventional energy investments. Meanwhile, investments in afforestation and reforestation, sustainable agriculture, and biodiversity protection will help climate change mitigation and adaptation, poverty reduction and food security. Greater international policy coordination will be needed, especially to finance investments in sustainable development and to enable needed technology transfers.

The ILO has been effectively advancing the "Decent Work" agenda by promoting a global jobs pact with which the stimulus should be aligned. This pact seeks to make the recovery job-intensive, leading to sustainable growth based on stronger and better functioning labor markets and social protection. A "social protection floor" is also being sought to ensure access to basic social services and protection for the poor and other vulnerable people. Developing countries generally lack the level of social protection found in most developed countries where some measures also serve as automatic economic stabilizers during economic downturns. The international community should support developing countries in creating a social protection floor to ensure access to basic social services and income security (including through cash transfers).

Reform of the International Financial System and Global Economic Governance

The current crisis is ultimately due to fundamental weaknesses in global economic governance; overcoming these defects is necessary for progress. These weaknesses led to inappropriate financial deregulation and residual regulation, the growth of global imbalances and vulnerabilities, and irresponsible behavior. Hence, fundamental changes are needed to reform the international financial system to improve safeguards against such crises, and to create a more equitable multilateral framework for global economic governance in line with contemporary realities.

Marginal changes in regulation and more IMF funding will not be enough to ensure a stable international monetary system. Progress towards a new international financial system and more equitable global economic governance should be urgently promoted through inclusive multilateral institutions and processes, especially the United Nations. The United Nations Conference on Monetary and Financial Affairs in 1944 created the Bretton Woods system and key institutions for the post-war period, but later developments, especially since the 1970s, have been *ad hoc*, resulting in what Robert Triffin called a "non-system". The current crisis, and the development emergency it has precipitated, highlight the urgent need to address systemic failure to sustain "growth, jobs, security"—the G20 slogan at London—and to create more conducive conditions for sustainable development more generally.

The 2002 UN Conference on Financing for Development (FfD)'s Monterrey Consensus, as well as its follow-up 2008 Doha Declaration, both emphasized the need to enhance the coherence of the international monetary, financial and trading systems, to achieve the internationally agreed development goals "to eradicate poverty, achieve sustained economic growth and promote sustainable development"[26] and to "advance to a fully inclusive and equitable global economic system."[27] This formulation provides the purpose of global economic system and governance reform.

The IMF Articles of Agreement reflect a shared understanding, present at Bretton Woods in 1944, of the desired features of the international economic system. First was ensuring the "expansion and balanced growth of international trade, and to contribute thereby to the promotion and maintenance of high levels of employment and real income and to the development of productive resources of all members as primary objectives of economic policy"[28]; second, "to promote exchange stability, to maintain orderly exchange arrangements among members, and to avoid competitive exchange depreciation"; and third, to create conditions favorable for post-war reconstruction and sustained post-colonial economic development, as reflected in the official name of the World Bank, viz. the International Bank for Reconstruction and Development.

Regulating Financial Markets

A macro-prudential regulatory system should be based on countercyclical capital provisioning and inclusive, effective and accountable institutions for better supervision of all financial market segments contributing to systemic risk. Recent regulatory reforms have been largely confined to improved disclosure, prudential controls and risk management, but these are now recognized as inadequate and insufficient in mitigating the inherent pro-cyclicality of financial markets, which tends to give rise to asset price bubbles. G20 leaders have also recognized the need for regulatory reform, but have made modest progress so far in furthering actual reforms to overcome the inherent weaknesses of existing mechanisms. Priority should be given to the following policy and institutional reform objectives:

- *Eliminating pro-cyclicality*: The pro-cyclical elements of the changing Basel II framework need to be replaced with more counter-cyclical tools to limit credit expansion during cyclical upswings and to provide for losses when they occur.

- *Regulating cross-border flows*: Such mechanisms should apply to all financial institutions and transactions, including cross-border capital flows. It is necessary to ensure comprehensive and appropriate regulation to reduce gaps and inconsistencies in regulatory regimes among countries, and to address systemic vulnerabilities due to uneven regulation of the financial system. International macro-prudential and regulatory arrangements need to be much better coordinated. Standards and procedures should be harmonized with greater clarity of responsibilities and objectives. Closer and more effective cross-border collaboration will be essential to enhance effective supervision.
- *Safeguarding against excessive risk taking*: Financial regulation should ascertain the safety of financial instruments, especially derivatives. There is a growing consensus on the need for tighter regulation of financial incentives and remuneration and for eliminating existing incentives which encourage excessive risk taking and short-termism.
- *More effective monitoring*: The 1999 international standards and codes initiative introduced after the 1997-1998 Asian crisis failed to provide adequate early warning signals for regulatory short-falls. Defining standards as well as designing effective monitoring, subject to independent peer-review, should be prioritized. Standard setting, implementation and monitoring are recognized as inter-related, and should be sensitive to the variety of country-specific conditions.
- *Reform of credit-rating agencies*: The current crisis has exposed the weaknesses of existing credit-rating arrangements. Governance of credit rating agencies needs to ensure more appropriate risk assessment processes. The G20 proposed a regulatory oversight regime in line with the IOSCO Code of Conduct by the end of 2009 to improve prudential regulation. Ratings should reflect differences in products and countries in a transparent manner to capture the actual risk of the product or country in question.
- *Capital account management should be encouraged*: The crisis has strengthened the case for the macro-prudential deployment of capital account regulatory tools for (counter-cyclical) macroeconomic management, especially in developing countries. The current crisis has again exposed the macroeconomic risks associated with capital account liberalization in the face of inherently volatile international finance.
- *Aligning financial regulation with the multilateral trading system*: The liberalization of financial services of recent decades has been advanced by multilateral and bilateral trade and investment agreements. The

WTO/GATS Financial Services Agreement (FSA) needs to be reviewed in light of its likely contribution to the fragility and vulnerability of international financial arrangements.

Tax Evasion and Fiscal Space

International tax cooperation must be strengthened for more effective financial regulation globally. Such cooperation should help reduce tax evasion, also associated with money laundering, corruption, terrorism financing, and drug trafficking. Considerable potential fiscal resources have evaded the tax systems of both developed and developing countries. Hence, improved international cooperation to combat pervasive tax evasion will boost the fiscal capacities and space of all governments.[29] Recognizing the critical role of fiscal space for effective government responses to the crisis and the implications of recent tax evasion scandals, the international community should ensure that the IMF and the OECD effectively support the UN to reduce international tax evasion and enhance tax revenues, especially of developing countries.

Sovereign Debt Sustainability

Better international mechanisms for sovereign debt restructuring and relief need to be established. In response to the current crisis, a more flexible approach to debt sustainability while providing additional funding is urgently needed. Many countries' balance of payments have rapidly deteriorated with the global crisis, as governments need to undertake massive countercyclical responses. Standstill agreements and temporary debt-payment moratoriums should give countries some additional space. Such efforts would also reduce the requirements for new funding. A more orderly sovereign debt workout mechanism and a framework for handling related cross-border issues are needed.

Global Governance Reform

The governance structures of the Bretton Woods institutions need fundamental reform. At the Doha Conference on Financing for Development, member states agreed in December 2008 that such reform must be comprehensive to more adequately reflect changing economic weights in the world economy, be more responsive to current and future challenges, and strengthen the legitimacy and effectiveness of these institutions.

Existing inequities in voting weights in these institutions prevent them from adequately incorporating the needs of users in their operations and conflict with their role as facilitators of international cooperation. Increases in the resources of these institutions should have been preceded by accelerated equitable governance reform.

Improved international macroeconomic policy coordination will require harmonization of the roles and functions of the Bretton Woods institutions. Global responses so far have been coordinated by the G7, G20 and other *ad hoc* and unaccountable initiatives. But all such exclusive groupings lack legitimacy, and hence effectiveness, to provide acceptable and effective global leadership and coordination, especially to make fundamental institutional governance reforms and to address systemic challenges. Redundancy among international institutions should also be addressed while enhancing the role of and scope for complementary regional monetary and financial cooperation.

IMF quota increases have been made on an ad-hoc basis over the decades, only leading to marginal changes, thus failing to shift the balance of power between developed and developing countries. Even the April 2008 decision by the Board of Governors to adopt a new quota formula is not broadly acceptable for making future adjustments in quotas and votes. The new formula actually shifts voting weight to rich countries at the expense of middle- and low-income ones, with a modest shift in favor of developing countries, achieved largely due to voluntary and *ad hoc* decisions on the part of some developed countries. Progress towards more equitable and representative IMF governance requires an improved quota formula, giving more weight to GDP at purchasing power parity (PPP), better reflecting actual trade vulnerability, and taking the size of national populations into account.

Governance reform should also strengthen the influence of low-income countries by restoring the weight of basic votes in the Bretton Woods institutions. When the IMF was established in 1944 with 44 members, basic votes were set at 250 votes for each member, and together represented 11.3 percent of total voting power. With quota increases over the years, the share of basic votes fell considerably, reaching its nadir of 2.1 percent of total voting power for 184 members before the most recent reforms. The IMF Board of Governors' April 2008 decision to triple basic votes only increased the share of basic votes to 5.5 percent of total voting power, falling far short of restoring the total share, let alone the country weight of basic votes. Strengthening basic votes would encourage powerful members to more meaningfully consult with poorer countries.

The extension of double majority voting to a broader set of decisions would also compensate for these gross voting imbalances at the Fund. At present, a double majority—85 percent of voting power and 60 percent of members—is required to amend the Articles of Agreement. Double majority voting (quotas and chairs) could be extended to the selection of the Managing Director and the chair of the International Monetary and Financial Committee (IMFC), as well as for key policy decisions and to approve access to lending. These changes would strengthen the sense of ownership in the Fund by requiring a significant majority of members to support key decisions that determine the direction of the organization.

Such a reform can only be successful if more effective participation by developing countries correspondingly reduces the excessive power of the Funds major shareholders. To be credible, the reform must eliminate effective veto powers over decisions to amend the Articles of Agreement. These basic principles for IMF governance reform should be considered in reforming the other international financial institutions, such as the World Bank. It may also be appropriate to have a 50-50 weight distribution between contributors and users of funds—as is the case with UNDP and the Inter-American Development Bank. Also, the World Bank's specific mandate as a development bank is distinct from the IMF's role, and should be reflected in its governance. Hence, distinct World Bank governance arrangements should be considered for determining the rights of its members.

Macroeconomic policy coordination should be embedded in an institutionalized representative multilateral framework. The IMF could provide this after adequate reform of its governance and appropriate revision of its functions. Its policy-making International Monetary and Financial Committee (IMFC) could mediate international policy coordination, including measures to avoid future unsustainable global imbalances by strengthening IMF surveillance, recognizing macro-financial linkages and extending its vulnerability exercises to all countries.

Broader global economic governance reforms are clearly needed. The crisis and search for adequate responses have underscored the urgent need for better governance of the international financial architecture, the multilateral trading system, the development agenda, the framework for addressing climate change, as well as peace and security.

The United Nations is the most legitimate forum for achieving greater coherence among different actors. Given the specific institutional foci of the IMF, the World Bank and other international economic institutions, there is need for better coordination and political accountability, and a forum for consensus building to guide their policy agendas. Such coordination could take place through a new Global Economic Council overseeing the UN system with the WTO joining. Such a body can provide coordination and oversight to address a broad range of global challenges. With more inclusive representation and accountability, the GEC could provide the required political legitimacy for effective global responses to emerging crises and ensure greater coherence among all major institutions involved in global economic governance.

Global Monitoring and Accountability

Mechanisms for assessing global economic and social vulnerability and for facilitating concerted policy actions need to be improved and better integrated. The world economy has long been in a state of great uncertainty, and many did not see this crisis coming. Existing monitoring mechanisms do not adequately address systemic risks and transmission channels to the real economy. Monitoring frameworks for identifying country vulnerabilities, environmental impacts and effects on living conditions of specific population groups are almost all fragmented. This makes assessing policy effectiveness challenging. Tax payers want to know the effectiveness and distributional consequences of the vast public resources allocated to deal with the crisis. Better monitoring should enhance accountability for national and internationally coordinated actions undertaken by Governments, thus helping to maintain broad social and political support for such actions. In contrast, if the measures do not have a visible impact within a reasonable time horizon, and tax payers are insufficiently informed of how public resources are being deployed, there is a danger of increased social unrest and threats to security.

Reforming the Global Reserve System

A new global reserve system should no longer rely on a single national currency as the major reserve currency. The dollar has not proven to be a stable store of value, a requisite for a stable reserve currency. In the face of global instability and the inability of the international financial institutions to address this instability, as well as inadequate collective protection and insurance mechanisms for balance-of-payments crises, many developing countries have accumulated vast reserves for self-protection. This has led to "uphill" capital flows from developing to developed countries. Overcoming the major inadequacies of the current system requires even broader reform measures. A new system—which allows for better pooling of reserves at the regional and international levels and is not based on a single or even multiple national currencies, but which ensures international liquidity (with Special Drawing Rights or their equivalent) to create a more stable global financial system—needs to be developed. For Special Drawing Rights (SDRs) to play this role, several further reforms and policy measures are needed[30]:

- First, given that IMF quota allocations, currently the basis for SDR issues, are not in line with current world economic realities, SDRs would need to be issued asymmetrically, favoring countries with the greatest need for reserves.
- Second, the issuance of new SDRs should be combined with a new international financing mechanism during crises, which would allow the IMF to lend unused SDRs to countries in need.
- Third, such a new SDR-based mechanism could be complemented by a stronger role for regional reserve and financial cooperation arrangements among developing countries.

Summary of Main Recommendations

- In the face of the world financial and economic crisis, the multilateral system must deploy considerable resources and capacities to achieve rapid and effective responses. Unprecedented global responses have already been taken, but more is still needed.
- Additional fiscal stimulus measures, which should be better internationally coordinated in a medium-term financing framework, are needed, giving due consideration to the problems of global imbalances and destabilizing exchange-rate movements, and the need to adequately finance countercyclical responses by developing countries.
- Financial sector rescue operations should be more effective in restoring credit flows especially to the productive sectors. Much more of the new international liquidity for emergency financing should be for developing countries, responding flexibly to country needs, especially to support countercyclical responses. Inter alia, this should be done through ex-post reallocation of new SDRs issued and greater reserve pooling through regional mechanisms of financial cooperation.
- Development lending and official development assistance need to be scaled up substantially, ensuring reliable financing for developing countries to respond swiftly to the crisis while making long-term investments in human development and global public goods, especially for climate change, requiring new capital replenishments for the

multilateral development banks and accelerated delivery on existing aid commitments.

- Comprehensive regulatory reforms of the international financial system should be undertaken, leading to a macro-prudential framework covering all financial market segments, credit-rating agencies and other systemically important institutions, eliminating existing pro-cyclical measures and perverse incentives for excessive risk taking, and developing improved monitoring mechanisms.
- Broader global economic governance reforms are also needed. The United Nations should have the authority to ensure greater coherence among all major areas of global governance, including those for the international financial system, the multilateral trading system, the development agenda, and the framework for addressing climate change, protection of human rights, and peace and security.
- The Bretton Woods institutions need to be fundamentally reformed to increase their legitimacy as well as their capacity to prevent and manage future crises. Financial reforms should also strengthen international tax cooperation and establish an international mechanism for sovereign debt restructuring and relief. A new global reserve system needs to be established that is no longer based on a single national currency, but rather, on a new SDR-based mechanism, complemented by regional mechanisms for international reserve pooling.
- The United Nations has proposed[31] a global green new deal to address the triple challenges of climate change, development and the financial crisis. A key element of the proposal is the front-loading of internationally subsidized renewable energy investments in developing countries, especially the poorest ones, as part of a "big push" to address global warming with support for sustainable development pathways, which will attract or 'crowd-in' complementary private investments deterred by the absence of basic energy infrastructure. In light of the huge overhang of under-utilized capacity owing to earlier over-investments thanks to the availability of cheap credit before the crisis, such an investment-based approach will enable economic recovery to resume in the poorest countries on the basis of their need, which is not currently reflected by market demand owing to their poverty.

Notes

1. See United Nations (2009). *World Economic Situation and Prospects. Chapter 1, released on 2 December 2009.*

2. United Nations University World Institute for Development Economics Research (2006). *The World Distribution of Household Wealth*. UN WIDER, Helsinki; United Nations (2005). *The Inequality Predicament: Report on the World Social Situation 2005*. New York: UNDESA; Jomo K.S. with Jacques Baudot [eds] (2007). *Flat World, Big Gaps: Economic Liberalization, Globalization, Poverty and Inequality*. Zed Books, London.

3. For some years, the United Nations system, in various publications such as the *World Economic Situation and Prospects* and the *Trade and Development Report*, has repeatedly warned that mounting household, public sector and financial sector indebtedness in the United States and elsewhere—reflected in the growing global financial imbalances—would not be sustainable over time. Together with the Bank of International Settlements, it also warned of the growing "fragility" of international finance. The G24 caucus of developing countries at the Bretton Woods institutions published a policy brief warning of the fragility of the US sub-prime mortgage market segment in the second quarter of 2007, well before its meltdown (Andrew Cornford [2007]. Sub-prime mortgages: Is the worse yet to come? Policy Brief no. 6, June).

4. The estimate includes financial bailout packages (including government guarantees on bad debts) and liquidity injections into financial systems between 1 September 2008 and 31 March 2009. See UN/DESA *Monthly Briefing on the World Economic Situation and Prospects* No. 7 (2 April 2009) (http://www.un.org/esa/policy/publications/wespmbn/sgnote_7.pdf).

5. Source: *Capital Flows to Emerging Market Economies*. October. http://www.iif.com/emr/article+204.php. Estimates of net private capital flows vary. In contrast to the IIF, the IMF's World Economic Outlook Database suggests that net private capital flows to emerging and developing economies declined from US$617.5 billion in 2007 to US$109.3 billion in 2008, and are estimated to fall to -US$190.3 billion in 2009. http://www.imf.org/external/pubs/ft/weo/2009/01/weodata/weoselagr.aspx

6. See United Nations (2006). *World Economic and Social Survey 2006: Diverging Growth and Development* (Sales No. E.06.II.C.1) and World Bank (2009). "Swimming against the tide: how developing countries are coping with the global crisis". Background paper prepared for the G20 Finance Ministers and Central Bank Governors Meeting, Horsham, United Kingdom, March 13-14.

7. See United Nations (2008). *Delivering on the Global Partnership for Achieving the Millennium Development Goals: MDG Gap Task Force Report 2008* (http://www.un.org/esa/policy/mdggap/mdg8report_engw.pdf)

8. See United Nations (2009). *World Economic Situation and Prospects as per mid-2009.*

9. Remittances are down in nearly all countries studied (Bangladesh, Benin, Bolivia, Cambodia, Ghana, Indonesia, Kenya, Nigeria, Uganda and Zambia) by Dirk Willem te Velde and others (2009). "The global financial crisis and

developing countries: Synthesis of the findings of 10 country case studies". ODI Working Paper, No. 306, Overseas Development Institute, London.

10. For example, in 2007, remittances accounted for almost half of national income in Tajikistan. There are several developing countries where remittances account for over 20 percent of their national income.

11. World Bank (2009). *Migration and Development Brief 11*, November 3.

12. Massimiliano Calì and Salvatore Dell'Erbal (2009). "The Global Financial Crisis and Remittances: What Past Evidence Suggests". ODI Working Paper 303, Overseas Development Institute, London.

13. See International Office of Migration. *The Impact of the Global Financial Crisis*. Policy Brief, January 2009.

14. Although there have been some modest improvements in recent fiscal conditionalities, several studies by the Center for Economic Policy Research (CEPR), Third World Network (TWN) and Eurodad argue that the Fund's monetary policies remain as restrictive as ever. After reviewing IMF agreements with 41 countries that include Stand-By Arrangements (SBA), Poverty Reduction and Growth Facility (PRGF), and Exogenous Shocks Facility (ESF), the CEPR concluded that 31 of them contain pro-cyclical macroeconomic policies. See Mark Weisbrot, Rebecca Ray, Jake Johnston, Jose Antonio Cordero and Juan Antonio Montecino (2009). "IMF-Supported Macroeconomic Policies and the World Recession: A Look at Forty-one Borrowing Countries". October, Center for Economic Policy Research, Washington, D.C.

15. The delay—or inside lag—is the time between a shock to the economy and corrective government action responding to the shock. The impact—or outside—lag is the time between government actions responding to a shock to the economy and the resulting effects on the economy. The length of the outside lag is primarily based on the speed of the multiplier process or the size of the multiplier. The size of the fiscal multipliers critically depends on key characteristics of the economy (closed versus open, predetermined versus flexible exchange rate regimes, high versus low debt) or the types of aggregates being considered (government consumption versus government investment). In a January 2009 *Wall Street Journal* op-ed piece, Robert Barro argued that peacetime fiscal multipliers are essentially zero. Christina Romer, Chair of President Obama's Council of Economic Advisers, used multipliers as high as 1.6 to estimate job gains that will be generated by the US$787 billion stimulus package approved by the US Congress in February 2009. The difference between Romer's and Barro's views comes to a staggering 3.7 million jobs by the end of 2010. In the March 2009 IMF Staff Note prepared for the G20 Ministerial Meeting, a range of multipliers was used. The low set of multipliers included 0.3 on revenue, 0.5 on capital spending, and 0.3 on other spending, while the high set included 0.6 on revenue, 1.8 on capital spending, and 1.0 for other spending. The estimates of fiscal multipliers in low income countries

range from negative to 0.5. (Christina Romer and Jared Bernstein [2009]. The Job Impact of the American Recovery and Reinvestment Plan. Testimony to the US Senate/Congress on January 9)

16. See International Labour Organization (2009). "The Financial and Economic Crisis: A Decent Work Response". Paper submitted to ILO Governing Body Committee on Employment and Social Policy, Geneva (document GB.304/ESP/2).

17. The 2001 recession experience suggests that it took about four years for unemployment rates to return to pre-crisis levels. This is because massive increases in long-term unemployment and greater labor market "casualization" are very difficult to reverse. See the work of the ILO in this regard, especially by the International Institute of Labour Studies in Geneva. Also see FAO (2009). *The State of Food Insecurity in the World* http://www.fao.org/docrep/012/i0876e/i0876e00.htm

18. The generic IMF recommendation is 2 percent of GDP.

19. See United Nations (2009). *World Economic Situation and Prospects as per mid-2009.*

20. For instance, the US fiscal stimulus will significantly increase US public debt, contributing to depreciation of the dollar, the world's major reserve currency. This is likely to have highly disruptive effects on financial markets.

21. According to UN forecasts, average developing country growth (excluding China and major oil-exporters) is expected to drop by almost four percentage points from the more robust growth of 2003-2007. Assuming a multiplier effect of about 1.7 from well-designed fiscal stimulus packages, a stimulus of about 3 percent of the combined GDP *per year* would be required for developing countries.

22. The World Bank's IDA concessional window was already replenished by US$30 billion in 2008 to cover three years of credits and grants. This could be frontloaded to make these resources available during 2009 and 2010. Similarly, concessional lending windows of regional development banks (ADB, AfDB, ADB and others) could be frontloaded to provide the additional US$20 billion.

23. Meeting the Gleneagles aid commitments should bring total ODA to US$160 billion per year and provide an extra US$80 billion over 2009-2010. Greater delivery of the agreed UN target of 0.7 percent of annual GNI could provide the remaining US$120 billion needed over 2009-2010. This would bring ODA to about US$220 billion per year, or 0.55 percent of the GNI of OECD-DAC members by 2010.

24. One study finds that the aid system generates massive negative income shocks to some developing countries. The deadweight loss associated with aid volatility is estimated to be between 15 and 20 percent of the total value of aid. At current aid levels, this loss is about US$16 billion. From the average recipient's perspective, the deadweight loss is about 1.9 percent of GDP. See Homi Kharas

(2008). "Measuring the Cost of Aid Volatility". Working Paper 3, Wolfensohn Center for Development, Brookings Institute, Washington, DC.

25. *Paris Declaration on Aid Effectiveness: Ownership, Harmonisation, Alignment, Results and Mutual Accountability.* High Level Forum, Paris, February 28-March 2, 2005. http://www.oecd.org/dataoecd/11/41/34428351.pdf

26. *The Monterrey Consensus of the International Conference on Financing for Development, March 2002*, paragraph 1.

27. *Ibid.* The formulation, from the Monterrey Consensus of 2002 was first enunciated in the Millennium Declaration of 2000 and similarly in many other international agreements.

28. IMF Articles of Agreement, Article I (iii).

29. The Monterrey Consensus and Doha Declaration on Financing for Development both emphasized that improved tax collection would greatly enhance financing for development. Both the United Nations Committee of Experts on International Cooperation in Tax Matters and the Organization for Economic Cooperation and Development (OECD) have taken steps in this direction, though the latter is limited to OECD members and financial centers that have entered into bilateral agreements to exchange information on tax matters. See United Nations, Report of the International Conference on Financing for Development, Monterrey, Mexico, 18-22 March 2002 (A/CONF.198/11, chapter 1, resolution 1, annex) and *Doha Declaration on Financing on Development: outcome document of the Follow-up International Conference on Financing for Development to Review the Implementation of the Monterrey Consensus* (A/CONF.212/L.1/Rev. 1*).

30. For further details, see Chapter VI of United Nations (2005). *World Economic and Social Survey 2005: Financing for Development* (Sales No. E.05.II.C.1).

31. United Nations (2009). *World Economic and Social Survey 2009: Promoting Development, Saving the Planet.*

4

The Unnatural Coupling:
Food and global finance

*Jayati Ghosh**

It has been clear for some months now that the global food crisis, which has been simmering for some time even if it first attracted international attention only around a year ago, is not something that can be treated as discrete and separate from the global financial crisis. On the contrary it has been intimately connected with it, particularly through the impact of financial speculation on world trade prices of food.

This is not to deny the undoubted role of other real economy factors in affecting the global food situation. While demand-supply imbalances have been touted as reasons, this is largely unjustified given that there has been hardly any change in the world demand for food in the past three years. In particular, the claim that food grain prices have soared because of more demand from China and India as their GDP increases, is completely invalid, since both aggregate and per capita consumption of grain have actually fallen in both countries. Supply factors have been—and are likely to continue to be—more significant. These include the short-run effects of diversion of both acreage and food crop output for bio-fuel production, as well as more medium term factors such as rising costs of inputs, falling productivity because of soil depletion, inadequate public investment in agricultural research and extension, and the impact of climate changes that have affected harvests in different ways.

Two policy factors affecting global food supply require special note. The first is the bio-fuel factor: the impact of both oil prices and government policies in the US, Europe, Brazil and elsewhere that have promoted bio-fuels as an alternative to petroleum. This has led to significant shifts in acreage to the cultivation of crops that can produce bio-fuels, and diversion of such output to fuel production. For example, in 2007, the US diverted more than 30 percent of its maize production, Brazil used half of its sugar cane production and the European Union used the greater part of its vegetable oil seeds production as well as imported vegetable oils, to make bio-fuel. In addition to diverting corn output into non-food use, this has also reduced acreage for other crops and has naturally reduced the available land for producing food.

The irony is that bio-fuels do not even fulfill the promises of ensuring energy security or retarding the pace of global warming. Ethanol production is extremely energy-intensive, so it does not really lead to any energy saving. Even in the most "efficient" producer of ethanol—Brazil—where sugar cane rather than corn is used to produce ethanol, it has been argued that the push for such production has led to large-scale deforestation of the Amazon, thereby further intensifying the problems of global warming. Indeed, recent scientific research suggests that the diversion of land to growing bio-fuel crops can produce an enormous "CO_2 debt" from the use of machinery and fertilizers, the release of carbon from the soil and the loss of CO_2 sequestration by trees and other plants that have been cleared for cultivation (Beddington, 2008). Yet, as long as government subsidies remain in the US and elsewhere, and world oil prices remain high, bio-fuel production is likely to continue to be encouraged despite the evident problems. And it will continue to have negative effects on global food production and availability.

The second factor is the policy neglect of agriculture over the past two decades, the impact of which is finally being felt. The prolonged agrarian crisis in many parts of the developing world has been largely a policy-determined crisis. Inappropriate policies have several aspects, but they all result from the basic neoliberal open market-oriented framework that has governed economic policy making in most countries over the past two decades. One major element has been the lack of public investment in agriculture and in agricultural research. This has been associated with low to poor yield increases, especially in tropical agriculture, and falling productivity of land. Greater trade openness and market orientation of farmers have led to shifts in acreage from traditional food crops that were typically better suited to the ecological conditions and the knowledge and resources of farmers, to cash crops that have increasingly relied on purchased inputs. But at the same time, both public provision of different inputs for cultivation and government regulation of private input provision have been progressively reduced, leaving farmers to the mercy of large seed and fertilizer companies, input dealers. As a result, prices for seeds, fertilizers and pesticides have increased quite sharply. There have also been attempts in most developing countries to reduce subsidies to farmers in the form of lower power and water prices, thus adding to cultivation costs. Costs of cultivation have been further increased in most developing countries by the growing difficulties that farmers have in accessing institutional credit, because financial liberalization has moved away from policies of directed credit and provided other more profitable (if less productive) opportunities for financial investment. So many farmers are forced to opt for much more expensive informal credit networks that have added to their costs.

The lack of attention to relevant agricultural research and extension by public bodies has denied farmers access to necessary knowledge. It has also been associated with other problems such as the excessive use of ground water in cultivation; inadequate attention to preserving or regenerating land and soil quality; the over-use of chemical inputs that have long run implications for both safety and productivity. Similarly, the ecological implications of both pollution and climate change, including desertification and loss of cultivable land, are issues that have been highlighted by analysts, but largely ignored by policy makers in most countries. Reversing these processes is possible, and of course essential. But it will take time, and also will require not only substantial public investment but also major changes in the orientation and understanding of policy makers.

While these remain urgent issues that require global and national policy interventions, the intensity of the food crisis that hit many developing countries in 2008 was particularly on account of the dramatically high global prices of important food items, which adversely impacted upon national food security for food deficit countries, and their partial pass-through to national economies, which in turn affected the food security of vulnerable groups within countries. It is now quite widely acknowledged that financial speculation was the major factor behind the sharp price rise of many primary commodities, including agricultural items over the past year (UNCTAD, 2009; IATP, 2008, 2009; Wahl, 2009). Similarly, the subsequent sharp declines in prices were also related to changes in financial markets, in particular the need for liquidity to cover losses.

However, the subsequent decline in global trade prices of important food commodities has induced some amount of complacency about the food crisis. Yet, it continues apace and is even likely to be exacerbated in many developing countries. One significant reflection of this continuing crisis is the fact that, even though global trade prices of wheat, rice, maize and other food items have fallen dramatically since mid/late 2008, the retail or wholesale prices of these commodities in many developing countries have not fallen and in many cases continue to increase. There are other mechanisms through which the financial crisis itself operates to increase food insecurity. These work through the constraints the current crisis is imposing on fiscal policies in balance of payments constrained developing countries and the effects of capital flows upon exchange rates, as well as through the adverse impact upon livelihoods and employment, which reduces the ability of vulnerable groups to purchase food.

In this chapter, some of these issues are explored in more detail. In the second section, the role of speculation in determining the recent volatility of prices of food and other agricultural commodities in global trade is discussed. In the third section, the conundrum of persistent high food prices in much of the developing world despite falling global prices, and the implications of this tendency, are explored, along with a consideration of how some developing countries have managed to avoid the more adverse effects. The fourth section contains a discussion of the various interconnections between finance and food that continue to generate food insecurity for a large part of the world's population. In this section, some proposals for regulating finance specifically in order to enable effective strategies for food security are also briefly noted.

Speculation and the Global Trade in Food Crops

For much of the period between mid-2007 and mid-2008, as global prices in oil and other commodity markets zoomed to stratospheric levels, various eminent economists joined bankers, financial market consultants and even policy makers, in emphasizing that these price rises were all about "fundamentals" that reflected real changes in demand and supply, rather than the market-influencing actions of a relatively small group of large players with enough financial clout and a desire to profit from changing prices.

In the case of oil, the arguments ranged from "peak oil", which pointed to the eventual (and imminent) problem of world oil consumption exceeding supply and known reserves, at one extreme, to the perfidious actions of the OPEC cartel in restricting supply so as to push up prices, at the other extreme. In between were other arguments such as the easing of monetary policy in the largest economy, the United States; the weakening US dollar, which caused oil prices to rise since oil trade is largely denominated in dollars; and rapid economic growth worldwide, but especially in China and India. Such arguments were widespread even though the period when global oil prices more than doubled was one in which total world oil demand had scarcely changed and if anything fell to some extent, and global oil supply increased slightly.

Similarly, the dramatic rise in food and other primary commodity prices was also traced to real economic causes and processes, even though 2008 has turned out to be a year of record grain production internationally. In the case of food grain and similar commodities, it is certainly true that rising costs of cultivation (partly affected in turn by high oil prices), inadequate policy support for agriculture resulting in falling yields, acreage diversion to produce bio-fuels, reduced government grain stockpiles, crop failures that could be traced to adverse weather conditions related to climate changes, all meant that there were imbalances that could explain some of the price rise. Nevertheless, even for food grains, the very rapid rise in prices over just a few months was hard to explain without bringing in some role of speculation. But even such speculation was excused, on the grounds that this also meant good times for the direct producers, not only oil exporting countries, but small farmers producing food grains that had become highly valued internationally.

The most common argument in favor of allowing continued speculation was simply that the economics of speculation require such activities to be stabilizing, rather than destabilizing, if they are to be profitable. The vital function of speculators is to predict future market patterns and thereby reduce the intensity and volatility of change. Because speculators are supposed to buy when prices are low and sell when prices are high, they thereby serve to make prices *less* volatile rather than more so. Futures markets in commodities play a similar role: they allow both producers and consumers (farmers and food purchasers in the case of food grain) to hedge against future price changes and therefore allow them to get on with their real work instead of worrying about possible price changes.

According to this perception, therefore, the presence of speculation has a positive effect on the markets, cannot be blamed for rising prices, and certainly should not be curbed in any way. Taken to its logical conclusion, this argument also suggests that the price rises witnessed in the first half of 2008 were inevitable, reflecting economic fundamentals and requiring adjustment by governments and societies.

But this apparently plausible argument dissolved completely in the face of more recent trends in prices, as prices that had risen very sharply in the first half of 2008 then peaked around the middle of the year and fell drastically to levels that completely wiped out the earlier increases and in some cases were even below the level of more than two years previously. This is evident from Figures 4.1 and 4.2, which plot the average monthly

Figure 4.1 Index numbers of world trade prices of food grains

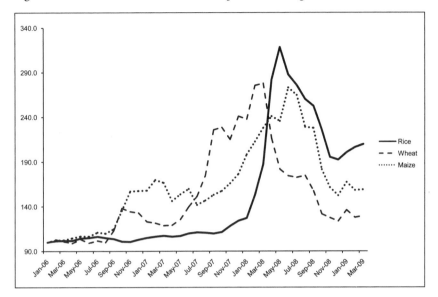

Source: www.fao.org/faostat (accessed on 29 March 2009).

Figure 4.2 Index numbers of world trade prices of some cash crops

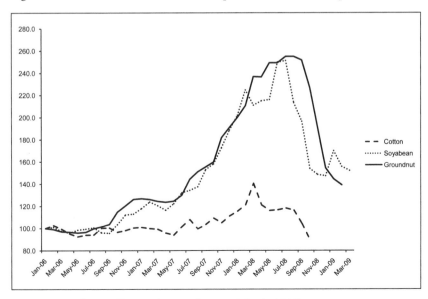

Source: www.fao.org/faostat (accessed on 29 March 2009).

prices of major food and cash crops in world trade since January 2006. These also happen to be the major agricultural commodities that have been increasingly subject to trade in the commodity futures exchanges.

Two general points are worth noting. First, there is a general absence of very large seasonality effects on prices in these major global crop markets, partly because of more generalized global stock holding, but largely because the differing weather conditions in various parts of the world ensure varying harvest times. Second, while commodity prices had been increasing since 2003, the very sharp increases were really evident only from late 2006 or some time in 2007. In the case of rice, the sharp increase in prices was from the beginning of 2008, but it was so dramatic as to cause an increase of more than two and a half times in the traded price between December 2007 and June 2008. The abrupt fall in price in the second half of 2008 was equally startling, bringing rice prices down by 40 percent compared to their peak, but still around 12 percent higher than their level of a year earlier. Wheat prices peaked in March 2008, at more than double that of previous year, and then fell almost to the levels of early 2007. It had been assumed that maize prices would continue to increase, essentially because of the impetus provided by bio-fuel subsidies in the US and EU, but even these peaked in August/September 2008 and have fallen thereafter.

In the case of cash crops, the trends are similar, with slightly later peak months for prices. The major oilseeds, soybean and groundnut, which also have other popular food uses, peaked in price in the third quarter of 2008. In July 2008, soybean prices were more than two and half times their level of January 2006, and more than 187 percent of their level of the previous year. But then they fell quite drastically by 40 percent from that peak in the subsequent 8 months, to be back at the levels of early 2007. A similar trend is evident for groundnut prices.

These sharp spikes are historically unprecedented even in the volatile price history of primary commodities. Such wild swings in prices obviously cannot be explained by short term supply and demand factors or any other "real economy" tendencies. Instead, these acute price movements are clearly the result of speculative activity in these markets. But then what explains all this speculation in the recent past, when it was not so evident before? And what form does it take? Why is it not stabilizing, as predicted by so many economic theories? The answer must relate such market involvement with broader tendencies in terms of changes in national and global financial markets, patterns of government regulation and other developments such as the eruption and persistence of the credit crisis in the US and other major capitalist economies.

Global commodity prices have always been volatile to some degree and prone to boom-bust cycles, which is one of the many reasons why developing countries have been encouraged to diversify away from dependence on such exports. In the 1950s and 1960s, commodity boards and international commodity agreements were seen as one means of stabilizing global prices. Since their decline from the mid-1970s, and especially as financial deregulation and innovation became more pronounced from the early 1980s, the emergence of commodity futures markets was touted as providing the advantages of such agreements in a more market-friendly framework. There were several features of such futures markets that were perceived to be of value: they allowed for better risk management through hedging by different layers of producers, consumers and intermediaries; they enabled open-market price discovery of commodities through buying and selling on the exchanges; they were therefore perceived to lower transaction costs.

Financial deregulation in the early part of the current decade gave a major boost to the entry of new financial players into the commodity exchanges. In the US, which has the greatest volume and turnover of both spot and future commodity trading, the significant regulatory transformation occurred in 2000. While commodity futures contracts existed before, they were traded only on regulated exchanges under the control of the Commodity Futures Trading Commission (CFTC), which required traders to disclose their holdings of each commodity and stick to specified position limits, so as to prevent market manipulation. Therefore they were dominated by commercial players who were using it for the reasons mentioned above, rather than for mainly speculative purposes. In 2000, the Commodity Futures Modernization Act effectively deregulated commodity trading in the United States, by exempting over-the-counter (OTC) commodity trading (outside of regulated exchanges) from CFTC oversight. Soon after this, several unregulated commodity exchanges opened. These allowed any and all investors, including hedge funds, pension funds and investment banks, to trade commodity futures contracts without any position limits, disclosure requirements, or regulatory oversight. The value of such unregulated trading zoomed to reach around US$9 trillion at the end of 2007, which was estimated to be more than twice the value of the commodity contracts on the regulated exchanges. According to the Bank for International Settlements, the value of outstanding amounts of OTC commodity-linked derivatives for commodities other than gold and precious metals increased from US$5.85 trillion in June 2006 to US$7.05 trillion in June 2007 to as much as US$12.39 trillion in June 2008 (BIS, 2009).

Unlike producers and consumers who use such markets for hedging purposes, financial firms and other speculators increasingly entered the market in order to profit from short-term changes in price. They were aided by the "swap-dealer loophole" in the 2000 legislation, which allowed traders to use swap agreements to take long-term positions in commodity indexes. There was a consequent emergence of commodity index funds that were essentially "index traders" who focus on returns from changes in the index of a commodity, by periodically rolling over commodity futures contracts prior to their maturity date and reinvesting the proceeds in new contracts. Such commodity funds dealt only in forward positions with no physical ownership of the commodities involved. This further aggravated the treatment of these markets as vehicles for a diversified portfolio of commodities (including not only food, but also raw materials and energy) as an asset class, rather than as mechanisms for managing the risk of actual producers and consumers. At the height of the boom, it was estimated by the hedge fund manager Michael Masters in a testimony to the US Congress that even on the regulated exchanges in the United States, such index investors owned approximately 35 percent of all corn futures contracts, 42 percent of all soybean contracts, and 64 percent of all wheat contracts in April 2008. This excluded all the (unregulated) ownership through OTC contracts, which were bound to be even larger.

As the global financial system became fragile with the continuing implosion of the US housing finance market, large investors, especially institutional investors such as hedge funds and pension funds and even banks, searched for other avenues of investment to find new sources of profit. Commodity speculation increasingly emerged as an important area for such financial investment. The United States became a major arena for such speculation, not only because of the size of its own crisis-ridden credit system, but because of the deregulation mentioned above that made it possible for more players to enter into commodity trading.

This created a peculiar trajectory in international commodity markets. The declared purpose of forward trading and of futures markets is to allow for hedging against price fluctuations, whereby the selling of futures contracts would exceed the demand for them. This implies that futures prices would be lower than spot prices, or what is known as *backwardation*. However, throughout much of the period January 2007 to June 2008, the markets were actually in *contango*, in which futures prices were higher than spot prices. This cannot reflect the hedging function and must imply the involvement of speculators who are expecting to profit from rising prices. Indeed it has been argued that contango was so strong that the futures markets were essentially driving the spot prices up in this period.

Then, by around June 2008, when the losses in the US housing and other markets became intense, it became necessary for many funds to book their profits and move resources back to cover losses or provide liquidity for other activities. UNCTAD (2009: 25) notes the sharp decline of financial investment in commodity markets from mid-2008. This caused futures market prices to fall, and this transmitted to spot prices as well.

Thus international commodity markets increasingly began to develop many of the features of financial markets, in that they became prone to information asymmetries and associated tendencies to be led by a small number of large players. Far from being "efficient markets" in the sense hoped for by mainstream theory, they allowed for inherently "wrong" signaling devices to become very effective in determining and manipulating market behavior. The result was the excessive volatility displayed by important commodities over 2008 — not only the food grains and crops mentioned here, but also minerals and oil. Such volatility had very adverse effects on both cultivators and consumers of food. This was not only because it sent out confusing, misleading and often completely wrong price signals to farmers that caused over sowing in some phases and under cultivation in others. In addition, it turns out that while the pass through of global prices was extremely high in developing countries in the phase of rising prices, the reverse tendency has not been evident in the subsequent phase as global trade prices have fallen. So both cultivators and food consumers appear to have lost in this phase of extreme price instability, with the only gainers from this process therefore being the financial intermediaries who were able to profit from rapidly changing prices.

Food Prices and Food Crises in the Developing World

Around the middle of 2008, when international recognition of the global food crisis was at its height and had not yet been displaced from the public radar by the financial crisis, there were actually visible signs of the crisis that went beyond the silent hunger of the poor that generally characterizes the unequal global food situation. For obvious reasons, the impact of the sharp food price increases, which generally transmitted at least to some degree to retail prices in the developing world, was felt most sharply in poor countries where most people tend to spend around half of their family budgets on food items. There were food riots in countries as far apart as Haiti, Guinea, Mauritania, Mexico, Morocco, Egypt, Senegal, Uzbekistan,

Yemen, Bangladesh, Philippines and Indonesia. And many more countries were threatened by social unrest as rising food prices caused not merely dissatisfaction but even the spread of hunger among social groups who were not inured to it. In several countries in Asia, such as Pakistan and Thailand, troops had to be deployed to guard food stocks and prevent seizure of grain from warehouses. Even the multilateral institutions (the same ones that had encouraged policies that brought the situation to this pass) had to sit up and take notice. For example, the World Bank President estimated in October 2008—ironically, when global prices were already falling—that the global rise in food prices could cause more than 100 million people in low-income countries to be pushed back into deeper poverty.

Subsequently, the decline in world trade prices of important food grains and other items, as well as the even more dramatic implosion of global finance after the collapse and closure of Lehmann Brothers in September 2008, pushed such concerns to the background. It is currently perceived by many international commentators that the food crisis is effectively over, because global food prices started falling around the middle of 2008, and it is presumed that this would have also led to declining food prices including in those parts of the developing world where the food crisis was most acute.

However, this is not the case, and, the food crisis has actually grown more intense in many developing countries since the middle of 2008. At the end of December 2008, the FAO estimated that 33 countries were experiencing severe or moderate food crises, with conditions in at least 17 countries worse compared to October 2008 (FAO, 2008). *This was **not** because of overall deteriorating conditions of global supply or suddenly increased global demand.* Indeed, as Table 4.1 indicates, aggregate conditions with respect to global food grain markets were generally favorable in terms of increased supply, which would have warranted expectations of stable and even slightly declining prices.

There are several points of interest in Table 4.1, such as the evidence that supply of wheat and coarse grains has increased at around the same rate as utilization, and for rice somewhat faster than utilization. End of season stocks have increased significantly for grains other than coarse grains as a group, and especially for the major wheat exporters. Aggregate food use has increased very little, and less than both production and supply. China and India continue to exhibit falling food grain consumption both in per capita terms as well as in the aggregate, completely belying the view that increased demand from these countries had contributed even partially to the global price rise.

Table 4.1 Basic facts of the world cereal situation (million tonnes)

	2006-07	2007-08	2008-09	% change: 2008-09 over 2007-08
Production[1]	2010.4	2129.2	2244.8	5.4
Wheat	596.6	610.8	682.2	11.7
Coarse grains	985.1	1078.4	1111.5	3.1
Rice (milled)	428.7	440.0	451.0	2.5
Supply[2]	2481.1	2553.4	2675.5	4.8
Wheat	776.3	767.9	832.4	8.4
Coarse grains	1171.0	1240.9	1282.5	3.4
Rice	533.8	544.7	560.6	2.9
Utilization	2064.3	2125.2	2198.3	3.4
Wheat	622.0	617.5	647.6	4.9
Coarse grains	1015.3	1070.9	1106.1	3.3
Rice	427.1	436.8	444.5	1.8
Per capita cereal food use (kg/yr)	151.8	152.3	152.4	0.1
Trade[3]	256.8	271.6	265.0	-2.4
Wheat	113.3	111.2	120.0	7.9
Coarse grains	111.2	129.6	114.0	-12.0
Rice	32.3	30.9	31.0	0.3
End of Season Stocks[4]	424.3	430.7	474.3	10.1
Wheat	157.0	150.2	182.9	21.8
– main exporters[5]	36.6	27.7	42.7	54.1
Coarse grains	162.5	171.0	175.2	2.5
– main exporters[5]	62.3	73.7	64.8	-12.1
Rice	104.7	109.6	116.2	6.0
– main exporters[5]	23.1	26.0	29.2	12.2
Cereal production[1]	887.2	916.6	934.9	2.0
excl. China and India	306.4	303.5	313.7	3.3
Utilization	935.5	960.2	978.3	1.9
Food use	650.4	663.5	673.1	1.5
excl. China and India	276.5	283.7	290.8	2.5
Per capita cereal food use (kg/yr)	155.5	156.3	156.3	0.0
excl. China and India	157.3	158.1	158.9	0.5
Feed	166.8	172.0	176.4	2.6
excl. China and India	48.9	49.2	50.1	1.9
End of season stocks[4]	238.2	255.9	278.1	8.7
excl. China and India	58.0	52.4	53.0	1.2

Notes: [1] Data refer to calendar year of the first year shown.

   [2] Supply refers to production plus opening stocks.

   [3] For wheat and coarse grains, trade refers to exports based on July/June marketing season. For rice, trade refers to exports based on the calendar year of the second year shown.

   [4] May not equal the difference between supply and utilization because of differences in individual country marketing years.

   [5] The main wheat and coarse grain exporters are Argentina, Australia, Canada, the EU and the United States. The main rice exporters are India, Pakistan, Thailand, the United States and Viet Nam.

Source: FAO (2008).

With respect to food vulnerability, of course, the relevant indicator need not be global supply and demand, but rather the supply conditions of the low-income food deficit countries (LIFDCs). These include food deficit countries with per capita GDP below the level used by the World Bank to determine eligibility for cheap International Development Association (IDA) loans and other assistance, for example US$1675 in 2005. For such countries, grain output continued to increase at a decelerating rate, amounting to 2 percent in 2008. Furthermore, as will be discussed in the following section, there are other aspects of the current global economy that have prevented easy access to imported food. As a result, in many developing countries food prices have remained high and even continued to increase, despite various policy measures taken by governments to limit the impact of high international prices on domestic markets. As noted by FAO (2008), "In countries where prices have declined the reductions have been modest compared to those in export markets and, generally, national cereal prices remain above their levels of a year earlier. Persistent high food prices in the developing world continue to affect access to food of large numbers of vulnerable population in both urban and rural areas."

Therefore many developing countries in which widespread and persistent hunger was already a problem, have experienced significant increases in the prices of staple foods in the past two years, and there has been hardly any decline even after global trade prices started falling. Table 4.2 provides some idea of the overall changes in food prices in some countries in the period January 2007 to December 2008.

Obviously, therefore, food prices in many developing countries are in general considerably higher than they were two years ago, and much higher than increases in nominal wage incomes in most of these countries. (In fact, it turns out that nominal wages also barely increased in many countries despite high rates of GDP growth and reasonable rates of inflation in these

Table 4.2 Changes in food staple prices in some developing countries

Country and food item	*% increase in price* *Jan 2007-Dec 2008*
Zimbabwe wholesale white maize	994
Ethiopia wholesale white maize	141
Malawi wholesale white maize	107
Kenya wholesale white maize	81
Zambia wholesale white maize	32
South Africa wholesale white maize	-38
Honduras retail white maize	36
Guatemala retail white maize	25
Ethiopia wholesale wheat	119
Eritrea wholesale wheat	114
Sudan wholesale wheat	4
Afghanistan retail wheat flour	114
Pakistan retail wheat flour	82
Thailand wholesale rice	73
Colombia wholesale rice	76
Bolivia wholesale rice	30
Senegal imported rice	85
Burkina Faso imported rice	65
Niger imported rice	44
Sri Lanka retail rice	30
Haiti retail rice	94
Nicaragua retail rice	54
Brazil retail rice	43

Source: FAO (2008).

two years, but that is another story.) Therefore food insecurity was clearly on the rise in most of these countries (and probably others for whom data are not so readily available) simply expressed in terms of the real price of food relative to wages.

Of course such overall increases mask the trends over time, and it is worth examining the extent to which food price changes in different countries have followed trends in global trade prices. Figures 4.3 and 4.4 provide evidence on rice prices in various developing countries. It is evident that these countries were all affected by the extraordinary world price movements, although they were able to avoid the extremely sharp spike that cause global prices to increase by around three and half times in the

18 months between January 2007 and June 2008. China appears to have handled the matter the best, with rice prices broadly stable over the entire period despite the high global volatility. It is tempting to explain this in terms of domestic food self sufficiency that allowed China to insulate its population from the effects of high world prices in this basic food item. But this need not be the only reason. By way of contrast, India which is also a large economy with domestic rice production several times the total volume of world trade, has experienced quite significant increases in price of rice. Furthermore, these have not decreased commensurately with the global price, to the point that retail rice prices were 60 percent higher in January 2009 than their level two years earlier. In an economy in which more than 90 percent of workers' incomes are not indexed, such a substantial increase obviously has a big impact upon food access. Given the large proportion—around half—of those who are calorie deficient among the Indian population, this is obviously a matter of great concern.

Figure 4.3 Index numbers of rice prices in some Asian countries

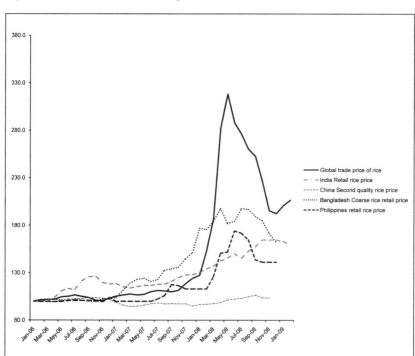

Source: www.fao.org/giews/pricetool/ (accessed on 29 March 2009).

Figure 4.4 Index numbers of rice prices in some developing countries

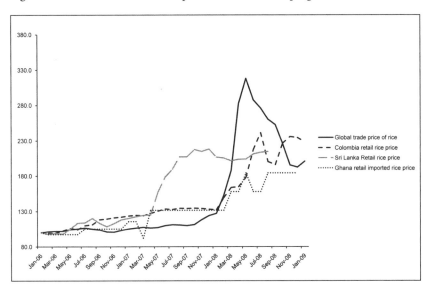

Source: www.fao.org/giews/pricetool/ (accessed on 29 March 2009).

Figure 4.4 describes developing countries that have been even less able to manage the global price hike in terms of the impact upon their own population. It should be noted that in these countries as well, prices went up as global prices increased—albeit to a lesser degree (which is only to be expected because it is hard to imagine any country in which food price increases of 350 percent in 18 months would be politically sustainable). But the subsequent equally sharp decline—which obviously affected rice exporting countries and their farmers adversely—did not get reflected in any real declines in rice prices in these countries. Similar tendencies are evident in some Latin American countries. For example, in Bolivia, retail rice prices increased by about 35 percent between January 2007 and June 2008 and subsequently have stayed at that level. In Brazil, the increase was by around 45 percent, and once again, there has been hardly any fall from that level since then.

Similarly, wheat and maize prices in most developing countries increased sharply when world prices increased, but did not come down after global prices declined. Between January 2007 and December 2008, retail wheat prices increased by 119 percent in Ethiopia and 114 percent in Eritrea. In Pakistan, retail flour prices increased by between 63 percent (Karachi) and 82 percent (Peshawar). In Afghanistan, the price increase was in the order of 114 percent. Retail maize prices increased by 141 percent in Ethiopia and by 81 percent in Kenya. Once again, some differing trends deserve to be noted: some apparently vulnerable countries, such as Sudan, were able to withstand the volatility and to keep prices relatively stable: retail wheat prices in Khartoum increased by only 4 percent throughout the period.

Mechanisms and Strategies

How has this peculiar process occurred, whereby developing countries find that their domestic prices of food go up when international prices go up, but do not come down as global trade prices fall? And what explains how some countries have managed to escape the worst effects of this volatility and keep their own prices relatively stable? The answers obviously lie largely with how domestic policies have functioned, but more importantly, also with the space for effective domestic policies that is determined by both the external environment and the country's mode of global economic integration. And in the latter, once again we find direct and indirect roles of international finance.

The most direct link is through trade, with both food importers and food exporters affected. Countries in which a very large proportion of the basic food requirement is met through domestic supply (China, India) are therefore less likely to experience the volatility *if* they have in place adequate institutional arrangements to ensure domestic production and distribution. By contrast, food importers are obviously more vulnerable. It used to be thought that "large" economies—those with the capacity to affect global prices through their entry or exit into world trade—should be more worried, but with the advent of financial players in the grain markets, it is no longer evident that this would have a direct impact on price. Rather, the impact is more likely to be indirect, through the impact upon the expectations of the financial players. But the lesson here is unpleasantly straightforward: no country, however small and open, can afford to neglect domestic food production and must ensure at least some domestic supplies, if it does not want to get caught in a vortex of price volatility that can dramatically affect national food security. This has important implications for trade negotiations, since the WTO rules have forced aggressive trade liberalization upon agriculture in developing countries and arguably created significantly higher food insecurity in the developing world. Future negotiations, if they do indeed occur, must take this into account and reverse such requirements accordingly.

But how have some importing countries managed to cope better than others? FAO (2008) has documented the range of measures undertaken by 101 developing countries in response to the global food crisis, with varying degrees of success. These interventions have ranged from the reduction or suspension of import tariffs and taxes, to the imposition of export restrictions, support for domestic production with agricultural inputs and credit, intervening heavily in food markets, introducing food assistance programs and increasing subsidies. The countries that have managed to do these more effectively are those that have also managed to restrain or stabilize food price increases to some extent. In addition, some countries have taken measures to contain domestic speculation in food markets, either through banning commodity futures markets in grain trade (India).

The case of China is especially significant, because with its large population, any significant entry into global markets through additional import demand would naturally affect spot prices. Despite this, China has managed the food situation the most effectively among all developing countries, and this reflects not only its internal policies but two features that are particularly noteworthy: the greater strength and viability of its fiscal strategy, and its control over internal and external flows (through the large state banking sector and extensive capital controls). Why these matter so much is noted below.

It is evident of course, that effective state intervention for food price stability and food security requires fiscal resources. This has become an important barrier to successful intervention to contain food price rises in many countries. Many, if not most, developing countries today are experiencing much larger fiscal deficits than before or than they had planned for. This is a typical outcome of financial crisis, when both government deficits and public debt increase substantially. Reinhart and Rogoff (2009), on the basis of a long and comparative historical review, argue that in the post-crisis scenario the real value of government debt tends to explode, rising an average of 86 percent in the major post World War II episodes of crises in both developed and developing countries. According to them, "the big drivers of debt increases are the inevitable collapse in tax revenues that governments suffer in the wake of deep and prolonged output contractions, as well as often ambitious countercyclical fiscal policies aimed at mitigating the downturn."

The difficulty is that many developing countries cannot engage in "ambitious countercyclical fiscal policies" because they are themselves constrained by internal and external deficits. In particular, governments of developing countries increasingly find themselves crowded out of international credit markets because of the voracious demands of the US and other major developed economies, as they guarantee more and more private debt within their own countries and expand their own fiscal deficits. Without the required external resources in particularly, governments cannot import more food. So they are simply not in a position to spend more and take the measures necessary to ensure adequate food for the population. International creditors in the current situation have been both unjust and contradictory to their own proclamations, punishing developing countries that have hitherto maintained "fiscal discipline" and otherwise adhered to the rigid precepts of neo-liberal policies, and rewarding irresponsible behaviors of public and private agents in countries like the US, because of their greater faith in the backing of the US state.

This is particularly true in private international financial markets. One of the more remarkable features of the recent months has been the recovery of the US dollar in international currency markets, despite all the evidence of continuing decline and the negative feedback loops that are feeding from financial to real sectors and back, creating possibilities of a severe depression in that economy. By contrast, many developing countries whose "fundamentals" appear to be much stronger in terms of continuing GDP growth, better managed banking systems and so on, have experienced rapid and large outflows of private capital, thereby causing sharp currency depreciations. For example, in the period between June 2008 and January 2009, the Indian rupee depreciated by 23 percent *vis-à-vis* the US dollar as portfolio capital moved back to the US. Similar declines are evident in most other developing countries, barring the exceptional case of China. And obviously this has led to rising prices of imported food (the trade of which is still mostly denominated in dollars) in domestic currency.

The food crisis in developing countries is therefore something that has been created and is currently being exacerbated by the workings of deregulated international finance, that continues to have an adverse impact even when these financial markets are themselves in crisis. Developing countries are caught in a pincer movement: between volatile global prices on the one hand, and reduced fiscal space and depreciating currencies on the other hand.

In this context, it is clear that the resolution of the food crisis requires not only strong government interventions to protect developing country agriculture, to provide more public support for sustainable and more productive and viable cultivation patterns and to create and administer better domestic food distribution systems. It also requires international arrangements and cooperative interventions, such as strategic grain reserves, commodity boards and other measures to stabilize world trade prices. And it definitely requires specific controls on finance, to ensure that food cannot become an arena of global and national speculation. These controls should include very strict limits (indeed bans) on the entry of financial players into commodity futures markets; the elimination of the "swap-dealer loophole" that allows financial players to enter as supposedly commercial players; and the banning of such markets in countries where public institutions play an important role in grain trade. In addition, because it has been seen that broader mechanisms, such as the impact of portfolio finance flows in affecting exchange rates, can also affect the food situation indirectly, it is important to impose capital controls of different sorts on short-term capital flows, not only for their own sake, but to prevent their destabilizing impact on domestic food prices.

Note

* I am indebted to participants in the IDEAs Conference on "Re-regulating global finance in the light of global crisis", Tsinghua University, Beijing, on 9-11 April 2009 for discussions, and especially to Jan Kregel for helpful comments.

References

Beddington, John (2008). Chief Scientific Advisor to UK Government, Speech to Govnet Sustainable Development UK Conference, quoted in *The Guardian*, 7 March. http://www.guardian.co.uk/science/2008/mar/07/scienceofclimatechange.food

BIS (2009). Statistics on amounts outstanding of OTC equity-linked and commodity derivatives, by instrument and counterparty. http://www.bis.org/statistics/otcder/dt21c22a.pdf, accessed on 18 April 2009.

FAO (2008). *Crop Prices and Food Situation*. Food and Agriculture Organization, Rome. http://www.fao.org/docrep/011/ai476e/ai476e01.htm, accessed on 26 March 2009.

IATP (2008). *Commodities Market Speculation: The Risk to Food Security and Agriculture*. Institute for Agriculture and Trade Policy, Minneapolis.

IATP (2009). Betting against food security: Futures market speculation. Trade and Global Governance Programme Paper, Institute for Agriculture and Trade Policy, Minneapolis, January.

Kregel, Jan (2008). The impact of changing financial flows on trade and production in developing countries. Presentation to Seminar on "Estructura productiva y dinámica de precios: efectos macro-micro y respuestas de política", Escuela de Verano de Economías Latinoamericanas, CEPAL, Santiago, August 6-7.

Reinhart, Carmen, and Kenneth Rogoff (2009). The aftermath of financial crises. Paper presented at American Economic Association meetings, 3 January, San Francisco.

UNCTAD (2009). *The Global Economic Crisis: Systemic Failures and Multilateral Remedies*. United Nations Conference on Trade and Development, Geneva.

Wahl, Peter (2009). Food speculation: The main factor of the price bubble in 2008. Briefing Paper, World Economy, Ecology and Development, Berlin.

5

Policy Responses to the Global Financial Crisis: Key issues for developing countries

Yılmaz Akyüz

The global financial crisis, triggered by widespread speculative lending and investment in major international financial centers, poses two sets of policy challenges. First, it calls for an immediate policy response in order to stabilize financial markets and international capital flows, halt economic decline and initiate recovery. So far, major industrial countries have taken a range of measures for these purposes, including bailout operations through infusion of capital into weakened financial institutions and industrial firms and government guarantees for impaired financial assets and bank deposits; significant easing of monetary conditions and speedy and sharp reductions in interest rates; and large fiscal stimulus packages. Developing and emerging economies (DEEs) have also adopted measures to ease credit conditions and stimulate private spending to counter destabilizing and deflationary impulses from the crisis. However, several of them face resource constraints in responding to the crisis with countercyclical policies. There is a strong rationale and some scope for using trade and financial policies to ease the resource constraint. But, in many cases, effective policy responses depend crucially on the provision of adequate international liquidity on appropriate terms and conditions through multilateral financial institutions.

Secondly, this crisis has indicated once again, the need for a fundamental reform of the international financial system in order to secure greater stability and prevent virulent crises with global ramifications. A consensus appears to have emerged among the major players in the world economy on the need for reform, and a number of *ad hoc* initiatives have been launched and proposals put forward in various forums including the United Nations, the Group of 20 and the Bretton Woods Institutions. But to what extent these will result in the kind of changes needed is highly uncertain. The past record in this respect is not very encouraging. Despite a wide agreement on a systemic reform to bring about more effective governance to international finance after a series of crises in emerging economies in the 1990s and proliferation of proposals for reform, the *Financing for Development* initiative launched has yielded no significant outcome in this respect in the past seven years.[1] DEEs have a considerably greater stake in such a reform in view of the disproportionately large damage that international financial instability inflicts on them. It is therefore important that they lead the process and form a coherent view for real change in a broad range of areas of crucial interest to them, including the mandate, resources, operational modalities and governance of the IMF, so as to reduce their vulnerability to financial instability and crises while preserving adequate policy autonomy in managing their integration into the international financial system, as well as capital flows and exchange rates.

These two sets of issues overlap in certain respects. In particular, many of the shortcomings in the immediate policy response to the crisis by the international community have their roots in the deficiencies in global institutional arrangements for crisis management and resolution. The next section will discuss the constraints DEEs are facing in responding to deflationary and destabilizing impulses from the crisis, making an assessment of the international initiatives undertaken so far to provide support. This is followed by a discussion of the reform of the international financial architecture under two headings—crisis prevention and crisis intervention and resolution. Discussion will focus on issues that are viewed as of particular importance for stability and growth in DEEs, rather than on every issue raised by the current crisis. The final section will give a summary of the policy proposals advanced.

Policy Response in DEEs: Payments Constraint and International Support

Crisis Impact and Domestic Policy Options

The fallouts from the global financial crisis are wreaking havoc in DEEs. The combination of sharply declining commodity and manufactured export earnings, collapse of remittances, reversal of private capital flows, rising risk spreads, an extreme degree of credit squeeze affecting even trade finance and losses of asset values is giving rise to a sharp economic slowdown and even contraction in many parts of the developing world. According to the most recent projections by the IMF, average growth in DEEs is expected to be as low as 1.6 percent in 2009, down from 8.7 percent in 2007. At more than 6 percentage points, the expected loss of growth in these economies exceeds that in the centre of the crisis, the United States economy, where output is projected to contract by 2.8 percent in 2009 after growing by 2 percent in 2007. This deceleration will result in sizeable drops in per capita incomes in most developing regions and countries. Consequently, there is a risk of reversal of many of the benefits achieved in poverty alleviation and development as a result of intense policy efforts and reforms carried out in recent years.

There is now a broad agreement on the need for expansionary, countercyclical macroeconomic policy response to deflationary impulses emanating from the crisis. It is also agreed that under current conditions of extreme liquidity preference and risk aversion, monetary policy would have very little impact on credit expansion and private spending. Consequently, the burden falls primarily on expansionary fiscal policies, particularly increased public spending.

The main impediment to countercyclical macroeconomic policy in many DEEs is the balance-of-payments constraint. Although several middle-income countries have succeeded in building up relatively strong payments positions and large stocks of international reserves during the preceding expansion, the balance-of-payments constraint has generally become tighter, with declines in exports earnings and the reversal of private capital flows. Indeed, reserves have been falling almost everywhere in the developing world, and even strong surplus economies, such as China, have been experiencing capital outflows. An acceleration of growth based on the expansion of domestic demand would certainly drain reserves further as imports pick up, exerting pressure on the currency and threatening external and financial stability. This means that for resource-constrained DEEs, expansionary macroeconomic policies would depend crucially on the provision of adequate external financing. For poorer countries where official flows are directly linked to the budget, injection of additional external financing would also help ease the fiscal constraint which has generally become tighter as a result of adverse effects of declines in export earnings and incomes on government revenues and of currency depreciations on public external debt servicing.

According to the World Bank (2009: 6), external financing needs in 2009 are expected to exceed private sources of financing in 98 of the 102

DEEs. In the absence of adequate official financing to fill the gap, these countries would have to use whatever domestic policy instruments they have under their control in order to weather the crisis with minimum damage. But options are quite limited. Currency adjustments would not be very effective in promoting exports when markets abroad are shrinking. Sharp devaluations in countries with extensive liability dollarization could also create deleterious effects on private balance sheets with large currency and maturity mismatches.

By contrast, selective restriction of non-essential, luxury imports, as well as of imports of goods and services for which domestic substitutes are available, could be more effective in easing the payments constraints and facilitating expansionary macroeconomic policies by allowing increased imports of intermediate and capital goods needed for the expansion of domestic production and income. For some DEEs, the space between applied and WTO-bound tariffs can provide adequate room for such an action, but the margins are generally quite narrow and even non-existent for a large number of DEEs. By contrast, under current conditions prevailing in many countries, there is a strong rationale, as a last resort, for invoking GATT (and GATS) balance-of-payments safeguard provisions, notably those of Article XVIIIB which are particularly directed at payments difficulties arising from a country's efforts to expand its internal market or from instability in its terms of trade.

Ideally, when global deflationary forces are at work, it would be highly desirable to avoid restrictive trade measures, particularly those of a discriminatory nature. Indeed, the interwar experience shows that *ad hoc*, discriminatory trade restrictions, together with beggar-thy-neighbor exchange rate policies, can aggravate, rather than ease economic difficulties and lead to conflicts. The recent G20 summit pledged not to "repeat the historic mistakes of protectionism of previous eras" and to "refrain from raising new barriers to investment or to trade in goods and services, imposing new export restrictions, or implementing World Trade Organization (WTO) inconsistent measures to stimulate exports" (G20, 2009c: para 22). However, there was no indication of what kind of actions would be considered as protectionist and what kind as WTO-consistent. Nor was there any specific commitment.

Whether or not a particular trade measure can be considered as protectionist depends on the conditions under which it is adopted. In this respect, a distinction should be made between restrictions applied by reserve-currency and reserve-rich countries, and those applied by DEEs facing balance-of-payments constraints. Import restrictions in the former cases would effectively imply exporting unemployment abroad, since by raising net exports, such an action would substitute foreign for domestic demand. But this would not be so for restrictions applied by DEEs facing shortages of international liquidity. In the latter case, the alternative would be to face stagnation or contraction, and hence, reduced demand for foreign goods and services. Selective restrictions over imports would allow allocation of scarce foreign exchange to facilitate domestic expansion without reducing the overall demand for foreign goods. This cannot be considered as a protectionist action.

Thus, resource-constrained DEEs should not be denied their rights embodied in multilateral trade agreements to use legitimate measures to avoid contraction in economic activity. Such trade measures should be distinguished from beggar-thy-neighbor import restrictions and subsidies, including those used by some major industrial economies—such as the "buy American" provisions and industrial subsidies in United States stimulus and bailout packages—which serve to protect jobs at home, rather than facilitate expansionary policy actions, and beg the question of conformity to the WTO rules.

A second set of measures that could be employed by countries facing a shortage of international liquidity to support domestic expansion relates to the capital account. DEEs are now experiencing net outflows on portfolio investment and international bank lending. Furthermore, residents in several of these countries have joined international lenders and investors in capital flight. This is, in large part, the outcome of widespread liberalization of resident investment abroad in recent years, often in an effort to relieve the upward pressure of the surge in capital inflows on currencies. Clearly, to the extent that reserves, exports earnings and official lending are used to finance capital flight, international liquidity available for current account financing would be reduced. Furthermore, under present conditions, capital flight would also compromise the ability to use monetary policy for expansion. Thus, there is a strong case for restricting capital outflows in countries facing the rapid loss of reserves. Restrictions would also widen the space for countercyclical monetary and fiscal policy responses to the crisis in order to stabilize economic activity and restrain declines in currencies and the consequent dislocations in private balance sheets.

International Liquidity Support

The extent to which trade and financial restrictions would need to be applied by resource-constrained DEEs depends on the speed with which international trade, financial markets and capital flows are stabilized, and on the availability of adequate financing from multilateral financial institutions. In the latter respect, a number of initiatives have been taken in the G20 and the Bretton Woods institutions in recent months, seeking improvement in three main areas: increased funding for multilateral financial institutions, widened access of DEEs to multilateral financing, and improvements in the terms and conditions of multilateral lending. Some of these initiatives have implications that go beyond matters of immediate policy response to the crisis, and could, in fact, entail systemic and more permanent changes in the way the IMF intervenes in financial crises. These features will be discussed in the subsequent section in the context of the reform of the international financial architecture. Here, a brief description will be given of the steps taken so far in the three areas, an assessment will be made of their adequacy in meeting immediate policy challenges for stabilizing economic conditions in DEEs and preparing the ground for recovery, and proposals will be made for further action.

Regarding new resources, according to the agreement reached in the April 2009 G20 Summit, commitments have been secured for an additional US$1.1 billion for international support. This includes a decision to allocate US$250 billion of Special Drawing Rights (SDRs), approved in the subsequent meeting of the IMF; trebling of resources available to the IMF to US$750 billion; an additional US$100 billion for multilateral development banks, presumably to be raised through bond issues;[2] and US$250 billion trade finance from various public and private institutions including export credit agencies. Of the additional US$500 billion for the IMF, only US$250 billion is readily available through bilateral lending by some of its major shareholders, to be subsequently incorporated into the "expanded and more flexible" New Arrangements to Borrow (NAB).[3] However, there does not seem to be an agreement on how the rest should be raised. While some major shareholders favor increasing the NAB by an additional US$250 billion and encourage reserve-rich economies to make bilateral loans, major emerging economies, notably China, India, Russia and Brazil, appear to insist that these resources be raised by borrowing from the markets, and have expressed interest in buying short-term notes (bonds) that the Fund could issue for this purpose.[4] This matter is now under consideration in the Fund.

Regarding access of DEEs to multilateral financing, the major recent initiatives include, in addition to the agreement on the SDR allocation noted above, doubling the normal access limits in the IMF; doubling the borrowing limits for the poorest countries eligible for the Poverty Reduction and Growth Facility (PRGF) and the Exogenous Shock Facility (ESF);

and a new Flexible Credit Line (FCL) established for crisis prevention in emerging economies facing contagion from the global crisis. The FCL is said to be available "for countries with strong fundamentals, policies and track records of policy implementation", to be assessed by the IMF according to several pre-determined criteria. It can be drawn or used as a precautionary instrument. Unlike the Short-Term Liquidity Facility (SLF) it replaces, the FCL has no hard cap.[5] However, it is not clear if this implies that the Fund will act as a lender-of-last-resort to countries it deems eligible, lending in unlimited amounts and without conditions except for penalty rates. So far, a US$47 billion FCL arrangement has been approved for Mexico. Poland has requested some US$20 billion as a precautionary FCL arrangement and Colombia has expressed interest in a similar arrangement for US$10 billion.

Finally, certain steps have been taken for "modernizing IMF conditionality for all borrowers" as part of the overhaul of the IMF lending framework.[6] First, access to the FCL will be based on *ex ante* rather than *ex post* conditionality. Second, decision has been taken to discontinue structural performance criteria in all Fund arrangements including those with low-income economies. This is expected to allow the Fund to focus on its core objectives.

It is difficult to make a precise judgment on whether these initiatives will meet the external financing needs of DEEs since this crucially depends on the effectiveness of the measures adopted by the advanced economies responsible for the crisis in restoring stability and growth. According to the World Bank (2009: p. 6), the total external official financing needs of the 98 DEEs with shortfalls are expected to be at least US$270 billion, and this figure could go up significantly, reaching US$700 billion. According to UNCTAD (2009), the gap could turn out to be US$2.000 billion. While the G20 summit claimed to have come up with a commitment for an extra US$1.1 trillion, the real additional amount readily available appears to be lower.[7] It is notable that despite these highly-publicized initiatives for additional financing for DEEs, the April 2009 growth projections by the IMF for these economies show downward revisions by 1.7 percentage points for 2009 and 1 percentage point for 2010 from those given in January 2009—more or less by the same amounts as for advanced economies (IMF, 2009b: Table 1.1).

The volume, terms and conditions of additional financing to be made available by the multilateral financial institutions can be expected to show considerable variations among DEEs according to their access limits to and eligibility for different categories of financing. Of the US$250 billion SDR allocation DEEs would receive some US$80 billion of which less than a quarter should be available to low-income countries. These amounts are small fractions of the estimated external financing needs of the developing world. Any additional IBRD lending funded by bond issues would not be available to a large number of poor countries, including those in low-income and lower-middle income categories. On current rules, additional IMF lending, financed by bilateral and/or market borrowing, should in principle be non-concessional. Judging on the basis of the established pre-qualification criteria, a very large number of DEEs, including several market-access countries with large current account deficits, high levels of public debt, high and unstable inflation etc. should not be eligible for the FCL.

It is generally agreed that when the balance-of-payments difficulties of a member of the Fund result from external shocks of a permanent nature, or from excessive expansion of domestic absorption, IMF financing should be accompanied by domestic policy adjustments to reduce the deficits. However, when payments difficulties are due to temporary external shocks, they need to be financed, rather than reduced through policy adjustment. The current financial crisis appears to contain both permanent and temporary elements of change. It can be expected that the crisis will bring a durable adjustment to the external deficits of the United States resulting from the long-awaited consumer retrenchment. This certainly calls for an adjustment in surplus countries, including the Asian developing countries, notably China, but not resource-constrained DEEs.[8] This means that deficit DEEs should not be subjected to pro-cyclical macroeconomic policy conditionality for any additional borrowing needed to meet their balance-of-payments shortfalls resulting from trade and financial shocks from the crisis. However, despite the "recent modernization of conditionality", the Fund has continued to impose pro-cyclical macroeconomic tightening in almost all recent standby programs—fiscal tightening in Pakistan, Hungary and Ukraine, and interest rate hikes in Latvia and Pakistan (TWN, 2009). Even though some of these countries may have had large budget deficits when they approached the Fund for loans, recessions are not the best times to undertake fiscal adjustment.

Nor should multilateral financing made available to DEEs to meet their balance-of-payments difficulties due to a global crisis for which they have no responsibility, place a heavy burden on them. This means that a high degree of concessionality would be needed. Indeed, the IMF had established two highly concessional oil facilities in the 1970s as deliberate countercyclical devices to prevent oil price hikes from triggering a global recession, with countries enjoying almost automatic access without counter-cyclical macroeconomic conditions.

Low-income countries should be compensated, not burdened with additional debt and debt servicing because of financing they receive to meet the shocks from the crisis. For political reasons as well as effectiveness, official development assistance (ODA) grants are not the best way to achieve this. An option would be to make a one-off permanent SDR allocation to these countries, based on some criteria of need.[9] The cost of drawing on such allocations could be financed collectively from the IMF resources, including gold sales. This should be combined with a moratorium on servicing debt owed by these countries to official creditors, without any additional interest charges.[10]

A no-cost SDR allocation to low-income countries can be combined with a large reversible SDR allocation to other DEEs, to be repurchased when the crisis is over, to provide them with low-cost, no-conditionality resources. Proposals for reversible SDR allocations were made in the 1990s in order to allow the IMF to act as a lender-of-last-resort for financial bailout operations in emerging economies hit by financial crises. The rationale for such an allocation is no doubt much stronger now given the sharp contraction in global output and trade.

A large and reversible SDR allocation would extend the policy of "quantitative easing" to the global level, widely used by some major economies in stabilizing conditions in domestic credit and financial markets and stimulating spending. Reversibility would also provide automatic exit, thereby preventing inflationary pressures once recovery is under way. Furthermore, relying mainly on SDR allocations to meet external financing needs would also help avoid several undesirable consequences of funding IMF lending with bilateral loans from its shareholders, discussed in the subsequent section. Finally, a large SDR allocation could allow surplus emerging economies, such as China, to diversify their reserve holdings and reduce their vulnerability to dollar instability.

The exact purpose and use of IMF lending under current conditions also need to be scrutinized. As in the past, the existing standby programs of the Fund appear to be premised on maintaining open capital accounts and ensuring that developing country debtors stay current on their payments to private creditors. Of all the countries with IMF stand-by programs, only Iceland has widespread capital controls over resident and non-resident outflows, introduced in the early days of the crisis. None of the emerging markets with IMF programs has introduced similar measures despite continued capital outflows. Even though the Fund may no longer be actively promoting capital account liberalization, its aversion to restrictions seems to continue unabated.

There can be little doubt that the rationale for capital controls over outflows in countries facing severe balance-of-payments difficulties is much stronger than that for trade restrictions. However, the latter have proliferated, both in DEEs and advanced economies after the outbreak of the credit crunch, while capital accounts have remained largely open, even in countries facing large and continued outflows.[11]

In such cases, the Fund should not only support, but also recommend the use of temporary exchange restrictions, preventing the burden of adjustment falling disproportionately on trade. These restrictions should also include temporary debt standstills. It is true that the international community has not been able to establish orderly mechanisms for the protection of debtors against litigation in such cases—an issue to be taken up later. But the IMF can express its support by "lending into arrears", thereby deterring potential hostile action by private creditors.

Such restrictions should also be applied in FCL-eligible countries if the precautionary access provided by the FCL fails to stem speculative attacks and there are large and persistent outflows. Outflows can indeed accelerate if emerging economies lag in recovery behind advanced economies. Borrowing from the IMF to finance such outflows could lead to considerable increases in government debt burden, particularly where an important part of foreign claims are on the private sector, as in Asia during the 1997-1998 crisis. Besides, there are serious risks in the Fund acting as a lender-of-last-resort to any country—an issue discussed later. It would thus be prudent to take up this matter at some length in the context of the broader systemic reform of the international financial architecture.

Reform of the International Financial Architecture

For DEEs, there are two key issues in the reform of the international financial architecture. The first relates to crisis prevention: how best to reduce their vulnerability to international financial instability and crises while retaining adequate policy autonomy in determining the pattern and degree of their integration into world financial markets and managing capital flows and exchange rates. Prevention of crises with global repercussions requires addressing three major sources of instability: policies, markets and the current international reserves system centered on the dollar. More specifically it calls for:

- Effective multilateral discipline over financial, macroeconomic and exchange rate policies in systemically important countries.

- Establishment of an international reserves system not based on a national currency or currencies;
- Effective regulation and supervision of financial markets and capital flows.

It should, however, be kept in mind that while effective multilateral arrangements are important for reducing the likelihood of crises with global spillovers, they cannot fully protect DEEs against instability and crises. They are not substitutes for national policies and institutions for crisis prevention. This makes it all the more important to retain adequate national policy space while setting up a new multilateral framework for the governance of international finance.

The second area of reform relates to crisis response. It is generally agreed that regardless of the measures that may be adopted to secure greater stability, crises with global ramifications will continue to occur. The damage they inflict on the world economy and its incidence will depend on policy responses at the national and international levels. The current crisis shows that closer multilateral cooperation and tighter discipline are needed to ensure that national policy responses take into account their impact on other countries and to avoid negative international spillovers and beggar-thy-neighbor policies. Even more importantly, there is a need to improve international interventions in the balance-of-payments, currency and debt crises in DEEs. This calls for *inter alia*, a fundamental reform of the mandate, operations and funding of the IMF.

Areas of Reform for Crisis Prevention

Multilateral Policy Discipline in Money and Finance

National policies almost always play a central role in financial instability and crises. Misguided deregulation of domestic financial markets, premature liberalization of the capital account, and unsustainable macroeconomic and exchange rate policies are often the proximate causes of currency and balance-of-payments instability and financial crises. This is true, both for DEEs and advanced economies. However, the global repercussions of financial crises and currency instability in systemically important countries are much more serious than those in DEEs, even though there is often regional contagion from crises in emerging economies, as witnessed in East Asia during 1997-1998.

Boom-bust cycles in capital flows to developing countries and major international financial crises are typically connected to large shifts in macroeconomic and financial conditions in the major industrial countries. The sharp rise in United States interest rates and the appreciation of the dollar were major factors in the debt crisis of the 1980s. Likewise, the boom-bust cycle of capital flows in the 1990s, which devastated many countries in Latin America and East Asia, were strongly influenced by shifts in monetary conditions in the United States and the exchange rates among the major reserve currencies (UNCTAD *TDR* 1998, Part II, chap. IV; and 2003, chap. II). This is even more visible in current conditions where the boom-bust cycle in the United States financial markets has produced the most serious post-war global financial and economic crisis.

It must now be evident that adverse international spillovers from macroeconomic, exchange rate and financial policies in advanced economies are much more damaging to DEEs than shocks from their trade policies. But unlike trade, there is no effective multilateral discipline in money and finance. The IMF members have the same *de jure* obligations to maintain orderly macroeconomic and balance-of-payments conditions and stable exchange rates. But the Fund's policy oversight is confined primarily to its poorest members who need to draw on its resources because of their lack of access to private finance and, occasionally, to emerging economies experiencing interruptions in their access to private financial markets. By contrast, the Fund is totally unable to impose meaningful disciplines over the policies of its major shareholders who exert a disproportionately large influence on global monetary and financial stability.

There are problems regarding not only effectiveness and even-handedness but also the quality of surveillance. After a series of crises in emerging economies the Fund's Interim Committee (now the International Monetary and Financial Committee, IMFC) agreed in April 1998 that the Fund "should intensify its surveillance of financial sector issues and capital flows, giving particular attention to policy interdependence and risks of contagion" (IMF, 1998). However, the Fund's intensified surveillance over emerging economies was not able to prevent further crises in Argentina, Russia and Turkey, all operating at the time under Fund programs, in large part because it failed to diagnose and act on the root causes of the problem. Indeed, according to an independent assessment of Fund surveillance, the policy makers interviewed had important reservations regarding the quality of the Fund's analysis of capital account issues (IMF/GIE, 1999: 13).

Similarly, in the run up to the present crisis, the Fund failed to identify the nature and extent of potentially destabilizing speculative build-up and to provide adequate early warning. In its Article IV Consultations with the United States throughout 2005-2006, the Fund staff was preoccupied with reducing fiscal and external deficits and maintaining control over inflation as the main policy challenges facing the United States economy, while reassuring that the "US financial sector has proven exceptionally resilient in recent years" (IMF, 2005: 31; 2006: 23). Even a month before the beginning of the credit crunch, the IMF staff argued that "the most likely scenario is a soft landing as growth recovers and inflation falls, although both are subject to risks" (IMF, 2007a: 26). In the same month, July 2007, the IMF staff assessment of economic conditions in Iceland was also highly upbeat, maintaining that "Iceland's medium-term prospects remain enviable" while adding some caveats about downside risks associated with large current account deficits, increasing indebtedness and high inflation (IMF, 2007b: 17).

This failure in adequately assessing the risks of instability and providing early warning appears to be deep-seated in the belief of the Fund secretariat, encouraged by some of its major shareholders, that disequilibria and imbalances generated by freely functioning financial and currency markets are self correcting, without entailing severe social and economic costs of adjustment. It has an obsession with budget deficits and inflation as the main threats to macroeconomic stability and growth, ignoring that inflation in asset markets driven by speculative lending and investment, both nationally and internationally, tends to pose even greater threats, despite mounting evidence from recurrent crises in emerging and mature markets alike.

A key question is, therefore, how to overcome the problems regarding the quality, effectiveness and even-handedness of IMF surveillance. The G20 (2009c: para 12) expressed its support for "candid, even-handed, and independent IMF surveillance" without making specific recommendations as to how these could be achieved. Subsequently, the IMFC reaffirmed the emphasis on "candor, evenhandedness, and independence" and the need "to enhance the effectiveness of surveillance" (IMF 2009c: para 11). However, this has little credibility since the IMFC is known to have come up with similar pronouncements in almost every other meeting, particularly those held after episodes of instability in international currency and financial markets.[12]

There can be little doubt that problems regarding the quality, effectiveness and even-handedness of IMF surveillance cannot be resolved without addressing its governance-related shortcomings. There is no ready-made solution and further reflection is needed on the ways and means of achieving these objectives. Given that the existing mechanisms within the Fund have so far failed to do so despite repeated pronouncements of intention, such a process should best be conducted outside the Fund.

A notable suggestion for improving surveillance, made by a senior British Treasury official, is its formal separation from decisions about program lending and the use of IMF resources so as to establish the Fund as independent from political influence in its surveillance of economies as an independent central bank is in the operation of monetary policy (Balls, 2003). It is rightly argued that the current structure of the IMF treats program design as an extension of surveillance, but the lack of a clear distinction between lending and surveillance activities creates the wrong incentives and diminishes the effectiveness of surveillance. Moreover, there is currently no formal regular mechanism for assessing whether the Fund is providing objective, rigorous, and consistent standards of surveillance across all member countries—program and non-program countries. While responsible for ensuring the effectiveness of the Fund's activities, Executive Directors also have responsibilities to their authorities. This creates a conflict of interest where Executive Directors tend to collude in surveillance in defense of the countries they represent, turning peer pressure into peer protection. Surveillance should thus rest with authorities who are independent of their governments and who are not involved in lending decisions, making it impartial, legitimate, authoritative, transparent and accountable.

A Stable International Reserves System

A reserves system, based on a national currency as a means of international settlement and a reserve asset, suffers from a major dilemma. This was pointed out by Triffin (1960) almost half a century ago, questioning the viability of the Bretton Woods arrangements based on the United States dollar. In a dollar-based system, net holdings of dollar assets by the rest of the world depend on the United States running current account deficits. If the United States stopped running deficits, the shortage of international liquidity would stifle global trade, investment and growth. If, on the other hand, the United States runs growing deficits and supplies adequate liquidity to the world economy, the accumulation of liabilities could undermine confidence in the dollar, depressing its value *vis-à-vis* other reserve assets—namely gold under the Bretton Woods system. Restoring confidence and overcoming inflationary pressures would then call for United States interest rates to rise and for deficits to fall, depressing economic activity and employment. Therefore, while issuing a reserve currency gives the country an advantage in financing its deficits, it can also become problematic. With the accumulation of liabilities abroad, the country can lose its monetary policy autonomy and be forced to adopt deflationary policies.

Indeed, the Bretton Woods system of exchange rates collapsed as the immediate post-war dollar shortage was translated into a dollar glut with the growing United States deficits, which made it impossible to maintain gold convertibility at a fixed rate, leading to a unilateral suspension in 1971—the first and the most significant post-war default of international obligations by any country. The move to floating exchange rates, rapid growth of international financial markets and capital flows, and the rise of Germany and Japan as industrial powers did not challenge the dominance of the dollar. As explained by the IMF historian Boughton (2001: 937) Germany and Japan "were reluctant to see their currencies 'internationalized' and used as reserves.... Moreover, the prospect of a system of multiple reserve currencies was widely viewed, both inside and outside the Fund, as a potentially destabilizing development that was to be avoided if possible. If central banks held several different currencies, then they would be likely to shift the composition of their portfolios to optimize expected returns. Such speculation could magnify the effects of market shifts in confidence or in expected relative returns". At the time of the suspension of gold convertibility, the estimated share of the dollar in all official reserves other than gold was 70 percent, compared to around 65 percent at present.

In the post-Bretton Woods era, instability in the United States' balance-of-payments has continued unabated, even aggravated by the absence of effective multilateral discipline over its macroeconomic policies—a discipline that the Bretton Woods system had sought to establish through gold convertibility. This resulted in recurrent gyrations of the dollar *vis-à-vis* other reserve currencies and played a major role in increased global financial instability.

After the collapse of the Bretton Woods system, the need for reserves was expected to lessen as countries gained access to international financial markets and became more willing to respond to balance-of-payments shocks by adjustments in exchange rates. However, capital account liberalization in DEEs and their greater access to international financial markets have produced exactly the opposite result. International capital flows have undoubtedly allowed running larger and more persistent current account deficits beyond the levels that could be attained by relying on international reserves. But this has also resulted in an accumulation of large stocks of external liabilities and the growing presence of foreigners in domestic securities markets. The debtor countries have thus become increasingly vulnerable to sudden stops and reversals in capital flows, with grave consequences for stability, growth and development. This became increasingly visible after the Asian crisis in 1997 when the only collective insurance available, namely IMF lending, proved to be highly unreliable and even counterproductive.

Thus, the combination of increased capital account liberalization in DEEs, accumulation of external liabilities, pro-cyclical behavior of international financial markets, and the absence of effective multilateral arrangements for the provision of international liquidity and for orderly debt workout procedures has forced DEEs to look for self-insurance by accumulating large stocks of international reserves, mostly held in dollars. While reserves covering three months of imports were traditionally considered adequate for addressing the liquidity problems arising from time lags between payments for imports and receipts from exports, it has become common wisdom that in order to avoid a liquidity crisis, international reserves in DEEs should at least meet their short-term external liabilities.[13]

At the end of 2008, total international reserves of DEEs reached some US$5.5 trillion, or 7 months of imports. Even though DEEs taken together have been running current account surpluses in recent years, only about half their total reserves are earned from current account surpluses, mainly by China and fuel exporters. The rest came from capital inflows—that is, they are borrowed reserves.[14] In a few countries such as China, current account surpluses and reserve accumulation have been associated with rapid growth. But in a large number of DEEs, additional reserves came either from capital inflows or from trade surpluses achieved by cutting growth for fear that a possible downturn in commodity prices or reversal of capital flows would necessitate additional international liquidity.

These reserves are invested in low-yielding assets, mainly the United States treasury bills and bonds. On the basis of average historical spreads between the borrowing rate and the return earned on reserves, the annual carry cost of borrowed reserves to DEEs alone is estimated to be in the order of some US$130 billion. This constitutes a net transfer of resources to reserve-currency countries, notably the United States, and exceeds total official development assistance to developing countries.[15] The cost borne by DEEs would be greater if allowance is made for foregone growth by using export surpluses to buy United States treasuries rather than invest and import. Furthermore, DEEs could incur losses on their dollar holdings if the large build up of United States government liabilities, resulting from bailout and fiscal stimulus packages, were to produce inflation and dollar depreciation.

Both the G20 summit and the IMFC remained silent on reform in this key area. There are various options for establishing an international reserves system not based on national currencies so as to avoid these difficulties. One proposal is to go back to the gold standard. Another is to revisit Keynes's proposal, made at the Bretton Woods conference, of introducing a global currency, the *bancor*, exchangeable with national currencies at fixed rates, issued by a global central bank—the International Clearing Union—to provide countries with liquidity for international payments clearance as well as overdraft facilities by amounts based on the value of their trade.[16] However, building on existing mechanisms and institutions and a gradual move away from the dollar towards the SDR (or expanded SDR) appear to be a more practical solution.

An important advantage of SDRs, particularly for DEEs, is that unlike dollar reserves, holding SDRs does not entail costs; costs are only incurred when they are used. Under the present arrangements, the IMF may allocate SDRs to members in proportion to their quotas. Members obtain or use SDRs through voluntary exchanges or by the Fund designating members with strong external positions to purchase SDRs from those with weak external positions. When members' holdings rise above or fall below their allocations, they earn or pay interest respectively, with the interest rate being determined as the weighted average of interest rates on short-term debt in money markets of the SDR basket currencies.

The cost advantage of SDRs has given rise to calls for regular distribution to alleviate the burden of holding reserves on low-income countries. Indeed, a former IMF Director of Research, Jacques Polak argued, in a joint paper, that the only principle that should now guide the allocation of SDRs should be "the benefits of permitting low-income countries to acquire and hold reserves at a much lower interest rate than they would have to pay in the market and a reduced dependence of the system on borrowed reserves that are liable to be recalled when they are most needed."[17]

Regular allocations of SDRs on the basis of existing rules cannot promote the SDR to be a major reserve asset and address the inequities and instability resulting from the current system based on national currencies, even if such allocations are done more often than has been the case. A way forward is to make the IMF an SDR-based organization, and to allow SDRs to replace quotas and GAB and NAB as the single source of funding for the IMF. The Fund could be permitted to issue SDRs to itself up to a certain limit which should increase over time with the growth in world trade. Under such a scheme, the present practice of allocations to countries according to their quotas would be discontinued. Unconditional access limits (the so-called reserve tranche or gold tranche) would need to be redefined and widened considerably, based *inter alia* on some criteria of need.

In such an arrangement, the demand for SDRs (or drawings from the IMF in SDRs) can be expected to be inversely related to buoyancy in world trade and income and the availability of private financing for external payments. Thus, allocations could be altered in a pro-cyclical way, accelerating at times of global slowdown. This would help counter deflationary forces in the world economy and provide an offset to fluctuations in private balance-of-payments financing.

Several issues of detail would still need to be worked out, but once an agreement is reached to replace traditional sources of funding with the SDR, the IMF could, in fact, be translated into a technocratic institution of the kind advocated by Keynes during the Bretton Woods negotiations. Its funding would no longer be subjected to arduous and politically charged negotiations dominated by the major industrial countries. Nor would it need to borrow from some of its members in order to lend to others. Such an arrangement could thus considerably improve the governance of the IMF, allowing it to stay at equal distance from all its members and help to perform policy surveillance even-handedly and effectively.

Making the Fund an SDR-based institution would undoubtedly result in a considerable increase in the supply of SDRs compared to the existing stock or the growth that could be expected with current practices. It would allow major surplus countries to invest their reserves in SDRs instead of reserve currencies. It is also possible to supplement this with a mechanism to remove the dollar overhang by allowing countries to rapidly replace their existing stocks of dollar reserves with SDRs without causing disruption in currency markets. Such a proposal was made by the Governor of the People's Bank of China. According to this proposal, the IMF would "set up an open-ended SDR-denominated fund based on the market practice, allowing subscription and redemption in the existing reserve currencies by various investors as desired" (Zhou, 2009).

This proposal corresponds to what came to be known as the substitution account, extensively discussed in the IMF in two previous episodes of considerable dollar weakness, but abandoned for several reasons; first, in the early 1970s by the Committee of 20 in an effort to replace the Bretton Woods system with something more viable, and then in the late 1970s and early 1980s, as the dollar weakened considerably.[18] The idea is a simple one: the IMF would issue interest-bearing certificates denominated in SDRs against dollar reserves handed over by central banks at the market exchange rate, and invest these reserves in interest-bearing United States Treasury bills and bonds. The operation would not affect the total volume of international reserves, but only its composition—thus, no "inflation" fears. Countries can use these certificates to settle international payments or to acquire reserve currencies. The substitution would result in a withdrawal of a large stock of dollar reserves from the market and put them into IMF coffers. It would eliminate the risk of monetary turmoil that could result from a potential widespread unloading of dollar reserves by central banks.[19]

Several issues of importance to DEEs would need to be sorted out.[20] First and foremost, there is the question of who will bear the exchange rate risk. A change in the dollar/SDR exchange rate would create losses and gains for the IMF since, by definition, a substitution account would mean a currency mismatch between assets and liabilities. A sustained decline in the dollar against other currencies that make up the SDR will imply losses. The exposure of the Fund can be considerable if the account is open-ended, rather than restricted in size. There is no guarantee that interest differentials between the dollar and the SDR would provide cover for such losses.[21] This is true whether the interest on SDRs is calculated as at present, or set in the market established for SDRs.

In previous discussions of this proposal, the IMF gold was proposed to be used for cover. But this would mean pushing the losses onto all members of the Fund, rich and poor alike. If, on the other hand, the exchange rate risk was to be borne by holders of the SDRs, the operation would be meaningless—there would be no incentive for holders of dollar reserves to subscribe to the account. An alternative would be for the United States to bear the risk—that is, to supply more interest-bearing dollar assets to cover exchange losses if the dollar falls against the other currencies. A more equitable solution would be to share the risk between the United States and the central banks subscribing to the substitution account, rather than to pass it onto the Fund, including its poorer members.

A second issue relates to the privatization of the SDR. Establishing a private market for SDRs by allowing banks to hold them, and using them in currency interventions would certainly improve its liquidity and status as a reserve asset. This is also seen as necessary for the substitution account to be attractive to central banks, not only for replacing dollar reserves but also reserves held in other currencies, including potential ones such as the Chinese yuan. However, this could also make the SDR a new instrument of speculation and a source of instability. In other words, it might be difficult to reconcile a high degree of liquidity with stability of its exchange value. It is therefore important to strike the right balance between the two and to ensure that SDRs are used mainly for the settlement of payments linked to international trade and investment.

Regulation of International Financial Markets and Capital Flows

Past experience shows that even when monetary and fiscal discipline is secured and a relatively high degree of price stability is attained, unbridled financial markets are capable of generating instability and crises with serious consequences for the real economy, notably jobs and incomes. The global financial turmoil triggered by the sub-prime debacle has shown once again that the Anglo-American view that financial markets regulate themselves—is not only wrong, but also highly damaging.

There is now broad agreement on the need for tighter regulation than has been the case, but views differ about how best to regulate and the degree of regulation. Moreover, regulation of international capital flows is highly contentious. The dominant view still entertained in the mainstream is that once financial markets and institutions are properly regulated; there is no need to restrict international capital flows. However, this does not stand against ample evidence that prudential rules do not necessarily bring greater stability to international capital flows, nor can they prevent such flows from inflicting serious damage to an economy (Akyüz, 2008b).

Several reasons are usually given why financial regulation should be international. First, since financial instability often has adverse global spillovers, national regulatory practices should be subject to multilateral disciplines. Second, multilateral rules would provide a level playing field and prevent regulatory arbitrage—that is, business moving from tightly to lightly regulated jurisdictions. Finally, they would reduce the influence of politicians over regulators and give them a certain degree of independence—a concern now widely shared after the hands-off approach that the previous United States administration had adopted *vis-à-vis* financial markets.

While these considerations are basically valid, there are both political and technical difficulties in establishing multilateral discipline in financial regulation and supervision. A supreme international body, with fully-fledged regulatory and supervisory powers over all financial institutions, is not on the agenda. However, it is increasingly held that global and systemically important institutions should be regulated and supervised internationally rather than nationally. Several proposals have been made for establishing global regulators for credit rating agencies and transnational banks over a certain size.[22]

An option would be to leave the conduct of regulation and supervision to national authorities within a framework established according to the same principles as the WTO.[23] This would involve binding multilateral agreements on a set of rules and regulations for financial institutions including banks, institutional investors, rating agencies, and bond and credit insurance companies. There would be a commitment by governments to implement such rules and regulations through national regulators. Finally, there could be a multilateral body to oversee implementation and impose sanctions for non-compliance, such as denying access of financial firms from non-complying countries to the markets of other members.

However, it is still quite unrealistic to expect systemically important countries, including some emerging economies, to give up national policy autonomy to the extent required. It is notable that even the EU has not managed to establish a unified regulatory system. Furthermore, serious difficulties could be faced in reconciling and integrating different legal systems and conceptual frameworks in arriving at a uniform set of rules for economies at different levels of financial development and with different financial institutions and culture.

More importantly, such an arrangement would carry risks and drawbacks for DEEs. It is not realistic to envisage that a global institution with genuine clout over major advanced economies could be established on the basis of a distribution of power markedly different from that of existing multilateral financial institutions. Thus, it may not be wise to create another multilateral body before satisfactorily solving the governance-related problems that pervade existing institutions such as the IMF, WB and WTO.

Second, there is the familiar one-size-fits-all problem. In all likelihood, rules and regulations to be agreed to in such a setting would be shaped by the exigencies of financial markets and institutions of the more advanced economies. These would not always be suitable for DEEs. On the other hand, as the experience of the WTO shows, special and differential treatment that may be granted to DEEs may not mean much in practice.[24]

Furthermore, entering into comprehensive multilateral negotiations could open the Pandora's Box of market access in financial services, liberalization of capital flows and multilateral agreement on FDI, resulting in further restrictions of policy space in DEEs. The real danger for DEEs is that a process designed to broaden the scope of global governance over finance may end up extending the global reach of financial markets. It is notable that one of the recommendations of a G20 working group on international cooperation was for Financial Stability Forum (FSF) member countries to "maintain the openness of the financial sector" (G20, 2009a: 7). It is not clear if this is meant to be liberalization of market access in financial services or if it would apply to new developing-country members of the expanded FSF. But it is a clear sign that global arrangements for financial regulations may entail new obligations for DEEs for opening up their financial sectors to foreign firms.

A less ambitious approach would be to extend the mandate and improve the governance of existing bodies such as the FSF, the BIS, the Basle Committee on Banking Supervision, the International Association of Insurance Supervisors, and the International Organization of Securities Commissions. Indeed, most existing proposals for improving global governance of finance envisage a voluntary process of closer coordination among national regulators, based on an agreed framework within such institutions, rather than a rules-based system with sanctions.[25]

The G20 also appears to be moving in that direction, emphasizing the need for "internationally agreed high standards", "common and coherent international framework, which national financial authorities should apply in their countries consistent with national circumstances" and "systematic cooperation between countries" (G20, 2009b: para 4; 2009c: paras 13-15). It proposes "to establish supervisory colleges for all major cross-border financial institutions" (G20, 2009a: 5). The Group has also agreed to transform the FSF into a Financial Stability Board by extending its membership to include all G20 countries and its mandate to the regulation and oversight of all systemically important financial institutions, instruments and markets, including the hedge funds and credit rating agencies.

There are also proposals to give a greater role to the IMF in financial surveillance. However, this role should not be extended to setting regulatory standards or overseeing financial markets and institutions. In this area, the task of the Fund is to monitor macroeconomic and financial developments and to provide early warning of risks of instability and crises. Its ROSC (Report on the Observance of Standards and Codes) exercises, introduced after the Asian crisis and undertaken as part of Article IVC consultations and in conjunction with the joint FSAP (Financial Sector Assessment Program) activities with the World Bank, are meant to help promote global financial stability. However, these activities have been highly ineffective because of several shortcomings in the design and application of codes and standards.[26] Therefore, before the IMF may be given new roles in the financial architecture, it is important to have a reasonably good understanding of the factors that have made existing instruments and mechanisms ineffectual and to remove them through appropriate reform.

A possible guiding principle for DEEs in the reform of the global financial architecture in the area of financial regulation and supervision could be to allow and retain considerable autonomy in setting standards for financial institutions without significant border-crossing activities. A multilateral framework for national regulatory systems or global regulators should be introduced only for transnational financial institutions. The nature and extent of regulations of different transnational financial activities and institutions needed are a highly complex issue that would require considerable deliberations. Even where developing countries do not have transnational financial institutions, they should have voice in setting global rules and standards since they often do business with those from advanced economies. For instance, supervisors from DEEs should always fully and directly participate in supervisory colleges proposed by the G20, rather than wait to be invited to such bodies as host supervisors "where appropriate", as envisaged by a G20 working group (G20, 2009a: para 4).

In the regulation of transnational financial institutions, the main objective of DEEs should be to ensure that the proposed mechanisms address their vulnerability to external financial instability and shocks. This calls for attention, at least to the following areas:

- First, international lenders to DEEs behave in a highly pro-cyclical way and this increases their susceptibility to external shocks. At times of boom, they lower their standards in lending to financial and non-financial firms in developing countries, and governments are not always fully able to prevent such surges creating serious currency and maturity mismatches in private balance sheets. When times change and market sentiment becomes pessimistic, lending is rapidly withdrawn, often leading to currency collapses and widespread bankruptcies, with the state often taking over private liabilities. Therefore, the main interest of DEEs in the much emphasized and fashionable countercyclical prudential measures for international banks is their potential impact on pro-cyclical behavior in international lending.

- Second, governments and private firms in DEEs face similar difficulties when they borrow abroad through international security issues. Rating agencies are not only pro-cyclical, but also biased against borrowers from DEEs. Before, the sub-prime credit crunch, ratings of many Asian emerging economies with sound payments, reserve and fiscal positions were below those of some advanced economies with serious vulnerabilities on these fronts, e.g. Iceland. Therefore, removing such rating bias and pro-cyclical behavior should be the primary objective of DEEs in regulating international rating agencies.

- Third, DEEs are not only borrowers from international markets. They are also investors in securities issued in advanced economies by both public and publicly sponsored institutions and private firms. Several central banks in DEEs are known to have invested large amounts in debt issued by the United States government-sponsored enterprises, including the mortgage firms Fannie Mae and Freddie Mac. Again, the so-called toxic assets issued by private financial institutions have found their way into the portfolio of banks and institutional investors in DEEs. In fact, because of increased liberalization of capital outflows by residents, such exposure has been on the rise. Therefore, DEEs have a growing stake in greater transparency and objective assessment of the quality of such securities. This calls for an overhaul of accounting, regulatory and underwriting standards and a fundamental reform of rating agencies. A Global Financial Products Safety Commission may also be established for this purpose with equal and full participation of DEEs.

- Fourth, a growing source of instability of capital flows in developing countries is due to international portfolio investors, including institutional investors and highly-leveraged institutions, notably hedge funds. The task of delimiting the nature and extent of their operations within their borders naturally falls on national governments and regulators. However, their task would be greatly facilitated by increased transparency of investors. The minimum requirement is registration with national financial authorities. Access to information on the degree and nature of leverage as well as the size and composition of portfolios and investment strategies of these investors would also be highly important for financial authorities in DEEs to make a reasonably sound assessment of the risks entailed by their entry into domestic asset markets.

Crisis Intervention and Resolution

Regardless of measures that may be taken to discipline policies in systemically important countries and to regulate systemically important financial institutions, instruments and markets, it is almost a certainty that crises will continue to occur. For countries which do not enjoy reserve currency status, notably the DEEs, balance-of-payments and debt crises will also continue to necessitate international interventions, except where there are effective regional alternatives. Under current arrangements this task falls on the IMF.

However, there are several contentious and unresolved issues regarding IMF interventions in crises in emerging economies, including their objectives, funding and policy conditionalities. Considerable dissatisfaction has been expressed by several developed and developing countries at the way interventions were designed and implemented in the late 1990s, and several proposals were made, both within and outside the Fund, for improvement (Akyüz, 2005). But these were put aside as a result of opposition from its major shareholders and the complacency created by quick resumption of growth in most countries hit by financial crises and strong recovery of capital flows in the early years of this decade.

The Fund's crisis intervention in the past typically involved injection of liquidity designed to keep countries current on their debt payments to private creditors, to maintain capital account convertibility and to prevent default, accompanied by monetary and fiscal tightening to restore confidence. Rescue packages amounted to several times the accepted quota limits and were often combined with bilateral contributions by the major industrial countries. As noted, recent interventions do not diverge in a significant way from this pattern: capital accounts are kept open despite rapid outflows and depletion of reserves, policy conditionality continues to be pro-cyclical and the IMF is increasingly relying on funds borrowed from its main shareholders.

This approach is troublesome for several reasons. Pro-cyclical policies add to contractions in economic activity brought about by external trade and financial shocks, leading to increased unemployment and poverty. Relying on major shareholders for funding increases their influence in the design of IMF programs and even allows them to pursue their national interests, as observed in Korea during the 1997 crisis. More importantly, bailouts undermine market discipline, create moral hazard and encourage imprudent lending since creditors and investors are not made to bear the consequences of the risks they take. They shift the burden of the crises almost entirely onto debtors, particularly governments in DEEs, which are often compelled to assume the external liabilities of private debtors who can no longer service their debt. Moreover, the financial integrity of the Fund is jeopardized, particularly as the scale of operations increases with the rapid growth in cross-border lending and investment.

As these problems became increasingly visible in IMF interventions in the recurrent crises of the 1990s and early 2000s, a proposed solution was to "bail-in", or involve international creditors and investors in the resolution of financial crises and to restrict IMF lending in order to encourage it. This received support from some G7 countries such as Canada, England and Germany. Various voluntary and involuntary schemes were proposed to achieve this, including temporary debt standstills and exchange controls.

The IMF Board recognized that "in extreme circumstances, if it is not possible to reach agreement on a voluntary standstill, members may find it necessary, as a last resort, to impose one unilaterally", and that since "there could be a risk that this action would trigger capital outflows… it might be necessary to resort to the introduction of more comprehensive exchange or capital controls", with the Fund signalling its "acceptance of a standstill imposed by a member… through a decision… to lend into arrears to private creditors."[27]

The Fund secretariat was also moving towards establishing a formal mechanism for involving private creditors in the resolution of sovereign debt crises through a Sovereign Debt Restructuring Mechanism (SDRM). Countries facing severe balance-of-payments and sovereign debt difficulties were expected "to come to the Fund and request a temporary standstill on the repayment of its debts, during which time it would negotiate a rescheduling with its creditors, given the Fund's consent to that line of attack. During this limited period… the country would have to provide assurances to its creditors that money was not fleeing the country, which would presumably mean the imposition of exchange controls for a temporary period of time" (Krueger, 2001: 7). However, because of opposition from its major shareholders and financial markets, and the lack of strong support from some developing countries, this proposal was first diluted—considerable leverage was granted to creditors, and provisions for standstills were dropped—and subsequently abandoned altogether.

In response to the adverse impact of the crisis on trade and capital flows in DEEs, the international community has now chosen to establish a new facility, the Flexible Credit Line (FCL), to allow the Fund to lend large amounts of liquidity to certain countries deemed eligible on the basis of some pre-determined criteria. However, this has not been accompanied by measures to meet the consequent risks of moral hazard, unequal burden sharing and the potential threat to the financial integrity of the Fund. The latter is a particular cause of concern since the majority of Fund members are excluded from access to this facility. This makes it all the more important to establish parallel arrangements to involve private creditors and investors in the resolution of balance-of-payments and debt crises in emerging economies.

Central components of such arrangements are recognition of the rights of countries facing large and sustained capital outflows to impose temporary debt standstills and exchange controls, and provision of statutory protection to them in the form of a stay on litigation. The decision for a standstill should be taken unilaterally by the country concerned and sanctioned by an independent panel, rather than by the IMF, because the countries affected are among the shareholders of the Fund, which itself is also a creditor. There can be little doubt that countries will resort to standstills with considerable prudence and discretion. As noted by a former Deputy Governor of the Bank of England, a "well-articulated framework for dealing with sovereign liquidity problems... would be no more likely to induce debtors to default than bankruptcy law is to induce corporate debtors to default" (Clementi, 2000).

Fund lending should focus on current account transactions, and there should be limits to lending to countries experiencing large and persistent capital outflows—notwithstanding that money is fungible and, in practice, it is not always possible to clearly identify the need catered for by a particular loan. Lending at progressively higher (penalty) rates, as the Fund now seems to be practicing, may not dampen the demand for liquidity from the FCL-eligible countries. Instead, the Fund should encourage involvement of private creditors by recommending—and even requiring—use of temporary standstills and exchange controls where needed.

Such restrictions should be introduced whether payments difficulties have their origin in private or sovereign debt, or the rapid exit of foreign investors; and whether they are due to liquidity or solvency problems—a distinction which is not always clear-cut. In cases of strong signs of insolvency, limits on IMF lending should be tighter—that is, countries should not borrow from multilateral sources to finance unpayable debt to private creditors, as happened extensively during the debt crisis in the 1980s (Sachs, 1998: 53).

Because of the absence of a multilaterally agreed legal system for debt workouts, the practice tends to be disorderly and *ad hoc*, and to favor creditors. Very often, the IMF is involved in coordinating and resolving debt servicing difficulties, whether due to solvency or liquidity problems, based on an adjustment program agreed to with the debtor country. The Fund generally seeks a voluntary agreement with creditors, but its position is asymmetrical—while it has significant leverage *vis-à-vis* sovereign debtors, it cannot impose appropriate terms and conditions on creditors. Even in bond contracts with collective action clauses (CACs), bondholders can hold out and opt for litigation in search of a better deal. Such *ad hoc* restructuring has rarely achieved sustainability where there were problems of solvency. In cases where debt servicing difficulties were due to liquidity shortages, it provided relief through maturity rollover at penalty rates, but this often came very late in the crisis and failed to prevent the damage.[28]

Multilateral arrangements for orderly workouts of sovereign debt should be efficient in that they should seek to contain the damage inflicted by debt servicing difficulties on the debtor and allow rapid recovery and growth, as facilitated by national bankruptcy procedures in many advanced economies, such as Chapter 11 of the United States Bankruptcy Code. They should also be fair in the distribution of the burden, making creditors bear the full consequences of the risks they have taken—risks already compensated for by handsome premiums. To the extent possible, debt restructuring, including rollovers and write-offs, should be based on negotiations between the debtor and creditors, and facilitated by the introduction of automatic rollover and CACs in debt contracts. However, impartial arbitration is needed to settle disputes in case of failure to reach agreement over the terms of restructuring.

Existing procedures for official debt workouts also need a fundamental change. Decisions on restructuring such debt are currently left to a club of creditors—the Paris Club—and tied to IMF structural adjustment programs and sustainability assessments. Sustainability is often judged on the basis of how much debt and debt servicing a country can tolerate without adequate attention to its implications for development and poverty. Furthermore, political considerations often dominate debt-relief outcomes. It might be highly desirable to de-link official debt restructuring from the IMF, and to leave debt sustainability analysis to an independent body of experts, appointed with the consent of the debtors. The Fund, the Bank and United Nations agencies could provide inputs to this process in their respective areas of work. Debtor countries should also be allowed to submit their own analyses of sustainability. Consideration should also be given to establishing impartial arbitration for official debt disputes along the lines of Chapter 9 of the United States Bankruptcy Code which deals with public debtors and applies the same principles as Chapter 11.[29]

Summary of Policy Conclusions and Proposals

Immediate Policy Responses

a.   DEEs should not incur heavy burdens in order to respond to fallouts from a crisis they cannot be held responsible for.

b.   DEEs facing payments' constraints should not be denied the right to use legitimate trade measures in order to mitigate the impact of the crisis on jobs, incomes and poverty. Such actions should not be put in the same pot as import restrictions and subsidies introduced in advanced economies not facing similar constraints.

c. DEEs should be encouraged to use temporary capital account restrictions and debt standstills to stem large and sustained outflows of capital. These should be supported by the IMF, where necessary, through lending into arrears.

d. Any additional financing DEEs may need in order to respond positively to shocks from the crisis should be unconditional, non-debt creating and/or at low-cost. This can best be achieved by SDR allocations, rather than grants, or IMF lending funded by bilateral borrowing from its shareholders:

- A one-off permanent SDR allocation to low-income countries based on their needs, with the interest costs of withdrawals being financed internally by the IMF.
- A large reversible SDR allocation to other DEEs.

e. There should be a moratorium on debt servicing by low-income countries to official creditors, including the Bretton Woods institutions, at no additional cost.

Crisis Prevention: Multilateral Policy Surveillance

a. There is a need to significantly improve the effectiveness, even-handedness and quality of IMF surveillance over macroeconomic, financial and exchange rate policies. This is needed to secure greater multilateral discipline over policies in systemically important countries and to ensure greater coherence between trade and finance in this respect. Improvements are also needed to provide early warning for risks of macroeconomic and financial instability.

b. Meeting these objectives depends very much on addressing the governance-related shortcomings of the Fund. Current arrangements suffer from a conflict of interest whereby Executive Directors pass judgment on surveillance of policies of the countries they represent. A solution could be formal separation of surveillance from lending decisions, entrusting it to an independent body.

Crisis Prevention: International Reserves System

a. The current multiple-currency reserves system centred on the dollar is highly unstable. It is very costly for DEEs which are compelled to hold large amounts of reserves for self-protection at the expense of growth and development. It should be replaced by a system not based on national currencies.

b. An SDR-based reserve system appears to be the most viable option. This calls for fundamental changes in current arrangements regarding the allocation and use of SDRs.

c. A way forward is to make the IMF an SDR-based institution by allowing it to allocate SDRs to itself to replace quotas, GAB and NAB, and to become the only source of funding. This would also improve the governance of the IMF by removing its dependence on major countries for funding. SDR allocations could be linked to growth in world trade in a countercyclical manner. Under such an arrangement, non-conditional access limits should be redefined and widened significantly.

d. This could be supplemented by an arrangement to allow existing reserve currency holdings to be replaced with SDRs without causing disruptions in currency markets. This can be done through a substitution account at the IMF, extensively discussed following two previous episodes of significant dollar weakness in the early 1970s and the mid-1980s.

e. However, care should be taken in following this course, particularly to ensure that the exchange rate risk does not fall on the IMF, including its poor members, and that the SDR does not become a new instrument of speculation.

Crisis Prevention: Regulation of International Financial Markets

a. The principle that could guide the approach of the DEEs to regulation of financial institutions, markets and instruments would be to retain sufficient domestic policy autonomy while seeking to reduce their vulnerability to instability and crises through regulation and supervision of transnational players with border-crossing activities.

b. A supreme international body with fully-fledged regulatory and supervisory powers is neither realistic nor desirable. This is also true of replicating the WTO in the area of finance, with binding multilateral agreements on rules and standards to be applied by national governments and sanctions for non-compliance.

c. Such an arrangement could entail serious loss of autonomy and lead to one-size-fits-all. Moreover, there is the risk that the process designed to broaden the scope of global governance over finance may end up extending the global reach of financial markets, forcing DEEs into granting greater market access in financial services than would be appropriate.

d. In assessing various proposals for regulatory reform of global financial institutions and markets, DEEs should pay attention to what these proposals could offer in reducing their vulnerability by:
    *   reducing pro-cyclicality in international bank lending to DEEs;
    *   reducing the bias against DEEs and the pro-cyclicality of ratings by international rating agencies;
    *   improving the quality of assets in which DEEs invest their reserves and private savings;
    *   improving the information on international portfolio investors in DEEs.
e. DEEs should also resist giving the IMF a greater role in financial surveillance and monitoring before undertaking a thorough examination of the reasons why its ROSC and FSAP activities have been highly ineffective, and removing them through appropriate reforms.

Crisis Intervention and Resolution

a. In providing international liquidity the Fund should not impose structural conditions; nor should it insist on macroeconomic policy adjustments when payments imbalances are due to temporary external shocks beyond the control of the borrowing country.
b. IMF bailouts of international lenders and investors in countries facing rapid exit of capital undermine market discipline, encourage imprudent lending, shift the burden onto debtors and threaten the Fund's financial integrity. The IMF should not finance large and sustained capital outflows, but should encourage involving private creditors and investors in the resolution of balance-of-payments and debt crises in emerging economies.
c. The rights of countries experiencing large and sustained capital outflows to exercise temporary debt standstills and exchange controls should be recognized; and they should be granted statutory protection in the form of stay on litigation.
d. To the extent possible, restructuring of sovereign debt should be based on negotiations with private creditors and facilitated by inclusion of rollover and collective action clauses in debt contracts. But an international system of impartial arbitration is needed to settle sovereign debt disputes.
e. Sustainability analyses in official debt restructuring exercises should be taken away from the IMF and given to an independent body of

experts. Consideration should be given to introducing arbitration for restructuring the official debt of DEEs.

Further Areas of IMF Reform

a. Several of the above measures needed for reducing the likelihood of financial crises with global repercussions and for ensuring better crisis intervention call for fundamental changes in the IMF. There are also additional reforms that need to be undertaken, particularly in its governance and mandate, in order to enhance its effectiveness and relevance.

b. There has been considerable debate on the shortcomings in the Fund's governance in several areas, including the selection of its head, the distribution of voting rights, transparency and accountability, and no further remarks are needed here. However, it should be emphasized that reforms in at least in two areas discussed above may produce significantly greater improvement in the governance of the Fund than changes in some of the other areas emphasized in the public debate:

    • Ending the dependence of the IMF on its shareholders for funding through quotas and bilateral lending (GAB and NAB) by transforming it into an SDR-based institution.

    • The separation of surveillance from program lending, giving the former task to authorities who are independent of their governments and not involved in lending decisions.

c. The Fund needs to focus on its main responsibility for safeguarding international monetary and financial stability. Consequently:

    • It should stay out of development finance and policy, including poverty alleviation. This is an unjustified digression into an area that belongs to the multilateral development banks. All IMF facilities created for this purpose should be transferred to the World Bank as the Fund terminates its activities in development and long-term lending.

    • It should also stay away from trade policies. Its attempts to promote unilateral trade liberalization in DEEs drawing on its resources undermine the bargaining power of these countries in multilateral trade negotiations. In this area its main task is to ensure a predictable global trading environment by helping secure stable payments positions and exchange rates.

Notes

1. See Akyüz (2002) for the issues raised and proposals made after the Asian financial crisis.

2. The World Bank has also set up the Vulnerability Financing Facility for countries hardest hit by the food and financial crises, but its potential contribution to crisis response in the DEEs is not very clear.

3. The Fund has two agreements for bilateral borrowing from its shareholders—the General Arrangements to Borrow (GAB) and the New Arrangements to Borrow (NAB). GAB was established in 1962 on the basis of the provisions of the Articles of Agreement (Article VII, Section 2) for replenishment of scarce currencies, which gave birth to the G10. It has been renewed ten times, raised from the original amount of SDR6 billion to SDR17 billion in 1983 in response to the debt crisis. NAB was established in 1998 as a set of credit arrangements with 26 members, for a total of SDR17 billion and renewed twice since then. In both GAB and NAB, commitments by individual countries are based on their quotas. Between the two the total amount available to the Fund is around US$50 billion.

4. See *New York Times*, "IMF Planning to Sell Bonds to Finance New Loans", April 26.

5. The SLF was introduced in October 2008 with the deepening and global spread of the crisis for members with "solid policy track records and strong fundamentals", and access was based on *ex-ante* qualification. Unlike the FCL, it had a cap of 500 percent of the quota, and could not be used as a precautionary credit line. It remained unused until replaced by the FCL. Members who do not qualify for the FCL can use the so-called High-Access Precautionary Stand-by Arrangements (HAPAs) on a precautionary basis, with a cap and frontloading subject to *ex-post* review; see IMF (2009a).

6. See IMF Press Release 09/85, 24 March 2009.

7. In particular, the additional US$250 billion for the Fund is not yet in sight, the source of the additional US$100 billion for the World Bank is not clear, and the so-called US$250 additional money for trade financing seems to be fictitious; see Giles (2009) and Khor (2009).

8. For implications of the current crisis for external adjustment in the United States and China, see Akyüz (2008a).

9. For a discussion of SDR allocation to poor countries as a way of reducing the costs of holding reserves, see Polak and Clark (2006).

10. UNCTAD has also called for a temporary moratorium on official debt servicing by DEEs, see UNCTAD (2009).

11. On trade restrictions, see Gamberoni and Newfarmer (2009) and World Bank (2009).

12. For instance, in September 2000, the Committee emphasized "enhancing Fund surveillance, and promoting stability and transparency in the financial sector"; in April 2002, it encouraged the Fund "to press ahead with the range

of recent initiatives designed to enhance the effectiveness of surveillance and crisis prevention, including the Financial Sector Assessment Program"; in October 2004, it allocated four paragraphs on "making surveillance more effective and strengthening crisis prevention"; and in April 2006, it proposed a "new framework for IMF surveillance" which included, *inter alia*, making the staff "accountable for the quality of surveillance".

13. This is known as the Guidotti-Greenspan rule formulated after the Asian crisis. For a discussion of adequate level of reserves, see UNCTAD *TDR* (1999: chap. V).

14. "Borrowed" in the sense that they accompany increased claims by non-residents in one form or another, including direct and portfolio equity investment, which entail outward income transfers.

15. The method used here to estimate reserve costs differs from that in the literature in that a distinction is made here between borrowed and earned reserves. Polak and Clark (2006) also refer to borrowed reserves in their estimation of the cost to the poorest developing countries.

16. For a recent discussion of this proposal in relation to the current crisis, see Monbiot (2008). Ironically, this proposal is now revisited for addressing the problems associated with the dollar-based reserve system and United States indebtedness, while at the Bretton Woods, it was opposed by the US because it was the biggest creditor at the time and Keynes proposed taxing current account surpluses. By contrast, in a recent speech on *Reform of the International Monetary System*, proposing adoption of the SDR as a global reserve currency, the governor of the People's Bank of China, the country with the biggest surplus, referred to Keynes's bancor proposal as "farsighted"; see Zhou (2009).

17. See Polak and Clark (2006), which also addresses whether SDRs should be issued to all members or to low-income countries alone.

18. For an account of these deliberations, see Boughton (2001: 936-943). See also Bergsten (2009).

19. Kenen (2005) suggests that a widespread unloading of dollar reserves into euro could be absorbed by establishing a similar substitution account at the European Central Bank so as to avoid the undesirable effects of a flight from the dollar on interest rates and exchange rates.

20. These are discussed in Boughton (2001, 2007) and Bergsten (2007a, 2007b).

21. An alternative would be for the IMF to invest dollar reserves in long-term Treasury bonds which normally carry higher interest rates. But this would not necessarily cover the exchange rate losses.

22. Several authors in Eichengreen and Baldwin (2008) propose a single global regulator for large highly leveraged institutions and banks with significant border-crossing activities.

23. A proposal made after the Asian crisis was to establish a World Financial Authority (WFA) or to turn the BIS into such a mega-agency "with major powers to establish best practice financial regulation and risk management

throughout international financial markets… to enforce regulatory standards, backed by high-profile surveillance… [and] monitor and mediate the imposition of capital controls by national governments"; see Eatwell and Taylor (1998). For a more detailed discussion, see Eatwell and Taylor (2000), and for an assessment, Akyüz and Cornford (2002).

24. Eichengreen (2008) proposes the creation of a World Financial Organization where members would undertake obligations for regulation and supervision set out in its charter and agreements, but would be free in deciding how to meet them. This would permit regulations to be tailored to the structure of individual financial markets. An independent body of experts would then decide whether the members have met their obligations, imposing sanctions such as denying access of banks from non-complying countries to the markets of other members. However, such a loose arrangement without clearly defined rules and obligations may not provide adequate safeguards for DEEs, or prevent regulatory arbitrage.

25. See, for example, G30 (2008) and the proposals made in several chapters in Eichengreen and Baldwin (2008).

26. For these shortcomings, see Cornford (2002), Schneider and Silva (2002) and Schneider (2005).

27. For the discussion of this issue in the IMF, see Akyüz (2005: 9-15).

28. For a discussion of Fund-led debt restructuring in emerging market crises, see Akyüz (2002).

29. For the rationale for an international chapter 9 insolvency, see Raffer (1993).

References

Akyüz, Yılmaz (ed.) (2002). *Reforming the Global Financial Architecture: Issues and Proposals*. Zed Books, London.

Akyüz, Yılmaz (2005). Reforming the IMF: Back to the drawing board. G-24 Discussion Paper 38, UNCTAD, Geneva.

Akyüz, Yılmaz (2008a). The current global financial turmoil and Asian developing countries. ESCAP Series on Inclusive & Sustainable Development 2, Bangkok; reprinted in TWN *Global Economy Series* 11, Penang.

Akyüz, Yılmaz (2008b). Managing financial instability in emerging markets: A Keynesian perspective. *METU Studies in Development*, 35 (10).

Akyüz, Yılmaz, and Andrew Cornford (2002). Capital flows to developing countries and the reform of the international financial system. In Deepak Nayyar (ed.). *Governing Globalization*. Oxford University Press, New York.

Balls, Edward (2003). Preventing financial crises: The case for independent IMF surveillance. Remarks made at the Institute for International Economics, 6 March, Washington, DC.

Bergsten, C. Fred (2007a). How to solve the problem of the dollar. *Financial Times*, 11 December.

Bergsten, C. Fred (2007b). Objections do not invalidate substitution account benefits. *Financial Times*, 29 December.

Bergsten, C. Fred (2009). We should listen to Beijing's currency idea. *Financial Times*, 8 April.

Boughton, James M. (2001). *Silent Revolution: The International Monetary Fund, 1979-89*. International Monetary Fund, Washington, DC.

Boughton, James M. (2007). Third time lucky for scheme to support dollar? *Financial Times*, 14 December.

Clementi, David (2000). Crisis prevention and resolution – Two aspects of financial stability. *BIS Review*, 11 September.

Cornford, Andrew (2002). Standards and regulations. In Yılmaz Akyuz (ed.). *Reforming the Global Financial Architecture: Issues and Proposals*. Zed Books, London.

Eatwell, John, and Lance Taylor (1998). *Why We Need a World Financial Authority*. Wider Angle 2/98, WIDER, Helsinki.

Eatwell, John, and Lance Taylor (2000). *Global Finance at Risk: The Case for International Regulation*. Polity Press, Cambridge.

Eichengreen, Barry (2008). Not a New Bretton Woods but a New Bretton Woods process. In Barry Eichengreen and Richard Baldwin (eds). *What G20 Leaders Must Do to Stabilise Our Economy and Fix the Financial System*. Centre for Economic Policy Research, London. Available at www.voxeu.org.

Eichengreen, Barry, and Richard Baldwin (eds) (2008). *What G20 Leaders Must Do to Stabilise Our Economy and Fix the Financial System*. Centre for Economic Policy Research, London. Available at www.voxeu.org.

Gamberoni, Elisa, and Richard Newfarmer (2009). Trade protection: Incipient but worrisome trends. 4 March. Available at www.voxeu.org

Giles, Chris (2009). Large numbers hide big G20 divisions. *Financial Times*, 2 April.

G30 (2008). *Financial Reform: A Framework for Financial Stability*. Group of Thirty, Washington, DC. Available at www.group30.org

G20 (2009a). *Enhancing Sound Regulation and Strengthening Transparency. Final Report, Working Group 1*. Group of Twenty. Available at www.g20.org

G20 (2009b). *Reinforcing International Cooperation and Promoting Integrity in Financial Market. Final Report, Working Group 2*. Group of Twenty. Available at www.g20.org

G20 (2009c). The global plan for recovery and reform. Communiqué of the G20 Summit, London, 2 April, Group of Twenty. Available at www.g20.org

IMF/GIE (IMF Group of Independent Experts) (1999). *External Evaluation of IMF Surveillance*. Report by a Group of Independent Experts, International Monetary Fund, Washington, DC.

IMF (1998). Interim Committee communiqué. 16 April. International Monetary Fund, Washington, DC.

IMF (2005). United States: Staff report for the 2005 Article IV Consultation. 30 June. International Monetary Fund, Washington, DC.

IMF (2006). United States: Staff report for the 2006 Article IV Consultation. 30 June. International Monetary Fund, Washington, DC.

IMF (2007a). United States: Staff report for the 2007 Article IV Consultation. 11 July. International Monetary Fund, Washington, DC.

IMF (2007b). Iceland: Staff report for the 2007 Article IV Consultation. 26 July. International Monetary Fund, Washington, DC.

IMF (2009a). Review of Fund facilities—Analytical basis for Fund lending and reform options. 6 February, International Monetary Fund, Washington, DC.

IMF (2009b). *World Economic Outlook*. April, International Monetary Fund, Washington, DC.

IMF (2009c). Communiqué of the International Monetary and Financial Committee of the Board of Governors of the International Monetary Fund. Press Release 09/139. 25 April, International Monetary Fund, Washington, DC.

Kenen, Peter B. (2005). Stabilizing the international monetary system. *Journal of Policy Modelling*, 27 (4), June: 487-493.

Khor, Martin (2009). Reality behind the hype of the G20 summit. TWN Info Services on Finance and Development, 7 April, Third World Network, Penang. Available at: www.twnside.org.sg

Krueger, Anne O. (2001). International financial architecture for 2002: A new approach to sovereign debt restructuring. Address given at the National Economists' Club Annual Members' Dinner, 26 November, American Enterprise Institute, Washington, DC.

Monbiot, George (2008). Keynes is innocent: The toxic spawn of Bretton Woods was no plan of his. *The Guardian*, 18 November.

Polak, Jacques J., and Peter B. Clark (2006). Reducing the costs of holding reserves. A new perspective on special drawing rights. In Inge Kaul and Pedro Conceição (eds). *The New Public Finance: Responding to Global Challenges*. Oxford University Press, New York.

Raffer, Kunibert (1993). What's good for the United States must be good for the world: Advocating an International Chapter 9 Insolvency. *From Cancún to Vienna: International Development in a New World*. Bruno Kreisky Forum for International Dialogue, Vienna.

Sachs, J.D. (1998). External debt, structural adjustment and economic growth. In *International Monetary and Financial Issues for the 1990s*. Vol. IX. UNCTAD, Geneva.

Schneider, Benu (2005). Do global standards and codes prevent financial crises? Some proposals on modifying the standards-based approach. UNCTAD Discussion Paper 177, Geneva.

Schneider, Benu, and Sacha Silva (2002). Conference report on international standards and codes: The developing country perspective. Conference paper, 21 June, Commonwealth Secretariat, Overseas Development Institute, London.

Triffin, Robert (1960). *Gold and the Dollar Crisis: The Future of Convertibility.* Yale University Press, New Haven.

TWN (2009). The IMF's financial crisis loans: No change in conditionalities. 11 March, Third World Network, Penang. Available at www.twnside.org.sg

UNCTAD (various issues). *Trade and Development Report* (*TDR*). United Nations, Geneva.

UNCTAD (2009). Temporary debt moratorium needed for some poor nations, UNCTAD Chief says. UNCTAD Press Release PR/30/2009/13, Geneva.

World Bank (2009). Swimming against the tide: How developing countries are coping with the global crisis. Background Paper prepared by World Bank staff for the G20 Finance Ministers and Central Bank Governors Meeting, 13-14 March, Horsham, United Kingdom.

Zhou Xiaochuan (2009). Reform the international monetary system. 24 March, People's Bank of China, Beijing. Available at: www.pbc.gov.cn/english

6

Reforming Financial Regulation:
What needs to be done

Jane D'Arista and Stephany Griffith-Jones[1]

> The more free-market oriented our economy, the greater its need for
> official financial supervision.
>
> Henry Kaufman, *Financial Times*, 6 August 2008

A short look at history indicates that, unless governed by appropriate
regulation, financial markets tend to cause costly and damaging crises.
This does not imply that financial crises are inevitable; they can, in fact, be
prevented, or ameliorated, by appropriate public policy and, especially, by
regulation.

After the Great Depression, the financial sector—particularly, but not
only in the US—was re-regulated for soundness by adopting such measures
as the US Glass-Steagall Act of 1933. During the next forty years, with the
global financial sector highly regulated and capital accounts fairly closed,
there were practically no financial crises. In the 1970s, and especially during
the 1980s and 1990s, there was massive de-regulation, both at national and
international levels. Since the 1980s, there have been very frequent and very
deep financial crises, both in the developing and developed world. These
have been extremely costly in terms of growth and development.

The only silver lining that appears during these costly crises is that
they provide a political opportunity to carry out desirable regulatory
reforms. The depth of the current crisis in the developed economies
represents such an opportunity. It has led to massive bail-outs, public
recapitalizations of many financial institutions and large costs to taxpayers
which generated a great deal of anger. The crisis threatens to lead to an

unacceptably serious and possibly long recession globally. Developing economies, though innocent bystanders, have been seriously affected. As a consequence, there is significant political appetite for more and better regulation. Furthermore, it is increasingly clear that effective regulation is not just in the interests of the real economy; it is also critical for the stability and competitiveness of the financial system itself, as well as of individual financial institutions.

The key question in policy circles at present is therefore not whether to regulate, but how best to do it. In thinking about the future shape of the financial system and its regulation, it is important to be clear about its purpose. The financial sector should be seen as a means to an end: it should serve the real economy, and thus the needs of households and enterprises to consume and invest. While governments should encourage the financial sector to innovate and create instruments that support growth and development in a sustainable way, they should also use regulation to dampen the potential for systemic risk. Future crises must be prevented because of their impact on lost output and investment and, above all, on the lives of people, many of whom are poor and bear no responsibility for what has occurred.

The global financial crisis that started in 2007 follows many costly crises in developing economies over the last 30 years. Like previous ones, it is the result of both inherent flaws in the way financial markets operate—such as their inherent tendency toward boom-bust behavior—and insufficient, incomplete and sometimes inappropriate regulation. The new systems of financial regulation should attempt to deal with these problems as well as the emergence of new and unregulated actors and instruments, and increased globalization of financial markets. To do this adequately and to avoid regulatory arbitrage, regulation has to be both comprehensive and countercyclical. These two broad principles—*comprehensiveness* and *counter-cyclicality*—provide the framework for our proposals detailed below.

Comprehensiveness

In order for regulation to be efficient, it is essential that the domain of the regulator is the same as the domain of the market being regulated. Furthermore, lender-of-last resort type facilities, provided by national central banks and the European Central Bank are increasingly being extended to new actors and instruments during the current turmoil. As a result, a corresponding expansion of regulation to actors and activities that have been, or are likely to be, bailed out, is essential to avoid moral hazard. The internationalization of lender-of-last resort facilities seems both inevitable and desirable, given European and globalized private financial players, but needs to be accompanied by a strengthening of the international dimension of financial regulation to prevent the growth of financial activity and risk-taking in areas where international regulatory gaps exist. Thus, we see a global regulatory institution as an essential condition to efficiently implement comprehensive international regulation of institutions that engage in international transactions. Such an institution would be particularly desirable from the perspective of developing countries if they are appropriately and effectively represented in such international regulatory fora.

The necessary pre-condition for comprehensive regulation is *transparency*. It should be required of all actors and activities and entail registration of relevant variables for all financial institutions. Requiring transparency will benefit other financial market participants and investors, as well as macroeconomic authorities.

Instituting *comprehensive* and equivalent regulation will require covering all entities that invest or lend on behalf of other people, and all activities which they undertake. Such regulation needs to be done in ways that protect both liquidity (by imposing liquidity requirements on individual institutions as well as required reserve holdings by all institutions with national or regional central banks), and solvency (based on capital requirements that would significantly improve and modify the existing Basel banking regulatory framework, while widening solvency requirements to other financial institutions). Adequate liquidity and capital buffers are, in fact, linked as sufficient reserves—implying higher levels of liquidity in individual institutions and in the whole system—will alleviate pressure on capital in times of stress.

Counter-cyclicality

The pro-cyclical behavior of most financial actors leads to excessive risk-taking and financial activity in good times, followed by insufficient risk-taking and financial activity in bad times. As a consequence, regulation needs to be countercyclical to compensate for the inherent pro-cyclical behavior of capital and banking markets. This implies varying regulatory requirements for reserves, loan to asset value ratios, capital, provisioning against losses, etc. according to the phase of the economic cycle. Regulatory requirements such as capital or reserves could thus be varied according to the growth of total assets, and/or the expansion of assets in particular sectors, e.g. loans for housing. As former BIS Chief Economist, William White (2007) pointed out, this would use "monetary and credit data as a basis for resisting financial excesses in general, rather than inflationary pressure in particular."

The next section briefly outlines the lapses in regulation of systemically important institutions in the advanced economies seen as the primary causes of the crisis, and how the problems generated were transmitted to developing economies. In the following section, we develop what we believe are the key principles and criteria for a regulatory framework that minimizes systemic risk. The concluding section develops our main regulatory proposals for liquidity and solvency.

Channels for Crisis Transmission: Lessons for Reform

In April 2009, the G20 meeting and the Financial Stability Board both agreed that the failure or absence of appropriate financial regulation were major causes of the crisis. Some of the factors seen as among the most damaging include:

– excessive leverage funded by short-term borrowing;
– changes in the structure of the financial system that increased the volume and importance of marketable assets relative to loans and resulted in what the Financial Stability Board (2009) characterizes as "extensive application of fair value accounting";
– the proliferation of opaque, non-public markets for asset-backed securities and derivatives;
– off-balance sheet operations that eroded regulatory constraints and systemic transparency and depleted capital reserves;
– unconstrained growth in global debt; and
– deceptive lending and fraud.

Like the sub-prime mortgage crisis itself, these are factors that originated in markets and institutions located in advanced economies. But they contributed to developments that, in time, precipitated losses for the financial sectors and economies of countries far removed from the sources of the problem as capital flows to developing economies drew these countries into the web of speculation that institutions in the advanced economies created. Preventing a repetition of the disturbances they precipitated is critical for the future growth and prosperity of developing countries and advanced economies.

Excess Liquidity Set the Stage for the Crisis

Much of the blame for the hands-off regulatory environment that allowed excessive speculation and risk-taking to flourish in the decade before the crisis has been directed at central banks in advanced economies. But central banks also abandoned the quantitative tools of monetary policy—such as lending limits, and liquidity and reserve requirements—and allowed credit flows to respond to the pro-cyclical pressures of market forces. As they lost their ability to moderate the explosion in debt that unchecked credit expansion produced or to prevent the asset bubbles it fuelled, they helped create conditions that led to the crisis. The explosion in leverage that fed the massive increase in the volume of capital flows could not have occurred without the excessive liquidity they created.

The build-up in liquidity began in the aftermath of the collapse of the major stock indices in 2000. In its 2004 *Annual Report*, the Bank for International Settlements (BIS) called attention to quantitative measures such as the monetary base, broad money and credit to the private sector which had expanded rapidly since 1999 in a large group of countries. The resulting low interest rate environment intensified investors' so-called "search for yield" and the unprecedented increase in the availability of funding spurred escalating amounts of leveraged speculation that narrowed risk premiums and eased credit standards. As the BIS correctly warned, a rising volume of leveraged speculation in domestic and international financial systems was fuelling credit expansion and creating unsustainable levels of debt in the global economy (BIS *Annual Report*, 2003, 2004).

Leveraged Capital Flows Undermined Policy Initiatives

Sizable, pro-cyclical capital flows over the last two decades played an important role in weakening the impact of changes in policy rates on the availability of credit in financial markets in both advanced countries and emerging market economies. In the US, for example, the Fed's efforts to revive credit flows and economic activity with infusions of liquidity and lower interest rates were undermined by capital outflows during the recession in the early 1990s. As interest rates fell, the search for higher yields by domestic and foreign holders of US assets prompted outflows—mostly to Mexico—that prolonged the recession. Credit growth resumed when the Fed raised interest rates in March 1994 and US and foreign investors returned to US assets, leaving Mexico in crisis (Federal Reserve System (FRS) *Flow of Funds*, 2006; US Department of Commerce, 2006). This shows how increases in US interest rates, on their own, were not effective in curbing credit growth in the US, but had very negative effects on Mexico.

By the middle of the 1990s, the growth of cross-border carry trade strategies, triggered by interest rate differentials on assets denominated in different currencies, increased the amount of leveraged speculation by financial institutions and further undermined central banks' ability to expand or curtail the transmission of liquidity to their national markets.[2] From 2004 through to the first half of 2007, for example, borrowing reached truly massive proportions, both in the US and abroad. Rather than halt rising debt levels, the Fed's increases in policy rates spurred foreign private inflows into dollar assets by encouraging carry trade strategies that borrowed low interest rate yen to purchase higher yielding dollar assets.

Thus, the pattern that has developed over the last two decades suggests that relying on changes in interest rates as the primary tool of monetary policy in advanced and emerging economies can set off pro-cyclical capital flows that tend to reverse the intended result of the action taken. As a result, monetary policy no longer reliably performs its countercyclical function and its attempts to do so by changing the policy rate may even exacerbate instability.

Capital Flows, Leveraged Speculation and Bubble Inflation

In the period 2004-2007, borrowing in international as well as national financial markets set new records in virtually every quarter. The majority of cross-border lending in these high-volume years were inter-bank loans and loans to financial institutions in offshore centres. Commenting on a particularly large surge in lending as early as 2005, both the BIS and the International Monetary Fund (IMF) warned that downward pressure on interest rates resulting from excessive global liquidity had created an environment in which borrowing for speculative purposes had come to dominate cross-border transactions (BIS, 2005, 2006; IMF *Global Financial Stability Report* (*GFSR*), 2005). The ongoing growth in borrowing by financial institutions within the financial sector underscored the extent to which rising financial leverage posed systemic risks to asset markets— symbolized by Long Term Capital Management's failure in 1998.

Meanwhile, as capital flows into the US in 2005 rose to twice the amount needed to finance the current account deficit, the US assumed an *entrepot* (recycling centre) function for global markets. Excess flows into dollar assets triggered sizable outflows for investment in higher-yielding emerging market assets (US Department of Commerce, 2006). With an excess of dollars from foreign capital flows on top of current account surpluses flooding their markets, central banks in these countries bought dollars to prevent their conversion into local currencies. Their sterilized intervention strategies moderated the build-up in domestic liquidity and helped mitigate the appreciation of their currencies.

But, needing to invest the dollars they had acquired, emerging market countries bought US treasury securities and other dollar assets and re-exported the problem back to the US. The accumulation of dollar reserves by these countries augmented the highly liquid conditions in US financial markets, exerted downward pressure on medium and long-term interest rates, fuelled another round of capital outflows from the US back to emerging markets and facilitated continued binge borrowing by US residents, possible mainly due to the deregulation of financial markets.

Rising liquidity and debt in the years from 2004 through 2007 reflected a new dynamic introduced by the advent of monetary easing after 2000: the generation of liquidity through the spillover effects of leveraged cross-border investment flows. The round-robin (circular) nature of those flows constituted a dangerous scenario that was bound to lead to crisis when uncertainty—for any reason—threatened the highly leveraged financial sector's need for funding.

Meanwhile, the rising debt levels of private financial and non-financial sectors were threatening to burst the asset bubbles they had created. The housing bubble that had become apparent in the US and was to burst in the second half of 2007 was fuelled by an extraordinary growth in debt. Outstanding credit reached 352.6 percent of GDP by year-end 2007, up from 255.3 percent in 1997. The rise in household debt over the same decade (from 66.1 to 99.9 percent of GDP) was both a key indicator of the debt bubble and of the growing threat it posed for future spending as debt service took a larger share of disposable income. But the most dramatic development, and yet another indicator of the growth in leveraged speculation, was the jump in the debt of the US financial sector to 113.8 percent of GDP from 63.8 percent only a decade earlier (FRS *Flow of Funds*, 2007).

Lessons for Emerging and Developing Economies

As early as 2005, the BIS' *Quarterly Review* expressed concern that record low spreads on carry trade investments in emerging economies could make these countries vulnerable to re-pricing if there were changes in interest rates. The IMF also warned that economic and market developments that had reduced risks in the near term were storing up potential vulnerabilities for the future (IMF *GFSR*, 2005). Those vulnerabilities became abundantly apparent in the fourth quarter of 2008 in the aftermath of the largest reduction in international bank claims for a single quarter on record.[3] As noted in the IMF's April 2009 *GFSR*, the collapse of international financing had spread the crisis to emerging and developing economies.

The reversal in flows and the collapse in global trade hammered emerging economies and triggered an equally large (US$298 billion) drop in the foreign exchange deposits they held in external banking markets to offset the loss of credit from international banks (BIS, 2009; IMF *GFSR*, 2009). The scale of the credit collapse in late 2008 was intensified by the amount of leverage in the system. Inflated by leverage, capital flows to these countries in the period 2005-2008 increased their vulnerability as speculative objectives determined the size and timing of inflows, and distorted domestic prices and the distribution of credit. In addition, the rising volume of marketable assets in national and external markets increased the impact of the downward pressure on prices.

While financial systems in emerging and developing countries remain primarily bank-based, the tilt toward market-based systems in advanced economies and the international markets means that developing countries must participate actively (and be given space to participate) in making decisions about ways to impose effective constraints on leverage related to capital flows and in derivatives and commodities markets. Although reinstating capital controls would moderate some of the damage inflicted on recipient countries by pro-cyclical inflows, the overall stability of the global financial system is no less important to their well being and will require controlling the scale of leveraged speculation through curbs on hedge funds and other highly leveraged institutions that engage in the carry trade.

Moreover, all countries must also join in efforts to reinstate tools that monetary authorities need to implement countercyclical policy initiatives and channel liquidity more effectively over the business cycle. And, as has been apparent since the Mexican crisis in 1994, central banks in emerging and advanced countries must reassess the ways in which capital requirements are designed. Capital should protect financial institutions from the boom and bust pressures of pro-cyclical market forces, not act as a stimulus to excessive credit expansion or a conduit to insolvency.

Finally, it is clear that more—and more careful—monitoring of external markets will be necessary. Regulatory strategies must be developed that can reach into these large and critical markets that flourish outside national borders and provide the stability needed to promote sustainable growth in the global economy. Whether or not national regulators have the ability to control the leveraged speculation that has dominated external markets in recent years is not clear. Eatwell and Taylor (2000) argue for establishing a global regulator. Discussion of this proposal is crucial, and should be undertaken as part of the effort to construct a framework that can constrain the damaging effects of excessive pro-cyclical capital flows (see D'Arista and Griffith-Jones, 2009).

Criteria and Principles for Financial Regulatory Reform

As discussed earlier, two broad principles—comprehensiveness and counter-cyclicality—need to be adhered to, so that financial regulation is effective in ensuring financial stability and avoiding crises. Since late 2008, there has been growing support from G20 leaders and finance ministers as well as from international regulatory bodies—such as the Financial Stability Board and the Basel Banking Committee—for these two principles. A key issue is the extent and way in which they will be implemented; in particular, will the implementation of new regulations be "cosmetic", or will the measures taken be strong enough to deal with the market imperfections at the heart of the current crisis?

Furthermore, though we focus on the two basic principles of prudential regulation, there are other, well-established ones: consumer protection and restricting monopoly power. Suffice it to say that even these well established principles were not followed in recent years. The first of these functions, consumer protection, should be considerably enhanced to avoid the supply of toxic mortgages and highly risky investment vehicles offered to unsophisticated agents. Restricting monopoly power is also very important, as the crisis has shown that very large financial institutions are difficult to regulate (given their large power), are very costly (and may become impossible) to bail-out, and also are too big to fail because of their interconnectedness with the rest of the financial system.

Regulation has to be Comprehensive

One of the main causes of the current crisis is the fact that effective regulation covers a diminishing share of total capital and banking markets. In particular, in the USA and other developed countries, there was a massive shift of savings from banks to capital markets. By 2007, only 25 percent of the US financial system's assets belonged to commercial banks, which is a major change from previous periods. However, commercial banks were the only part of the financial system that was regulated on a global basis for capital requirements, and even that regulation was partial, as off-balance sheet mechanisms went unregulated. Investment banks were very lightly regulated, and had less stringent capital requirements, while other financial actors—like hedge funds—were not regulated at all. Off-shore actors are subject to no or very light regulation. As a result of these regulatory shortages, a massive "shadow financial system" was allowed to emerge, with no or little transparency or regulation.

Because of regulatory arbitrage, growth of financial activity (and risk) moved to unregulated mechanisms (structured investment vehicles—SIVs), instruments (derivatives) or institutions (hedge funds). However, though unregulated, those parts of the shadow financial system were *de facto* dependent on systemically important banks.

A clear example of when the lack of capital requirements led to excessive growth of unregulated mechanisms is in the case of SIVs. It is very interesting that the Spanish regulatory authorities allowed Spanish banks to have SIVs, but required them to consolidate these special purpose vehicles in their accounting, implying they had the same capital requirements as other assets (Cornford, 2008: interviews). This eliminated the incentive for such vehicles to grow in Spain, and thus prevented them from becoming a major problem for banks as SIVs were in the United States.

Unlike Basel I, Basel II requires banks to set aside capital to support liquidity commitments to these vehicles; however, such commitments have lower capital requirements for short maturities. A more comprehensive solution would be for all vehicles and transactions to be put on banks' balance sheets; then there would be no regulatory arbitrage, as risk-weighted capital requirements would be equivalent for all balance sheet activities; furthermore, transparency could become more comprehensive.

In capital markets, there was little formal regulation for systemic risks, with the focus mainly on individual investor protection. Private actors, such as insurance companies, pretended that they were able to sell systemic risk insurance, like credit default swaps (CDSs). Some of those major insurance companies, like AIG in the USA, had to be rescued, as they essentially became bankrupt. This was because they did not have sufficient capital and reserves to fulfill contracts that had a massive amount of systemic risk. Indeed, no entity—except the government—is capable of credibly fulfilling such a contract once the crisis spread. Thus, the government not only became the lender of last resort, but also the insurer of last resort (see Mehrling, 2009).

It is encouraging that the G20 Working Group on Regulation and Transparency (G20 WGRT) agreed in March 2009 that: "All systemically important financial institutions, markets, and instruments should be subject to an appropriate degree of regulation and oversight, consistently applied and proportionate to their local and global systemic importance. Consideration has to be given to the potential systemic risk of a cluster of financial institutions which are not systemically important on their own. Non-systemically important financial institutions, markets, and instruments could also be subject to some form of registration requirement or oversight." The timeline for implementing this will be two years after the fall of 2009. In *Lessons of the Financial Crisis for Future Regulation* (IMF, 2009), the IMF takes a similar approach: "The perimeter of financial sector surveillance needs to be expanded to a wider range of institutions and markets...."

While it is welcome that the G20 and the IMF recognize the need for regulating *all* systemically important institutions, markets, and instruments (which implies significant progress in relation to the past), it seems problematic to define "systemic importance" *ex ante*. For example, would Bear Stearns have been defined *ex ante* as a systemically important institution? Furthermore, the risk is that market actors will take advantage again of regulatory gaps, and that the *de facto* less regulated parts of the system will again create systemic risk. In this sense, we prefer the stronger statement of 14 March 2009 by Brazil, Russia, India and China (the BRICs) which calls for "all financial activities—especially those of systemic importance—to be subject to adequate regulation and supervision, including institutions that are in the shadow banking system... and strongly support... to intensify supervision of hedge funds and private pools of capital."

Indeed, we believe that the task of defining equivalent regulation on assets for *all* financial institutions and activities, both for solvency and liquidity, is essential.[4] To be more specific, *all* entities that invest or lend on behalf of other people—using other people's money and providing some type of leverage—need to have both relevant transparency requirements and need to be regulated, especially as regards their leverage, but also their liquidity. Within institutions, all their activities need to have equivalent regulation. Therefore, institutions like hedge funds need to be brought into the regulatory domain, as do all off-balance activities of banks.

As regards comprehensive regulation of solvency, equivalent regulation of different actors, instruments and activities should especially refer to leverage, as excessive leverage has been such a major source of systemic risk.

However, as the longevity of funding is an important variable, it may be desirable to restrict leverage more (and thus require more capital) for assets funded by short-term liabilities. This will not just protect the solvency of financial institutions, but also encourage them to seek more long-term funding.

Persaud (2009) has argued that tying leverage requirements to maturity of funding will also encourage diversity of behavior amongst different actors, thus discouraging herding across different categories of financial actors, and contributing to financial stability. In this regard, he proposes that, whatever they are called, financial institutions with short-term funding should follow bank capital adequacy requirements. Those with long term funding, according to Persaud, could have a different long term "solvency" regime, that would take into account their long-term obligations and assets. This interesting proposal deserves further study. It is key however that the equivalent regulation of leverage, for all actors, instruments, and activities, is designed and implemented in a simple way, as complexity makes implementation difficult and may ease regulatory arbitrage. Separate and sufficient minimum liquidity requirements should be an essential part of regulation, an aspect neglected in recent years.

Specific steps have already been taken towards more comprehensive regulation; the US authorities are addressing regulatory gaps, for example in the oversight of entities that originate and fund mortgages. The US Treasury's March 2009 plea for future regulation was clearly summarized by US Treasury Secretary Timothy Geithner (2009): "All institutions and markets that could pose systemic risk will be subject to strong oversight, including appropriate constraints on risk-taking."

As pointed out above, there is a great deal of broad support—from the G20, FSF, as well as major governments—for comprehensive regulation, including of hedge funds and private equity. Furthermore, an influential and detailed European Parliament (2008) report argues that financial regulation should be comprehensive; it especially emphasizes the need to regulate hedge funds and makes specific recommendations to limit the leverage of hedge funds to preserve the stability of the EU financial system. However, though the resulting proposed European Commission Directive says it favors regulation of hedge funds and private equity, it is extremely weak *de facto* on direct regulation; for example, it proposes only to directly regulate, and require capital, from fund managers (which is minimal), and *not* from the funds themselves. This would *de facto* mean no direct regulation of hedge funds and private equity leverage, key sources of systemic risk.

Reducing Information Asymmetries for Better Regulation

A key pre-condition for comprehensive regulation is comprehensive transparency of the relevant variables. Transparency also has advantages for other stakeholders such as investors, other market agents and macroeconomic authorities. The March 2009 G20 WGRT has been clear in endorsing comprehensive transparency and recognizing it as a pre-condition for effective regulation "in order to determine the appropriate degree of regulation or oversight, national authorities should determine appropriate mechanisms for gathering relevant information on all material financial institutions, markets, and instruments."

OTC Derivatives

One example is the complex and totally opaque over-the-counter (OTC) derivatives, which have reached massive levels. Possible solutions would attempt to standardize such instruments and channel them through clearing house based exchanges, as Soros (2008) was among the first to suggest, especially for the US$45 trillion worth of credit default swap contracts; if transactions are not channeled through exchanges, those that hold the contracts do not even know whether the counterparties are properly protected with capital. This requirement of trading in either clearing houses or exchanges should be obligatory for all OTC derivatives. This would have the benefit of ensuring appropriate margin and capital requirements for each transaction, as well as many other advantages, including those of transparency.[5]

It is encouraging that the US administration moved forward in May 2009 by proposing the requirement that all "standardized" OTC derivatives be cleared through regulated central clearing houses (*Financial Times*, 14 May 2009, "Geithner in push on derivatives regulation"; US Treasury Press Release, 13 May 2009, "Regulatory Reform Over-The-Counter (OTC) Derivatives"). This would reduce the risk to investors of being dangerously exposed to a single counterparty. In the proposed plan, their regulated central counterparties (CCP) would impose robust margin requirements and ensure that customized OTC derivatives are not used as a means to avoid using a CCP. All OTC derivatives dealers and counterparties would be subject to conservative capital requirements. These "standardized" derivatives, estimated at present to represent the largest part of the market, would also have to be traded on regulated exchanges via electronic systems. Central clearers will be required to produce publicly available data on trading volumes and reveal to regulators the trades of individual counterparties.

However, several concerns remain. First, exchange trading would only be made mandatory in the US for "standardized" derivatives, not all derivatives. Second, global coordination of transparency and regulation of derivatives is essential, as these markets are particularly global. Finally, if several competing clearing houses are created in the US, and even more internationally, these could increase risks.

Hedge Funds

Another somewhat related example of the need for increased transparency involves hedge funds. On this, there is a growing consensus—including in the hedge fund industry itself—that improved information on hedge funds and other highly leveraged institutions (HLIs) would also be valuable to investors and counterparties, as well as regulators. Griffith-Jones, Calice, and Seekatz (2007) have pointed out that it seems appropriate for hedge funds to report market, liquidity, and credit risk. It also seems essential that hedge funds report aggregate worldwide and country positions, the aggregate levels of leverage, especially the levels of long and short positions, and the level of trading.

It is also important to decide the frequency of disclosure and to whom such information is to be disclosed. Positions can be reported in real time or with lags. Although real time reporting would be more useful, it could be much more costly, though much of the information is already privately available. Real time reporting, if publicly available, can enhance market stability by encouraging contrarian positions; however, it also risks encouraging herd behavior if other market actors mimic the positions of large actors (see de Brouwer, 2001). One problem of fixed point in time disclosure is the risk of "window dressing" for such moments. It would seem best if information be made publicly available. It may be sufficient if positions are reported in aggregate by class of institution, e.g. bank, securities firms, hedge funds, other HLIs, etc.

It seems important to find an institution that would be efficient at collecting and processing such data in a timely manner without compromising confidentiality. The institution with the best experience of similar data gathering is the Bank for International Settlements (BIS). Although we have discussed issues of transparency and disclosure in relation to the most opaque actors (hedge funds) and transactions (derivatives), similar criteria need to apply to opaque parts of the banking system.

Regulation has to be Countercyclical

The most important manifestation of market failure in financial markets through the ages has been pro-cyclicality. In fact, risk is mainly generated during booms, even though it becomes apparent during busts. Therefore, the time for regulators to act—to prevent excessive risk taking—is during booms. This needs to happen through simple rules which cannot be easily changed by regulators so that they will not be "captured" by the general over-enthusiasm that characterizes booms that have so often led to the dangerous relaxation of regulatory standards. Unfortunately, Basle II bank regulation does exactly the opposite. Particularly in the advanced approach, Basle II calculates required capital based on the banks' own models. This perversely incorporates the inherent pro-cyclicality of bank lending into bank regulation—thus accentuating boom-bust patterns—and interacts with the use of mark-to-market pricing to accentuate asset booms with excessive leverage.

Countercyclical regulation implies that the traditional microeconomic focus of prudential regulation and supervision be complemented by a macro-prudential perspective, particularly by introducing explicit counter-cyclical features in prudential regulation and supervision that would compensate for the pro-cyclicality of financial markets. The simplest recommendations are to increase capital and/or provisions for loan losses during booms, and to avoid mark-to-market asset pricing from feeding on greater leverage, with countercyclical limits on loan-to-value ratios and/or rules to adjust the value of collateral for cyclical asset price variations. The requirement of a countercyclical perspective in prudential regulation would go a long way to address some of the major criticisms of Basle II. It also implies that financial institutions should be urged to adopt risk management practices that take better account of the evolution of risk over the full business cycle, and less sensitive to short-term variations in asset prices.

It is very encouraging that the G20 leaders, the Basel Committee, the April 2009 Financial Stability Forum (FSF) Report and several recent major reports on financial regulation—such as the United Nations (2009), De Larosière (2009) and Turner (2009) Reports—all very clearly emphasize counter-cyclicality as a key principle of regulation. The April 2009 FSF Report on Addressing Pro-cyclicality in the Financial System is particularly insightful and complete in addressing issues of pro-cyclicality (see the discussion in D'Arista and Griffith-Jones (2009), from which this chapter is abridged).

Countercyclical bank regulation can be easily introduced, either through banks' provisions or through capital adequacy requirements. It is important that countercyclical rules are simple, and done in ways that regulators cannot loosen the rule in boom times, when they can be captured, not just by vested interests, but also by the exuberance that characterizes booms. On the other hand, some flexibility may be required, especially to add requirements for more capital and/or other provisions when new more risky activities emerge.

Countercyclical Regulation of Non-banking Institutions: The Carry Trade

Some of the least regulated parts of the financial system may have some of the strongest pro-cyclical impacts, including on emerging economies. One such example is the role that hedge funds and other actors as well as instruments, such as derivatives, play in the carry trade. Speculative positions are taken, whereby there is borrowing in a low interest currency and investing in a high interest currency, when it is assumed that there is a strong correlation between both currencies, or if the high yielding currency is appreciating. The countries' vulnerability is further increased by the fact that national companies borrow uncovered in low interest rate foreign currencies, benefiting even more in the short term due to the appreciating local currency. There is increasing empirical evidence that the carry trade has very pro-cyclical effects (for over- or under-shooting) on the exchange rates of both developed and developing economies, often with negative effects on the real economy.

UNCTAD (2008) describes how the carry trade contributed in a major way between 2004 and 2008 to the sharp appreciation of currencies that had high interest rates, including those of many developing countries such as the Brazilian *real*, the Turkish *lira*, the South African *rand* and the Korean *won*, as well as several Central and Eastern European currencies. This allowed large speculative gains. Dodd and Griffith-Jones (2006; 2008) provide in-depth analysis of the Brazilian and Chilean experience. The global financial crisis provoked a "flight to quality" spurred by increased perception of risk; as a result, there was a large unwinding of the carry trade, including in developing country currencies, as well as several problems and even bankruptcies of large companies in countries like Mexico and Brazil. Naturally, those countries, companies and individuals who had borrowed in foreign currencies were particularly hard hit.

Developing and emerging regulators can, on their own, attempt to restrict the activities of those involved in the carry trade, especially in boom times. This can be done by imposing minimum capital requirements on

derivative dealers and collateral (margin) requirements on derivative transactions. As discussed below, this regulation can even have countercyclical
elements. However, it seems unlikely that developing countries (and
individual countries in general) can totally or effectively regulate the carry
trade on their own, given that such a large part of these transactions are
carried out by internationally mobile actors, often formally operating from
off-shore centers, with low or no regulation.

This is precisely the type of issue that needs to be dealt with globally.
Currently, the FSF coordinates actions with national authorities, and
eventually, a global regulator could do so. The significantly increased
presence of several major developing counties in bodies like the FSF and
the BCBS needs to be used to raise issues such as international regulation
of the carry trade, which is of particular—but not exclusive—interest to
developing countries.

For regulation to be comprehensive, there should be minimum capital
requirements for all derivatives dealers and minimum collateral requirements
for all derivatives transactions, so as to reduce leverage and lower systemic
risk. Collateral requirements for financial transactions function much like
capital requirements for banks. However, the 2009 FSF report emphasizes
that regulators should ensure that collateral and margin requirements should
be cycle-neutral, that is they do not decline in booms. An issue to explore
is whether the regulation of derivatives' collateral and capital requirements
should go beyond this, and also have countercyclical elements. This would
be desirable as it would imply that when derivatives' positions, either long or
short, are growing excessively (for example, well beyond historical averages),
collateral and capital requirements should be increased.

In addition, prudential regulation needs to ensure adequate levels
of liquidity for financial intermediaries to handle the mismatch between
the average maturities of assets and liabilities inherent in the financial
system's essential role of transforming maturities, but which generates
risks associated with volatility in deposits and/or interest rates. This
underscores the fact that liquidity and solvency problems are far more
closely interrelated than traditionally assumed, particularly in the face of
macroeconomic shocks.

Reserve requirements, which are strictly an instrument of monetary
policy, provide liquidity in many countries, but their declining importance
makes it necessary to find new tools. Moreover, their traditional structure
is not geared to the specific objective of ensuring financial intermediaries'
liquidity in the face of the inherent maturity mismatches in their portfolios.
The best system could be one in which liquidity or reserve requirements

are estimated on the basis of the residual maturity of financial institutions' liabilities, thus generating a direct incentive for the financial system to maintain an appropriate liability structure.

Currency Mismatches and Capital Account Regulations

In developing countries, these countercyclical measures should be supplemented by more specific regulations aimed at controlling currency mismatches (including those associated with derivatives operations). The strict prohibition of currency mismatches in the portfolios of financial intermediaries is probably the best rule (as discussed in Griffith-Jones and Ocampo, 2009). Authorities should also closely monitor the currency risk of non-financial firms operating in non-tradable sectors, which may eventually pose credit risks for banks. Regulations can be used to establish more stringent provisions and/or risk weighting (and therefore, higher capital requirements) for these operations, or a strict prohibition on lending in foreign currencies to non-financial firms and households without revenues in those currencies.

Complementarily, and as long as there is no international lender of last resort, international rules should continue to provide room for the use of capital account regulation by developing countries. Capital account regulations can, in fact, play a dual role. They can be used as a complementary tool of macroeconomic and domestic regulatory policy. But they can also help to improve debt profiles, and in this way reduce the risks associated with liability structures biased towards short-term capital flows.

In practice, capital market regulations segment domestic and international markets. Traditional "quantity" controls—of the type used in China and India (but being gradually dismantled in these countries, as in others before)—differentiate between residents and non-residents, and between corporate and non-corporate agents among the former.

Another option is to introduce price-based regulations that effectively tax inflows or outflows. Taxing inflows was the choice pioneered by Chile in 1991 and Colombia in 1993 using the mechanism of unremunerated reserve requirements (URRs) on capital inflows. Argentina and Thailand have also used this approach in recent years, and taxing financial (including external) transactions has been common in Brazil. The basic advantage of price-based over traditional regulations is their non-discretionary character.

A large literature on these experiences leads to five main conclusions. First, controls on both inflows and outflows can work, but the authorities must be able to administer regulation while closing loopholes and avoiding corruption. *Permanent* regulatory regimes that can be tightened or loosened in response to external market conditions are probably the best option. Second, exchange controls and quantitative restrictions may be the best means to reduce domestic sensitivity to global financial cycles, as reflected in China's and India's avoidance of the Asian crisis in the late 1990s. URRs and similar measures may only have temporary effects on capital inflows (especially if they are not ratcheted up during a surge), but do seem to influence interest rate spreads. Third, URRs and other reserve requirements help hold down short-term debt, which is highly volatile, and thus a significant source of vulnerability. Fourth, and perhaps foremost, controls are a complement to sound macroeconomic policies, not a substitute for them. Fifth, for capital controls—as for domestic regulation—good data availability is essential.

Capital controls obviously have costs. During surges, they increase the cost of financing, which is precisely what they are supposed to do. Longer term costs are more important. They can discourage operations by foreign institutional investors who may act as market makers for domestic bond and stock markets.

Despite their advantages, capital account regulations were not widely used during the recent boom. The trend has continued towards capital account liberalization, reflected in the gradual liberalization that has taken place in China and India. Liability policies in developing countries have, however, played an important role in recent years, particularly prudential instruments aimed at mitigating currency mismatches and active liability management by public sectors.

Liquidity and Solvency

Reform proposals put forward by national and international regulatory authorities have included calls for banks to raise capital to offset losses and write-downs on assets that have fallen in value. In these discussions, capital is viewed as the sole cushion for financial institutions and their shrinking capital base is increasingly seen as a threat to systemic solvency. Moreover, the ongoing pressure on capital has impeded efforts to revive credit flows and restart economic activity. But despite growing recognition that the increase and decline in financial capital responds pro-cyclically to market forces and tends to exacerbate pro-cyclicality, the focus on capital as the primary macro-prudential tool in the global system over the last two decades has crowded out discussion of alternatives that could augment capital in protecting both the system and individual institutions.

Reform proposals must now focus on ways to make capital as well as provisioning requirements countercyclical. But they must also include discussions of alternative macro-prudential tools that readily respond to countercyclical monetary strategies and can act as systemic safeguards across the credit cycle. These tools include dynamic provisioning, lending limits (including limits on total leverage) and liquidity, margin, and reserve requirements.

These alternative tools would enhance monetary authorities' ability to stabilize both the financial system and the economy—an ability called into question by the current crisis. The severity of the threat to institutional solvency led many to question whether central banks could defuse the credit crunch and stem the decline in asset prices. In the US, for example, what had been viewed as a liquidity crisis had become a solvency crisis by the fall of 2008. A continuation of liquidity support was seen as necessary, but that support appeared to be of limited value in terms of either ending the crisis or moderating its current and potential negative impact on the real economy. Solutions increasingly turned to proposals for government intervention to protect the solvency of systemically important institutions by supplying capital.

But beyond the immediate issue of crisis management, the complementary roles of central bank liquidity as well as capital and holdings of liquid assets as cushions for private financial institutions remain critical issues for reform in both advanced and emerging economies. Moreover, the shift in savings and investment flows from banks to capital markets in advanced countries and the international financial system requires that the transmission belt for both regulatory and monetary policy initiatives be extended to reach all segments of the financial system.

The Role of Capital in a Market-based System

Assessments of the role capital plays in guarding the soundness of the financial system have tended to focus on the balance sheets of depository institutions. It should be noted, however, that before 1983, there had been no statutory basis in the US for proscribing the amount of capital banks were required to hold against assets and capital requirements had tended to be ignored in most other countries as well. With the threat of default and the proliferation of non-performing loans to developing countries in the early 1980s, the US Congress directed the Fed to set limits on banks' assets in relation to capital and this, in turn, led to negotiations with other developed countries that resulted in the adoption of the Basel I Agreement on Capital Adequacy in 1988.

But, as noted above, rules governing capital adequacy for banks have not provided the systemic protection that was expected. Because of the rapid increase in outstanding securitized mortgages and other asset-based securities as well as the explosive growth of derivatives, trading and investment in marketable securities has come to dominate the major national and international financial markets. However, as has been demonstrated repeatedly since the crisis erupted in the summer of 2007, marketability does not mean that an asset can be sold at the expected price—or even sold at all—and the wider applicability of fair value accounting associated with trading activity intensified the inherent pro-cyclical bias of the increasingly market-based global system.

One requirement of traded financial assets is that they be marked to market as prices change. Unlike bank loans held in portfolio at face value, such traded assets—including those held by banks—change the value of the capital held by an institution as their prices fluctuate. When prices fall, an institution is required to write down the value of its capital to reflect the change in the value of the asset. As the amount of credit channeled through capital markets expanded, capital charges applied to a larger share of total credit, exacerbating the pressure on capital as the sub-prime mortgage crisis spread. Thus, the greater applicability of market-based rules increased the likelihood that the credit crisis would deteriorate into a solvency crisis more rapidly than in earlier periods and affect a larger group of institutions in a wider group of countries.

Indeed, resulting threats to the solvency of systemically important non-depository institutions have made clear that the focus on banks' capital position is incomplete. The role of capital in a transformed, market-based system is a parallel concern. Thus, there is need to systemically re-examine the role of capital and to ensure that the strategies and tools used to bolster the soundness of financial institutions apply equally to all engaged in the activity. But how much capital should be held by individual institutions and when are increasingly related to the level of liquidity in the system as a whole, as well as the level of their holdings of liquid assets.

Maintaining Liquidity in a Market-based System

As capital is a scarce resource that is automatically depleted when losses are written off, liquidity requirements were used by central banks and regulators as a critical tool to protect capital before deregulation eroded their effectiveness. The Federal Reserve's August 2008 call for investment banks to shore up their balance sheets with more liquid assets underscored its belated recognition that capital alone is an insufficient cushion against the threat of insolvency (Guerrera and van Duyn, 2008). However, the systemic nature of the current crisis suggests that efforts by individual institutions or sectors to increase their holdings of liquid assets may be ineffectual if the central bank is unable to inject liquidity into critical markets.

Designing a countercyclical regulatory system will require re-examining the role and effectiveness of liquidity requirements for individual institutions and sectors as well as the channels the central bank uses to provide liquidity. The shift from a bank-based to a market-based system has obscured the fact that the systemic cushion for the financial sector in the US before the 1980s was bank reserves. Creating and extinguishing reserves by undertaking open market operations was the primary tool that allowed the Fed—as former Fed officials phrased it—to lean against the winds of the credit cycle. It reflected an ongoing commitment to countercyclical monetary policy that had evolved within the Fed in its formative years.

In 1951, when US banks held 65 percent of financial sector assets and liabilities, their reserve balances with the Fed accounted for 11.3 percent of bank deposits and constituted a remarkably comfortable cushion for a segmented financial system in which banks loaned to other financial sectors with which they were not in competition. Fifty years later, however, the shift in credit flows away from banks and banks' use of borrowed funds and strategies such as sweep accounts to reduce holdings of deposits subject to reserve requirements, had virtually wiped out that cushion. By year-end 2001, banks reserve balances had shrunk to 0.2 percent of their deposits and banks' holdings of credit market assets had fallen to less than half the share they held fifty years before (FRS *Flow of Funds*, 2002).

Going into the current crisis, the missing monetary cushion weakened individual financial institutions and made them more vulnerable to stops in external funding. Borrowing and lending among financial institutions through repurchase agreements—another rapidly expanding market in recent years—ceased to be an efficient channel for distributing liquidity as institutions' confidence in the solvency of their financial counterparties eroded. But the missing monetary cushion also impeded the Fed's ability to provide liquidity to the system as a whole. Despite the number of lending programs it created and the run-up in its balance sheet to include a more than ten-fold increase in bank reserves over a four month period, success in addressing the collapse of liquidity in funding markets remained elusive.

Capital infusions also failed to revive a stable funding channel for the financial sector, and credit to the real economy remained blocked.

The Fed's struggle to ensure a systemic reach for its efforts suggests that central banks should attempt to build a source of systemic funding within the monetary system that, like reserves, is renewable, and will be immediately available to all financial institutions in a downturn—especially those that have extensive counterparty relationships with others within the financial sector. While capital is and will remain a critical tool as a cushion against insolvency for individual institutions, capital alone cannot protect the financial sector as a whole in the event of a systemic crisis.

A new system-wide reserve management regime—that will take into account the reduced role of the traditional banking conduit for policy implementation and the increased integration of institutions and markets—is needed. Such a regime would require imposing reserve requirements on all financial institutions and authorizing the central bank to increase and reduce liquidity by supplying and withdrawing reserve accounts with the central bank held on the liability side of institutions' balance sheets. This would restore the effectiveness of countercyclical monetary strategies—a reform no less important than the regulatory reforms we and others have proposed—and help mitigate the pro-cyclical impact of the rise and fall in financial capital.[6]

In summary, we argue that there is a critical link between liquidity and solvency; that liquidity protects solvency, and that financial stability will require reforms that include comprehensive, countercyclical regulatory and monetary strategies like those suggested here.

Notes

1. We are grateful to Ariane Ortiz Marrufo and Stefano Pagliari for excellent research assistance.

2. Low interest rates in one national market provided an incentive for carry trade strategies that used borrowings in that currency to fund investments in higher-yielding assets denominated in other currencies.

3. This figure is for consolidated claims on an ultimate risk basis—that is, after taking into account net risk transfers related to credit derivatives, guarantees and collateral.

4. The technical aspects of calculating equivalent liquidity (e.g. reserves) and solvency (e.g. capital) requirements across different institutions and activities require further study, both by institutions like the BIS and the FSF, by national regulators, from both developed and developing countries, and by academics.

5. It is interesting that Brazil, an emerging country, has been effective in using regulations and other measures to encourage derivatives to move to established exchanges (Dodd and Griffith-Jones, 2008).
6. For discussions of proposals to extend reserve requirements to all financial institutions, see Thurow, 1972; Pollin, 1993; D'Arista and Schlesinger, 1993; D'Arista and Griffith-Jones, 1998; Palley, 2000, 2003; and D'Arista, 2009. For a discussion of the liability reserve management regime, see D'Arista, 2009.

References

Bank for International Settlements (BIS) (2002, 2003, 2004, 2005, 2008). *Annual Report*. Basel Committee on Banking Supervision, Basel.

Bank for International Settlements (BIS) (June 2005, March 2006). *Quarterly Review: International Banking and Financial Market Developments*. Basel Committee on Banking Supervision, Basel.

Cornford, Andrew (2008). An agenda for financial system reform. *SUNS-South-North Development Monitor* #6511, 7 July, Geneva.

D'Arista, Jane (2009). Setting an agenda for monetary reform. Working paper number 190, Political Economy Research Institute, University of Massachusetts, Amherst.

D'Arista, Jane, and Stephany Griffith-Jones (1998). The boom of portfolio flows to emerging markets and its regulatory implications. In Stephany Griffith-Jones, Manuel Montes and Anwar Nasution (eds). *Short-Term Capital Movements and Balance of Payments Crises*. World Institute for Development Economics Research, Helsinki.

D'Arista, Jane, and Stephany Griffith-Jones (2009). Agenda and criteria for financial regulatory reform. G-24 working paper, Washington, DC. www.g24.org

D'Arista, Jane, and Tom Schlesinger (1993). The parallel banking system. In Gary Dymski, Gerald Epstein and Robert Pollin (eds). *Transforming the U.S. Financial System: Equity and Efficiency for the 21st Century*. M.E. Sharpe, Armonk, NY.

De Brouwer, Gordon (2001). *Hedge Funds in Emerging Markets*. Cambridge University Press, Cambridge, MA.

De Larosière, Jacques (2009). *The High-Level Group on Financial Supervision in the EU (Larosière Report)*. Brussels.

Dodd, Randall, and Stephany Griffith-Jones (2006). Report on Chile's derivatives markets: Stabilizing or speculative impact. www.stephanygj.net (accessed 19 July 2009).

Dodd, Randall, and Stephany Griffith-Jones (2008). Brazil's derivatives markets: Hedging, central bank intervention and regulation. Working Paper, Economic Commission for Latin America and the Caribbean, Santiago.

Eatwell, John, and Lance Taylor (2000). *Global Finance at Risk: The Case for International Regulation*. The New Press, New York.

European Parliament, Committee on Economic and Monetary Affairs (2008). *Draft Report with Recommendations to the Commission on Hedge Funds and Private Equity*. 18 April, Brussels.

Federal Reserve System (FRS) (various years). *Flow of Funds Accounts of the United States*. Board of Governors of the Federal Reserve System, Washington, DC.

Financial Stability Forum (2009). *Addressing Pro-cyclicality in the Financial System*. Financial Stability Forum, Basel.

Geithner, Timothy (2009). Testimony at the Committee on Financial Services Hearing in the US House of Representatives. *Financial Times*, March 25.

Griffith-Jones, Stephany, Pietro Calice and Carmen Seekatz (2007). New investors in developing countries: Opportunities, risks and policy responses, the case of hedge funds. http://www.stephanygj.net (accessed 24 September 2008).

Griffith-Jones, Stephany, and José Antonio Ocampo (2009). Global governance for financial stability and development. UNDP Paper Series: Development Dimensions of Global Economic Governance, United Nations Development Programme, New York.

Guerrera, Francesco, and Aline van Duyn (2008). Fed presses Wall Street banks on liquidity. *Financial Times*, 11 August, p. 13.

G20 (2009). Working Group 1 – Enhancing sound regulation and strengthening transparency. Treasury, London.

IMF (2009). *Lessons of the Financial Crisis for Future Regulation*. International Monetary Fund, Washington, DC.

Kaufman, Henry (2008). The principles of sound regulation. *Financial Times*, 6 August: 11.

Mehrling, Perry (2009). Credit default swaps (CDSs): The keys to financial reform. In Stephany Griffith-Jones, J.A. Ocampo and J.E. Stiglitz (eds). *Time for a Visible Hand: Lessons from the 2008 World Financial Crisis*. Oxford University Press, New York.

Palley, Thomas (2000). *Stabilizing Finance: The Case for Asset-Based Reserve Requirements*. Financial Markets Center, Howardsville, VA.

Palley, Thomas (2003). Asset price bubbles and the case for asset-based reserve requirements. *Challenge*, 46 (3), May/June.

Persaud, Avinash (2009). The role of policy and banking supervision in the light of the credit crisis. In Stephany Griffith-Jones, J.A. Ocampo and J.E. Stiglitz (eds). *Time for a Visible Hand: Lessons from the 2008 World Financial Crisis*. Oxford University Press, New York.

Pollin, Robert (1993). Public credit allocation through the Federal Reserve: Why it is needed; how it should be done. In Gary Dymski, Gerald Epstein and Robert Pollin (eds). *Transforming the U.S. Financial System: Equity and Efficiency for the 21st Century*. M.E. Sharpe, Armonk, NY.

Soros, George (2008). *The New Paradigm for Financial Markets: The Credit Crisis of 2008 and What it Means*. Public Affairs, New York.

Thurow, Lester (1972). Proposals for re-channeling funds to meet social priorities. In *Policies for a More Competitive Financial System*. Conference proceedings, Federal Reserve Bank of Boston.

Turner Review (2009). *The Turner Review: A Regulatory Response to the Global Banking Crisis*. March, Financial Services Authority, London.

UNCTAD (2008). Rebuilding financial multilateralism with stability. Policy Brief, 4 October, Geneva.

United Nations (2009). Report of the Commission of Experts of the President of the United Nations General Assembly on Reforms of the International Monetary and Financial System. United Nations, New York. www. josephstiglitz.com

US Department of Commerce, Bureau of Economic Analysis (2006). The U.S. international investment position. *Survey of Current Business*. U.S. Department of Commerce, Washington, DC.

US Treasury Department (2009). *Regulatory Reform Over-The-Counter (OTC) Derivatives*. March, U.S. Treasury Department, Washington, DC.

White, W.R. (2007). The need for a longer policy horizon: A less orthodox approach. In Jan Joost Teunissen and Age Akkerman (eds). *Global Imbalances and Developing Countries: Remedies for a Failing International Financial System*. Forum on Debt and Development (FONDAD), The Hague.

7

The Basel 2 Agenda for 2009: Progress so far

Andrew Cornford

The revisions of Basel 2, the international standards for banks' regulatory capital developed by the Basel Committee on Banking Supervision (BCBS) to replace the 1988 Basel Capital Accord (Basel 1), are now beginning to take shape. The 2006 text of Basel 2, which was the culmination of a drafting process which began at the end of the 1990s, had been considered closed before the credit crisis which began in mid-2007.[1] This crisis has indicated major shortcomings in the regulatory framework for financial institutions which are now the subject of an agenda of wide-ranging reform.[2] Strengthening Basel 2 is an important item on this reform agenda. (An outline of the Basel capital accords can be found in the Annex to this chapter.)

Two of the major subjects of the revisions of Basel 2, discussed in this chapter, are the rules for securitization exposures and the Market Risk Framework. These are covered by consultative documents issued by the Basel Committee on Banking Supervision in January 2009. The documents on the Market Risk Framework follow up earlier July 2008 consultative documents concerning the strengthening of the regulatory capital charges for the market risks of banks' trading books. The new documents supplement the proposals of July 2008 with recommendations concerning the incorporation in the Framework of the proposed rules for banks' securitization exposures whose strengthening is an important part of the Committee's response to the major part played by such exposures in the recent financial turmoil.

Other revisions of Basel 2 still to come include supplementing the risk-based minimum regulatory requirements of Basel 2 with simpler overall measures (such as banks' aggregate leverage ratios) and the inclusion in the rules or guidelines for banks' capital "additional shock absorbers" (such as through-the-cycle or countercyclical reserves) (Wellink, 2008).

Basel 2's Rules on Securitization

Techniques of Securitization

The term "securitization" denotes one of a number of different financial operations involving the substitution of securities for other debt or the decomposition of large loans into loan shares or participations for distribution among financial institutions. The best known form of securitization consists of pooling loans and other debt obligations by banks and other financial institutions and the sale to investors of interests in the pool (asset-backed securities).

Investment instruments collateralized by pools of mortgage loans have a long history in the United States going back to the nineteenth century. In the 1980s the asset backing in securitization was extended to several other kinds of debt such as computer leases, automobile and truck loans, credit cards, trade receivables, junk bonds, and unsecured consumer loans. Initially, the mortgages in the pools of asset-backed securities were overwhelmingly prime, i.e. made to individuals with good credit histories. With the expansion of markets for assets with greater credit risk in the 1990s, the pools began to include sub-prime mortgages made to individuals with less highly rated credit histories. Initial development of markets for asset-backed securities took place mainly in the United States, but more recently, such markets have also taken off in other developed countries and in some emerging-market countries. (Concerning the development of markets for assets-backed securities in emerging-market countries, see Box 9.1.)

Owing to the different categories of debt obligation included in asset-backed securities and to the development of legal terminology associated with their regulation, securitization is associated with a bewildering number of different acronyms to denote the different instruments. The discussion which follows focuses primarily on Collateralized Debt Obligations (CDOs), here used as a generic term to cover pools of debt instruments serving as the collateral of asset-backed securities.

In cash-flow CDOs debt instruments are transferred by a bank or another financial institution to a special purpose entity (SPE), a legal structure established to sell shares in the asset-backed securities to investors. Payments due to the investors through these SPEs are made according to various formulas.

Box 9.1   Securitization in Asia and Latin America

In comparison with levels in the developed countries of North America and Western Europe, investments in asset-backed securities in emerging markets are still small. According to figures from the Bank of England, outstanding asset-backed securities in mid-2006 in the United States and Western Europe amounted to US$10.7 trillion (of which commercial mortgage-backed securities accounted for US$0.7 trillion, residential mortgage-backed securities for US$6.5 trillion, and non-mortgage asset-backed securities for US$3.5 trillion (Bank of England, 2007: 20). Issuance of asset-backed securities in United States reached US$200 billion in 2000 and subsequently expanded to nearly US$800 million in 2005, while issuance in EU member countries rose from a little under US$100 billion in 2000 to over US$300 billion in 2005 (Gyntelberg and Remolona, 2006: 67-69).

In the emerging-market countries of Asia, only in the Republic of Korea were substantial amounts of asset backed securities issued to domestic investors during 2000-2005, with the figures varying between about US$20 billion and about US$30 billion. Asset-backed securities in smaller amounts (less than US$5 billion a year) were also issued during this period to international investors by Hong Kong (China), Malaysia, Philippines, Singapore, Taiwan (Province of China) and Thailand as well as the Republic of Korea. In China, following regulatory initiatives in 2005 aimed at encouraging securitization, domestic issuance of asset-backed securities increased from a negligible amount to more than US$2 billion. As of 2006, there had been little use of credit tranching to produce asset-backed securities with different risk profiles (Gyntelberg and Remolona, 2006: 67-72).

In the emerging-market countries of Latin America, the market for asset-backed securities was dominated by issuance to foreign investors before 1998. Such issuance fell sharply thereafter to less than US$4 billion in 2006. However, this fall was accompanied by a rise in asset-backed securities issued in domestic markets to a level of US$16 billion in 2006. Two countries, Brazil and Mexico, accounted for three-quarters of those issued in 2006 (Scatigna and Tovar, 2007: 73-74).

In Asian emerging-markets, much of the initial impetus behind securitization was provided by the 1997-1998 financial crisis. Necessary changes in the legal and regulatory framework were spurred by governments' perceptions that securitization could play a useful role in the disposal of the large amounts of non-performing loans generated by the crisis. In both Brazil and Mexico, the growth in asset-backed securities also followed changes in the legal framework. In Mexico, the changes were part of policy initiatives aimed at alleviating a housing shortage, in this case through improving mechanisms for mortgage financing damaged by the financial crisis of the mid-1990s (Zanforlin and Espinosa, 2008).

The simplest of these formulas is pass through. In this case, investors have a pro-rata share in the pooled assets and a corresponding pro-rata share in the cash flows which they generate. Under the pay-through or tranched arrangements which have been a prominent feature of the credit crisis, the CDOs are sold to investors after reconfiguration of the cash flows from the original assets into a number of tranches in the form of structured notes. While each tranche is entitled to payments from the pool, this entitlement is subject to different degrees of seniority. Likewise, losses on the original assets are allocated according to rules under which the first losses up to a specified percentage are borne by the most junior (equity) tranche and subsequent proportions successively by the mezzanine and senior tranches. The rates of return for investors in the tranches reflect the different risk levels and thus are substantially higher for lower-grade tranches.

The principles entailed in tranching for a cash-flow CDO can be illustrated with a simple numerical example in which four tranches or structured notes are created from a pool of loans and bonds.[3] The first (equity) tranche is based on 5 percent of the total pool and absorbs losses from the pool, until they have reached 5 percent. The second tranche is based on the next 10 percent of the pool and absorbs losses in excess of 5 percent up to a maximum of 15 percent. The third tranche absorbs losses in excess of 15 percent of the pool up to a maximum of 25 percent. The fourth (or senior) tranche absorbs residual losses in excess of 25 percent of the pool.

Under the resulting distribution of risks, a one-per-cent loss for the pool as a whole becomes a 20-per-cent loss for investors in the equity tranche. The return on their investment, which may be as much as or more than twice that on the second tranche and a much higher multiple of the return on the senior fourth tranche, will henceforth be paid only on 80 percent of their initial investment. A 5-per-cent loss on the pool wipes out the first tranche, and with it, the return to investors, and a 10-per-cent loss also wipes out 50 percent of the value of investments in the second tranche. And so on.

Various alternatives to classic, cash-flow CDOs are also available. For example, in synthetic CDOs, the risks associated with a pool of assets, rather than the assets themselves, are transferred to the SPE. The payments to investors depend on the structuring of the synthetic CDO. In a funded CDO, investors pay in the principal corresponding to their tranches, and this principal is invested in government or other highly rated securities. Defaults lead to a write-down of this principal. The returns to investors are generated by the interest payments on government and highly rated securities and by the premiums on the credit derivatives (credit default swaps) also held in the portfolio backing the CDO. In an unfunded synthetic CDO, no payments of principal are made by investors, and their returns are generated exclusively by the credit derivatives backing the portfolio. Synthetic CDOs also come in the form of hybrid instruments, of which some tranches are funded, but the lowest-risk (super senior) tranche is unfunded. Large banks themselves often held such super senior tranches in their investment portfolios.

The Approach of Basel 2 to Securitization

The lack of rules for banks' securitization exposures in the 1988 Basel Capital Accord (Basel 1) was one of the shortcomings which led to the decision to start the process leading to Basel 2. The concern of regulators antedated the widespread sale to investors of the more baroque investment instruments just described and focused on securitization's role as a vehicle for regulatory arbitrage under Basel 1.

More profitable, but riskier loans and other exposures were not necessarily associated with higher regulatory capital charges according to the risk calibration of Basel 1. This created incentives for regulatory arbitrage under which banks reduced their holdings of less profitable assets whose risks were overestimated under the capital charges of Basel 1 and increased their holdings of more profitable assets whose risks were underestimated, thus increasing profits without a corresponding allocation of capital to cover the greater exposure to credit risk (losses from which would probably take time to appear). Securitization was one of the techniques used by banks and other originating institutions to manage their exposure to credit risks and regulatory capital charges by choosing which loans to keep on their own balance sheets. They also pocketed fees associated with origination and management.

Faced with various national regulatory approaches to securitization, the Basel Committee opted in Basel 2 for rules based on economic substance, rather than legal form, thereby avoiding problems linked to differences in national legal regimes for derivatives. A major objective of the rules was to ensure that securitization exposures were no longer the result of artificial incentives to regulatory arbitrage. But the result in the 2006 version of Basel 2 was a particularly complex set of rules for minimum regulatory capital charges.

In these rules, the reality of risk transfer served as the basis for the stringent conditions which had to be met if an operation was to be accepted as a securitization. If these conditions were not met, Basel 2's minimum regulatory capital requirements were set as if the securitization operation had not occurred and the assets were still held on the balance sheet.

The 2006 version of Basel 2 specified a number of alternative ways of measuring the credit risk of securitization exposures. Under the Standardized Approach to securitization exposures, the rules follow lines similar to those for the attribution of risk weights under the Standardized Approach to the credit risk of non-securitized positions, but prescribing higher capital charges for securitization exposures with low credit ratings than for non-securitized exposures with equivalent ratings. Thus, for long-term securitization exposures to corporates rated BB+ to BB– (according to the scale of Standard & Poor's) the risk weights are 350 percent as opposed to 100 percent for non-securitized exposures to similarly rated corporates.[4]

Under the Internal Ratings-Based Approach to securitization exposures, there were three options. The Ratings-Based Approach (like the simpler Standardized Approach) maps external ratings of exposures into weights for credit risk, but on the basis of a finer calibration of risk than for non-securitized exposures as well as of rules which also take account of the seniority of the tranche of asset-backed securities and of concentrations of risks in the pool of underlying assets (the "non-granularity" of the pool, to use Basel 2's term). The Internal Assessment Approach applies mainly to exposures due to the sponsorship of securitizations where investments are liquid asset-backed commercial paper (ABCP) and where a bank's own internal ratings of the exposures can be mapped into the external ones of a credit rating agency.

The Ratings-Based Approach can be illustrated for an exposure with an AAA (according to the scale of Standard & Poor's). For a senior securitized exposure the risk weight is 7 percent, and for a non-senior securitized exposure, the risk weight is 12 percent if it meets the granularity criterion (i.e. is sufficiently diversified) and 20 percent if it does not meet the granularity criterion. (Concerning the relation between seniority and risk, see the example of a tranched CDO discussed later.)

When neither the Ratings-Based Approach nor the Internal Assessment Approach is possible, recourse is to be had to a third option, the Supervisory Formula. Owing to its complexity, this last option was expected to be used only by sophisticated banks.

In the context of subsequent developments, two points about these rules deserve emphasis. Firstly, most of the rules depend, directly or indirectly, on credit ratings and thus on the integrity of the ratings process.

Secondly, the rules assume that the different forms of securitization are an inevitable part of modern banking practice.

However, at the national level, regulatory approaches more restrictive of securitization have in fact been tried. Spain, for example, has adopted rules which mandate the same regulatory capital requirements for securitized and on-balance-sheet exposures, thus removing a major incentive for banks to participate in the "originate and distribute process" for securitized assets whose dysfunctioning was at the origin of the sub-prime crisis (Tett, 2008). The Spanish approach is consistent with the supervisory guidelines for securitization exposures under Pillar 2 of Basel 2 (the minimum regulatory capital charges being part of Pillar 1). Pillar 2 of Basel 2 provides considerable scope for supervisory discretion, and in a section entitled "significance of risk transfer", the text states that "If the risk transfer is considered to be insufficient or non existent, the supervisory authority... may deny a bank from obtaining any capital relief from the securitizations" (BCBS, 2006: paragraph 786).

Securitization and the Credit Crisis

Although the 2006 version of Basel 2 covers the different dimensions of banks' exposures to securitization, developments during the credit crisis have led regulators to decide that further strengthening of the rules was nonetheless necessary. The proposed revisions of Basel 2 concerning securitization are complemented by the Basel Committee's rules for the management and supervision of liquidity risk which are not part of Basel 2, but are closely connected to several of its rules (BCBS, 2008c).

Features of the credit crisis especially noteworthy in this context have involved the financing of the SPEs used for securitization and the pricing, rating and valuation of structured investment products.[5]

Problems associated with financing have arisen in connection with two vehicles commonly used in securitizations. The structured investment vehicle (SIV) is an entity whose assets consist of highly rated medium and long-term assets such as mortgages and CDO tranches financed with highly-rated short-term commercial paper. The bank or other financial institution sponsoring a SIV makes money through management fees and the spread between the funding cost and the return on the assets. In addition to the usual credit, market and interest-rate risks, the SIV is exposed to liquidity risk owing to the maturity mismatch between its short-term liabilities and its longer-term assets. In the typical SIV, the sponsor does not provide credit enhancement through back-up liquidity.

ABCP (asset-backed commercial paper) conduits have balance sheets similar to SIVs, but are usually backed by liquidity commitments, often from the sponsoring institution, i.e. pledges by a financial institution to provide funding when alternative sources are not available.

The credit crisis affected SIVs and conduits in various ways. Losses due to the sub-prime crisis reduced the return on their assets. The contraction of liquidity adversely affected their refinancing. In these circumstances, the sponsoring banks and other financial institutions found themselves constrained to provide back-up financing or to consolidate the SIVs and conduits on their own balance sheets. This applied to the sponsors of SIVs as well as of conduits, despite the lack of legal liability in their case, owing to the reputational risk entailed by the insolvency of entities with which their names were associated. Purchase or consolidation could lead to losses for sponsors as a result of the shortfall of the fair (accounting) value of the assets of the SIVs and conduits in comparison with their original par value.

The pricing and marketability of securitized investment products has to depend on disclosure regimes and credit ratings which have proved to be subject to serious shortcomings. For example, in the United States, detailed disaggregated information on the loans in the portfolio backing securitized investment products is not publicly available, and there is no obligation regarding public disclosure for synthetic CDOs. In consequence, for initial valuation and pricing of CDOs, investors must rely on the ratings of credit rating agencies. But such reliance is believed to have reduced the incentives, not only to investors, but also to institutions participating in the originate-and-distribute procedures for structured products to properly monitor the quality of the debt in portfolios backing CDOs.

Both the performance and the independence of the credit rating agencies have attracted adverse comment during the credit crisis. Under the first heading, critics have focused on deficiencies in the agencies' procedures for taking account of events causing the clustering of defaults and of the impact of credit migrations leading to the downgrading of the rating of structured investment products. Under the second heading, critics have emphasized the potential for conflicts of interest due to the combined role of the agencies as advisers as well as raters of these products.[6]

Traditional credit ratings are based solely on the intrinsic qualities of issues and issuers. However, the dependence of the ratings of structured notes not only on the quality of the debt instruments in the underlying pool, but also on default correlations and on the seniority of the tranches in CDOs, has typically left them more vulnerable to rapid ratings changes.

During the credit crisis, such changes have contributed to the—often extreme—price volatility of super senior and other highly rated tranches.

This price volatility, in turn, has been associated with large accounting losses for banks and other financial institutions carrying structured products on their balance sheets. Under United States and international accounting rules, investments in the trading book (financial instruments and commodities held, either with trading intent or to hedge other positions in the trading book) are re-valued according to their fair value (the amount for which the assets could be exchanged between knowledgeable, willing parties in an arm's length transaction). Resulting losses (or gains) are reflected in reported income. Fair value is estimated on the basis of either market prices for these or similar investments or of models of the cash flows which the investments are expected to generate. In illiquid markets, it is questionable whether either of these procedures is capable of serving as a basis for reasonable estimates of investments' fair value.

In Asia, the direct impact on developing countries of the collapse in the values of asset-backed securities which began in the United States in 2007 has been limited by the size of the exposure of their banks to such securities in relation their equity. This can be illustrated by selected data from mid-2007 (Fitch Ratings, 2007; Tucker, 2007).

- The largest Chinese banks had exposure to sub-prime-related assets, mostly small in relation to their equity. The largest such exposure was that of the Bank of China at 17.7 percent of shareholder equity.
- Banks in Hong Kong (China) had some limited exposure to sub-prime-related assets through their investments in SIVs. Bank of East Asia had holdings of CDOs amounting to 20 percent of its equity which, however, were not backed by sub-prime mortgages.
- In India, available information suggests that sub-prime-related investments were unlikely to be material in relation to their capital.
- Indonesian banks had no significant exposures to sub-prime-related assets.
- The exposure of banks of the Republic of Korea to sub-prime-related assets was likely to have been well below one percent of their equity.
- A selection of large Malaysian banks reported no direct and only small indirect exposure to sub-prime-related assets.
- Banks in Philippines held, in aggregate, CDOs amounting to about 1.5 percent of their equity, but these CDOs were not backed by mortgages.
- Three large banks in Singapore reported holdings of CDOs (backed only partly by sub-prime-related assets) varying from 0.5 to 2 percent

of their equity. Exposures to CDOs elsewhere in the banking sector were too small to be capable of seriously reducing institutions' capital.

- The banks of Taiwan (Province of China) had aggregate exposures to sub-prime-related assets which were likely to be well below 2 percent of their equity.
- In Thailand, Bank Thai had sub-prime-related exposures amounting to 21 percent of equity, but other major banks had exposures to CDOs amounting to 6 percent of their equity at most.

Elsewhere in developing countries, banks' holdings of foreign currency denominated assets are mostly small, so that there was little scope for exposure to asset-backed securities in North America or Western Europe.

Proposed Revisions of Basel 2

The Basel Committee's proposals for strengthened rules on securitization under Pillar 1 (Minimum Capital Requirements) of Basel 2 cover both the requirements which must be met if exposures are to be removed from a bank's balance sheets and the capital charges for the exposures which remain.

In the 2006 version of Basel 2, the requirements which had to be met if the removal of assets from a bank's balance sheet was to be recognized by its supervisors concerned such subjects as the absence of residual control by the transferor over, or residual obligations connected with, the transferred exposures, and the autonomy of the transferee SPE with respect to exchanging or pledging the assets involved. Under the strengthened rules, banks would also have to meet requirements designed to ensure that they conduct their own due diligence concerning the assets being securitized and not simply rely on the ratings of credit rating agencies. These requirements are intended to reduce failures regarding risk management and due diligence in connection with the originate-to-distribute model during the credit crisis, to which the consultative document (BCBS, 2009c) draws repeated attention.

For the purpose of estimating capital charges, the calibration of securitization exposures has been refined to take better account of risks connected to such exposures. To the categories used as part of the attribution of risk weights in the 2006 version of Basel 2 (senior, non-senior, and granular securitization exposures) has been added re-securitization exposures. These are defined as securitization exposures for which one or more of the assets backing structured investment products are themselves securitization exposures.

This definition would classify as re-securitization exposure CDOs whose asset backing included other CDOs. Re-securitization exposures would mostly be subject to higher capital charges than other securitization exposures to which equivalent ratings have been attributed under Basel 2 rules. Re-securitizations themselves are classified as senior or non-senior according to conditions which exclude those which are themselves re-securitizations from the senior category. The document of the Basel Committee itself provides an extreme instance of the sort of practices which are the target of the new rules. "This would preclude the situation whereby a bank took a mezzanine [non-senior] re-securitization exposure, created two tranches (e.g. a junior tranche of 0.1 percent and a senior tranche of 99.9 percent), and claimed that the senior tranche should qualify for the senior column of re-securitization weights" (BCBS, 2009c: 3).

Other new rules concern the capital charges for a bank's exposures in the form of back-up liquidity support for securitizations (liquidity facilities). Under the simpler Standardized Approach to credit risk of Pillar 1 of Basel 2, the capital charge for such off-balance-sheet exposures meeting certain conditions is estimated by multiplying them by a credit conversion factor (CCF) of less than 100 percent to convert them to their on-balance-sheet equivalents. Under the new rules for securitized exposures the CCFs are standardized at a single level of 50 percent; the 20-per-cent CCF for short-term exposures, previously part of the rules, is suppressed. The rules for CCFs in other approaches to securitization exposures are also tightened and various options permitting low CCFs suppressed. Now, this applies in particular to market disruption lines which are liquidity facilities available to support securitizations only in the event of general market disruptions. The suppression of the low CCF here is clearly a response on the part of the Basel Committee to heightened awareness of the risks associated with market disruption lines revealed by the credit crisis.

Consequences of the proposed revision can be illustrated as follows. In the Standardized Approach for re-securitization exposures rated BB+ to BB– (according to the Standard & Poor's scale), the risk weight is increased from 350 percent to 650 percent. In the Ratings-Based Approach for long-term exposures rated AAA (according to the Standard & Poor's scale), there are now two new risk weights for re-securitization exposures, 20 percent for senior tranches and 30 percent for non-senior tranches, in addition to the risk weights for less complex securitization exposures (7 percent for senior granular, 12 percent for non-senior granular, and 20 percent for non-granular exposures).

The additional recommendations of the consultative document (BCBS, 2009c) under Pillar 2 of Basel 2 (Supervisory Review) cover the responsibilities of both supervisors and management, not only for better oversight and control of securitization, but also more generally. Implicit in one of the recommendations concerning board and senior management oversight is a criticism of the lack of professionalism displayed during recent events by several boards of directors. As the Basel Committee puts it, "The board of directors should possess sufficient knowledge of all major business lines to ensure that appropriate policies, controls and risk monitoring systems are effective. They should have the necessary expertise to understand the capital markets activities in which the bank is involved—such as securitization and off-balance sheet activities—and the associated risks" (BCBS, 2009c: para. 17). Hopefully, this recommendation will serve as a clarion call regarding the qualifications of board members, which can be incorporated in the process for selecting them, either by law or as part of a code of corporate governance.

The Pillar 2 recommendations also run through shortcomings on the front of risk management of securitization exposures during the credit crisis. Of special interest here is the digest here of points raised in the Basel Committee's September 2008 document, *Principles for Sound Liquidity Risk Management and Supervision* (BCBS, 2008c). The Basel Committee has often been criticized for not sufficiently integrating its rules for regulatory capital for credit risk, on the one hand, and those for liquidity management and supervision, on the other. (The rules for market risk naturally incorporate liquidity risk since liquidity determines the marketability and prices of the items in banks' trading books at which these rules are directed.) While the tightening of the rules on CCFs for liquidity facilities described above represent a step forward on this front, the Basel Committee's critics are none the less unlikely to be satisfied until liquidity risk becomes part of an overall regulatory framework which integrates macro- and micro-prudential considerations and recognizes more fully the link of liquidity risk to other major banking risks, including those covered by Basel 2.

The recommendations under Pillar 3 of Basel 2 (Disclosure Requirements) cover additional requirements regarding the disclosure of securitization exposures. Particularly noteworthy here are the inclusion of new mandatory disclosures concerning "all securitization activities which the bank sponsors, regardless of whether they are in the banking or trading book, on- or off-balance sheet, and whether or not they are subject to the securitization framework". In the 2006 version of Basel 2, disclosure of sponsorship activities was encouraged, but still voluntary.

Market Risk Framework

Approaches to Estimating Market Risk

The Market Risk Framework of Basel 2 was the subject of two consultation documents of July 2008, *Guidelines for Computing Capital for Incremental Risk in the Trading Book* and *Proposed Revisions to the Basel II Market Risk Framework* (BCBS, 2008a and 2008b). These consultation documents have been revised in two new consultation documents covering the same subjects published in January 2009 (BCBS, 2009a; 2009b).

The Market Risk Framework is now part of the regulatory rules for banks' capital in developed countries and in several developing countries and transition economies of Eastern Europe—more than 15, for example, in the sample of developing countries covered in the 2007 Global Survey of the New York based Institute of International Bankers (2007: 8). Banks in the great majority of these countries are also permitted by their regulators to use internal models (see below) to measure market risks for their minimum regulatory capital requirements.

The Market Risk Amendment was added in 1996 to Basel 1. The Amendment is directed at risks associated with banks' trading books, i.e. positions in financial instruments and commodities held either with trading intent or to hedge other positions in the trading book (as opposed to the institutions' banking books which contain assets such as loans and selected off-balance-sheet or contingent positions that were the main target of the 1988 Accord). Positions in the trading book are regularly re-valued and actively managed. The most important risks of these positions are due to movements in their market prices or values.

The Market Risk Amendment was the Basel Committee's response to the increase in the involvement of banks generally in trading (particularly of derivatives) and brokerage as compared to the more traditional business of receiving deposits and other repayable funds from the public and granting credits for their own account. The rules eventually adopted followed a long consultation period, in which banks themselves played an active role, and were designed to incorporate banks' own experience and practices.

The rules of the 1996 Amendment allow two approaches to calculating the minimum regulatory capital requirement for market risk. The standardized approach uses a series of conversion factors for different instruments and positions. This approach is cumbersome and likely to generate a higher minimum regulatory capital requirement than the alternatives. Under the internal models approach, banks use their own internal risk models to estimate the requirement.

In addition to general market risk, i.e. that due to overall changes in financial markets in such indicators as equity prices or interest rates, trading books are exposed to specific market risk, i.e. that due to changes in the value of particular instruments such as stocks or bonds. In the 1996 Amendment, capital requirements for specific market risk under the Standardized Approach vary for different instruments and positions. Under the internal models approach, calculation of specific market risk by means of a bank's own models may be permitted by regulators. If not, capital charges for specific market risk are calculated according to rules given in the Standardized Approach and are added to that for general market risk.

Under the internal-models approach, exposure to general market risk is calculated on the basis of a measure of Value at Risk (VaR). This makes possible a statement of the following form: the bank is X percent (for example, 99 percent in the Market Risk Framework) certain that it will not lose more than a specified amount due to general market risk during the holding period, i.e. the period required to liquidate the trading positions, thus stopping further losses. More colloquially, VaR is an answer to the question of how bad things can get (Hull, 2006: 436).

For the purpose of such a calculation, the bank requires a statistical frequency distribution or models for the profits and losses due to factors to which its trading book is exposed. These tools are then used to identify the maximum loss to the bank corresponding to the chosen level of probability for its VaR.

Three alternative techniques are used for this purpose: historical simulation, Monte Carlo simulation, and the model-building approach.

Under historical simulation, a frequency distribution is derived empirically from the effects on the bank's trading book of actual movements in market variables. In Monte Carlo simulation, the frequency distribution of profits and losses in the trading book is generated by sampling values for profits and losses on positions in different instruments which have themselves been generated by statistical modeling. Both of these processes are highly time-consuming and costly in terms of computer power.

Under the internal model-building approach, the inputs to the estimates of VaR for trading positions in particular instruments are the sensitivity of the value of the positions to changes in market prices or values and hypothetical maximum changes in these prices or values corresponding to the level of probability selected for the VaR. The VaR of trading positions in particular instruments are then combined into an estimate of the VaR of the trading book as a whole, after taking account of reductions in aggregate VaR due to diversification across particular positions.

Modeling and assumptions about the statistical properties of the distributions of prices or values enter at three stages in the model-building approach: (1) the estimation of the sensitivities of the values of positions to the determinants of changes in market prices or values; (2) the frequency distribution generating the hypothetical maximum changes in prices or values; and (3) the correlations between different positions used to estimate the benefits from diversification.

Estimates of VaR are not infallible guides to market risk so that, for the purpose of calculating capital levels in the 1996 Amendment, a bank's VaR is multiplied by a factor of at least three, which is set by the bank's supervisor on the basis of assessment of its model. A key test of the performance of the bank's model is provided by the results of back-testing, a procedure which compares actual profits and losses with those generated by the model. For VaR corresponding to a 99 percent confidence level, there should be only one period out of 100 for which the loss exceeds that calculated by the VaR model. Under the 1996 Amendment, a failure to meet this standard leads to an increase by the bank's supervisor in the multiplicative factor used to set its capital requirement. A bank is also to have in place a stress-testing program providing for computer-based scenario analysis of disturbances capable of having a major impact on the market risks faced by a bank. Such scenarios could include the crash in stock markets of October 1987 and the exchange-rate crisis in the European Union in 1992-1993.

Several reservations have been expressed about the model-building approach and VaR of the Market Risk Framework. Some of these reservations are primarily technical and concern the models and the hypothetical changes in prices and values used to calculate VaR. Others concern their relation to market stability. Thus, for example, the experience of the impact on financial markets of the Russian default and the collapse of the hedge fund, LTCM, in 1998 heightened misgivings about the potential of risk management based on VaR to exacerbate markets' pro-cyclicality.

As a senior risk manager at Goldman Sachs characterized the experience of 1998 at the time, "Consider a situation when volatilities rise and there are some trading losses. VaRs would be higher and tolerances for risk would likely be lower. For an individual firm, it would appear reasonable to reduce trading positions; however, if everybody were to act similarly it would put pressure on their common trading positions" (Dunbar, 2000: 203). The increased orders to sell into the market would coincide with a drying-up of buying orders and liquidity.

Revisions in Response to Shortcomings of the 1996 Framework

Recent revisions by the Basel Committee have been directed at some, but not all of the Market Risk Framework's perceived shortcomings.

Revisions in 2005 were directed at preventing the gaming of minimum regulatory capital through the shifting of exposures between banking and trading books to reduce capital requirements, at the valuation of trading positions and the need during times of stress to establish special reserves for illiquid positions in the trading book, and at fleshing out the capital requirements for specific risk. In the preamble to the text of these revisions, the Basel Committee acknowledged problems due to the observed assignment by banks to the trading book of an increasing number of instruments related to the management and trading of credit risk and of other structured and exotic products. These practices were the result of financial innovations whose importance had increased during the long process of drafting Basel 2. As the Basel Committee put it, "These products are generally less liquid and give rise to risks that were not entirely contemplated in the market risk framework when it was introduced" (BCBS, 2005: paras 258-263).

The Market Risk Framework in the revised 2006 version of Basel 2 included, in the internal models approach, a requirement for additional capital in the form of an incremental default charge designed to capture the impact of default risk on trading positions not already covered by the charge for specific market risk (BCBS, 2006: paras 718 (xcii) and 718 (xciii)).

The revisions proposed in the 2008 documents of the Basel Committee are the result of agreement reached in March 2008 that, reflecting the experience of the credit crisis, the scope of the incremental default charge in the internal models needed to be expanded to become an Incremental Risk Charge to capture the impact on trading positions, not only of default, but also of other sources of price risk.

As the Basel Committee put it, "The decision [to propose an Incremental Risk Charge] was taken in the light of the recent credit market turmoil where a number of major banking organizations have experienced large losses, most of which were sustained in banks' trading books. Most of those losses were not captured in the 99 percent/10-day VaR. Since the losses have not arisen from actual defaults but rather from credit migrations [transfers of positions in the trading book between different risk classes in banks' systems for rating credit risk], combined with widening of credit spreads [due to increased credit risks] and the loss of liquidity, applying an incremental risk charge covering default risk only would not appear adequate. For example, the incremental default risk charge would not have captured recent losses of CDOs of ABS and other re-securitizations held in the trading book... the current VaR framework ignores differences in the underlying liquidity of trading book positions. In addition, these VaR calculations are typically based on a 99 percent/one-day VaR which is scaled up to 10 days. Consequently, the VaR capital charge may not fully reflect large daily losses that occur less frequently than two to three times per year as well as the potential for large price movements over periods of several weeks or months" (BCBS, 2008b: paras 1-2).

The Incremental Risk Charge is intended to address these short-comings. But the Basel Committee acknowledged that there is not yet an industry standard for addressing and thus measuring the risks covered by the Incremental Risk Charge. Thus its guidelines for setting the Charge take the form of high-level principles with considerable flexibility for banks as to how they implement them.

The documents of January 2009 on the Market Risk Framework (BCBS, 2009a; 2009b) contain the results of a consultation process which is still incomplete. The document, which provides an overall review of pro-posed revisions of the Market Risk Framework (BCBS, 2009a), is primarily devoted to extension of the Market Risk Framework to incorporate the new rules for securitization exposures into estimates for specific risk, as well as to a consolidation of Basel 2's rules for the prudential valuation.

The proposed rules for the capital charges for the specific risk of securitization exposures are prescriptive, following, as they do the standardized, rather than the internal models approach to market risk. (See the discussion of alternative approaches to estimating capital charges for market risk earlier in this section.) Refusal to permit the internal models approach here is due to the absence, in the Basel Committee, of a consensus as to a methodology for such an approach to estimating the specific risks of securitized products in the trading book. As in the case of the new rules for securitization exposures, for the purpose of setting regulatory capital charges, the new rules being proposed distinguish between securitization exposures and re-securitization exposures (i.e. those for which one or more of the assets backing structured investment products are themselves securitization exposures), attributing higher capital charges to the latter.

Under prudent valuation, the rules of Basel 2 concerning the subject would be extended to all positions subject to fair-value accounting. Thus, the rules of Basel 2 would apply to fair-value positions in the banking book as well as those held for trading. The rules for prudent valuation of Basel 2 generally follow the analogous international accounting rules: mark-to-market valuation, when feasible, i.e. valuation at market prices in orderly market conditions; and when market prices are not available, marking-to-model, for example, on the basis of market inputs and discounted expected cash flows. However, prudent valuation according to the rules of Basel 2 is also to include—in addition to international accounting rules—adjustments of valuation to allow for illiquidity "which may be in addition to any changes to the value of the position for financial reporting purposes" (para 718 (xcxx) of the version of Basel 2 which will incorporate post-2006 revisions).

The July 2008 consultative document on guidelines for computing the Incremental Risk Charge (BCBS, 2008b) was somewhat tentative and discursive. The sequel of January 2009 (BCBS, 2009b) clarifies and simplifies the guidelines of the earlier document. "Specifically, for all IRC-covered positions, a bank's IRC model must measure losses due to default and migration at the 99.9 percent confidence interval over a capital horizon of one year, taking into account the liquidity horizons [the times required to sell the position or to hedge all material risks covered by the IRC model in a stressed market] applicable to individual positions or sets of positions" (BCBS, 2009b: para 13). The model for the Incremental Risk Charge is not to incorporate securitization positions since in the Basel Committee's judgment, "for the purpose of quantifying default and migration event risks, the state of risk modelling in this area is not sufficiently reliable as to warrant recognizing hedging or diversification benefits attributable to securitization positions" (BCBS, 2009b: para 10).

Preliminary Assessment and Implications for Developing Countries

The proposed new rules for securitization exposures and for the Incremental Risk Charge would refine the calibration of the risks covered by the Market Risk Framework and would lead to higher minimum regulatory capital requirements, and thus reduced leverage for banks. The new charges would thus meet the commitment in the 2008 reform agenda of the Financial Stability Reform (FSF, 2008) to strengthen the treatment in Basel 2 of structured credit and securitization activities and to issue specific proposals for raising capital requirements for certain complex structured credit products such as CDOs of asset-backed securities.

The proposed new rules for securitization exposures, including those which contribute to specific risk in the Market Risk Framework, incorporate credit ratings as an integral part of the estimation of capital charges. Changes in the rating process and in the oversight and regulation of the credit rating agencies introduced as part of the overall agenda of financial reform will thus affect how these rules work out in practice. Progress in the agenda of financial reform in related areas will also affect Basel 2's new rules on prudent valuation since these rules link the valuation of exposures under Basel 2 to international accounting standards.

In the absence of an industry consensus on the measurement of the risks covered by the Incremental Risk Charge of the Market Risk Framework, implementation of the Charge can be expected to lead to still greater variation in the minimum capital requirements accepted by regulators under Basel 2. The Charge is thus likely to further undermine one of the underlying objectives of Basel 2, namely "maintaining sufficient consistency that capital adequacy regulation will not be a source of competitive inequality among internationally active banks". However, this objective has already been compromised by the multiplicity of options and approaches elsewhere in Basel 2, and would appear to be part of the price to be paid for the achievement of agreement on global capital standards.

From the point of view of risk management generally, special interest attaches to the questioning of the effectiveness of VaR implicit in the Basel Committee's acknowledgement that the Incremental Risk Charge is intended to address VaR's shortcomings. Since the early 1990s, VaR has been one of the principal jewels in the crown of quantitative financial risk management. Its downgrading in the Basel Committee's new guidelines may point towards further reassessment of ways of managing and supervising market risk.

For developing countries which introduce the Market Risk Framework the Incremental Risk Charge will represent a challenge to their supervisors additional to the others posed by the implementation of Basel 2, even though the Basel Committee does also propose a simpler fall back option in its guidelines.

The introduction of Basel 2 is already proceeding, or about to proceed, in a large number of emerging market and other developing countries.[7] However, as is evident from the data in Box 9.1, issuance of asset-backed securities is still small in emerging market countries. Similarly, only a relatively small minority of such countries has introduced the rules of the Market Risk Framework, including those covering the internal model-building approach, the subject of the proposed revisions discussed in the last section. As a result, the main effects on these countries of the revised rules of Basel 2 concerning securitization exposures and the Market Risk Framework are likely to be indirect—in the form of the rules' contribution to greater stability in international financial markets.

Nevertheless, in both cases the rules proposed by the Basel Committee draw attention to problems which may arise in future. For example, in the case of securitization, financial institutions in Asia already depend on credit rating agencies for rating the risks involved (Gyntelberg and Remolona, 2006: 74). Similar dependence can also be observed in Mexico (Zanforlin and Espinosa, 2008: 17-18). The agencies may be domestic ones, rather than the international majors. But in either case, the Basel 2 rules are relevant.

Moreover, in the absence of appropriate controls, banks may be exposed to risks associated with cross-border asset-backed investments as well as investments linked to operations in their own financial markets. As noted in the second section, the supervisory guidelines of Pillar 2 of Basel 2 provide governments with scope for introducing rules more stringent than those of Pillar 1 for controlling exposures to certain risks, if they judge such rules to be necessary. Thus, Pillar 2 can justify restricting domestic financial institutions' cross-border investments in the opaque and complex financial products which may still be available in the financial markets of industrial countries even after the introduction of regulatory reforms currently under way.

Annex: The Basel Capital Accords

Basel 2 is designed to replace the 1988 Basel Capital Accord (Basel 1). Both agreements were drawn up by the Basel Committee on Banking Supervision, a body of banking regulators of the countries of the G10 and selected other developed and emerging market countries, originally established in 1974 and linked geographically and organizationally to the Bank for International Settlements in Basel (an organization which dates from 1930, primarily to serve the functions of bank and meeting-place for national central banks).

Basel 1 and Basel 2 are agreements on frameworks for assessing the capital adequacy of banks. The framework sets rules for the allocation of capital to banks' exposures to risks through its lending and other operations. The agreements have two objectives. One is prudential, namely to help to ensure the strength and soundness of banking systems. The other is to help to equalize cross-border competition between banks (provide "a level playing field") by eliminating competitive advantages due to differences among countries in their regimes for capital adequacy (a special concern of United States and European banks *vis-à-vis* competitors from Japan in the 1980s).

As a measure of the difference between the value of a bank's assets and liabilities, capital serves as a buffer against future, unidentified losses. The capital of banks consists of equity and other financial instruments which have the properties of being available to support an institution in times of crisis. Financial instruments classified as capital are usually associated with higher rates of return and are thus a more costly way of financing banks' assets than other liabilities such as deposits. The rate of return on capital is a determinant of banks' pricing of loans and other transactions involving exposure to risk, and as such, is a factor in their competitiveness *vis-à-vis* other banks.

Capital under the initial version of Basel 1 agreed to in 1988 was to serve as a buffer against credit risk, i.e. that of the failure of borrowers or parties to the other banking transactions to meet their obligations. Under the accord, capital was to constitute 8 percent of banks' risk-weighted assets.

Measurement of these risk-weighted assets was based on the attribution of weights reflecting the credit risk of different classes of counterparty (sovereign, OECD or non-OECD, other public sector, corporate, etc.). Off-balance sheet exposures (such as guarantees, various contingent liabilities, and interest-rate and exchange-rate derivatives) were converted to their on-balance-sheet equivalents by multiplying them by factors specified for this purpose. The resulting figures were then weighted according to the class of counterparty as for on-balance-sheet exposures. For example, collateralized documentary credits received a credit conversion factor of 20 percent, and the resulting on-balance-sheet equivalent would be multiplied by the risk weight of the counterparty to which the documentary credit was made available.

The attribution of credit risk weights (0, 10, 20, 50 and 100 percent) followed a scheme which favored governments and certain other entities from OECD countries over those from non-OECD countries, and banks over other commercial borrowers. Thus, a weight of 0 percent was attributed to claims on OECD governments and central banks, and one of 20 percent to claims on banks incorporated in OECD countries and to banks incorporated in non-OECD countries with a residual maturity of up to one year. A weight of 100 percent was attributed to claims on private sector entities not otherwise specified, such as non-financial corporations and non-OECD governments.

Through an amendment in 1996, Basel 1 was extended to cover market risks, i.e. those due to the impact on a bank's portfolio of tradable assets of adverse changes in interest and exchange rates and in the prices of stocks and other financial instruments. The procedures for setting minimum regulatory capital levels under this amendment were described in the third section.

Basel 1 was originally designed for internationally active banks. However, by the second half of the 1990s, it had become a global standard and had been incorporated into the prudential regimes of more than 100 countries. But, owing to its crude calibration of credit risk and to the growing importance of securitization and other financial innovations, Basel 1 was also the subject of increasingly widespread dissatisfaction among both banks and regulators so that a decision was taken to initiate what proved to be the lengthy process of drafting a successor agreement. What was intended to be the definitive version of the new accord, Basel 2, became available in mid-2006. However, as part of the policy response to the credit crisis, this text is now being revised.

Basel 2 consists of three Pillars. Under Pillar 1, minimum regulatory capital requirements for credit risk are calculated according to two alternative approaches—the Standardized and the Internal Ratings-Based. Under the simpler of the two, the Standardized Approach, the measurement of credit risk is based on ratings provided by external credit assessment institutions. According to the text of the agreement, export credit agencies as well as credit rating agencies are indicated for this purpose. However, the expectation of both the Basel Committee and of national authorities is clearly that the role will most frequently be assumed by credit rating agencies.

Under the Standardized Approach of Basel 2 entities from OECD countries are no longer favored over those from non-OECD countries. Both banks and non-financial corporations are now differentiated according to their credit ratings (for which the BCBS uses the scale of Standard & Poor's for illustrative purposes). Thus, non-financial corporate borrowers rated between AAA and AA– are attributed a weight of 20 percent, those rated between A+ and A– one of 50 percent, those rated between BBB+ and BB– one of 100 percent, and those rated below BB– one of 150 percent. Unrated non-financial corporate borrowers are attributed a weight of 100 percent.

Under the Internal Ratings-Based Approach, subject to supervisory approval for the satisfaction of certain conditions, banks use their own rating systems to measure some or all of the determinants of credit risk, i.e. the probability of default, loss given default, exposure at default and the remaining maturity of the exposure. Under the Foundation version of the Internal Ratings-Based Approach, banks calculate the probability of default on the basis of their own ratings, but rely on their supervisors for measures of the other determinants of credit risk. Under the Advanced version of the Internal Ratings-Based Approach, banks also estimate their own measures of all the determinants of credit risk. Pillar 1 also contains rules for regulatory capital requirements for market risk which follow those of the 1996 amendment of Basel 1.

Unlike Basel 1, Basel 2 contains regulatory capital requirements for operational risk which covers losses due to events such as human errors or fraudulent behavior, computer failures, or disruptions from external events such as earthquakes. Under the Basic Indicator Approach, the simplest of the three options in Basel 2, the capital charge for operational risk is a percentage of banks' gross income. Under the Standardized Approach to operational risk, the capital charge is the sum of specified percentages of banks' gross income or loans for eight business lines. Under the Advanced Measurement Approach to operational risk, the most sophisticated option of Basel 2, subject to the satisfaction of more stringent supervisory criteria, banks estimate the required capital with their own internal measurement systems. Also unlike Basel 1, Basel 2 contains detailed rules concerning securitization exposures explained in the second section.

Under Basel 2, the minimum regulatory capital ratio remains at the 8 percent figure of Basel 1. The denominator of this ratio consists of estimated exposures for credit, market and operational risk. The numerator consists of capital, as in Basel 1, but after adjustment in certain ways. Conceptually, the most important of these adjustments is the exclusion of risks corresponding to several categories of expected losses from the denominator of the ratio and of banks' corresponding loss provisions from capital in the numerator. This exclusion brings Basel 2 more into line with traditional banking practice according to which expected losses are covered by loss provisions, while capital is intended to cover unexpected losses.

Pillars 2 and 3 of Basel 2 are concerned with supervisory review of capital adequacy and the achievement of discipline in banks' risk management through disclosure to investors. Under the guidelines of Pillar 2, supervisors are to prescribe additional regulatory capital not only for the credit, market and operational risks of Pillar 1, if they judge this to be necessary for supervisory reasons, but also for risks not covered under these three headings, such as liquidity risk (which covers banks' ability to obtain funding and the prices at which it can sell assets in financial markets) and interest-rate risks due to changes in the margins between the rates at which banks lend and borrow.

Pillar 3 specifies rules for the disclosure of information concerning banks' capital and risk management. These rules are intended to enable financial market participants, such as investors and analysts as well as supervisors, to subject these to scrutiny which will reinforce the effectiveness of Pillars 1 and 2.

Notes

1. The full text of Basel 2, now being revised, is the 2006 version (BCBS, 2006).
2. Major features of the reform agenda can be found in FSF (2008).
3. The example is taken from Hull (2006: 516-517).
4. The capital charge for the exposure is estimated by multiplying the standard or benchmark ratio of 8 percent by the risk weight. Thus, a risk weight of 350 percent corresponds to a capital charge of 28 percent of the value of the exposure, while a risk weight of 100 percent corresponds to a capital charge of 8 percent of the value of the exposure. A risk weight of 1250 percent corresponds to a capital charge of 100 percent of the value of the exposure. Such a weight is equivalent to deducting the value of the exposure from a bank's capital under Basel capital rules.
5. The discussion which follows makes extensive use of the account of the sub-prime crisis in Scott (2008: chapter 12).
6. The importance of structured-products business to credit rating agencies can be illustrated with the example of Fitch. Revenue from the rating of structured products accounted for 51 percent of the agency's revenue in the first quarter of 2007 (Westlake, 2007).
7. Evidence on the global introduction of Basel 2 from surveys of the Basel-based Financial Stability Institute and other national sources is discussed in Cornford (2008).

References

Bank of England (2007). *Financial Stability Report*, 22, October, Bank of England, London.

Basel Committee on Banking Supervision (BCBS) (2005). *The Application of Basel II to Trading Activities and the Treatment of Double Default Effects*. July, Bank of International Settlements, Basel.

BCBS (2006). *International Convergence of Capital Measurement and Capital Standards: A Revised Framework Comprehensive Version*. Bank of International Settlements, Basel.

BCBS (2008a). *Proposed Revisions to the Basel II Market Risk Framework*. July, Bank of International Settlements, Basel.

BCBS (2008b). *Guidelines for Computing Capital for Incremental Risk in the Trading Book*. July, Bank of International Settlements, Basel.

BCBS (2008c). *Principles for Sound Liquidity Risk Management and Supervision.* September, Bank of International Settlements, Basel.

BCBS (2009a). *Revisions to the Basel II Market Risk Framework.* January, Bank of International Settlements, Basel.

BCBS (2009b). *Guidelines for Computing Capital for Incremental Risk in the Trading Book.* January, Bank of International Settlements, Basel.

BCBS (2009c). *Proposed Enhancements to the Basel II Framework.* January, Bank of International Settlements, Basel.

Cornford, Andrew J. (2008). Introduction of Basel 2: The mid-2008 state of play, paper prepared for the Technical Group of the Group of 24, 2008.

Dunbar, Nicholas (2000). *Inventing Money.* John Wiley, Chichester.

FSF (2008). *Report of the Financial Stability Forum on Enhancing Market and Institutional Resilience.* April, Financial Stability Forum.

Fitch Ratings (2007). Banks/Asia Pacific limited direct impact on Asia-Pacific banks from sub- prime exposure. 24 August.

Gyntelberg, Jacob, and Eli M. Remolona (2006). Securitization in Asia and the Pacific: Implications and credit risks. *BIS Quarterly Review*, June.

Hull, John C. (2006). *Options, Futures, and Other Derivatives.* Sixth edition. Pearson Prentice Hall, Upper Saddle River, NJ.

Institute of International Bankers (2007). *Global Survey.* New York.

Scatigna, Michela, and Camilo E. Tovar (2007). Securitization in Latin America. *BIS Quarterly Review*, September.

Scott, Hal S. (2008). *International Finance Transactions, Policy, and Regulation.* Fifteenth edition. Foundation Press, New York.

Tett, Gillian (2008). Spain's banks weather credit crisis. *Financial Times*, 31 January.

Tucker, Sundeep (2007). Asia crosses its fingers on exposure to sub-prime. *Financial Times*, 24 August.

Wellink, Nout (2008). The importance of banking supervision in financial stability. Keynote address of the Chairman of the Basel Committee on Banking Supervision at the High level Meeting, "The Role of Banking and Banking Supervision in Financial Stability", 17 November, Beijing.

Westlake, Michael (2007). Rating agencies brace for rough regulatory ride. *Global Risk Regulator*, September.

Zanforlin, Luisa, and Marco Espinosa (2008). Housing finance and mortgage-backed securities in Mexico. IMF Working Paper WP/08/105, April, International Monetary Fund, Washington, DC.

8

Should Financial Flows Be Regulated? Yes

*Gerald Epstein**

Prior to the First World War—in the late 19th and early 20th centuries—the industrialized economies of Europe and the United States were characterized by a high degree of global financial integration, a relatively large role for markets, and a philosophy based on limited government regulation (*laissez-faire*). Capital could flow freely with very light regulation both within and between countries, and there were relatively low barriers to trade in goods and services. Many countries' monetary systems were based on a gold standard, which fixed countries' exchange rates relative to one another. The Bank of England "orchestrated" the system with help from central banks in France and elsewhere on the European continent. This system helped bring great wealth to bankers and industrial capitalists in the richer countries, and spread investments in infrastructure and other projects to the colonial and semi-colonial countries of the New World, enriching some elites in those countries as well.

However, in the 1930s, this system of free capital mobility collapsed, as did most of the world economy. Figure 8.1, due to Reinhart and Rogoff, shows the rise of capital flows in the late 19th and early 20th century, and then their dramatic collapse in the 1930s. Among the key causes of the collapse were the excesses allowed by the *laissez-faire* approach to financial markets, which led to excessive accumulations of debt and highly speculative investments—a significant number of which failed spectacularly. Equally important was the role of international capital flows in worsening the crisis as it broke out, with capital fleeing those countries perceived to be in trouble and flooding into those seen as safe havens (Block, 1977; Kindleberger, 1986 Eichengreen, 1992). Figure 8.1 also shows that international capital flows tend to precede banking crises.

Figure 8.1 Capital mobility and the incidence of banking crises: All countries, 1800-2008

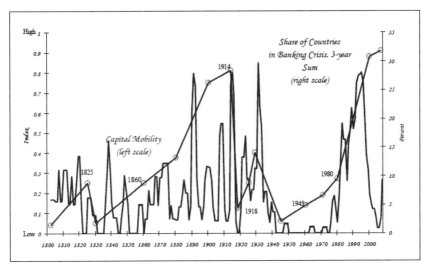

Source: Reinhart and Rogoff (2008, p. 23).

In the aftermath of the collapse and the ensuing, catastrophic Second World War, governments in most of the world—with the reluctant blessing of the newly created International Monetary Fund (IMF)—adopted government controls (exchange and capital controls) to manage the international flows of money and capital. This policy had been strongly advocated by John Maynard Keynes, the most important economist of the 20th century and co-architect of the Bretton Woods agreements that, in 1944, had established the IMF and the World Bank as well as a global system of fixed exchange rates (Crotty, 1983). For at least the first three decades following the Second World War, controls over the international flow of capital became the norm in most of the world.

Over time, as the world economy recovered and much of the developed world flourished in the so-called "golden age" of economic growth in the 1950s and 1960s, memories of the financial crises of the Great Depression faded, and governments began to relax restrictions on the international flow of capital and money (Helleiner, 1984). From 1971 to 1973, the post-war Bretton Woods system of fixed exchange rates broke down and exchange rates became more flexible. A general shift in economic fashion occurred, from an approach (prevalent from the 1940s to the 1960s) based on financial regulation of the market aimed at maintaining stability and achieving social goals to a return to a more *laissez-faire* approach in which the market dominates. This movement back toward *laissez-faire* accelerated with the oil crises and stagflation of the 1970s and the coming to power of Margaret Thatcher in the United Kingdom and Ronald Reagan in the United States—both very strong advocates of smaller government, less regulation, and more promotion of market dominance and the interests of business as the best approach for economic development (Diaz-Alejandro, 1985; Glyn, 1986). Naturally, these policies were strongly supported by banking and business interests, as well as by some workers and members of the middle class who had suffered during the stagflationary period of the 1970s.

The next 20 years witnessed a secular move toward more financial deregulation and the reduction of controls over financial flows in the United States, Canada, and Europe, as well as in many developing countries. Figure 8.2 shows the reductions in capital regulations and the corresponding increases in capital mobility, which rose in most types of countries in the 1980s. Note that Figure 8.2 is based on capital flow (account) *regulations* (*de jure* capital controls), whereas Figure 8.1 is based on *actual* flows of capital (*de facto* capital flows). At the same time, the frequency and severity of banking and financial crises accelerated as well,

Figure 8.2 Capital account liberalization, 1973-1995

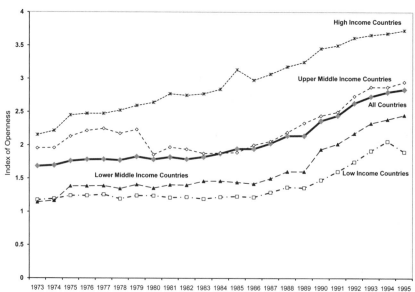

Source: Lee and Jayadev (2005: 26).

with most, but not all of them, primarily afflicting developing countries (Figure 8.1). Still, the majority of economists and the IMF continued to press for financial liberalization and the elimination of capital controls in the developing world.

Then, in 1997, the so-called Asian financial crisis hit, creating havoc in many highly successful Asian countries including Thailand, South Korea, and Malaysia. This crisis was soon followed by the Russian financial crisis. Figure 8.1 reflects these crises and illustrates a general rule. Prior to crises, international financial flows accelerate. Then, when the crisis hits, international capital flows tend to drop precipitously (so-called "sudden stops"), the inflows exacerbating the build-up to the crisis and then the outflows worsening its severity.

With the Russian and Asian crises, continued pressure for financial liberalization by bankers and economists collided head-on with the reality of unstable financial flows, which were clearly contributing to—and even causing—financial crises with alarming frequency. This clash was perhaps most apparent in the debate over a proposed amendment to the IMF bylaws that would have made capital account liberalization a requirement of membership; the proposal was made just as the Asian financial crisis was hitting. Dani Rodrik (1998) has been critical of full capital account liberalization, and has offered the following analogy:

> Imagine landing on a planet that runs on widgets.[1] You are told that international trade in widgets is highly unpredictable and volatile on this planet, for reasons that are poorly understood. A small number of nations have access to imported widgets, while many others are completely shut out even when they impose no apparent obstacles to trade. With some regularity, those countries that have access to widgets get too much of a good thing, and their markets are flooded with imported widgets. This allows them to go on a widget binge, which makes everyone pretty happy for a while. However, such binges are often interrupted by a sudden cut-off in supply, unrelated to any change in circumstances. The turnaround causes the affected economies to experience painful economic adjustments. For reasons equally poorly understood, when one country is hit by a supply cutback in this fashion, many other countries experience similar shocks in quick succession. Some years thereafter, a widget boom starts anew. Your hosts beg you for guidance: how should they deal with their widget problem? Ponder this question for a while and then ponder under what circumstances your central recommendation would be that all extant controls on international trade in widgets be eliminated. Substitute "international capital flows" for "widgets" above and the description fits today's world economy quite well.

Indeed, during the Asian financial crises, countries that had strong controls over international financial flows (for example, China and India) were much less negatively affected by the financial crisis than were countries that had few controls (see the discussion below). This observation led some economists in academia, the IMF, and other policy circles to question the conventional wisdom that free flows of international capital will lead to the best outcomes.

More than a decade after it was written, Rodrik's analogy is still highly relevant—perhaps even more so than in 1998. The financial crisis, which spread in 2008 from the "sub-prime" housing markets of the United States to many other financial markets via international capital (and trade) flows, has placed in focus once again the instability and difficulties that can be created across national borders by the unregulated flow of finance. Once again, then, the question is raised: Should financial flows be regulated? This chapter answers the question with a "yes".

The remainder of this chapter is organized as follows. The next section includes a brief discussion of the arguments for unregulated ("free") capital mobility and a comparison of these with the empirical evidence. The following section discusses the goals of regulating international capital flows and the types of controls that governments can use to manage these flows. The next section presents evidence regarding the costs, benefits, and effectiveness of different types of controls. The final section presents my conclusions.

Arguments for Unrestricted International Capital Flows

Economists' arguments in favor of minimal government restrictions on the international flows of money and capital stem from their basic faith in the efficiency of the market and the inefficiency and/or inefficacy of government regulation. While this faith is quite general, it is usually applied more specifically in specific contexts. In the case of financial markets, the arguments are rooted in the following perceived "functions" of money, finance, and financial markets: 1) to provide a medium of exchange, means of payment, and unit of account; 2) to allocate credit to its most productive uses; 3) to serve as an efficient intermediary between savers and investors; 4) to allow savers to reduce the risks associated with making investments; and 5) to provide an efficient means to save for the future (what economists refer to as "smoothing the consumption stream over time"). In effect, these economists argue that financial markets "free from government regulation" can achieve these aims better than regulated markets can (Neely, 1999).

Economists make a leap when they apply these arguments for the efficiency of the free flows of capital, taken from an analysis of a national economy, and apply them to international flows of finance between countries, despite the fact that there are big differences between purely domestic financial transactions and international ones. Moreover, these arguments are based on a *microeconomic* logic and do not take into account many key *macroeconomic* concerns, such as the impact on unemployment, and financial instability.

In any event, the upshot of these claims is that free capital mobility should be associated with the following, all relative to contexts in which there are more regulations and controls over capital flows: 1) higher levels of output and investment; 2) more rapid productivity growth and economic growth overall; 3) an allocation of financial resources away from those who need them less (rich countries) to those who need them more (poor countries); 4) less risk; and 5) an improved ability to smooth consumption over time.

What does the evidence show? There is now a large body of empirical literature that investigates these claims over time and across countries (see Lee and Jayadev, 2005; Reinhart and Rogoff, 2008; Rodrik and Subramanian, 2008; and Kose *et al.*, 2006).[2] A number of studies have attempted to examine the link between free capital mobility and growth. Overall, this literature shows a lack of any compelling evidence for a positive link between capital account liberalization and growth. Perhaps the most careful and detailed summary of this literature is provided by Kose and others (2006: 8), who conclude that, "taken as a whole, the vast empirical literature provides little robust evidence of a causal relationship between financial integration and growth".

As Figure 8.1 shows, there is a strong correlation between capital mobility and financial crisis. Moreover, there is strong evidence that financial crises result in permanent losses of output (Cerra and Saxena, 2008).

In short, capital account liberalization and integration do not appear to increase economic growth or investment; instead, they contribute to financial crises that can have devastating short-term effects as well as costly long-term effects on output. Furthermore, capital account liberalization and crisis can increase inequality (Lee and Jayadev, 2005). There is very little to no evidence that free capital mobility delivers the benefits suggested by advocates. Still, it is possible that controlling flows with government regulation could make the situation even worse, or, at best, is unnecessary. Moreover, there are many different ways to manage flows and many different types of flows to manage.

In light of these findings, it is not surprising that many countries use capital controls to manage the flows of finance across borders. What are the main goals of these policies? What types of policies work best, and under what circumstances?

Goals and Mechanisms for Controlling International Financial Flows[3]

Types of Controls

First, it is important to be aware of the techniques that are available for controlling and managing the quantity, type, and impact of international financial flows. Table 8.1 presents a list and typology of controls. Controls, first of all, are simply types of government regulations or taxes that affect inflows or outflows of capital or the effects of the latter on the domestic economy. Types of capital flows that are affected are most easily thought of as the buying by domestic residents of foreign assets (outflows) or the selling of assets by domestic residents to foreigners (inflows). These assets are usually financial assets—stocks, bonds and securities of various types, currency, and bank deposits—but they can also refer to real assets, such as land. These securities and assets can be short term and highly liquid, such as bank deposits and short-term government bonds, or they can be longer term and less liquid, such as significant ownership of businesses (foreign direct investment), long-term government bonds, or real estate. Currency itself (dollars, euros, pesos, and so on) is the most short term and liquid. Increasingly, complex financial assets and liabilities (debts) called derivatives are involved in the flows of capital in and out of countries; these are hard to control, mostly because they are almost completely unregulated and relatively little is known about the roles of these securities in many financial transactions (Dodd, 2002; Garber, 1998).

Typologies for understanding controls usually distinguish between controls on *outflows* (domestic buying of foreign assets, including foreign currency) and those on *inflows* (the buying by foreign residents of domestic assets, including domestic currency). Another key distinction is between controls that work mainly through price measures, such as taxing inflows or outflows, and those that work primarily through quantitative measures, such as placing a quota on buying or selling assets, restricting the types of assets that can be bought or sold, or placing an absolute ban on the buying or selling of particular assets. This distinction is similar to the distinction in international trade, where economists distinguish between restrictive

Table 8.1 Objectives and types of capital management techniques

	Objectives	Price-based	Quantity-based	Prudential
Inflows	• Keep a stable and competitive real exchange rate • Limit excessive debt and maturity or locational mismatch to prevent financial instability • Alter the composition of inflows to attract desired inflows • Limit foreign ownership of assets for sovereign purposes or to protect domestic industries	• Tobin tax (tax on foreign exchange transactions) • Reserve requirements on inflows of capital (e.g. URR, unrequited reserve requirements) • Taxation of capital inflows	• Quantitative limits on foreign ownership of domestic companies' assets • Reporting requirements and quantitative limits on borrowing from abroad • Limits on ability to borrow from offshore entities	• Keynes tax (tax on domestic financial transactions) • Reporting requirements and limitations on maturity structure of liabilities and assets • Reserve requirements on deposits • Capital requirements on assets and restrictions on off-balance-sheet activities and derivatives contracts
Outflows	• Protect tax base by reducing capital flight • Maintain stability of exchange rate • Preserve savings to finance investment • Help in credit allocation mechanisms in order to support "industrial policy" and investments for social objectives • Enhance the autonomy of monetary policy in order to reduce inflation or expand employment and economic growth	• Tobin tax • Multiple exchange rates	• Exchange controls • Restrictions on purchase of foreign assets including foreign deposits • Limits on currency convertibility	• Limits on asset acquisition • Asset-backed reserve requirements
Inflows and Outflows	• All of the above			• "Trip wire and speed bump" approach (Grabel, 2004): identify a set of early warning signals and implement these various qualitative and quantitative policies gradually and dynamically, with an emphasis on controls on inflows.

measures that rely on tariffs (price-based measures) and those that rely on quotas (quantity-based measures) (see Neely, 1999).[4]

Finally, regulations that affect the inflows or outflows of capital directly can be distinguished from those that affect them and their impacts indirectly, by implementing *prudential regulations* on financial institutions. These prudential regulations can be capital regulations, regulations concerning maturity mismatches between short- and long-term assets and liabilities, regulations concerning derivative contracts, regulations concerning the borrowing of domestic currency from offshore banks, and so on. While such regulations might not affect the flows of foreign assets and liabilities directly, they will often affect them indirectly. In many countries, derivatives contracts are often entered into with foreign counterparties, for example, to correct maturity mismatches. These often involve creating foreign currency liabilities or assets which can ultimately generate changes in exchange rates or the buying and selling of foreign exchange.

The term "capital management techniques" is used to refer to the combination of capital and exchange controls plus the financial prudential regulations that indirectly affect these flows and their impacts. In the discussion that follows, we will move interchangeably between the terms "capital controls" and "capital management techniques" for ease of exposition.

Examples of controls that involve taxes are direct taxes on the buying or selling of foreign exchange. An example of this is the so-called "Tobin tax", named after Nobel prize-winning economist James Tobin, who proposed such a tax in the 1970s (see Tobin, 1978). The Tobin tax would place a small tax on all foreign exchange transactions, thereby discouraging the buying and selling of foreign exchange for very short-term purposes, which some economists argue tends to be for speculative purposes. The tax could raise significant amounts of revenue if implemented on an international scale. If that were to happen, some economists and policy makers have urged that any revenues generated be used for a variety of purposes, including aid for economic development (Chang and Grabel, 2004). A "Keynes" tax would implement a small tax on all domestic transactions and would serve similar purposes to the Tobin tax but on a domestic scale (Pollin, 2005).

Another example of a tax-based control is the so-called "unremunerated reserve requirement" (URR), or *encaje*, used in Chile and Colombia. In Chile, this policy required foreign investors who wanted to invest in the country to place some of the funds in a bank account for a period of time; they received no interest on the funds. This policy works like a tax, since the investors lose out on the interest they could have received if they were able to invest in interest-bearing securities or bank accounts.

Quantitative regulations include quotas on buying foreign exchange, limits on buying equity in certain industries, limits on ownership shares of firms, and an inability to borrow money from offshore banks unless the funds are used for particular purposes.

Another important distinction is whether countries utilize controls in a rigid or flexible way. Importantly, countries often use controls in a *dynamic* fashion, tightening or loosening them as circumstances demand rather than keeping them in place in a fixed—and therefore *static*—way. For example, when a crisis hits, countries may tighten controls; when the crisis eases, they may loosen them again.

Objectives of Capital Management Techniques

There are many ways to categorize the goals of capital management techniques (see Table 8.1 for a detailed list of goals). More generally, capital management techniques are used to achieve the following four objectives: to promote financial stability; to encourage desirable investment and financing arrangements; to enhance policy autonomy, including the maintenance of stable and competitive exchange rates; and to enhance national sovereignty and democracy. The more specific goals in Table 8.1 can be seen as particular means of achieving these objectives.

In order to understand the goals, challenges, and trade-offs associated with capital management techniques, we first need to understand the so-called "trilemma" problem of international finance.

The "Trilemma"

Capital mobility creates challenges for countries that want to set interest rates for domestic purposes. For example, central banks may want to lower interest rates to reduce the cost of borrowing in order to increase investment, employment, and economic growth. At other times, governments and central banks may want to raise interest rates to slow down an "overheated" economy and reduce inflation. International capital mobility can undermine these policies because, in integrated, global financial markets, domestic interest rates are strongly affected by foreign interest rates. Domestic and foreign investors will move capital from countries that have lower interest rates—adjusted for political and exchange rate risks—to countries that have higher interest rates. So if a central bank lowers its interest rate to try to encourage domestic investment, capital might leave the country in search of higher interest rates abroad, counteracting the policy. Similarly, if central banks try to raise interest rates to fight inflation, then investors might send capital flowing into the country, thereby driving down interest rates and undermining the policy.

Capital mobility also causes problems for countries wishing to fix or smooth their exchange rates. If investors think that risk has increased in a country, then they might sell their investments and take their money out of the country. When they do this, they sell their domestic currency assets and buy foreign exchange, thereby lowering the value (depreciating or putting pressure for a devaluation) of the domestic currency. If the country does not want its currency value to go down, then it will have to raise its interest rates to try to keep domestic assets more attractive and prevent the capital from leaving. But what if the country does not want to raise interest rates, because, say, it is facing a recession and wants lower interest rates to promote domestic investment?

Here, we see the "trilemma". Countries have a very difficult time maintaining all three of these goals—free capital mobility, autonomous monetary policy directed to domestic concerns, and fixed (or highly managed) exchange rates—at once. In general, they can have at most two out of the three. For example, they can choose free capital mobility and autonomous monetary policy, but then they must let the market determine the exchange rate. Or they can have free capital mobility and a fixed exchange rate, but then they must give up the autonomous monetary policy and use it to keep the exchange rate fixed in the face of market-determined capital flows.

This problem can also be explained by the so-called "interest parity relation", which says that in a financially integrated international economy, domestic interest rates are tied to foreign interest rates (adjusted for expected changes in exchange rates and risks associated with default or political instability).

If a country wants to have domestically oriented monetary policy and a fixed or highly managed exchange rate, then it must control capital mobility. That is where capital controls or capital management techniques come in.

Objectives of Capital Management Techniques

Capital Management Techniques can Promote Financial Stability

Capital management techniques can promote financial stability through their ability to reduce currency, flight, fragility, and/or contagion risks.

Capital management can thereby reduce the potential for financial crisis and attendant economic and social devastation (Grabel, 2003; Epstein, Grabel and Jomo, 2005).

"Currency risk" refers to the risk that a currency will appreciate or depreciate significantly over a short period of time. "Investor flight risk" refers to the likelihood that holders of liquid financial assets will sell their holdings en masse in the face of perceived difficulty. "Lender flight risk" refers to the likelihood that lenders will terminate lending programs or will only extend loans on prohibitive terms. "Fragility risk" refers to the vulnerability of an economy's private and public borrowers to internal or external shocks that would jeopardize their ability to meet current obligations. Fragility risk arises in a number of ways: borrowers might employ financing strategies that involve maturity or locational mismatch; agents might finance private investment with capital that is prone to flight risk; or investors (domestic and foreign) might over-invest in certain sectors, thereby creating overcapacity and fuelling unsustainable speculative bubbles. Finally, "contagion risk" refers to the threat that a country will fall victim to financial and macroeconomic instability that originates elsewhere. Capital management techniques can reduce contagion risk by managing the degree of financial integration and by reducing the vulnerability of individual countries to currency, flight, and fragility risks.

Capital Management Techniques can Promote Desirable Types of Investment and Financing Arrangements and Discourage Less Desirable Types of Investment/Financing Strategies

Capital management techniques can influence the composition of the economy's aggregate investment portfolio and the financing arrangements that underpin these investments. Capital management techniques—particularly those that involve inflow controls—can promote desirable types of investment and financing strategies by rewarding investors and borrowers who engage in them. Desirable types of investment are those that create employment; improve living standards; and promote greater income equality, technology transfer, learning by doing, and/or long-term growth. Desirable types of financing are those that are long term, stable, and sustainable. Capital management can discourage less desirable types of investment and financing strategies by increasing their cost or precluding them altogether (Nembhard, 1996).

Capital Management Techniques can Enhance the Autonomy of Economic and Social Policy

Capital management techniques can enhance policy autonomy in a number of ways. They can reduce the severity of currency risk, thereby allowing authorities to protect a currency peg. They can also keep exchange rates at competitive and stable levels. Capital management can create space for the government and/or the central bank to pursue growth-promoting and/or reflationary macroeconomic policies by neutralizing the threat of capital flight (via restrictions on capital inflows or outflows). Moreover, by reducing the risk of financial crisis in the first place, capital management can reduce the likelihood that governments will be compelled to use contractionary macro- and microeconomic policies, as well as social policy, as a signal to attract foreign investment back to the country or as a precondition for financial assistance from the IMF. Finally, capital management techniques can reduce the specter of excessive foreign control or ownership of domestic resources.

Capital Management Techniques can Enhance National Autonomy and even Democracy

It follows from the third point that capital management can enhance democracy by reducing the potential for speculators and external actors to exercise undue influence over domestic decision-making either directly or indirectly (via the threat of capital flight). Capital management techniques can reduce the veto power of the financial community and the IMF and create space for the interests of other groups (such as advocates for the poor) to play a role in the design of economic and social policy. Capital management techniques can thus be said to enhance democracy because they create the opportunity for pluralism in policy design.

Costs of Capital Management Techniques

Critics of capital management techniques argue that they impose four types of costs: they reduce growth; reduce efficiency and policy discipline; promote corruption and waste; and aggravate credit scarcity, and uncertainty. Critics argue that the benefits that derive from capital management (such as financial stability) come at an unacceptably high price.

In sum, many critics argue that there are significant costs associated with capital management techniques. However, there is little consensus in the empirical literature on the size—or even the existence—of these costs. More importantly, researchers have largely failed to investigate the relative weight of costs and benefits.

Evidence on the Costs, Benefits, and Effectiveness of Capital Management Techniques

There have been many studies of the impact, effectiveness, and costs and benefits of capital controls and capital management techniques (for recent surveys, see Epstein, Grabel and Jomo, 2005, and Magud, Reinhart and Rogoff, 2005). Some of these offer a statistical/econometric analysis, while others rely on case studies.

Case Study Evidence[5]

I first present case study evidence compiled by Epstein, Grabel and Jomo (2005) (see Tables 8.2 and 8.3). The researchers undertook case studies of capital management techniques in seven countries: Chile, Colombia, China, Taiwan, India, Malaysia, and Singapore. As Table 8.2 shows, these countries used quite specific combinations of the types of controls listed in Table 8.1, and for a variety of purposes (mostly those listed in Table 8.1).

First, consider six commonly held—and mistaken—ideas about capital management techniques. One is that these techniques can only work in the short run, not the long run. However, with the exception of Malaysia, all of the cases show that management *can* achieve important objectives over a significant period of time. Taking China and Singapore as two cases at different ends of the spectrum in terms of types of controls, both countries effectively employed capital management techniques for more than a decade in the service of important policy objectives.

A second common view is that, for capital management to work over a long period of time, measures have to be consistently strengthened. In fact, the reality is much more complex than this. In Malaysia, Chile, and China, during times of stress it proved necessary to strengthen controls to address leakages that were being exploited by the private sector. However, as these same cases demonstrate, controls can be loosened when a crisis subsides or when the international environment changes, and then reinstated or strengthened as necessary. In short, dynamic capital management techniques have been successfully utilized across a range of countries.

A third common (but misleading) view is that, for capital management to work, there must be an experienced bureaucracy in place. It is certainly

Table 8.2 Summary: Types and objectives of capital management techniques employed during the 1990s

Country	Types of capital management techniques	Objectives of capital management techniques
Chile	**Inflows:** – FDI and PI: One year residence requirement – 30% URR – tax on foreign loans: 1.2% per year **Outflows:** – no significant restrictions **Domestic financial regulations:** – strong regulatory measures	• Lengthen maturity structures and stabilize inflows • Help manage exchange rates to maintain export competitiveness • Protect economy from financial instability
Colombia	Similar to Chile	Similar to Chile
Taiwan	**Inflows:** *Non-residents* • Bank accounts can only be used for domestic spending, not financial speculation • Foreign participation in stock market regulated • FDI tightly regulated *Residents* • Regulation of foreign borrowing **Outflows:** • Exchange controls **Domestic financial regulations:** • Restrictions on lending for real estate and other speculative purposes	• Promote industrialization • Help manage exchange rates to maintain export competitiveness • Maintain financial stability and insulate itself from foreign financial crises

Table 8.2 (continued)

Country	Types of capital management techniques	Objectives of capital management techniques
Singapore	**Inflows:** "Non-internationalization" of the Singapore currency (Singapore$) **Outflows:** *Non-residents* – financial institutions can't extend S$ credit to non-residents if they are likely to use for speculation – if they borrow for use abroad, must swap first into foreign currency **Domestic financial regulations:** – restrictions on creation of swaps, and other derivatives that could be used for speculation against S$	• prevent speculation against S$ • support "soft peg" of S$ • help maintain export competitiveness • help insulate itself from foreign financial crises
Malaysia (1998)	**Inflows:** • Restrictions on foreign borrowing **Outflows:** *Non-residents* • 12-month repatriation waiting period • Graduated exit levies inversely proportional to length of stay *Residents* • Exchange controls **Domestic financial regulations:** *Non-residents* • Restrict access to Malaysian currency *Residents* • Encourage to borrow domestic borrowing and investment	• Maintain political and economic sovereignty • Kill the offshore ringgit market • Shut down offshore share market • Help reflate the economy • Help create financial stability and insulate the economy from contagion

Table 8.2 (continued)

Country	Types of capital management techniques	Objectives of capital management techniques
India	**Inflows:** *Non-residents* • Strict regulation of FDI and PI **Outflows:** *Non-residents* • None *Residents* • Exchange controls **Domestic financial regulations:** • Strict limitations on development of domestic financial markets	• Support industrial policy • Pursue capital account liberalization in an incremental and controlled fashion • Insulate domestic economy from financial contagion • Preserve domestic savings and foreign exchange reserves • Help stabilize exchange rate
China	**Inflows:** *Non-residents* • Strict regulation on sectoral FDI investment • Regulation of equity investments: segmented stock markets **Outflows:** *Non-residents* • No restrictions on repatriation of funds • Strict limitations on borrowing Chinese renminbi for speculative purposes *Residents* • Exchange controls **Domestic financial regulations:** • Strict limitations on residents and non-residents	• Support industrial policy • Pursue capital account liberalization in incremental and controlled fashion • Insulate domestic economy from financial contagion • Increase political sovereignty • Preserve domestic savings and foreign exchange reserves • Help keep exchange rates at competitive levels

Source: Epstein, Grabel and Jomo (2005: 304–305).

true that having experience helps; China, India, and Singapore are all examples of countries that have long-term experience with government direction of the economy. Malaysia, however, is an important counter-example. The country was able to successfully implement capital management even without having had a great deal of experience in doing so. In the case of Chile, to take another example, the central bank had no previous experience implementing the reserve requirement scheme, though it had had some negative experiences trying to implement capital controls in the 1970s. What is more important than experience is *state capacity* and *administrative capacity* more generally.

A fourth view, which has recently become popular, is that controls on capital inflows work but those on outflows do not. However, in our sample we have seen examples of policy success in both dimensions. For example, Chile and Colombia maintained controls on inflows, while China, India, and Malaysia maintained controls on outflows. In addition, Singapore and Taiwan maintain controls on the ability of residents and non-residents to use domestic currency offshore for purposes of "speculating" against the home currency. This is a control on outflows that has successfully insulated these countries from crises and helped their governments manage their exchange rates.

We now turn to the lessons to be drawn from the case studies, which are summarized in Tables 8.2 and 8.3. First and most generally, capital management techniques can contribute to currency and financial stability, macro- and microeconomic policy autonomy, stable long-term investment, and sound current account performance. There may also be some costs associated with capital management techniques, such as the fact that they can create space for public corruption.

Second, successful implementation of controls over a significant period of time depends on the presence of a sound policy environment and strong fundamentals. These include a relatively low debt ratio, moderate rates of inflation, sustainable current account and fiscal balances, consistent exchange rate policies, public sectors that function well enough to be able to implement coherent policies (administrative capacity), and governments that are sufficiently independent of narrow political interests to be able to maintain some degree of control over the financial sector (state capacity).

Third, we can see that causation works both ways: from good fundamentals to successful capital management techniques, and from successful capital management techniques to good fundamentals. Good fundamentals are important to the long-run success of capital management techniques because they reduce the stress on these controls and thereby.

Table 8.3 Summary: Assessment of the capital management techniques employed during the 1990s

Country	Achievements	Supporting factors	Costs
Chile	• Altered composition and maturity of inflows • Currency stability • Reduced vulnerability to contagion	• Well-designed policies and sound fundamentals • Neo-liberal economic policy in many domains • Good returns offered to foreign investors • State and administrative capacity • Dynamic capital management	• Limited evidence of higher capital costs for Small and Medium sized Enterprises
Colombia	• Similar to Chile, but less successful in several respects	• Less state and administrative capacity than in Chile, meaning that blunter policies were employed • Economic reforms in the direction of neo-liberalism	• No evidence available
Taiwan	• Competitive exchange rate and stable currency • Insulated from financial crises • Enhanced economic sovereignty • Debt burdens and financial fragility are insignificant	• High levels of state and administrative capacity • Policy independence of the central bank • Dynamic capital management	• Limited evidence of concentration of lending to large firms, conservatism of banks, inadequate auditing of books, and risk and project assessment capabilities • Large informal financial sector • Limited evidence of inadequate liquidity in financial system

Table 8.3 (continued)

Country	Achievements	Supporting factors	Costs
Singapore	• Insulated from disruptive speculation • Protection of soft peg • Financial stability	• Strong state capacity and ability to use moral suasion • Strong economic fundamentals	• Possibly undermined financial sector development • Loss of seigniorage
Malaysia (1998)	• Facilitated macroeconomic reflation • Helped maintain domestic economic sovereignty	• Public support for policies • Strong state and administrative capacity • Dynamic capital management	• Possibly contributed to cronyism and corruption
India	• Facilitated incremental liberalization of capital flows • Insulated from financial contagion • Helped preserve domestic saving • Helped maintain economic sovereignty	• Strong state and administrative capacity • Strong public support for policies • Experience with state governance of the economy • Success of broader economic policy regime • Gradual economic liberalization	• Possibly hindered development of financial sector • Possibly facilitated corruption
China	• Facilitated industrial policy • Insulated economy from financial contagion • Helped preserve savings • Helped manage exchange rate and facilitate export-led growth • Helped maintain expansionary macro-policy • Helped maintain economic sovereignty	• Strong state and administrative capacity • Strong economic fundamentals • Experience with state governance of the economy • Gradual economic liberalization • Dynamic capital management	• Possibly constrained the development of the financial sector • Possibly encouraged non-performing loans • Possibly facilitated corruption

Source: Epstein, Grabel and Jomo (2005: 328–329).

enhance the chance that they will be successful. On the other hand, capital management techniques also improve fundamentals. Thus, there is a synergy between capital management techniques and fundamentals.

Fourth, the dynamic aspects of capital management techniques are perhaps their most important feature. Policy makers need to retain the ability to implement a variety of management techniques and alter them as circumstances warrant.

Fifth, capital management techniques work best when they are coherent and consistent with the overall aims of the economic policy regime, or—better yet—when they are an integral part of a national economic vision. To be clear, this vision does not have to be one of widespread state control over economic activity. Singapore is a good example of an economy that is highly liberalized in some ways, but where capital management techniques are an integral part of an overall vision of economic policy and development.

Sixth, there is not one type of capital management technique that works best for all countries; in other words, there is no single "best practice" when it comes to capital management techniques.

As I suggested earlier, despite the economic crisis, there is still pressure on developing countries to liberalize their capital accounts more than they already have. Epstein, Grabel and Jomo (2005) suggest that, in many cases, it is not in the interests of developing countries to seek full capital account liberalization. The lesson of dynamic capital management is that countries need to have the flexibility to both tighten *and* loosen controls. Thus, if countries completely liberalize their capital accounts, they might find it very difficult to re-establish any degree of control when the situation warrants or even demands it. This is because market actors might see the attempt to re-establish capital management as *abandonment* of a liberalized capital account, and might then react rather radically to this perceived change. By contrast, if investors understand that a country is maintaining a system of dynamic capital management, they will expect management to tighten and loosen over time. It is therefore less likely that investors will overreact if management techniques are tightened in these circumstances.

Statistical Analysis of Capital Controls

Magud, Reinhart and Rogoff (2005) recently summarized and synthesized more than 30 statistical studies of the impact of capital controls. Their results are instructive, though subject to further scrutiny. They distinguish between controls on inflows and outflows, and find that while capital controls on inflows appear to "make monetary policy more independent; alter the composition of flows (to longer term); [and] reduce real exchange rate pressures", they "seem not to reduce the volume of net flows." As for outflows, the authors find that "there is Malaysia and there is everybody else. In Malaysia, controls reduce outflows and may give room for more independent monetary policy. There is little evidence of 'success' in other countries attempting to control flows, either in terms of altering the volume or regaining monetary independence" (Magud, Reinhart and Rogoff, 2005: 21-22).

Hence, there is a great deal of evidence in support of the ability of inflow controls to help achieve important goals; the evidence on the impacts of outflow controls is more mixed. One lesson from this is that capital management techniques that control the quantity—and especially the quality—of inflows are likely to reduce the necessity of countries engaging in outflow controls for lengthy periods of time if problems arise.

Conclusions

As the instability and difficulties associated with uncontrolled international financial flows become more apparent in the crisis of 1997, and now 2007-2009, interest in capital management techniques has been revived. Studies reveal that there are many different types of capital management techniques that can be custom fit to different countries' needs and circumstances. Of course, capital management techniques are no panacea for economic problems, and they will not work well unless they are part of an overall, appropriate framework of economic management. For countries navigating the treacherous waters of international finance, however, they can be useful components of the macroeconomic toolkit.

Notes

* The author thanks his co-authors and colleagues James Crotty, Ilene Grabel, Arjun Jayadev, and Jomo K.S. for their contributions to his understanding of capital management techniques and for their work, on which he draws liberally here. Of course, they are not responsible for any errors. Another version of this chapter will be published in *Macroeconomic Debates: Competing Views*, edited by Mario Seccareccia and Hassan Bougrine, Ottawa: Emond Montgomery Publications, 2009.

1. At the time this article was written, "widgets" simply meant "things"; this was before the current use of the term for cool programs connected to your desktop, blog, or cellphone.

2. Thanks to Arjun Jayadev for sharing some of his unpublished work in this area, which I have drawn on here.
3. This section draws heavily on my joint work with Ilene Grabel and Jomo K.S. (Epstein, Grabel and Jomo, 2005) and on the separate work of Grabel (2003, 2004).
4. Another distinction concerns measures that affect only the flows of capital (the so-called "capital account") and those that affect trade and inflows and outflows of returns from holding investments (the so-called "current account"). Since we will not discuss this distinction further, it is not reflected in Table 8.1.
5. This section draws heavily on Epstein, Grabel and Jomo (2005).

References

Block, Fred L. (1977). *The Origins of the International Economic Disorder: A Study of International Monetary Policy.* University of California Press, Berkeley.

Cerra, Valerie, and Sweta Chaman Saxena (2008). Growth dynamics: The myth of economic recovery. *American Economic Review,* 98 (1): 439-457.

Chang, Ha-Joon, and Ilene Grabel (2004). *Reclaiming Development: An Alternative Economic Policy Manual.* Zed Press, London.

Crotty, James (1983). Review: Keynes and capital flight. *Journal of Economic Literature,* 21 (1): 56-65.

Diaz-Alejandro, Carlos F. (1985). Good-bye financial repression, hello financial crash. *Journal of Development Economics,* 19 (1-2): 1-24.

Dodd, Randall (2002). Derivatives, the shape of international capital flows and virtues of prudential regulation. UNU WIDER Discussion Paper 2002/93. http://www.financialpolicy.org/dscwider2002.pdf

Eichengreen, Barry J. (1992). *Golden Fetters: The Gold Standard and the Great Depression, 1919-1939.* Oxford University Press, New York.

Epstein, Gerald, Ilene Grabel and Jomo K.S. (2005). Capital management techniques in developing countries. In Gerald A. Epstein (ed.). *Capital Flight and Capital Controls in Developing Countries.* Edward Elgar, Northampton, MA.

Garber, Peter M. (1998). Derivatives in international capital flows. NBER Working Paper W6623, National Bureau of Economic Research, Cambridge, MA. www.nber.org

Glyn, Andrew (1986). Capital flight and exchange controls. *New Left Review,* I/155 (January-February): 37-49.

Grabel, Ilene (2003). Averting crisis: Assessing measures to manage financial integration in developing countries. *Cambridge Journal of Economics,* 27 (3): 317-336.

Grabel, Ilene (2004). Trip wires and speed bumps: Managing financial risks and reducing the potential for financial crises in developing economies. G-24 Discussion Paper 33, UNCTAD, Geneva. http://www.unctad.org/en/docs/gdsmdpbg2420049_en.pdf

Helleiner, Eric (1984). *States and the Reemergence of Global Finance: From Bretton Woods to the 1990s.* Cornell University Press, Ithaca, NY.

Kindleberger, Charles, P. (1986). *The World in Depression, 1929-1939.* Revised and enlarged edition. University of California Press, Berkeley.

Kose, M. Ayhan, Eswar Prasad, Kenneth Rogoff and Shang-Jin Wei (2006). Financial globalization: A reappraisal. Harvard University, revised December 2006.

Lee, Kang-Kook, and Arjun Jayadev (2005). Capital account liberalization, growth and the labor share of income: Reviewing and extending the cross-country evidence. In Gerald A. Epstein (ed.). *Capital Flight and Capital Controls in Developing Countries.* Edward Elgar, Northampton, MA: 15-57.

Magud, Nicolas E., Carmen Reinhart and Kenneth Rogoff (2005). Capital controls: Myth and reality; A portfolio balance approach to capital controls. http://www.webmeets.com/files/papers/LACEA-LAMES/2006/168/Magud-Reinhart-Rogoff%20(May-09-06).pdf

Neely, Christopher J. (1999). An introduction to capital controls. *Review* (Federal Reserve Bank of St. Louis), 81 (6): 13-30.

Nembhard, Jessica (1996). *Capital Control, Financial Policy and Industrial Policy in South Korea and Brazil.* Praeger Press, New York.

Pollin, Robert (2005). Applying a securities transactions tax to the US: Design issues, market impact and revenue estimates. In Gerald A. Epstein (ed.). *Financialization and the World Economy.* Edward Elgar, Northampton, MA: 409-425.

Reinhart, Carmen, and Kenneth Rogoff (2008). Banking crises: An equal opportunity menace. NBER Paper No. 14587, December, National Bureau of Economic Research, Cambridge, MA. www.nber.org

Rodrik, Dani (1998). Who needs capital account convertibility? *Essays in International Finance* (Princeton University), 207: 55-65.

Rodrik, Dani, and Arvind Subramaniam (2008). Why did financial globalization disappoint? Processed, Harvard University. http://ksghome.harvard.edu/~drodrik/Why_Did_FG_Disappoint_March_24_2008.pdf

Tobin, James (1978). A proposal for monetary reform. *Eastern Economic Journal*, 4 (3-4): 153-159.

9

Financial Services, the WTO and Initiatives for Global Financial Reform

Chakravarthi Raghavan

The financial crisis that began in 2007, and has now spread globally affecting the real economy has evoked considerable discussions and views on its origins and nature, and proposals for rethinking and reforming national and international governance and regulation of the financial sector. For lack of a better term, all these are referred to here as Bretton Woods II.

There is now a general consensus that the reform of the financial sector, and a new global financial architecture, must include strong regulatory measures and their enforcement—though it is not at all certain that the final outcome will be in line with these objectives. In all these discussions, international trade and the trading system, has figured, if at all, only somewhat peripherally—in terms of the effects of the credit crunch on trade finance and the need to resist "protectionist pressures". The successful conclusion of the current Doha Round of negotiations at the World Trade Organization (WTO) is however presented and promoted as a panacea for the financial and economic crisis. There has been little attention to and focus on the finance-trade systems and their inter-linkages.

This contrasts with the discussions on the post-war Bretton Woods (BW) system, and the holistic view of Harry Dexter White for the US and John Maynard Keynes for the UK, who were the chief designers and architects of that system. At that time, Keynes and others in Britain noted that the policy of the US Administration on various issues of political and economic preparation formed a connected whole. In Britain, the monetary policy arrangements were seen as part of other arrangements—including a stabilization policy for the cost of living through steps to mitigate the fluctuations of the international prices of primary commodities, and a trade liberalization policy to remove obstacles to British exports. For Keynes, without currency agreements to prevent countries from altering the value of their currencies unilaterally and at short notice, there was no firm ground to discuss tariffs (Keynes, 1980). And in 1944, in the preparations for and at Bretton Woods, both Keynes and White took for granted the necessity for controls on capital movements. Keynes, in his own writings, noted that if finance capital was liberated, it would develop a life of its own and destabilize merchandise trade (Richardson, 1997).

It is not, however, easy or even possible to go back in time, and just adopt the same designs and views today. After the breakdown of BW-I in 1971, and since early 1980s, there has been a change of course in the overall political economy of the USA and other key nations, and each of them have pursued variegated economic liberalization policies and measures. Any reforms and regulatory measures to make the finance system serve the real economy have to deal not only with financial institutions such as banks and other credit and lending institutions, but a whole range of inter-connected sectors. Some of these have their own intergovernmental institutions for global coordination and oversight; others have mostly private bodies that lay down norms, standards and guidelines. All these raise important issues of coherence—of the multilateral trading system, the international monetary and finance system, and the over-arching UN system, the United Nations Organization (UNO) and its Charter whose obligations over-ride that of any other in international law.

Within this complex, an element that has received scant mention, or at best cursory attention, is the World Trade Organization's 1997 Financial Services Agreement (FSA) on international trade in financial services (banking, insurance, securities and other financial instruments, and many associated services) that entered into force on 1 March 1999. The FSA is a part of the General Agreement on Trade in Services (GATS), one of the agreements annexed to the Marrakesh Agreement Establishing the WTO. Under the Fifth Protocol, WTO members annexed new financial services schedules (replacing or modifying any earlier ones of 1993 and 1995) to their Uruguay Round services schedules. About 70 WTO members became parties to the FSA, and through the Fifth Protocol attached Schedules of Specific Commitments and List of Exemptions from the Most Favored Nation (MFN) Article II of GATS of about 70 WTO members who became parties to the FSA.

Since the FSA is a part of the GATS agreement, any reform of the financial services sector will have to be seen in the context of the WTO and its annexed agreements as a Single Undertaking, and the various panel and appellate body rulings in disputes at the WTO. Some "reforms" may need changes in the GATS itself.

The Marrakesh Agreement for the World Trade Organization, the outcome of the Uruguay Round (UR) of Multilateral Trade Negotiations covering a complex range of subjects and issues, entered into force on 1 January 1995. The WTO Treaty provides a common institutional framework for its annexed agreements listed in four Annexes. Every WTO member had to sign on to all the agreements in the first three annexes, while the fourth has some plurilateral agreements—among those who agree to be parties.

One of the main drivers behind the UR negotiations and of bringing services within its ambit, was a coalition of financial, audio-visual and other service enterprises of the United States led from about 1982 by the American Express (AMEX) Co, which with CitiCorp and the AIG (of insurance companies) formed a powerful trio. Even the idea for a trade agreement covering services began in 1979, with American Express initiating the moves, and roping in others (Freeman, 2000; Gould, 2008). The trio, with considerable lobbying clout and influence over the US Congress and administration, as well as in many developing countries emerged as a dominant influence in the financial services negotiations (of 1993, 1995 and 1997, and until recently, in the Doha talks).

The GATS sets out an overall framework of rules and disciplines on trade in services and has an annex on Financial Services (FS); but by the time of Marrakesh, the negotiations for market access commitments on FS were not complete, and these continued after Marrakesh, as part of the unfinished business, and were concluded in 1997 with the Fifth Protocol to the GATS, which entered into force in 1999, 17 years from the time the subject of services was first raised as an international trade issue. About 70 WTO members who became parties to the FSA, used the Fifth protocol to modify their GATS schedules, and file Specific Commitments under FSA and, in respect of these, file a List of Exemptions from the Most Favored Nation (MFN) Article II of GATS.

In the complex set of subjects and issues encompassed in the (UR) negotiations, the subject of services, resulting in the GATS, and within it, financial services, were perhaps the most difficult and controversial. Part of the problem was the changing view of the US over time on how to bring services into the multilateral framework on trade; but partly also it was due to the evolving views on services as something separate from goods, and how to trade them. Ironically, early in 2009, the issue has been raised that, in fact, the classification of services and goods is artificial (and entirely for the convenience of governments and statisticians), and that trade in services and goods may be treated alike (Economist, 2009; Lester, 2009). In the current Doha Round, the issue of classification of goods and services' trade is being considered in the context of cross-border electronic delivery.

The WTO and GATS

The FSA is a part of the GATS, which is an integral part of the WTO agreement. Some of the issues of the WTO and GATS, relevant to trade in financial services are just flagged below, but not dealt with in detail:

1.   The GATS, a framework agreement for international trade in services (with some sectoral annexes, including two on financial services), is an integral part of the Marrakesh Treaty (the WTO Agreement) and its annexed bundle of agreements in the area of Trade in Goods, Trade in Services, Trade-Related Intellectual Property Agreement (TRIPS), an integrated Dispute Settlement Understanding (DSU), and a Trade Policy Review Mechanism. The GATS is linked to the multilateral agreements on goods and to the TRIPS mainly through the DSU (Das, 1999: chapter VII, 1). There are also some related provisions between GATT and the GATS, such as Article V of GATS on economic integration and Article XII on restrictions to safeguard balance-of-payments.

2.   The Marrakesh Treaty is an umbrella agreement to provide an institutional and organizational framework for the administration of the multilateral and plurilateral agreements reached at the conclusion of the UR of multilateral trade negotiations. Under the Treaty a Ministerial Conference is the supreme governing body of the WTO and, in between sessions of the Conference, the General Council.

3.   The Treaty is a "Single Undertaking"—with members having to sign on to all the agreements annexed to it. Over the period 1986-1993, when the various agreements in the area of trade in goods, TRIPS and Trade in Services were negotiated, most participants and even key leading countries like the USA had no clear idea of their ultimate shape or the institutional arrangement. It was only at the very end, in November-December 1993, that all these were integrated, along with an integrated dispute settlement understanding, and brought under a single institutional framework. After the negotiations were concluded in December 1993 at the official level, during the subsequent legal scrutiny stage, some of the variations in language used on the same

issues in different agreements came to the fore; but the difficulties of changing them without upsetting the overall delicate balance resulted in things being left to later processes. Some of the current difficulties in the system can be traced to this.

4. The Treaty requires (Article XVI: 4) that each Member "shall ensure" the conformity of its laws, regulations and administrative procedures with its obligations as provided in the annexed Agreements; and (XVI: 5), "no reservations may be made (by any member) in respect of any provisions" of the Treaty, and reservations to any of the provisions of its Multilateral Trade Agreements "may only be made to the extent provided for in those Agreements."

4.1. For trade relations on matters dealt with under the WTO agreements, there is a prescriptive (mandatory) provision (Article III: 2) that the WTO is "the forum" for negotiations; on matters not dealt with, such as trade in commodities, the WTO "may be" a forum for negotiations, meaning negotiations may be held in any forum including the WTO.

4.1A. Under Article III: 3, "The WTO shall administer the Understanding on Rules and Procedures Governing the Settlement of Disputes (the 'Dispute Settlement Understanding' or 'DSU') in Annex 2 to this Agreement."

4.2. Since the GATS is an integral part of the WTO Treaty and the FSA is a part of the GATS, any changes to GATS or its FSA, so as to be compatible with any regulatory and/or administrative changes resulting from the Bretton Woods II processes, have to be effected through negotiations at the WTO as a forum, and changes or amendments to the agreements effected through the WTO amendment process set out in Article X of the WTO agreement. States and powerful private interests could frustrate this by forum games.

5.1. Article IX of the Treaty sets out that the WTO "shall continue the practice of decision-making by consensus followed by GATT 1947". And in a footnote, the treaty stipulates that "the body concerned shall be deemed to have decided by consensus on a matter submitted for its consideration, if no Member, present at the meeting when the decision is taken, formally objects to the proposed decision." This is generally referred to as "positive consensus"—as different from what is called "negative consensus"—when rulings of dispute panels and the Appellate Body (AB) are to be adopted automatically by the WTO membership in the Dispute Settlement Body (DSB), unless they decide, by consensus, not to adopt a particular report.

The Article also lays down that where a decision cannot be arrived at by consensus, the matter at issue shall be decided by voting. And various majority requirements are provided for various parts of the Agreement. So far, there has been no recourse to this and decisions taken by vote.

5.2. Under IX: 2, the Ministerial Conference of the WTO and the General Council have the "exclusive authority" to adopt interpretations of the Marrakesh Agreement, and its Multilateral Trade Agreements.

5.3.1. Under the DSU, panels that hear and give rulings and recommendations for settling disputes among parties about the impairment of their rights and obligations, and the AB that hears appeals against panel rulings on issues of law (as different from appreciation of evidence on facts), are required to "clarify" the existing provisions of the relevant WTO agreements in accordance with "customary rules of interpretation of public international law."

5.3.2. In terms of customary public international law, when states are parties to more than one agreement, they are expected to observe all of them. In interpreting conflicts among them, some well-known principles are followed: a later treaty on the same subject prevails over an earlier one, a treaty on a specific issue will prevail over a general one, etc.

5.3.3. At the WTO, the panels and the AB in purporting to follow public international law, have repeatedly said they would "clarify" the provisions of various separate agreements in such a way as to avoid conflicts and thus ensure all parties carry out obligations of all the agreements. And in this task, panels and the AB, have cited Article 31 of the Vienna Law of Treaties (codifying international public law) and delved into the "history of the negotiations" to "clarify" the meaning or find support for the meaning given by the panel or AB. However, at the end of the UR negotiations, the plenipotentiaries at Marrakesh did not establish and adopt a "negotiating history"—as was done at the end of the Tokyo Round; the "history" if any are in the internal files of the GATT secretariat which serviced those negotiations, but are not public documents. This has given rise to some complaints about the secretariat influences in dispute settlement processes.

5.4. Successive rulings and recommendations of the panels and the AB, adopted by negative consensus, have resulted in blurring any difference between "clarification", that dispute panels and the AB are mandated to do, and "interpretation", solely reserved for the

Ministerial Conference and the General Council. And since panel and AB rulings are automatically adopted by negative consensus, whilst actions by the Ministerial Conference and the General Council need a positive consensus, and/or forcing issues to a vote (but never done so far), the panels and the AB have, in practice, become more powerful than the supreme governing body of the WTO! However, when the Ministerial Conference or General Council provide an authoritative interpretation, it can only be changed by amending the agreement concerned; the *stare decisis* principle of law does not apply in international public law, and thus not to rulings of the panels and AB; in theory, they could thus be changed by another decision in another dispute.

5.5. Rulings of panels and the AB, adopted by negative consensus at the DSB resulting in a "GATT-acqui" status, and panels and the AB making legal determinations that a political body of the WTO is empowered to make, have resulted in the creation—by the dispute settlement processes—of new or additional rights and obligations (see Das, 2003: 96-97; Roessler, 2001; Raghavan, 2000; Colares, 2009).

Overall, the culture of the WTO—a member-driven and rules-based system in theory but largely driven by the secretariat—and its working— mostly in informal negotiations and processes—has made it difficult to distinguish and separate process from substance of the accords or any changes to them. This will have a bearing on how current processes for BW-II will be reflected in changes that will be needed in the WTO trading system, in particular the GATS and its FSA.

GATS

The GATS as mentioned earlier is a framework agreement of rules and disciplines governing the relationships of members in the area of trade in services and providing for periodic negotiations for liberalizing trade in services. The Agreement has 29 Articles and 8 sectoral annexes which are integral parts of the GATS (under Article XXIX). Two of the annexes relate to financial services (Annex on FS and Second Annex on FS); and there are six other sectoral annexes — on Article II (MFN) Exemptions; on Movement of Natural Persons Supplying Services; on Air Transport Services; on Negotiations in Maritime Transport Services; on Telecommunications; and, on Negotiations on Basic Telecommunications.

The GATS was the outcome of very difficult negotiations, and for most members, including those who initiated it, uncharted territory.

The GATT 1947, a part of the Havana Charter, had been put into force through the protocol of provisional application (pending entry into force of the Havana Charter). With the US not willing to ratify the Havana Charter, the GATT 1947 had remained a provisional treaty for 48 years (until the Marrakesh Treaty). This resulted in the initial grandfathering of existing legislation, and it became a privilege, in particular for the original signatories. However, the "grandfathered" privileges were gradually eroded over a period of years—through panel rulings that only changes towards compliance with GATT in pre-GATT mandatory law would be GATT-legal, but not retrogressive changes.

During the UR negotiations on GATS, the US sought to bring the grandfathering concept into GATS. The issue was discussed and rejected, except as reflected through GATS provisions on the MFN exemptions in one dimension, and limitations on market access and national treatment as reflected in the schedules in the other dimension.

In its schedule of commitments on Financial Services under the Fifth Protocol, the US filed "an additional commitment" to work with Congress for Glass-Steagall reform, and with states on other banking service reforms, as well as in the insurance sector. The repeal of Glass-Steagall—firewalls between banking activities and trading activities—was achieved in December 1999. In the context of the current financial and related economic crisis, there are moves in the US and elsewhere for financial sector reforms and for re-imposing the Glass-Steagall type of restrictions as part of the regulatory structures in the financial sector. If this happens, and a dispute is raised by another Member, it is unclear what view would be taken in the WTO dispute settlement system. It is difficult to predict whether the US additional commitment would be viewed as a firm or a best endeavor commitment (precluding a reversal once the "reforms" are achieved) or something else?

There has been no WTO jurisprudence on the FS Annex, the FSA (the Second and Fifth protocols to GATS) or the Understanding on Commitments in Financial Services, which is not even a part of the legal texts of the Marrakesh Agreement and Ministerial Decisions and Understanding, but may have a bearing in disputes involving those WTO members who expressly or indirectly made it a part of their schedule under the Fifth Protocol. The Understanding was accepted by only some 30 WTO members in scheduling their FSA commitments. But panels, in case of ambiguity in matters requiring clarification, have relied on past practices and any negotiating history.

The GATT-1947 encompassed the area of international trade in goods. Most of the concepts and principles of international trade in goods underlying the GATT framework—the MFN or non-discrimination principle, the national treatment principle, border controls (tariffs and quantitative and other measures), etc.—had evolved over more than a century or two of trade between and among nations. When the post-war system—the Havana Charter and, as its subset, the provisional GATT was negotiated (at a UN convened plenipotentiary conference), it was only a case of translating these principles and concepts into a treaty.

In the case of services, it was completely uncharted territory. The initial US proposal was for a Ministerial meeting to launch a new trade round to deal with investment and all attendant problems of liberalizing the movement of capital, liberalizing trade in services, including issues of capital investment and the free movement of capital, banking, insurance, shipping, consultancy, data systems, etc., and problems of technology (Raghavan, 1990: 70). At the 1982 GATT Ministerial, and the subsequent processes, the list of services put forward by the US ranged, at one end, from religious missionary activities and the work of philanthropic and charitable organizations to, at the other end, many tangible and intangible services provided for profit.

After considerable, lengthy, protracted and difficult negotiations, which at one stage threatened to split apart the GATT trading system itself, negotiations were launched on "trade in services", with negotiations to aim at establishing a multilateral framework of principles and rules for trade in services, including elaboration of possible disciplines for individual sectors, with a view to expansion of such trade under conditions of transparency and progressive liberalization and as a means of promoting economic growth of all trading partners and the development of developing countries. It was agreed that such framework "shall respect" the policy objectives of national laws and regulations applying to services and shall take into account the work of relevant international organizations (Raghavan, 1990).

From the outset of the preparatory processes and the negotiations on GATS, the US position was that services had to be provided on the spot to the consumers, and the only effective way to provide the service was through establishment or investment. At the same time, the US viewed its own services market as fully liberalized and thus having commercial value, and initially sought: (a) rights for its service providers to invest or establish in WTO member countries, and (b) national treatment in the WTO member countries for US foreign investor/service providers on the analogy of the GATT's "national treatment provisions" for imported goods. On the other hand, the US did not agree to the fundamental MFN principle of trade and wanted to provide only a reciprocally negotiated conditional MFN commitment for individual countries.

During the UR negotiations, the US kept repeatedly going back to some of its initial stances, in particular automatic right for investment and establishment, national treatment, and negotiated MFN only. This impasse ended when the concept of trade in services by four modes of delivery was evolved and agreed to. And as against the initial US position that a country should commit to allowing all services to be traded, subject only to specified listed exceptions by each country, the compromise was on the basis of the GATS framework—for periodic rounds of negotiations on liberalizing services, and the adoption of what is called a "positive listing" approach: countries agreeing to open their markets in specified service sectors or sub-sectors, and subject to limitations they would inscribe in their schedules—under national treatment, market access limitations, and MFN treatment exceptions. The removal or reduction of these limitations could be the subject of future rounds of GATS negotiations. In the current Doha round, there are both bilateral and plurilateral requests for removal or reduction of limitations set in country schedules in the UR outcome.

In the final stages, in the last quarter of 1993, when the newly elected Clinton administration turned its attention to the UR negotiations, on the issue of FS and negotiating market access, as part of the framework accord in GATS, the US withdrew all its "offers" on financial services and went back to its original stance, upsetting a very delicate balance that had been reached over six years of negotiations, and the tentative agreement in the UR package, including on the framework of the services accord, with bilateral market access negotiations in services set to begin on 26 November and working towards a final overall agreement by 15 December. The US Treasury argued that given its very large and open market for financial services, the US could not agree to commit itself to provide access in its markets to financial services providers of other Members on the basis of the MFN provision—namely, extending to all members the outcome of its bilateral market access accords with anyone. The US conceded that many developing countries did not have the regulatory structures and prudential regulations and systems in place, and this would take time to set up. But, the US sought and insisted upon "reciprocal commitments", with developing countries having to agree with the US to fully liberalize their markets for financial services over an agreed phased period of six to seven years, to be able to get a right for their own financial service institutions to set themselves up in the US and offer financial services.

These US positions were so fundamentally at variance with compromises that had been so painfully negotiated and tentatively agreed to, that other participants said that this would require a complete renegotiation of the GATS and, since there was no time, the services talks would have to be abandoned. Alternatively, the US was told, it would force every other participant to withdraw their own offers on the table, and enter similar reservations to that of the US, in effect nullifying GATS. On financial services in particular, a number of participants made clear that they too would withdraw all their financial services offers, limiting their MFN commitment in this sector to assuring existing market access, and reserving all future liberalizations to non-MFN basis. Some, like Egypt, actually withdrew their financial services offers, while others, like India, Brazil and some ASEAN countries stipulated that their own offers were conditional on the US changing its position. This would have resulted in a UR accord with a GATS component that would have virtually excluded a major "services sector", on whose liberalization much of the ostensible benefits of the Round seemed to depend, namely financial services. The non-MFN provisions in this, as in several other areas, would have made the UR a multilateral negotiation to get for the industrial world the right to derogate from the MFN principle. Finally, the accord on GATS became possible only when the US compromised on the GATS framework, but enabling continuance of the FS negotiations beyond Marrakesh (as unfinished UR negotiations).

Article XXVIII of GATS provides definitions for a number of terms used such as "supply of a service", "measures", "measures on trade in services", etc. However, GATS does not provide a definition of services as such. Under article 3 (b), "services" include any service in any sector "except services supplied in the exercise of government authority". Article 3 (c) provides that a "service supplied in the exercise of government authority" means any service which is supplied neither on a commercial basis nor in competition with one or more service suppliers.

Some of the key articles of the GATS framework agreement are: Article II, a general obligation for MFN or non-discriminatory treatment as between members (subject to some qualifications and initial exemptions), Article III on transparency, Article XVI on market access, Article XVII on national treatment, and Article XIX on progressive liberalization through specific commitments in periodic rounds of negotiations for liberalization.

The GATS adopts what is called a positive list or bottom-up approach to Members making commitments in sectors and sub-sectors that they specify in a schedule. This means that members agree to accept commitments to liberalize and provide market access for trade in services in specified sectors and sub-sectors. The initial US, Canadian, European and Japanese positions favored what is called negative list, or top-down approach; that is all tradable services are to be allowed, excepting those specified in a list as excluded and scheduled. This was unacceptable to developing countries for whom the whole area of trade in services was completely new.

[The negative list approach is being used by both the US and the EU in current and ongoing negotiations for free trade agreements (FTA) with developing countries—e.g., the EU-Cariforum agreement. And developing country governments agreeing to and joining such FTAs are short-changing themselves and their future.]

Under GATS, any limitations on MFN treatment were to be listed in a country's schedule of initial UR commitments and could be the subject of negotiations in subsequent rounds with a view to removal or dilution. Any limitation would be in terms of providing more favorable treatment to service suppliers of another country or countries or regional groupings under specific agreements.

Market access as such is not defined by GATS. However, six categories of measures are prohibited (Article XVI: 2) unless they are specified in a country's schedule for each of the four modes of supply. These prohibited categories are: a) limitations on the number of service suppliers—whether numerical quotas, monopolies, exclusive service-suppliers or requirements of an economic needs test; b) limitations on the total value of service transactions or assets in the form of quotas or the requirements of an economic needs test; c) limitations on the number of service operations or quantity of service output; d) limitations on the number of natural persons that may be employed; e) limitations on the type of legal entities through which a service is supplied; and f) limitations on the permissible size of foreign capital in terms of maximum percentage limits on foreign share-holding or total value of individual or aggregate foreign investment.

National treatment under GATS Article XVII is defined as treatment no less favorable than that accorded to a domestic service supplier. Deviations from national treatment are to be listed and included in a country's schedule of commitments. There are two provisions, in paragraphs (d) and (e) of Article XIV, "General Exceptions", that enable derogations from national treatment in some tax matters.

Other key provisions include: Article III: on transparency of relevant policy measures; Article IV: facilitation of increased participation of developing countries in services trade; Article X: emergency safeguard measures in certain circumstances, prescribing further multilateral negotiations on this subject in the future; Article XII: restrictions that may be imposed in the event of serious balance-of-payments difficulties of a country; Article XIV: exceptions dictated by requirements of public order, health, securing compliance with laws and regulations (not inconsistent with GATS) to prevent deceptive or fraudulent practices or default on a service contract and protection of privacy of individuals in processing and dissemination of personal data and confidentiality of individual records or accounts, and safety; and Article XIV bis: security exceptions. Article XV on subsidies recognizes that, in certain circumstances, subsidies may have distortive effects on trade in services and calls for ("shall enter into") negotiations to develop multilateral disciplines and appropriateness of countervailing (CV) measures, explicitly recognize the role of subsidies in the development programs of developing countries. For purposes of the negotiations on disciplines for subsidies, the article also requires members to exchange information on all subsidies related to trade in services provided to domestic service suppliers. No rules or disciplines have been set so far.

Some areas are envisaged for further GATS negotiations, and technically are on the Doha agenda.

Emergency Safeguard Measures (ESM) under Article X

In several developing countries, and in particular in Asia, domestic constituencies and stakeholders opposed liberalization measures in the financial sector, especially after their experiences during and after the 1997-98 Asian financial crisis. Here governments and their policy makers sought to reduce opposition by holding out reassurances to their domestic constituencies that they would arm themselves with powers to invoke ESM in the services trade, and in financial services in particular, before making any more concessions in the Doha Round.

Judging merely by the list of papers and documents on the issue before the negotiators, this is an area of GATS rules negotiations where there has been the most intensive engagement, and considerable work has been done at technical levels; yet until now, there is no clarity about "who is to be protected against what and how".

The ESM notion, embodied in the goods agreement, is difficult to operate in the structure of the GATS trade flows in four modes; and it will be even more difficult to prove or defend an ESM in the services area in a dispute, absent clear data for each of the modes. There are complicated methodological issues and problems, which make it almost impossible to devise an across-the-board set of disciplines applicable to all modes. The other trade-remedy instrument used in goods trade—anti-dumping and countervailing measures—is not foreseen in GATS.

Subsidies (Article XV of the GATS)

GATS envisages future negotiations for multilateral disciplines in services to avoid the trade-distortive effects of subsidization on trade in services, the appropriateness of CV measures, and to provide for such CV measures. GATS has no provisions analogous to GATT Article XVI (subsidies) and Article VI (CV measures)—concepts taken and expanded in the disciplines of the Subsidies and Countervailing Measures (SCM) Agreement. Framing the subsidies disciplines for GATS, especially for banking and financial services, would pose several methodological issues as complicated as for ESM. Article XV uses the mandatory "shall", both for entering into the negotiations and for recognizing the role of subsidies in the development programs of developing countries and the need for flexibility.

And, unlike in GATT, GATS has no analogous provisions on dumping and unfair trade. GATS has also no analogous provisions to GATT Article III: 8 (excluding national treatment for purchases by government or government agencies of products for government consumption, and excluding from subsidy disciplines government subsidies in such purchases).

Some of the requests in the Doha round, for example, include removal of the requirement for capital adequacy ratios of a foreign bank's operation as a "branch" in a country and the deposits, etc., in it, preferring instead to use the capital available to the principal that is presumably cheaper. However, the collapse of Lehman brothers, and its consequences in the absence of international bankruptcy arrangements, has led to rethinking, with some of these very same countries now "ring-fencing" the assets of foreign financial firms (whether branches or incorporated subsidiaries) operating within their jurisdiction.

And when, as now, the US, UK and other major developed countries have gone to the rescue of their banks and have provided them with subsidized credit from the governments and the central banks concerned, the subsidizing effects have aroused concerns, even among some global players. On the face of it, absent GATS disciplines on subsidies, nothing much can be done. However, such subsidies may be open to WTO challenge, where governments have made commitments on the basis of the Understanding, and without inscribing national treatment exceptions. The US and the EU, in Part 1 of their services schedules, Horizontal

Commitments, have entered some reservations on national treatment in respect of the provision of subsidies, limiting it generally to nationals, incorporated enterprises with national majority shareholding, etc. In the case of the US, on the face of it, the reservations do not appear to cover the current Troubled Assets Relief Program (TARP) and other funding for banks and other financial enterprises, including the latest moves of providing government guarantees and subsidies to private investors to buy the "toxic assets" of banks. Complicating the problems of interpretation, the US headnote to its Financial Services Schedule under the Fifth Protocol says: "Commitments in these sub-sectors are undertaken in accordance with the Understanding on Commitments in Financial Services (the "Understanding"), subject to the limitations and conditions set forth in these headnotes and the schedule below." This makes it a happy hunting ground for trade lawyers to argue whether the headnotes to the 1997 US FSA schedule in effect overrides the 1993 reservations in market access under Horizontal Commitments. But it may introduce another uncertainty for policy-makers, regulators and administrators.

There are equally difficult problems in the insurance area, in particular, in some non-life insurance and reinsurance sectors. All these may need revisiting, in the light of likely and forthcoming regulatory reforms: some of the GATS provisions and existing commitments by Members on subsidization, national treatment and admission of commercial presence in the form of branches as opposed to locally incorporated subsidiaries.

GATS Negotiating Rounds for Progressive Liberalization

Article XIX on progressive liberalization provides for periodic rounds of negotiations for liberalization, and for the WTO Council for Trade in Services (CTS), the WTO body mandated to facilitate the operation of GATS, to establish, for each round, negotiating guidelines on the basis of an assessment of trade in services, in overall terms and on a sectoral basis, with reference to the objectives of the agreement, including increased participation of developing countries in the services trade.

Absent adequate and relevant data on overall and sectoral trades in services and of participation by developing countries (the issue is discussed in detail in the G24 working paper), this important requirement has not been carried out in any measurable quantitative terms for the current Doha Round and cannot be undertaken for future rounds either. With the major developed countries the overwhelming exporters of services, particularly financial services, it has been part of the strategy of the leading US and

European service coalitions, and of the WTO/GATS secretariat, to "sell" liberalization in the services sector as essential for growth and development, lack of data notwithstanding (Freeman, 2000; see also Annexes 3A and 3B of the Working Paper, and Raghavan, 2002). Qualitative judgments on assessments of services trade, in overall and sectoral terms, tend to be theoretical and theological on liberalization and its benefits.

At a minimum for achieving the mandatory requirement under GATS Article XIX, and even for BW-II itself, the UN General Assembly needs to mandate UN statisticians, in a time-bound process (and without delegating it to others) and accountable to the UN membership, to revisit the issue of a manual for collection of data on trade in services, and ensure a way for data collection to reflect needs of governments in GATS negotiations. They must be asked to recommend a methodology for adoption by the UN General Assembly (UNGA) to be followed by UN members for collecting and reporting national and international data on trade in services according to the GATS definitions, and not in the manner it has been dealt with so far as explained in paragraphs 2.72, 2.73 and 2.74 of the 2001 manual (ST/ESA/STAT/SER.M/86; UN sales No.E.02.XVII.11). In effect, the manual suggests that the statisticians disregarded the mandate given to them to draw up guidelines to collect data on trade in services as defined in GATS, but adopted their own views on services and trade in services.

Also important to keep in mind, particularly in terms of the ongoing processes for BW-II and any regulatory, governance or other changes, would be Article XXI for the modification of schedules or withdrawal of concessions, and provisions of the Marrakesh Treaty if any changes are to be made in the GATS. Modification or withdrawal of concessions in a schedule would require renegotiation with interested members and provision of compensation; if any changes need to be made to the provisions of the GATS itself, it may involve the processes envisaged in the Marrakesh Treaty for amendments. The difficulties and challenges the US has been facing in withdrawing its initial commitments in GATS to provide access for gambling services—both in terms of compensating Antigua and Barbuda who won a dispute against the US over restrictions on Internet gambling, and in getting the agreement of other interested parties—bear this out. In its schedule at the end of the UR, the US had agreed to a market access commitment under "Recreational Services (except Sporting)" item 10D of the central product classification list, and the US had placed no limitations under supply modes 1, 2 and 3. "Internet Gambling services" was found by a panel to be covered under this item under mode 1 supply!

GATS and the Financial Services Agreement

As mentioned earlier, the GATS as an integral part of the WTO, and its FS Annex supplements and interprets some parts of the GATS in relation to financial services—definitions, prudential carve-outs, and some requirements in disputes. But the FS is not a stand-alone agreement, and parties have to conform to the FS, the GATS and other parts of the WTO agreements.

Paragraph 1 of the GATS Annex on financial services sets out the scope and definition of the annex; para 2 provides for a "prudential carve-out" for the sector from the disciplines on domestic regulation; in para 3, there is provision for recognizing the prudential measures of another Member; para 4 has a provision on dispute settlement, requiring panels in disputes on financial services and prudential issues to have the necessary expertise relevant to the specific financial service, and para 5 has the definition of financial services (Legal Texts, 1994: 355-358).

Para 5(a) of the Annex provides a definition of financial services that is both vague and all encompassing, and has an illustrative list of some 16 items that are declared to be "included" in the definition (Legal Texts, 1994: 355-358). However, the definition in 5(a) is much wider than the illustrative list: "A financial service is any service of a financial nature offered by a financial service supplier of a Member" (Gould, 2008; Cornford, 2004). Financial services include all insurance and insurance-related services, and all banking and other financial services (excluding insurance). According to Freeman (formerly of AMEX), who was prime mover in the GATS/FS negotiations and outcome, the term "financial services", encompasses not only banks, insurance companies and securities companies, and others enumerated, but also such enterprises as H&R Block, one of the largest, accounting firms in the United States and operating in about twenty countries; and so is EDS, which does back-office work for American Express Bank, Citibank, and others around the world; credit card processors, such as MBNA, Reuters Information, Standard & Poor's, which operates in 100 countries or something like that, and asset management companies are all financial services companies. (Most recently, a trade dispute between the US and EU on one side and China on the other, related to operations of Reuters, Bloomberg and AP Dow Jones financial news services in the Chinese market, and was settled as an issue involving Chinese commitment on market access to financial enterprises. At the time of writing, the actual terms of the settlement were yet to be notified to the WTO).

On "Domestic Regulations," the annex provides for a prudential carve-out. Under Para 2 of the Annex,

> "Notwithstanding any other provisions of this agreement, a Member shall not be prevented from taking measures for prudential reasons, including for protection of investors, depositors, policy-holders or persons to whom a fiduciary duty is owed by a financial service supplier, or to ensure the integrity and stability of the financial system". However, this is qualified by a second sentence in the same paragraph: "Where such measures do not conform to the provisions of this Agreement, they shall not be used as a means of avoiding the Members' commitments or obligations under the Agreement."

On the one hand, this is a wide-ranging and sweeping carve-out from any disciplines that may be fashioned under the GATS provisions for disciplines on regulations. The prudential carve-out, on the face of it, appears wide enough to cover any reforms out of the BW-II processes for closer oversight of the financial institutions from a fiduciary or systemic viewpoint. However, the measures and character of measures permitted under the heading "prudential measures" are not spelt out. In addition, the 30-odd countries that accepted the "Understanding" and signed the FSA and filed schedules under the Fifth protocol, have undertaken a standstill on "existing non-conformist measures" (Legal Texts, 1994: 478).

This leaves open the possibility of a challenge through a dispute process at the WTO, where three panelists (selected by the secretariat, and serviced and guided by the secretariat in the panel process) will decide on "facts", and the AB on WTO law, on whether the measures taken properly fall within the prudential carve-out provisions (see Stichele, 2005; 2006). In disputes, panels and the AB have adopted a case-by-case approach. This might inject a situation of uncertainty in as important a sector as a financial system, national and global.

One set of questions under this heading is likely to be measures taken as part of the restructuring of banking sectors in the aftermath of financial crises such as that which broke out in Asia in 1997. Such restructurings can take place over an extended period of time, thus posing the question whether all the actions involved can be classified as being covered by the reference to system integrity and stability. Moreover, the restructuring may also be accompanied by substantial injections of government money in forms which some may consider as distorting competition and discriminating against foreign suppliers of financial services (Cornford, 2004: 15).

This question, posed in the aftermath of the Asian financial crisis and the restructuring of financial institutions with considerable injections of government funds in South Korea, has now acquired much greater topicality in light of actions in the US, UK, France, etc. So far, there is no WTO/GATS jurisprudence (or panel rulings) on such an issue. In the South Korean case, the provision of government funds to recapitalize the banks and loans to industry were challenged under the SCM Agreement of the GATT/WTO. However, in the case of the US, and others who signed on to the Understanding and the negative list approach, and without a national treatment exception, some of the current measures may be open to challenge as de facto discrimination. The guidelines for scheduling commitments approved by the Council on Trade in Services say:

> "Article XVII [national treatment] applies to subsidies in the same way that it applies to all other measures. ...any subsidy which is a discriminatory measure within the meaning of Article XVII would have to be either scheduled as a limitation on national treatment or brought into conformity with that Article. Subsidies are also not excluded from the scope of Article II (MFN)". In line with this, the guideline adds: "a binding under Article XVII with respect to the granting of a subsidy does not require a Member to offer such a subsidy to a services supplier located in the territory of another Member."

Overall, the 1997 FSA (the Fifth Protocol of the WTO that entered into force on 1 March 1999) "is generally regarded as having contributed to more transparent policy regimes in the organization's member countries. But its contribution to the opening of markets to foreign suppliers varied greatly among the different parties to the agreement" (Cornford, 2004: 2). As a result of the 1997 Agreement and the Fifth Protocol, a total of 104 members had commitments of varying degrees in financial services. Three of them, the United States, India and Thailand withdrew their broad MFN exemptions based on reciprocity; a small number of countries submitted limited MFN exemptions or maintained existing broad MFN exemptions; several others reduced the scope of their MFN exemptions. The US submitted a limited MFN exemption in insurance, applicable in a circumstance of forced divestiture of US ownership in insurance service providers operating in WTO Member countries; this was principally aimed at Malaysia, but as a contingent, future conditional withdrawal of MFN, based on a US unilateral determination of another member's future measures, it is of doubtful WTO-GATS legality.

In scheduling their GATS commitments under the Fifth Protocol, various members (the vast majority) did so according to the provisions of Part III of the GATS (Articles XVI, XVII and XVIII), viewing the "alternative approach" promoted—in the Understanding—as only a voluntary guideline that could not be invoked against them, once their schedule of market access commitments (subject to limitations entered in their schedules) had been scrutinized, accepted and multilateralized. Some, like Japan, not trusting future jurisprudence on "prudential regulations and scope" under the Annex, entered them as limitations on market access and/or horizontal commitments.

The US took a different approach in scheduling its commitments: the headnotes to its schedule of commitments under the Fifth Protocol (GATS/SC/90/Suppl.3) has by reference incorporated the Understanding as part of its commitments—subject only to the limitations it has set out in the schedules. The US headnotes on "all insurance and insurance-related services" and "banking and other financial services (excluding insurance)" are set out in Annex 2 of the Working Paper.

However, the US has made no national treatment exception in its financial services schedule (though it has a horizontal national limitation on its services schedule as a whole), it is not clear whether the subsidies now being received as a result of the various rescue measures taken by the Treasury and the US Fed (TARP loans, and ability of some firms to raise loans on easier terms because of government guarantees, and other very non-transparent measures) in respect of the AIG conglomerate—resulting in the US government currently owning 80 percent of the company and *de facto* controlling it—fall within the national treatment exceptions in the US commitments. If the subsidies, *de jure* or *de facto*, are not available to all insurers, the US may be open to a WTO challenge by any other Member whose government-owned or government-controlled insurance enterprise is refused market access in any of the states enumerated in the US schedule, on the ground that it is "government-owned or government-controlled".

The US schedule also has an attachment titled: "Additional Commitments Paper II", which says in part: "(1) The Administration has expressed its support for Glass-Steagall reform on a national treatment basis and *will work with Congress to achieve an appropriate framework to accomplish this objective*" (emphasis added).

The US attachment itself is in the nature of a "best endeavor" commitment by the US administration implemented later. Subsequent to the entry into force of the Fifth Protocol, in 1999, the US repealed the Banking Act of 1933, more popularly known as the Glass-Steagall Act or the Second Glass Steagall Act; the first, in 1932, expanded the Federal Reserve's ability to offer rediscounts on more types of assets and issue government bonds as well as commercial paper. The 1933 Act had erected barriers between enterprises engaged in normal commercial banking operations and so-called investment bank enterprises engaged in securities and other trading operations. The repealing legislation, US Public Law 106-102, known as the "Gramm-Leach-Bliley Act", signed into law by President Clinton on 12 November 1999, became effective in mid-February 2000. An issue that arises in the context of the current discussions on course reversal, and putting in place strong regulatory measures and firewalls between normal banking activities and trading activities is whether the US can reverse course, by changing or amending the Gramm-Leach-Bliley Act? The jurisprudence on GATS in general, and in particular on financial services is rather sparse. Under the old GATT, in terms of the protocol of provisional application and the grandfathering of existing legal provisions in individual contracting parties, the jurisprudence developed after the mid-1950s seems to indicate that a contracting party can take steps fully or partially to change the grandfathered provisions of its laws to comply with GATT obligations, but may not reverse course. It is somewhat unclear whether any WTO member would raise a dispute and challenge the US in terms of the FSA commitments set out above, if and when (as seems likely) the US enacts domestic legislation to put some firewalls between purely banking operations, and trading operations—of investment banks, brokerage or security trading operations of banking enterprises.

Also, the European Commission (EC) and others who signed on to the Understanding and scheduled financial services commitments under the Fifth Protocol to the GATS, have thus committed themselves to a standstill on regulations. As such, some of their recent measures, purportedly claimed to fall under "prudential carve-out measures" such as bans on short-selling of shares in banks, etc., may be contrary to their WTO/GATS obligations, and thus subject to a dispute process (see SOMO, 2009).

Current Negotiations: The Doha Round

A new round of negotiations on trade in services (as mandated by Article XIX: 1 of GATS) technically began on 1 January 2000 and in March 2001, the Council on Trade in Services adopted Guidelines and the Procedures for the Negotiations on Trade in Services, 2002). The services negotiations were rolled over and made part of the single undertaking of the Work Programme and Negotiations launched at Doha in November 2001. The Doha Ministerial Declaration confirmed the CTS guidelines set in March. Current negotiations for further liberalization of the trade in financial services are part of this exercise; some of the issues covered in the general negotiations on services have implications for the trade in financial services too. A detailed analysis of the Doha Round services negotiations can be found in the WP, and are not detailed here. But two issues are highly relevant to the various moves for global restructuring of the financial sectors.

Even prior to the launch of the Doha Round, the GATS Council on Trade in Services has adopted (May 1997) in respect of "accountancy services" the Guidelines for Mutual Recognition Agreements or Arrangements in the Accountancy Sector, and following that in December 1998 by the Disciplines on Domestic Regulation in the Accountancy Sector. These will become effective as part of the Doha single undertaking.

While accounting and auditing services constitute the core activities of accountancy firms, a wide range of additional services may also be offered, most notably merger audits, insolvency services, tax advice, investment services and management consulting. Accountancy firms are among the world's largest suppliers of such consultancy services. One of the elements identified as having facilitated the current financial crisis has been the nexus between accountancy firms and the financial firms, they not only audit, but provide a range of other services—the most lucrative aspect of these firms. The same accountancy firms are retained over long periods of time, and sometimes only a new set of auditors uncover problems. This is what happened in the Parmalat scandal in Italy, where statutorily auditors have to be changed after nine years! In Switzerland, auditors of banking institutions have the primary statutory obligation to notify the authorities of any irregularities or violation of banking regulations that are found. If countries, members of WTO/GATS, attempt to introduce such provisions in their statutes on audit and accounting of firms, it may be violative of the agreed Disciplines on Domestic Regulation in the Accountancy Sector. Apart from this, Accountancy is included in the new services negotiations, which began in January 2000, and has been rolled into the Doha single undertaking.

As set out in the proposals and presentations of key members of the CTS, and in its subordinate bodies, including the Committee on Trade in Financial Services (CTFS), there are also attempts at clarifications (limitations) on regulatory powers (domestic regulations provisions of GATS). Also on the agenda are proposals for adoption by developing countries, and their enforcement through the WTO dispute settlement process, of so-called financial, accounting, insurance and other standards and practices set by "international" supervisory organizations, coupled with pressures for expanded market access through commercial presence (investment) for transnational corporate service providers. Parallel to these efforts at the WTO are the moves to use the IMF and its assistance packages or its Article IV surveillance to force "emerging markets" to adopt standards set by the Basel-based Bank for International Settlements (BIS), associated institutions such as the Basel Committee on Banking Standards (BCBS), the Financial Stability Forum (FSF), international security market supervisors and others, as a price for the IMF's positive assessment of their financial sectors.

Besides the proposals and demands for expansion and liberalization of financial services in the Doha Round, through pressure on developing countries to commit themselves to increased commercial presence without limitations and in any form the supplier deems appropriate, there are also demands for liberalization of accounting, auditing and other professional services. In terms of the current GATS negotiations, particularly over financial services, a whole range of new regulatory issues—at both national and international levels, such as the functioning of the US-sanctioned oligopoly of global rating agencies—have come up, with calls for regulating them. Each and every one of these will have an effect on the trade in financial services, and some of the regulatory reforms. And most of them may come in the way of reforms agreed in other forums.

In the current Doha Round, the leaked information on requests to major developing countries by some of the developed country demandeurs (oftentimes, acting in concert with the US and the EU) suggests that the major developing countries have been "requested" to undertake commitments "in accordance with the Understanding".

At least in hindsight, the source of the current financial crisis—whose contours and extent are still not clear, but which is overall estimated to involve a few trillion dollars of "assets"—appears to be in many cases, "the alphabet soup" of credit default swaps, collateralized debt obligations, "insurance contracts" guaranteeing their values and payments, and several trades in derivatives, whose markets are unregulated and non-transparent. If the requests made on them are accepted by developing countries, it will preclude regulation and banning of trade in such derivatives. And developing countries will be fully enveloped in the next financial crisis.

A question that needs to be seriously weighed in country capitals now, and more so in capitals of developing countries, is the real implications of GATS as an "agreement" of the WTO system. Within it, the wisdom of further market access openings and concessions—more so in mode 3, and to some extent, in modes 1 and 2, in a wide range of financial services, without reaching a clearer understanding, and arriving at prior agreements to strengthen and enforce regulations rather than reducing them—is also a question. Even the wisdom of financial globalization and its benefits would need to be re-assessed in capitals.

The Doha Round of negotiations are at an impasse (Raghavan, 2009), with major public attention focused on agriculture and non-agricultural market access issues. Notwithstanding the efforts to shift the focus away from financial sector reforms to the trade front, it is probable that the trade negotiations may not reach a conclusion for a year or two. This gives developing countries time and opportunity to examine their own particular situations, think through their particular needs, and, if needed, revisit proposals and partial tentative accords in the trade negotiations, including on financial services and GATS rules.

In theory, WTO governance structures and consensus decision-making, with every member having the theoretical right to object, enables developing countries to have an equal voice. However, in practice, while developing countries and their groups have been able to prevent certain actions and policy courses, they have not been so successful in prevailing in a positive way. Preserving the *status quo* will not be beneficial to the developing world.

References

Das, Bhagirath Lal (1999). *The World Trade Organization: A Guide to the Framework for International Trade*. Third World Network and Zed Books, Penang and London.

Das, Bhagirath Lal (2003). *The WTO and the Multilateral Trading System: Past, Present and Future*. Third World Network, Penang, and Zed Books, London.

Colares, Juscelino F. (2009). A theory of WTO adjudication: From empirical analysis to biased rule development. *Vanderbilt Journal of Transnational Law*, 42 (2): 383-439.

Cornford, Andrew (2004). The WTO negotiations on inancial services: Current issues and future directions. UNCTAD Discussion Paper 172, UNCTAD, Geneva.

Economist (2009). Coming in from the cold. *Economist*, 8 January.

Freeman, Harry (2000). Comments and discussion. Financial services and the GATS 2000 round. Brookings-Wharton Papers on Financial Services, Brookings Institution, Washington, DC: 455-461.

Gould, Ellen (2008). Financial instability and the GATS negotiations. Briefing Paper, Canadian Centre for Policy Alternatives, 9 (4), July: 1-22.

Keynes, John Maynard (1980) [1944]. *The Collected Writings of John Maynard Keynes Vol. XXVI*. Edited by Donald Moggridge. Macmillan and Cambridge University Press, London and Cambridge.

Legal Texts (1994). *Legal Texts. The Results of the Uruguay Round of Multilateral Trade Negotiations*. GATT Secretariat, Geneva.

Lester, Simon (2009). The GATT/GATS overlap. International economic law and policy blog. 15 January, http: //worldtradelaw.typepad.com/ielpblog/2009/01/should-the-gatt-and-the-gats-be-merged.html

Raghavan, Chakravarthi (1990). *Recolonization: GATT, Uruguay Round and the Third World*. Third World Network, Penang, and Zed Books, London.

Raghavan, Chakravarthi (2000). *The World Trade Organization and Its Dispute Settlement System: Tilting the Balance against the South*. TWN Trade and Development Series no. 9, Third World Network, Penang.

Raghavan, Chakravarthi (2002). *Developing Countries and Services Trade: Chasing a Black Cat in a Dark Room, blindfolded*. Third World Network, Penang.

Raghavan, Chakravarthi (2009). Round that no one wanted, now proving difficult to end. *SUNS*, 6622: 2-5; *Third World Economics*, 442: 14-16.

Richardson, Paul (1997). The general theory in an open economy. In G.C. Harcourt and P.A. Riach (eds). *'A Second Edition' of the General Theory, Vol. 2*. Routledge, London.

Roessler, Frieder (2001). The institutional balance between the judicial and political organs of the WTO. In R.B. Porter, P. Sauve, A. Subramanyan and A.B. Zampetti (eds). *Efficiency, Equity and Legitimacy: The Multilateral Trading System at the Millennium*. Brookings Institution Press, Washington, DC.

SOMO (2009). Dossiers on EPAs, GATS, investment and WTO. Centre for Research on Multinational Corporations, SOMO, Amsterdam. http: //somo.nl/dossiers-en/trade-investment

Stichele, Myriam Vander (2005). Critical issues in the financial industry. SOMO financial sector report, April 2005 (updated). SOMO, Amsterdam. http://www.somo.nl/html/paginas/pdf/Financial_sector_report_05_NL.pdf (accessed 22 March 2008).

Stichele, Myriam Vander (2006). GATS negotiations in financial services: The EU requests and their implications for developing countries. SOMO, Amsterdam. http: //somo.nl/publications-en/Publication_601/at_download/fullfile

10

Cross-Border Tax Evasion and Bretton Woods II[1]

David Spencer

Setting the Scene: The Issues of Cross-Border Tax Evasion

The problem of tax evasion and its cost to the community, and to development in developing countries, has a higher profile than ever. This has been given extra impetus by two recent events. One is the coming to light of Union Bank of Switzerland (UBS) employing practices that facilitated tax evasion by high wealth United States clients. These UBS practices included maintaining—for an estimated 19,000 US clients—"undeclared" accounts in Switzerland with allegedly US$17.9 billion in assets that were not disclosed to US tax authorities; assisting US clients in structuring their accounts to avoid US reporting requirements; and allowing its Swiss bankers to market securities and banking services on US soil without an appropriate license (*WSJ*, 2009a: A1; *NYT*, 2009a).

A second high profile tax affair arose when authorities obtained data about the clients of LGT Bank—owned by Liechtenstein's royal family—that led to high-profile investigations of prominent German citizens. Other countries also launched similar investigations (Spencer, 2008b; 2008c), and after considerable pressure on Liechtenstein, it agreed, in May 2009, to adopt global standards on transparency and information exchange in tax matters (*NYT*, 2009b).

Such instances bring home to a wider public the reality previously known only to those aware of international banking practices. On a larger scale, the current international financial crisis has highlighted the need for a historic and fundamental restructuring of the international financial architecture. The Financial Stability Forum (FSF)—re-established as the

Financial Stability Board (FSB)—and the G20 governments have been planning and are implementing this restructuring, which will hopefully broaden and intensify international regulatory cooperation, and limit regulatory arbitrage. This restructuring is expected to undermine non-transparent systems, including what the Bank for International Settlements (BIS) has referred to as the "shadow banking system", generally defined as involving "the setting up of banks, bank-like institutions and funds, including hedge funds, private equity operations, and structured investment vehicles—conduits used by mainstream investment banks and others—in jurisdictions ('tax havens') outside the main financial centers and outside their regulatory reach."[2]

One likely result of this restructuring of the international financial architecture will be more international tax cooperation, including increased efforts against cross-border tax evasion and other illicit cross-border financial flows. *First*, substantively, the restructuring will confront non-transparent systems, limiting the role of bank secrecy and confidentiality, and weakening the role and influence of tax haven jurisdictions, which at present facilitate and encourage cross-border tax evasion and other illicit financial flows. *Second*, procedurally, the restructuring will strengthen the framework of international financial cooperation, which will provide a more receptive setting for, and facilitate, increased international tax cooperation.

Initial Restructuring Steps

The call for negotiations for the proposed restructuring of the international financial architecture has been referred to as a "Bretton Woods II", referring to the 1944 conference in Bretton Woods, New Hampshire, that designed the post-Second World War international financial architecture.

A first step in the current restructuring was the issuance by the FSF in April 2008 of its Report on Enhancing Market and Institutional Resilience (FSF Report).[3] The FSF Report focused on systemic issues and the factors that have contributed to systemic risk in the global financial crisis. With 67 specific recommendations, the FSF Report proposed greater international regulatory coordination and cooperation by a variety of international organizations and national regulatory authorities (Spencer, 2008a).

A second step in the restructuring of the international financial architecture was the 15 November 2008, Summit on Financial Markets and the World Economy, a meeting in Washington, DC, of the G20 group of countries (2008 Financial Summit).[4] The decisions at that meeting appear in the Declaration of the Summit on Financial Markets and the World Economy.[5]

The 2008 Summit Declaration establishes five "common principles for reform", which were detailed in the Action Plan to Implement Principles for Reform attached to the Declaration. They are: (1) strengthening transparency and accountability, (2) enhancing sound regulation, (3) promoting integrity in financial markets, (4) reinforcing international cooperation, and (5) reforming international financial institutions. It also called for certain "immediate actions by 31 March 2009" and other "medium term actions".

The section on promoting integrity in financial markets states explicitly: "We will also promote information sharing, including with respect to jurisdictions that have yet to commit to international standards with respect to bank secrecy and transparency…. Tax authorities, drawing upon the work of relevant bodies such as the Organization for Economic Cooperation and Development (OECD), should continue efforts to promote tax information exchange. Lack of transparency and a failure to exchange tax information should be vigorously addressed" (2008 Financial Summit Declaration, p. 4).

Bretton Woods I: Control of Capital Inflows?

The 1944 Bretton Woods conference provides some guidance on how the present international financial architecture could be restructured with regard to international tax cooperation. The principal architects of the conference, John Maynard Keynes (of the United Kingdom) and Harry Dexter White (of the United States), were concerned about large scale capital flights from war-devastated Europe to the USA in the post-Second World War period. Keynes and White recognized the difficulty of implementing effective controls on capital outflows, but proposed that countries receiving capital inflows should share information about those capital inflows with the countries from which the capital came. The US financial community strongly opposed the proposals about governments sharing information to control capital flight, so the Articles of Agreement of the International Monetary Fund (IMF) ultimately did not require the exchange of information (Epstein, 2005).

Scope of Change

High profile figures, such as Christine Lagarde, the French Minister of Economic Affairs, Industry and Employment, have more recently noted the need for broader coverage of supervisory and regulatory regimes.[6]

Massive annual cross-border illicit financial flows—heavily laced with cross-border tax evasion—cannot continue to remain basically unregulated. They are, indeed, facilitated and encouraged by non-transparent OECD onshore financial centers and non-transparent offshore financial centers that the regulators in OECD countries permit to exist. Such cross-border illicit financial flows, including tax evasion, distort statutory tax burdens, undermine tax systems and the rule of law, and deprive governments of needed tax revenues and societies of socioeconomic programs.

Process of Change

Tax professionals normally work with "micro" issues and concentrate on existing tax and legal provisions ("the world as it is"). But they should also focus, and be required to focus, on "macro issues" and to better understand the relationship of taxation to financial markets, and the importance of reform or change ("the world as it can and should be").

Two major aspects of the process of change must be recognized in this area. *First*, changes in international finance and international financial laws are constant and natural. They may not be seen day to day, but when viewed over longer periods, e.g., three, five, ten years, the changes, often quite significant, become obvious. These developments in international financial laws have, in effect, been redesigning, step by step, the international financial architecture.[7] This process of change can be called the "Dance Rule" because there is only step-by-step progress.

In a world of constant change and ever-increasing globalization, the question arises: how do national regulators, and also the private sector, coordinate and implement policies and programs internationally? This is the structural mismatch issue. The structure of international regulation has not yet caught up with the international financial and economic changes. International financial law issues are complex, with many different governmental interests and private sector interests involved. So, it takes time to develop consensus and implement multilateral solutions—the responses therefore tend to lag significantly behind the problem they respond to.

The *second* relevant aspect of the process of change is that it will be propelled by unexpected events.[8] For example, the events of 9/11 led to greater efforts to combat terrorist financing and more regulation of some illicit financial flows. The Liechtenstein and UBS tax scandals, noted briefly above and discussed in greater detail elsewhere,[9] and the global financial crisis are three other unexpected events likely to lead to substantial regulatory changes. Just as such changes in international finance and international financial laws could not have been predicted a decade ago, similar unpredictability undoubtedly lies ahead.

Five Relevant Factors

The current international financial crisis is relevant to international tax issues, cross-border tax evasion and the process of change for at least five reasons.

First, as the non-government organization Christian Aid (2008: 11) has emphasized, "financial markets are fundamentally driven by the efficient use of information to price assets and liabilities appropriately. For more than a decade, new asset structures were allowed to develop where no one—not investors nor regulators, nor even market players themselves—could clearly see the underlying value. This complexity was made still more opaque by the deliberate use of tax havens—be it to hide from regulators, tax authorities, investors or competitors." Thus, as a result of lack of transparency, tax havens (secrecy jurisdictions) not only facilitate tax evasion, but also have exacerbated the current financial crisis.

Second, the epicenter of the global financial crisis has been the OECD financial centers, the United States in particular. The fact that governments in OECD countries, especially the financial centers, did not prevent or foresee this international financial crisis shows that regulators in OECD financial centers, and the IMF, are not as omniscient and above criticism as they would like the rest of the world to believe. This has particularly invigorated some OECD countries, perhaps especially those that are not financial centers or are comparatively more comfortable with "cultures of regulation". President Nicolas Sarkozy of France and Chancellor Angela Merkel of Germany have, for example, taken a very public stance against tax havens, especially in the context of the Group of 20 countries (G20) Summit in London on April 2, 2009, and in OECD forums (*FT*, 2009b: 3).

Third, several major financial institutions based in OECD jurisdictions helped cause the global crisis, due in part to non-transparent financial transactions. Those financial institutions required government financial support, were merged into other financial institutions, or were liquidated. If those financial institutions were so omniscient, why did they help cause the crisis? As the *Financial Times* noted so succinctly, "The financial services industry is chief villain in the global recession. As a result, political opinion is no longer comfortable with a weakly-regulated sector. Instead, it strongly favors a tightly restricted one" (*FT*, 2008k: 8).

Fourth, as a result of the worldwide impact of the crisis and its severity, many countries believe that they have an interest and want to participate in the proposed solutions. Initially, this led to the involvement of the G20, which includes Brazil, Russia, India and China (commonly referred to as the "BRICs"[10]), a broader group than the G7, which, over time, will presumably lead to an even larger group of countries becoming involved in designing a new international financial architecture, as evident in the calling for and convening of the United Nations Conference on the World Financial and Economic Crisis and its Impact on Development in New York on 24-26 June 2009.

The international financial crisis has certainly strengthened the positions of non-OECD countries—especially those such as the BRICs, that are G20, but not OECD Members—and has made more acceptable an objective critique of OECD policies and programs (*FT*, 2008e: 9; 2008g: 9). One key non-OECD but G20 country is Brazil, and its President, Luiz Ignacio Lula da Silva, has observed: "In the middle of an unprecedented global crisis, our [Latin American] countries are discovering that they aren't part of the problem. They can and should be fundamental players in the solution" (*NYT*, 2008c: A10). A *Financial Times* November 2008 editorial noted that the crisis has resulted in a shift in economic power, including through the involvement of key emerging economies in the G20 (*FT*, 2008h: 14). Whether that center of gravity shifts towards non-G20 developing countries is a more open question. It remains to be seen whether a real cooperative relationship emerges, or a G20 directed process—under the pretence of wider "ownership"—continues.

The 2008 G20 Summit Declaration stated explicitly in the section on Reforming International Financial Institutions that "The [FSF] must expand urgently to a broader membership of emerging economies, and other major standard setting bodies should promptly review their membership" (O'Neill, 2009). This happened with the April 2009 re-establishment of the Financial Stability Forum as the Financial Stability Board (FSB), with broader participation of all G20 countries (FSF, 2009). The FSB has the task of monitoring global financial stability and promoting medium-term reform.

This increased participation of emerging non-OECD countries could result in significant consequences in the tax area—it could lead them to focus on, and challenge, tax "rules" previously established by the OECD, such as (1) a preference for residence—rather than source—country taxation in the OECD Model Tax Convention, (2) the OECD Transfer Pricing Guidelines for Multinational Enterprises and Tax Administrations of 1995, (3) the OECD concept of exchange of information on request (rather than automatic exchange of information), and (4) tax haven "regimes" in OECD financial centers and offshore financial centers permitted to exist by OECD financial centers and the IMF, which have continued to facilitate massive cross-border illicit financial flows, including tax evasion from developing countries. This shift in power might also motivate emerging countries to become more energized in the UN Committee of Experts on International Cooperation in Tax Matters, whether or not that Committee is upgraded into an inter-governmental body, an issue currently under discussion.

Fifth, the systemic nature of the global crisis has led to greater concerns about systemic financial issues in general, and has resulted in a greater focus on systemic solutions. The proposed solutions will involve increased international regulatory cooperation, as evidenced by the FSF's April 2008 Report on Enhancing Market and Institutional Resilience, to ensure stability in the financial system, and to prevent regulatory arbitrage (*FT*, 2008a: 11; 2008c: 11; 2008d: 9; 2009f: 11).[11] The FSF Report of April 2008 and the 2008 Summit Declaration both demonstrate the extensive degree of international cooperation that needs to be developed to confront the international financial crisis.

The five factors mentioned above will hopefully help create a framework of more intensive international regulatory cooperation and coordination to avoid regulatory arbitrage (*FT*, 2008i). As this new regulatory framework takes shape, the idea of greater international tax cooperation will seem more realistic and acceptable. And this increased international regulatory cooperation and coordination will likely lead to and facilitate greater international tax cooperation.

Bretton Woods I vs. Bretton Woods II

As governments attempt to redesign the international financial architecture with a new Bretton Woods-type agreement, a major difference must be recognized between Bretton Woods I and Bretton Woods II. In the case of Bretton Woods I, the United States could, in effect, dictate the terms and impose its will on others. Philip Stephens has commented: "[t]he chaos speaks to a world in which the west is surrendering centuries of economic and political hegemony; to a globalization that has at once weakened nation states and demanded more of them; and to an emerging multi-polar system that has broken the multilateral boundaries of the old order (*FT*, 2008l: 19)."

Systemic Issues

Lessons from the October 1987 Stock Market Crash

Many who have looked at the crashes and crises of the past decades have recognized the systemic nature of the problems identified. A Presidential Task Force on Market Mechanisms,[12] considering the causes of the 1987 stock market crash, concluded in its report ("the 1987 Stock Market Report", also known as "the Brady Report") that traditional perceptions of the respective markets were incorrect, and that regulators had not adequately understood the relationship between different relevant markets (the markets for stocks, stock index futures, and stock options). It is clear from this report that the regulatory structure was characterized by fragmentation and a lack of systemic analysis; regulators needed a more inter-market, systemic focus/analysis/approach—the very basic concept of inter-market connectivity.

Paul Volcker, former chairman of the Federal Reserve Board, emphasized, to the Economic Club of New York on 8 April 2008, that there had been "at least five serious breakdowns of systemic significance in the past 25 years—on the average one every five years. Warning enough that something rather basic is amiss."[13] Similarly, in a 9 June 2008 presentation on the sub-prime crisis to the same audience, Timothy F. Geithner, current US Treasury Secretary and former President and Chief Executive Officer of the Federal Reserve Bank of New York, admitted that systemic issues were not receiving sufficient attention, noting that "the conventional risk-management framework today focuses too much on the threat to a firm from its own mistakes and too little on the potential for mistakes to be correlated across firms."[14]

Critically, over 20 years after the 1987 Stock Market Report, which emphasized the importance of a systemic regulatory approach to financial issues, US regulators have not effectively foreseen and confronted systemic risks with a sufficiently systemic approach (Spencer, 2008b). The Obama administration sent its regulatory plan to the Congress on 19 June 2009 (*Marketwatch*, 2009), with the US Federal Reserve proposed to regulate for systemic risk, able to oversee large financial firms based on size, leverage and interconnectedness to the financial system. The issue of regulation remains the subject of great debate, with intense lobbying in Washington, especially on whether and which hedge funds should be treated as "systemically important", and therefore subject to special scrutiny in terms of capital and reporting requirements (*NYT*, 2008a; *Washington Post*, 2009).

Cross-border Tax Evasion: Inconsistencies in a Systemic Approach

The messages of the 1987 Stock Market Report, of Paul Volcker, and of Timothy Geithner—noted above—are relevant to the problem of cross-border tax evasion. International financial regulators and norm setters (the OECD, IMF, World Bank) and US tax and banking authorities have had a fragmented approach to cross-border tax evasion. They have not confronted cross-border tax evasion with a coherent, coordinated, consistent, and systematic approach. For example:

1) The OECD considered Liechtenstein an "uncooperative" tax haven jurisdiction until May 2009[15] because Liechtenstein had not adopted the OECD rules on exchange of information on request (which, in any event, is not "effective" exchange of information). But the IMF, in its March 2008 report, "Liechtenstein: Detailed Assessment Report on Money Laundering and Combating the Financing of Terrorism", in effect, accepted and tacitly supported Liechtenstein's policy of bank secrecy/confidentiality and "favorable tax arrangements", that is, Liechtenstein's policy of not exchanging tax information, a policy which facilitates and encourages cross-border tax evasion;

2) The OECD has adopted the policy of exchange of information on request, but the Financial Action Task Force (FATF) generally has not adopted the use of relevant information about money laundering for tax purposes;

3) The proceeds of money laundering, corruption and other criminal activities are frequently invested cross-border in offshore and onshore financial centers that provide bank secrecy/confidentiality and tax-free treatment. That is, the proceeds of money laundering, corruption and other criminal activity are intertwined with tax evasion because these proceeds are frequently followed by cross-border tax evasion. However, the FATF and the UN Office on Drugs and Crime (UNODC), which administers the UN Convention Against Corruption, have not yet focused on the positive impact that the exchange of tax information (in particular, automatic exchange) would have in diminishing illicit cross-border financial flows, which are the proceeds of money-laundering, corruption and other criminal activities;

4) As Raymond Baker (2005) has pointed out, the international financial organizations (the World Bank, IMF and regional financial organizations, such as the Inter-American Development Bank, African Development Bank, and Asian Development Bank) have been concerned

about "official" capital flows, but these organizations have not focused on and confronted a major macroeconomic issue: the "unofficial" capital flows, the impact of capital flight and the resulting tax evasion (although the joint UNODC/World Bank StAR [Stolen Asset Recovery] Initiative Report[16] does consider cross-border tax evasion);

5) The OECD proposals for addressing tax havens, developed as a result of the 1998 OECD report, "Harmful Tax Competition: An Emerging Global Issue,"[17] focus on capital outflows from OECD countries and the resulting tax evasion in OECD countries. But these proposals do not confront capital flight from third countries to offshore financial centers and OECD financial centers and the resulting tax evasion in those third countries;

6) Similarly, the EU Savings Directive imposes the automatic exchange of information (or imposition of a withholding tax instead) on interest payments from payers in the EU to individual residents in the EU, but does not require exchange of information or impose a withholding tax on interest payments from payers in the EU to individual residents in non-EU countries. That is, the EC is concerned about tax evasion by residents of the EU, but not about tax evasion by residents of non-EU countries who invest in the EU; and

7) The United States has aggressively confronted cross-border tax evasion by US citizens and residents (*FT*, 2009c: 3), but facilitates and encourages foreign persons to evade foreign income tax by providing confidentiality and tax-free treatment for certain investments in the United States by foreign persons. The United States publicly asserts the need for exchange of information, while senior US officials have emphasized the "efforts [of the United States] to ensure that no safe haven exist anywhere in the world for the funds associated with illicit activities, including tax evasion (Comisky and Lee, 2009). But the US QI [qualified intermediary] program frustrates and, in effect, makes impossible the exchange of information by the United States for income derived by foreign persons from certain investments that qualify for the QI program.

This partial list shows that international regulators have not confronted cross-border tax evasion with a coherent, coordinated, consistent and systematic approach. The current international financial crisis—presumably leading to a Bretton Woods type redesign of the international financial architecture—should definitely lead to a more systematic confrontation with cross-border tax evasion.

Transfer Pricing

Transfer (mis)pricing is the manipulation of prices of goods or services that are exchanged among various divisions of a multinational corporation in order to reduce declared profits, and therefore tax payments in high tax countries, and to increase declared profits in low or no-tax countries. Such mispricing has become a major tax issue for at least three reasons. *First*, quantification of transfer mispricing has highlighted the seriousness of the problem. The May 2008 Christian Aid study, "Death and Taxes: The True Toll of Tax Dodging" ("Christian Aid Report") estimates that developing countries lose revenue of US$160 billion annually as a result of transfer mispricing and false invoicing.[18] According to the Report, some 60 percent of world trade is reported to take place within corporate groups, i.e., among related entities within the same corporate group,[19] and 50 percent of world trade is reported to take place—on paper, at least—through tax havens.[20]

Second, transfer mispricing can serve as a technique for money laundering, tax evasion, capital flight and import duty fraud. The final report of the Task Force on the Development Impact of Illicit Financial Flows, discussed below, refers[21] to transfer mispricing as a key element of illicit financial flows.

In March 2009, Christian Aid issued a further report, "False Profits: Robbing the Poor to Keep the Rich Tax Free", which quantifies the capital flight and lost tax revenue of individual countries due to trade mispricing.[22] The main points of the report are:

1) Transfer pricing is a major issue because 60 percent of world trade is now taking place within multinational corporations.

2) Developing countries lose about US$160 billion of tax revenues annually due to transfer (mis)pricing.

3) If that money was available to allocate according to current spending patterns, the amount going to health services could save the lives of 350,000 children under the age of five every year.

4) The total tax revenue lost by developing countries annually is more than the current annual global official development assistance (ODA) of about US$103 billion, and much greater than the US$40-60 billion that the World Bank estimates will be required annually to meet the UN's Millennium Development Goal (MDG) aimed at halving extreme poverty by 2015.

5) The developing countries attending the April 2009 G20 London Summit (Argentina, Brazil, China, India, Indonesia, Mexico and

South Africa) lost a total of US$172 billion in capital flight to the United States and the EU between 2005 and 2007, while the lost tax revenue of these developing countries during the same period was US$39.5 billion.

Christian Aid proposed two solutions to transfer (mis)pricing—namely country by-country reporting and the automatic exchange of information—and made three recommendations to implement them:[23]

- That the G20 should establish an international standard for cooperation in taxation. This would provide for comprehensive exchange of information for the assessment and collection of taxes, including automatic, on request and spontaneous exchanges of information.
- That the current system of bilaterally negotiated tax information exchange agreements (TIEAs) has demonstrably failed to deliver effective information exchange. A new standard would enable automatic sharing of information from both individual nationals and residents, and companies or trusts formed under the laws of, or resident in, each country. It would include a requirement that all banks and other financial institutions collect information, which should be available to the appropriate supervisors or regulators (including tax authorities), on the beneficial owners of all payments made, whether to residents or non-residents, individual and companies.
- That the G20 should request the International Accounting Standards Board to produce a draft standard on country-by-country reporting for multinational companies.

Country-by-country reporting by multinational corporations would indeed have a strong deterrent impact on transfer mispricing, especially in conjunction with automatic exchange of information. The International Accounting Standards Board (IASB) has an obvious role, as it determines the International Financial Reporting Standards (IFRS), which could include country-by-country reporting. More specifically, country-by-country reporting would require each corporation to disclose at least:

1) The name of each country where it operates.
2) The names of all of its companies (subsidiaries and affiliates) doing business in each country where it operates.
3) What its financial performance is in each country where it is doing business, including:
   - Its sales to both third parties and other group companies.
   - Purchases from both third parties and other group companies.

- Labor costs and employee numbers.
- Financing costs split between those paid to third parties and other group members.
- Its pre-tax profit in each country where it operates.
- How much it pays in tax and other payments to the government of each country where it is doing business.
- Details of the cost and net book value of its physical fixed assets located in each country where it is doing business.
- Details of its gross and net assets in total for each country where it is doing business.

Norwegian Task Force on Development Impact of Illicit Financial Flows

A plenary meeting of the Leading Group of Countries in Seoul (September 2007) assigned to Norway the responsibility of heading an international task force to study illicit financial flows and their impact on development. The Norwegian Task Force on the Development Impact of Illicit Financial Flows ("Norwegian Task Force") issued a final report in late 2008. This led to the formation of the Task Force on Financial Integrity and Economic Development[24]—a consortium of Governments and NGOs—focused on achieving greater transparency in the global financial system for the benefit of developing countries. This Task Force advocates five priorities in addressing the current global financial crisis, each one focusing on transparency and extending initiatives that have already been put in place:

1. Curtailment of mispricing in trade imports and exports;
2. Country-by-country accounting of sales, profits and taxes paid by multinational corporations;
3. Confirmation of beneficial ownership in all banking and securities accounts;
4. Automatic cross-border exchange of tax information on personal and business accounts;
5. Harmonization of predicate offences under anti-money laundering laws across all Financial Action Task Force cooperating countries.

In view of the proposed restructuring of the international financial architecture, the work of the Task Force on Financial Integrity and Economic Development should be significant, especially in view of the membership of the G20 and the expanded membership of the Financial Stability Forum.

UN Stiglitz Commission

The President of the UN General Assembly established a Commission of Experts on Reforms of the International Monetary and Financial System, chaired by Joseph Stiglitz, a Nobel laureate in economics. The Stiglitz Commission produced Recommendations on 29 April 2009[25] and a Preliminary Report of 21 May 2009.[26] The Recommendations[27] and Preliminary Report[28] emphasized the close link between regulatory arbitrage and tax evasion, and supported strengthening the UN Committee of Experts on International Cooperation in Tax Matters ("UN Tax Committee"). The Stiglitz Commission Recommendations (para. 55) supported the automatic exchange of tax information on the basis of efficiency, rather than the OECD's policy of exchange on request.

G20 London Summit

The "Declaration on Strengthening the Financial System", issued by the G20 leaders on 2 April 2009, at the London summit, affirmed that "[t]he era of banking secrecy is over."[29] The Declaration stated: "We are committed to developing proposals, by end 2009, to make it easier for developing countries to secure the benefits of a new cooperative tax environment". The official communiqué of the Summit does not explicitly refer to either automatic exchange of information or exchange of information on request, but the Declaration, in the paragraph titled "Tax Havens and Non-Cooperative Jurisdictions", refers to the "international standard for information exchange".

The Summit also called for proposals to be developed during 2009 to extend international tax cooperation to developing countries. These proposals could affect every investment bank and financial institution in OECD financial centers, and those in other onshore and offshore financial centers that receive funds from Latin America, Africa, or Asia.

A Role for the IMF?

The proposed US legislation in 1989 could serve as a guide for a future role for the IMF. Such proposed legislation in 1989, the International Development and Finance Act of 1989, Title IV, International Debt Provisions, would have required the Secretary of the Treasury to instruct the US Executive Director of the IMF to propose that the IMF conduct a study on multilateral means by which the banking industry might help reverse capital flight from countries engaged in debt restructuring, including:

1)   the feasibility of disclosing the names of account holders whose accounts may consist of flight capital, and the balances of such accounts;

2)   the usefulness of such disclosures in deterring the creation and maintenance of such accounts, and how such deterrence would operate or be defeated;

3)   the extent to which any such information is gathered and to whom such information is made available;

4)   the receptiveness of such countries to the disclosure of such information;

5)   the difficulties in, and the cost of, collecting such information and overcoming legal obstacles used to disguise the true ownership of such deposits, including the feasibility of using the threat of confiscatory penalties to prevent disguising the ownership of deposits;

6)   the usefulness of using taxes as a means to encourage the repatriation of flight capital; and

7)   the applicability (if any) of efforts to facilitate the identification, tracing, seizure and forfeiture of drug crime proceeds, and to prevent the use of the banking system and of financial institutions for the purpose of money laundering.[30]

The IMF has been opposed to becoming involved in adopting or supporting the OECD Project on Harmful Tax Practices against cross-border tax evasion. The reasons for this are detailed by Richard Gordon (2010), a senior IMF staff member from 1994 through 2003. However, with regard to the jurisdiction of the IMF, there is a strong argument that the IMF has jurisdiction over cross-border tax evasion and the resulting capital flight under Article 1(i) of the IMF Articles of Agreement, which includes as one of its purposes "To promote international monetary cooperation through a permanent institution which provides the machinery for consultation and collaboration on international monetary problems."

The traditional reluctance of the IMF to confront cross-border tax evasion resulting from capital flight (Gordon, 2010) could change over time as the OECD now claims that there is an "international standard for exchange of information" (Spencer, 2009g), relying upon the identical standard contained in the OECD Model Tax Convention Article[31] and the proposed next version of the UN Model Tax Convention Article[32] on exchange of information.

However, the "international standard" claimed is merely one of exchange of information upon request. As discussed below, governments and NGO advocates of automatic exchange of information assert that:

(1) the OECD's policy of exchange of information upon request is not an "international standard", and (2) in any case, exchange of information upon request is not effective. Nevertheless, if the IMF does accept the OECD's "international standard", at least as a first step, the IMF could become involved in confronting capital flight and other illicit financial flows, the resulting cross-border tax evasion and the consequential challenge to the international financial architecture.

UN Tax Committee

The members of the UN Committee of Experts on International Co-operation in Tax Matters ("UN Tax Committee") for the four year 2009-2013 term have been selected by the Secretary-General of the UN (E/2009/9/Add.17) following nominations by their respective governments. They act in their personal capacity, including for the next Annual Session of the UN Tax Committee in late October 2009. The following OECD countries will have experts on the new UN Tax Committee: Belgium, Germany, Italy, Japan, Korea, Mexico, New Zealand, Norway, Spain, Switzerland and United States. Non-OECD countries represented are Barbados, Brazil, Bulgaria, Chile (which has applied for OECD membership), China, Egypt, India, Malaysia, Morocco, Nigeria, Pakistan, Senegal and South Africa. However, some of these non-OECD countries are observers on the OECD Committee on Fiscal Affairs.

The inclusion of Brazilian and Indian experts on the new Committee is of interest (as is the return of a US expert) as is the broadening agenda of the Committee (which now has introduced transfer pricing issues for consideration, as well as the costs and benefits of corporate tax incentives). But a practical issue is whether members of the UN Tax Committee from developing countries, and also from non-financial centers, will act with greater coordination and assertiveness in the UN Tax Committee during the next four years.

The G-8 July 2009 Meeting and Tax Evasion

The Italian Minister of Finance, Giulio Tremonti, announced on 12 May 2009 that "[Italy] will have the development of international standards for fighting tax evasion the top priority at [the July 2009] Group of Eight Summit" at L'Aquila near Rome (Zagaris, 2009). However, in the G8 Declaration, "Responsible Leadership for a Sustainable Future,"[33] adopted at the L'Aquila Summit, there was little on tax issues directly. Obviously, the G8 was looking to the G20 to take matters forward. The G8 leaders nevertheless agreed on the objectives of a strategy to create such a comprehensive framework, the "Lecce Framework", and to "make every effort to pursue maximum country participation and swift and resolute implementation". The Global Standard draws on a wide range of instruments, established or under development, sharing a common thread related to propriety, integrity and transparency. It classifies them into five categories:

- corporate governance,
- market integrity,
- financial regulation and supervision,
- tax cooperation, and
- transparency of macroeconomic policy and data.

Relevant principles in the current draft are:[34]

4) Tax evasion and avoidance are harmful to society as a whole and companies and all business entities, irrespective of their legal form, should fulfill their fiscal duties, including by respecting the arm's length principle in transfer pricing practices....
9) Bribery, including bribery in international business transactions, should be established as a criminal offence and effectively prosecuted and punished.
10) Money laundering should be criminalized and the crime of money laundering should be applied to all serious offences, with a view to including the widest range of predicate offences.
12) Bank secrecy should not constitute an obstacle to the application of the above mentioned principles, including tax compliance worldwide.

OECD's Role?

The OECD has coordinated an "inventory of relevant legal instruments"[35] relevant to the so-called "Global Standard", in cooperation with the International Labour Organization, the International Monetary Fund, the World Bank, and the World Trade Organization. Although perhaps an indication of the limits and failings of international coordination, no attempt appears to have been made to refer to the relevant United Nations instruments, such as the widely used UN Model Tax Convention, or the widely adhered-to UN Convention against Corruption, there being no column in the inventory for UN instruments.

The OECD's 1998 report, "Harmful Tax Competition: An Emerging Global Issue" highlighted the cross-border tax evasion issue. The OECD has played a significant role in aggressively asserting, in the new Article 26 of the OECD Model Income Tax Treaty and in the OECD Model TIEA,[36] that bank secrecy and other confidentiality laws, and any domestic tax interest requirement, cannot serve as an obstacle to the exchange of tax information, but the OECD's proposals have serious flaws, which are explored below.

Capital Flight from South to North

The OECD's proposals address capital flight from OECD member countries to tax haven jurisdictions, including dependencies of OECD member countries ("Tax Haven Jurisdictions"), and the resulting tax evasion and loss of government revenue in OECD member countries. The OECD proposals do not constrain capital flight from third countries to OECD financial centers or to tax haven jurisdictions, and the resulting tax evasion and loss of government revenue to those third countries. The G20 London Summit possibly reflects a change of policy in its commitment to make it easier for developing countries to secure the benefits of a "new cooperative tax environment", but it remains to be seen what decision-making and norm-setting roles the OECD countries are genuinely willing to share.

Exchange of Tax Information upon Request

The OECD's program of exchange of information upon request is not really "effective" exchange of information. The standard OECD information exchange agreement (the TIEA) is nearly worthless. Information exchange under the standard agreement is sporadic, difficult and unwieldy for tax administrators, even under the best of circumstances. When a banking haven is the requested party, information exchange is nearly impossible. The information exchange article in the OECD model tax convention suffers from the same limitations. The OECD agreement is also not drafted to provide serious, real-time help with tax administration. The agreement only allows countries to ask for assistance in well-developed tax evasion cases. The UK *Guardian*, which has a long-running tax gap project, recognized the limited utility of these agreements: "This is not good enough. The much hallowed bilateral information-sharing deals require tax officials to request specific financial details and show why they want them. They take immense time and effort" (Shepherd, 2009a; 2009b).

A 9 February 2009 letter from Agustin Carstens, the Finance Secretary of Mexico and former Deputy Managing Director of the IMF, to US Treasury Secretary Geithner[37] is relevant. It calls for the US to exchange tax information automatically with Mexico about bank deposits held in the United States by Mexicans as "a powerful tool to detect, prevent and combat tax evasion, money laundering, terrorist financing, drug trafficking and organized crime". Although Mexico is an OECD member country, the Carstens letter urges the automatic exchange of information, rather than the OECD's policy of exchange on request. This reinforces the argument that automatic exchange of information is necessary for "effective" exchange of information, not the OECD's policy of exchange of information upon request (which is soft on OECD and non-OECD financial centers) (Spencer, 2009h). Of course, assistance may have to be given to some developing countries to administratively enable them to be able to share information automatically, but such assistance would be of obvious benefit, including for increasing the likelihood that other countries will be willing to automatically send information to the developing country and allow it to properly collect taxes due to it.

An International Standard

The OECD has tried to give the impression that its "standard on transparency and exchange of information" upon request has been universally endorsed. This is simply not so, as evidenced by the following:

*   *The European Union*: The EU has adopted automatic exchange of information with regard to cross-border interest income within the EU, and is trying to expand such automatic exchange of information to other types of income and to other jurisdictions (Council of the European Union, 2009).
*   *The Carstens Letter*: The letter from Agustin Carstens, Secretary of Finance of Mexico, is significant because although Mexico is an OECD member country, the letter urges the automatic exchange of information, rather than the OECD's basic policy of exchange of information on request.
*   *UN Stiglitz Commission*: The Stiglitz Commission recommended the automatic exchange of tax information rather than the exchange of information on request.

Implementation of the OECD Standard

The OECD has determined that if a tax haven jurisdiction signs at least twelve TIEAs based on the OECD Model TIEA (exchange of information upon request), that Tax Haven Jurisdiction will be considered to have "substantially implemented the internationally agreed tax standard". But twelve TIEAs is a small number considering that there are 30 OECD member countries and about 162 other countries. For example, Bermuda was elevated to the OECD's "White List" as Bermuda has signed TIEAs with the United States, Australia, the United Kingdom, New Zealand, Netherlands and the seven jurisdictions in the Nordic Group: Denmark, the Faroe Islands (non-OECD), Finland, Greenland (non-OECD), Iceland, Norway and Sweden. The Faroe Islands and Greenland have small populations and minimal economic activity. And there is not one developing country in that group of twelve. How could twelve such TIEAs constitute "substantial implementation" of any exchange of information program, whether exchange of information upon request or automatic exchange of information?

Summary

In summary, the international financial crisis has focused attention on systemic risks and systemic solutions. The crisis has resulted in unparalleled coordination and cooperation on financial law matters by governments, international financial organizations and other international organizations, though the real breadth and depth of such cooperation can sometimes be questioned.

The international financial crisis has also focused attention on cross-border tax evasion issues. First, there are several issues related to tax haven jurisdictions which are considered factors contributing to the international financial crisis or presenting actual or potential systemic risk problems: (1) regulatory arbitrage exacerbated by tax haven jurisdictions with low regulatory requirements; (2) entities organized in tax haven jurisdictions treated as off-balance sheet by financial institutions and other corporations based in major financial centers and other industrialized countries; and (3) hedge funds organized in tax haven jurisdictions, some of which had operated in other jurisdictions.

Second, several recent issues related to cross-border tax evasion have not been considered factors contributing to the international financial crisis, but these issues have become significant in the discussion about international regulatory reform; these issues have included:

1) The quantification of illicit cross-border financial flows into onshore and offshore centers, estimated to be between US\$800 billion to US\$1 trillion annually, highlights the seriousness of the problem for non-financial centers.

2) The pressure from developed countries with donor fatigue and budget deficits for developing countries to mobilize domestic resources for development, as mandated by the UN's Monterrey Consensus of March 2002. But that would mean developing countries have to crack down on capital flight and cross-border tax evasion, and reduce the resulting loss of tax revenue.

3) As a result, in part, of the Liechtenstein situation and the US case against UBS, there is a growing assertiveness against cross-border tax evasion—by France, Germany, other OECD countries which are not financial centers, and the Leading Group of Countries, in which Norway has a very active role.

4) The efforts by the EU to expand the EU Directive on the Taxation of Savings, and its program of automatic exchange of information, to cross-border income in addition to interest, and to expand its geographic scope.

5) The emergence of assertive non-government organizations well versed in international financial issues, such as Action Aid, Christian Aid, Eurodad, Global Financial Integrity, Global Witness, Oxfam, Publish What You Pay, and Tax Justice Network.

6) The impact of capital flight from India and the resulting cross-border tax evasion was a big issue in the mid-2009 Indian parliamentary elections.

(7) The recent assertiveness of the BRIC countries (Brazil, Russia, India and China) at the IMF as the influence of the BRIC countries has been growing (*FT*, 2009a: 11; 2008j: 3; O'Neill, 2009; Peel, 2009; *WSJ*, 2009b: C1; *NYT*, 2009c: A5; *FT*, 2009g: 2).

(8) The call by the UN's Stiglitz Commission for the automatic exchange between governments of tax information.

(9) Confirmation by the 2008 Report of the Norwegian Task Force on the Impact of Illicit Financial Flows on Development that illicit financial flows from corruption and criminal activity are intertwined with tax evasion because the perpetrators attempt to hide the proceeds of the illicit activities in onshore and offshore financial centers providing confidentiality and tax-free treatment.[38]

What is Next?

The collapse of the international financial system has resulted in two fundamental changes in its architecture. *First*, based on a concern with systemic risk, detailed proposals in the April 2008 Financial Stability Forum

Report for more intensive, systemic, international regulatory cooperation were adopted by the G20. *Second*, there has been a shift in power from the G7 to a broader group of countries, the G20, which includes Argentina, Brazil, China, India, Indonesia, Mexico and South Africa.

This new international regulatory framework and shift in power will probably outlast the current crisis. The question: after the storm has subsided, what will the impact on capital markets and international finance of these two fundamental changes be?

First, the new framework confirms that regulatory arbitrage, seeking the least regulated, most favorable jurisdiction, is not systemically healthy. This will encourage international cooperation on several financial law issues not directly related to the crisis, but which could benefit from cross-border cooperation such as: insolvency, corporate law and corporate governance, securities regulation, commodities regulation, codes of conduct for multinational companies, money laundering and illicit financial flows including corruption. At present, they do not seem to be a high priority, but will receive close attention in the future. Finance and trade have become globalized, and the new international regulatory framework will permit regulatory cooperation to catch up.

Second, and more important, the shift in power to a broader group of countries will bring into question the West's hegemony on regulation. If the US, UK and international financial organizations (the IMF, World Bank, Bank for International Settlements, etc.) could not prevent the crisis, why should they determine the response? (Spencer 2009h). Without China, India and others at the table, more established industrialized nations cannot properly address the global crisis. Some sort of new structure of global governance will be essential to reflect redistribution of power, and provide meaningful guidance and regulations (*FT*, 2009d: 8).

The Changing Regulatory Environment

The efforts by the G20 against regulatory arbitrage, and the more intense regulatory scrutiny of tax haven jurisdictions by the G20 will not only impact the use of such jurisdictions by hedge funds, private equity groups, financial institutions and multinationals for structured investment vehicles and off-balance sheet entities. These increased regulatory efforts will most likely have spillover effects on the use of tax haven jurisdictions in general to facilitate capital flight and other illicit financial flows from other jurisdictions.

In "Time for Calm on Secrecy", Philip Marcovici, Chair of the Global Private Banking Practice Group of Baker & McKenzie, wrote: "wealth owners need to understand that non-compliance with tax laws is simply not an option in today's environment. Breaking the law carries criminal, financial and reputational risks and all too often these are left to the younger generation to sort out. ...A solution to the issue of undeclared funds will need to involve financial institutions and government working together cooperatively" (*FT*, 2008b).

Bretton Woods I and Bretton Woods II

The wisdom of John Maynard Keynes and Harry Dexter White, the principal architects of Bretton Woods I, in suggesting full sharing of information between sending countries and receiving countries, should be remembered. In their initial drafts of the Bretton Woods agreement, both Keynes and White required the governments of receiving countries to share information with the governments of countries using capital controls about the foreign holdings of the latter's citizens. White went further in his draft to also suggest that the receiving counties should refuse to accept capital flights altogether without the agreement of the sending country's government.

Both of these proposals were strongly opposed by the US financial community, which had profited from the handling of flight capital during the 1930s and which feared that the proposals would affect New York's reputation as an international financial center. In the face of this opposition, the final IMF Articles of Agreement contained watered-down version of Keynes' and White's initial proposals. Cooperation among countries to control capital movements was now simply permitted, rather than required (Article 8-2b). The only requirement in this area was a limited one that IMF members had to ensure that all exchange contracts which contravened other members' exchange controls were "unenforceable in their territory" (Article 8-2B) (Epstein, 2005).

Conclusion

In concluding, it is useful to reflect upon the words of Agustin Carstens, Secretary of Finance of Mexico, in the letter noted above. Carstens confirmed the intertwined relationship between bank secrecy, tax evasion and other illicit financial flows. And he confirms a systemic approach: automatic exchange of information will not only help constrain cross-border tax evasion, but also other illicit financial flows.

A Bretton Woods II can include the automatic exchange of information proposed by Keynes and White at Bretton Woods, but then opposed by the US financial community. The serious problems caused by very substantial cross-border tax evasion and other illicit financial flows, exacerbated by the current international financial crisis, have led to a search for systemic solutions to confront such problems. In the new international financial architecture, who could be against the automatic exchange of information?

Notes

1. This chapter draws upon Spencer (2009a, 2009b, 2009c, 2009d, 2009e, 2009f). The assistance of Michael Lennard of the United Nations' Financing for Development Office in the Department of Economic and Social Affairs in abridging and updating the material for this publication is gratefully acknowledged.
2. Report by Christian Aid (2008: 10, 12). At footnote 40, the Report noted that: "The BIS [Bank for International Settlements] asked: 'How could a huge shadow banking system emerge without provoking clear statements of official concern?'", citing 78th Annual Report, Bank for International Settlements, page 138.
3. Available at http://www.financialstabilityboard.org/publications/r_0804.pdf
4. The G20 is made up of the finance ministers and central bank governors of 19 countries and EU representatives. The countries are: Argentina, Australia, Brazil, Canada, China, France, Germany, India, Indonesia, Italy, Japan, Mexico, Russia, Saudi Arabia, South Africa, South Korea, Turkey, United Kingdom, and the United States of America.
5. Available at http://www.g20.org/Documents/g20_summit_declaration.pdf
6. See *NYT* (2008b: B5) and *Sunday Business*, 16 November 2008, p. 2. See also *FT* (2009e: 2).
7. For example, a major issue is the regulation of derivatives trading, which financial institutions and the US government opposed in the 1990s. Now, regulators are calling for central clearing of derivative transactions. See, e.g., *FT* (2008f: 27); Lukken (2008: A15).
8. This can be termed the "Portuguese Revolution Factor": an unexpected revolution in Portugal resulted in a new government that unexpectedly gave independence to Portuguese colonies.
9. See Spencer (2009a, 2009b, 2009c, 2009d, 2009e, 2009f).
10. A term regarded as first coined by Jim O'Neill of Goldman Sachs and early referred to in the 2003 Goldman Sachs paper: "Dreaming With BRICs: The Path to 2050", http://www2.goldmansachs.com/ideas/brics/book/99-dreaming.pdf
11. See also *FT*, 2009f: 11: "Unfortunately bank regulation, such as the Basel accord [on risk-based bank capital], ignores systemic risk since it analyzes the risk of failure of each bank in isolation".

12. Available at http://ia310811.us.archive.org/1/items/reportofpresiden01unit/reportofpresiden01unit.pdf
13. http://econclubny.org/files/Transcript_Volcker_April_2008.pdf
14. http://www.newyorkfed.org/newsevents/speeches/2008/tfg080609.html
15. http://www.oecd.org/document/57/0,3343,en_2649_33745_30578809_1_1_1_37427,00.html
16. Available at http://www.unodc.org/pdf/Star_Report.pdf
17. Available at http://www.oecd.org/dataoecd/33/1/1904184.pdf
18. http://www.christianaid.org.uk/images/deathandtaxes.pdf, at page 2.
19. *Ibid.* at page 2.
20. *Ibid.* at page 2.
21. *Ibid.* at page 8.
22. Available at: http://www.christianaid.org.uk/Images/false-profits.pdf
23. *Ibid.* page 6.
24. http://www.financialtaskforce.org
25. http://www.un.org/ga/search/view_doc.asp?symbol=A/63/838&referer=http://www.un.org/ga/econcrisissummit/docs.shtml&Lang=E
26. http://www.un.org/ga/president/63/interactive/financialcrisis/PreliminaryReport210509.pdf, at p. 65ff.
27. At Recommendation 8(c).
28. At page 65 ff.
29. Available at http://www.g20.utoronto.ca/2009/2009-london-ifi-090402.html
30. Section 404, Study on Elimination of Capital Flight.
31. Available at http://www.oecd.org/document/53/0,3343,en_2649_33747_33614197_1_1_1_1,00.html
32. The UN Model, and the proposed new Article 26 are available at http://www.un.org/esa/ffd/tax
33. Available at http://www.g8italia2009.it/static/G8_Allegato/G8_Declaration_08_07_09_final,0.pdf
34. Available at http://www.oecd.org/document/6/0,3343,en_2649_34487_43268358_1_1_1_1,00.html
35. Available at http://www.oecd.org/dataoecd/35/63/42393042.pdf
36. Available at http://www.oecd.org/dataoecd/15/43/2082215.pdf
37. Available at: http://www.letemps.ch/rw/Le_Temps/Quotidien/2009/07/22/Finance/ImagesWeb/Lettre du Mexique aux US.pdf
38. See also "Tax Havens and Development". Norwegian Commission on Capital Flight from Developing Countries". 18 June 2009, available at: http://www.regjeringen.no/upload/UD/Vedlegg/Utvikling/tax_report.pdf.

References

Baker, Raymond W. (2005). *Capitalism's Achilles Heel: Dirty Money and How to Renew the Free-Market System.* John Wiley & Sons, Hoboken, NJ.

Christian Aid (2008). The morning after the night before: The impact of the financial crisis on the developing world. November: 10, 12.

Comisky, Ian M., and Matthew D. Lee (2009). Increased IRS scrutiny of offshore activity: Raising the stakes for US citizens with bank accounts abroad. *Journal of International Taxation*, January.

Council of the European Union (2009). Council conclusions on good governance in the tax area. 9 June, Brussels.

Epstein, Gerald A. (2005). *Capital Flight and Capital Controls in Developing Countries*. Edward Elgar, Cheltenham.

FSF (2009). Press release of 2 April 2009. Financial Stability Forum. Available at http://www.financialstabilityboard.org/press/pr_090402b.pdf

FT (2008a). Why financial regulation is both difficult and essential. *Financial Times*, 16 April, p. 11.

FT (2008b). Special supplement on private banking. *Financial Times*, 18 June, p. 18.

FT (2008c). The principles of sound regulation. *Financial Times*, 6 August, p. 11.

FT (2008d). The five lessons bankers must learn. *Financial Times*, 11 August, p. 9.

FT (2008e). The financial crisis marks out a new geopolitical order. *Financial Times*, 10 October, p. 9.

FT (2008f). Calls for derivatives clearing intensify. *Financial Times*, 15 October, p. 27.

FT (2008g). Why agreeing a new Bretton Woods is vital and so hard. *Financial Times*, 5 November, p. 9.

FT (2008h). G20 marks a shift in economic power — meeting is a big step towards a global response to crisis. *Financial Times*, 17 November, p. 14.

FT (2008i). Global initiative to revamp mortgage securities. *Financial Times*, 3 December.

FT (2008j). Brazil set to push for more influence. *Financial Times*, 5 December, p. 3.

FT (2008k). Shapiro takes on an unhappy legacy. *Financial Times*, 19 December, p. 8.

FT (2008l). Advice for seasonal seers: The future is not in the stars. *Financial Times*, 19 December, p. 19.

FT (2009a). Why Brazil and friends want the world to listen. *Financial Times*, 5 January, p. 11.

FT (2009b). French and Germans put foot down on tightening financial regulations. *Financial Times*, 9 January, p. 3.

FT (2009c). Congress aims to create systemic risk regulator. *Financial Times*, 16 January, p. 3.

FT (2009d). Risks rise in shift to a multipolar world. *Financial Times*, 28 January, p. 8.

FT (2009e). Paris toughens regulation line with call for clearing systems. *Financial Times*, 30 January, p. 2.

FT (2009f). A proposal to prevent wholesale financial failure. *Financial Times*, 30 January, p. 11.

FT (2009g). BRIC Summit: quartet defined by differences. *Financial Times*, 16 June, p. 2.

Gordon, Richard (2010). On the use and abuse of standards for law: Global governance and offshore centers. *North Carolina Law Review*, 88 (forthcoming).

Lukken, Walter (2008). How to solve the derivatives problem. *Wall Street Journal*, 10 October, p. A15.

Marketwatch (2009). Obama sends systemic regulator plan to Congress. 22 June. http://www.marketwatch.com/story/obama-sends-systemic-regulator-plan-to-congress-2009722165200

NYT (2008a). Hedge funds step up efforts to avert tougher rules. *New York Times*, 22 June.

NYT (2008b). France's Finance Minister in a crucial role at global economic talks. *New York Times*, 14 November, p. B5.

NYT (2008c). At meeting in Brazil, Washington is scorned. *New York Times*, 17 December, p. A10.

NYT (2009a). A Swiss bank, not by choice, will open files. *New York Times*, 18 February.

NYT (2009b). Tax havens likely to be target of G20 nations. *New York Times*, 12 May.

NYT (2009c). Seeking greater financial clout, emerging powers prepare to meet in Russia. *New York Times*, 16 June, p. A5.

Norwegian Commission on Capital Flight from Developing Countries (2009). Tax havens and development. 18 June, Oslo; available at: http://www.regjeringen.no/upload/UD/Vedlegg/Utvikling/tax_report.pdf

O'Neill, Jim (2009). Why it would be wrong to write off the BRICs. *Financial Times*, 6 January, p. 9.

Peel, Quentin (2009). Risks rise in shift to a multipolar world. *Financial Times*, 28 January, p. 8.

Shepherd, Lee (2009a). Ineffectual information sharing. *The Guardian*, 16 March.

Shepherd, Lee (2009b). Tax analysts. *Tax Notes Today* (122 Tax Notes 1411), 23 March, pp. 3-5.

Spencer, David (2008a). Why did no one do anything? *International Financial Law Review*, September, pp. 34-37.

Spencer, David (2008b). Liechtenstein and the subprime crisis: Systemic issues (Parts 1 and 2). *Journal of International Taxation*, 19 (9), September.

Spencer, David (2008c). Liechtenstein and the subprime crisis: Systemic issues (Parts 1 and 2). *Journal of International Taxation*, 19 (10), October.

Spencer, David (2009a). Cross-border tax evasion and Bretton Woods II (Part 1). *Journal of International Taxation*, 20 (5), May.

Spencer, David (2009b). Cross-border tax evasion and Bretton Woods II (Part 2). *Journal of International Taxation*, 20 (6), June.

Spencer, David (2009c). Cross-border tax evasion and Bretton Woods II (Part 3). *Journal of International Taxation*, 20 (7), July.

Spencer, David (2009d). Cross-border tax evasion and Bretton Woods II (Part 4). *Journal of International Taxation*, 20 (8), August.

Spencer, David (2009e). Cross-border tax evasion and Bretton Woods II (Part 5). *Journal of International Taxation*, 20 (9), September.

Spencer, David (2009f). Cross-border tax evasion and Bretton Woods II (Part 6). *Journal of International Taxation*, 20 (10), October.

Spencer, David (2009g). The G20 London Summit and tax haven jurisdictions. *Journal of International Taxation*, 20 (6), June.

Spencer, David (2009h). Watch for emerging nations: Imagine if developing countries aggressively coordinate on international finance: That could be the result of the G20. *International Financial Law Review*, June, p. 45.

WSJ (2009a). Swiss bank to give up depositors' names to prosecutors. *Wall Street Journal*, 19 February, p. A1.

WSJ (2009b). Brazil, Russia trade t-bills for IMF clout. *Wall Street Journal*, 11 June, p. C1.

Washington Post (2009). For hedge funds, biggest fear is more regulation. 25 June.

Zagaris, Bruce (2009). Italy prioritizes international tax enforcement for the next G8 meeting. *International Enforcement Law Reporter*, 25 (7), July, p. 270.

11

Learning from the Crisis:
Is there a model for global banking?

C.P. Chandrasekhar

One of the many noteworthy features of the evolving financial and economic crisis in the world economy is the belated recognition that the financial crisis is not restricted just to Wall Street or the mortgage-periphery of the financial system, but afflicts its core: the banking sector. When the sub-prime crisis broke, this was seen as confined to mortgage markets and to institutions holding mortgage-backed securities. Reasons that were implicitly contradictory were offered to justify this presupposition. It was on occasion argued that since banks were more regulated than players in other segments of the financial system they had stayed out of these markets for risky retail loans. At other times it was held that financial innovation in a liberalized banking system had allowed banks to transfer such risks off their balance sheets by securitizing those loans and selling them on to others. For reasons such as these, the banking system, the core of the financial sector, was seen as relatively free of the disease the sub-prime crisis came to epitomize.

However, in time, it became clear that the exposure of banks to these mortgage-backed and other asset-backed securities and collateralized debt obligations was by no means small. Because they wanted to partake of the high returns associated with those assets or because they were carrying an inventory of such assets that were yet to be marketed, banks had a significant holding of these instruments when the crisis broke. A number of banks had also set up special purpose vehicles for creating and distributing such assets which too were holders of what turned out to be toxic securities. And, finally, banks had lent to institutions that had leveraged small volumes of equity to make huge investments in these kinds of assets. In the event,

271

the banking system was indeed directly or indirectly exposed to these assets in substantial measure. Not surprisingly, it is now clear that banks too are afflicted by losses on derivatives of various kinds, resulting in write-downs that have wiped out their base capital.

Closure of these banks is clearly unacceptable for two reasons. First, banks are at the centre of the payments and settlements system in a modern economy, or the institutions, instruments and procedures that facilitate and ease transactions without large scale circulation and movement of currencies. If there is systemic failure in the banking system, the settlements system can freeze, causing damage to the real economy. Second, banks are designed to be the principal risk-carriers in an economy, because their intermediation is crucial to mobilizing financial savings in relatively small lots, from depositors who have a high liquidity preference and expect to be insured against risk and channeling these savings to borrowers looking for large sums of capital to be invested in illiquid assets characterized by significant risk. Even if banks lend largely for working capital purposes, this role they play is crucial for the real economy. If there is a banking crisis the credit pipe would get clogged with adverse implications for the real economy.

Recognition of these facts is prompting a structural transformation of the banking industry. An aspect of that transformation that has received much attention is the open or covert, "back-door" nationalization of leading banks in different countries. After having failed to salvage the crisis-afflicted banking system by guaranteeing deposits, providing refinance against toxic assets and pumping in preference capital, governments in the UK, US, Ireland and elsewhere are being forced to recapitalize them by subscribing to common equity capital. In the process they are required to hold a majority of ordinary equity shares in an expanded equity base. Most often this occurs not because governments want nationalization, but because there appears to be no option if the banks have to survive. Their survival matters not just for stakeholders in the individual banks concerned but for the economy as a whole, since their closure can send out ripple effects with systemic implications. The list of the banks subject to nationalization reads like a veritable who's who of global banking, covering among others, Citigroup, Bank of America, Royal Bank of Scotland and Lloyds Group.

This near-collapse and ongoing transformation of banking in the US and UK, even if perceived as temporary, raises not just the question of the appropriate form of ownership in the banking sector, but questions the form that banking structures, banking strategy and banking regulation took in the US and UK. From a developing country perspective, this is of considerable significance because financial liberalization and reform in developing countries has been geared to homogenize financial systems and restructure the still-dominant banking sectors in these countries to approximate the "model" that emerged and came to prevail in the Anglo-Saxon world since the late 1980s. The failure of the Anglo-Saxon model is now seen as indicative of the fact that a number of features of that system which governments and regulators in the developing world had chosen to move towards have lost their legitimacy.

The Original US Model

The crisis makes clear what has been known for long: the model of efficient markets that successfully mobilize savings, channel them into investment in the highest-yielding projects and ensure that those resources are successfully utilized is not real. The "real" Anglo-Saxon model is the imperfect, crisis prone system that emerged and consolidated itself in the US and the UK after the 1980s. Prior to that banking in the US was highly regulated and shaped by the Glass-Steagall Act of 1933. Regulation of this kind was necessitated by the crisis that engulfed the free banking regime that characterized the US in the early 20th century. During 1930-1932 alone, more than 5,000 commercial banks accounting for about a fifth of all banking institutions in the US suspended operations and in many cases subsequently failed.

The regulatory framework that Glass-Steagall defined was created to restore the viability of the banking system and prevent mass closures in future. It was designed to protect banks against failure by excluding them from competition of a kind that forces them to adopt risky strategies in search of larger business volumes and higher margins. Underlying the 1930s crisis was the competition that characterized the free banking era in which interest rate competition to attract deposits necessitated, in turn, investment in risky, high-return areas. This soon showed up in a high degree of financial fragility and almost routine bank closures. The Banking Act of 1933 limited competition with deposit insurance, interest rate regulation, and entry barriers which together rendered any bank as good as any other in the eyes of the ordinary depositor. This pre-empted the tendency to push up deposit rates to attract depositors that would require risky lending and investment to match returns with costs. The regulatory framework went even further to curb risky practices in the banking industry. Restrictions were imposed on investments that banks or their affiliates could make, limiting their activities to provision of loans and purchases of government securities. There was a ban on banks underwriting securities and serving as insurance underwriters or agents, besides limits on outstanding exposure to a single borrower and lending to sensitive sectors like real estate. Finally, solvency regulation involved periodic examination of bank financial records and informal guidelines relating to the ratio of shareholder capital to total assets.

There were two consequence of this structure of regulation. First, even though this regulatory framework was directed at and imposed principally on the banking sector, it implicitly regulated the non-bank financial sector as well. It is not often recognized that the size, degree of diversification and level of activity of the non-bank financial sector depends on the degree to which institutions in that sector can leverage their activity with credit delivered directly or indirectly from the banking system. Banks being the principal depository institutions are the first port of call for a nation's savings. So if direct or indirect bank involvement in a range of non-bank financial activities was prohibited, as was true under Glass-Steagall, then the range and scope of those activities are bound to be limited. Not surprisingly, right through the period of intensive regulation of the financial sector in the US, there was little financial "innovation" in terms of new institutions or instruments, though there were periods characterized by substantial and rapid growth in the financial sector. In the event, even by the 1950s, banking activity constituted 80-90 percent of that in the financial sector. And even at the end of the 1950s, savings accumulated in pension and mutual funds were small and trading on the New York Stock Exchange involved a daily average of three million shares at its peak as compared with as much as 160 million shares per day during the second half of the 1980s, when leverage became possible (Sametz, 1992).

A second consequence of the regulatory structure epitomized by Glass-Steagall was the implicit decree that banks would earn a relatively small rate of return defined largely by the net interest margin, or the difference between regulated deposit and lending rates adjusted for intermediation costs. Thus, in 1986 in the US, the reported return on assets for all commercial banks with assets of US$500 million or more averaged about 0.7 percent, with the average even for high-performance banks amounting to merely 1.4 percent. The net interest margin (to earning assets) was 5.2 percent for the high performance banks (Gup and Walter, 1991). This outcome of the regulatory structure was, however, in conflict with the fact that these banks were privately owned. What Glass-Steagall was saying was that because the role of the banks was so important for capitalism they had to be regulated in a fashion where, even though they were privately owned and socially important, they would earn less profit than other institutions in the financial sector and private institutions outside the financial sector.

This amounted to a deep inner contradiction in the system which set up pressures for deregulation. What is clear in hindsight is that Glass-Steagall type of regulation of a privately owned banking system was internally contradictory. It would inevitably lead to deregulation.

The Nature of Deregulation

The regulatory breakdown occurred finally in the 1980s and after when a host of factors linked, among other things, to the inability of the United States to ensure the continuance of a combination of high growth, near full employment and low inflation, disrupted this comfortable world. With wages rising faster than productivity and commodity prices—especially prices of oil—rising, inflation emerged as the principal problem in the 1970s. The fiscal and monetary response to inflation resulted in higher interest rates outside the banking sector, threatening the banking system (where interest rate regulation meant low or negative inflation-adjusted returns) with desertion of its depositors. Using this opportunity, non-bank financial companies expanded their activities. With US banking being predominantly privately owned, this situation where there were more lucrative profit opportunities outside of banking but banks were not allowed to diversify into those activities was untenable. The contradiction between private banking and strict regulation could no more be easily managed. The era of deregulation of interest rates and banking activity followed, paving the way for the transformation of the financial structure.

Once the specific response to the late-1960s and post-1960s crisis facing the US economy triggered the phase out of the regulated interest rate regime, a change in the institutional structure of the financial sector was inevitable. Initially money market funds grew in importance, stock market activity increased, market volatility was enhanced and new instruments to hedge against the risks associated with such volatility were created, triggering the process of securitization. The process of securitization intensified with instruments such as mortgage bonds.

With banks now having to cover the much higher interest rates they were paying on deposits, they had to have new avenues for investment. They saw their viability being dependent on entering non-bank businesses where profits were high. This included investment in junk bonds, real estate development loans and equity. Even though the risks involved were high banks were keen to enter these areas, emboldened by the US$100,000 per deposit coverage of deposit insurance. Thus the pressure to liberalize banking regulation was high.

This paved the way for the removal of restrictions on banking activity. The process of dismantling of the Chinese Walls separating different segments of the financial sector began in 1982, when the Office of the Comptroller of Currency permitted several banks to set up subsidiaries to engage in the discount brokerage business. Since then the process has continued. Bank holding companies were allowed to underwrite commercial paper, municipal revenue bonds, mortgage- and consumer loan-backed securities, and corporate bonds and equities through securities subsidiaries. The net result of these developments was a decline in the role of the banking business within financial markets.

Finally, to increase the flexibility that banks had in making invest-ments, bank solvency protection measures were diluted to make way for regulatory "forbearance". Capital standards were lowered, the intensity of supervision was relaxed and accounting rules simplified. Regulatory guidelines for banking increasingly imitated those for the securities business with requirements such as disclosure of information, mark-to-market accounting rules and risk-adjusted capital requirements.

Thus, by adopting a range of measures, the US state and federal governments and the Federal Reserve dismantled during the 1980s the system of regulation and the financial structure created by the policy framework put in place during and after the Great Depression.

The New Financial Framework

At the centre of the new financial framework was a set of beliefs on how financial markets functioned and therefore should be regulated. The first was that if norms with regard to accounting standards and disclosure were adhered to, capital provisioning, in the form of an 8 (or more) percent capital adequacy ratio, was an adequate means of insuring against financial failure.

Second, this was to be ensured by requiring that the size of regulatory capital was computed not on the actual value of assets but on a risk-weighted proxy of that value, where risk was assessed either by rating agencies or by the banks themselves by using complex algorithms. Risk-weighting was expected to achieve two results: it would inflate the size of regulatory capital required as the share of more risky assets in the portfolio of banks rises; it would discourage banks from holding too much by way of risky assets because that would lock up capital in forms that were near-barren.

Third, this whole system was to be made even more secure by allowing the market to generate instruments that helped, spread, insure or hedge against risks. These included derivatives of various kinds.

Fourth, use of the framework was seen as a way of separating out segments of the financial system that should be protected from excessive risk (for example, banks, in which depositors trusted their money) and those where sections which could be allowed to speculate (high net worth individuals) can legitimately do so (through hedge funds, private equity firms, and even investment banks).

Implicit in these beliefs was the idea that markets, institutions, instruments, indices and norms could be designed such that the financial system could regulate itself, getting off its back agencies that imposed structural and behavioral constraints to ensure the "soundness" of the financial system. The intervention of such agencies was seen as inimical to financial innovation and efficient provisioning of financial services. There was an element of systemic moral hazard involved here. If the system is seen as designed to self-regulate and is believed to be capable of self-regulation, then any evidence of speculation would be discounted. In fact, it would be seen as a legitimate opportunity for profit, leading to responses that reinforce such speculation.

The transformation of the financial framework, which unfolded over the last two decades and more, had many features. To start with, banks extended their activity beyond conventional commercial banking into merchant banking and insurance, either through the route where a holding company invested in different kinds of financial firms or by transforming themselves into universal banks offering multiple services.

Second, within banking, there was a gradual shift in focus from generating incomes from net interest margins to obtaining them in the form of fees and commissions charged for various financial services.

Third, related to this was a change in the focus of banking activity as well. While banks did provide credit and create assets that promised a stream of incomes into the future, they did not hold those assets any more. Rather they structured them into pools, "securitized" those pools, and sold these securities for a fee to institutional investors and portfolio managers. Banks transferred the risk for a fee, and those who bought into the risk looked to the returns they would earn in the long term. This "originate and distribute" model of banking meant, in the words of the OECD Secretariat (OECD, 2000), that banks were no longer museums, which "would take the asset and put it on their books much the way a museum would place a piece of art on the wall or under glass—to be admired and valued for its security and constant return", but parking lots which served as temporary holding spaces to bundle up assets and sell them to investors looking for long-term instruments. This meant that those who originated the credit assets tended to understate or discount the risks associated with them. Moreover, since many of the structured products created on the basis of these credit assets were complex derivatives, the risk associated with them was difficult to assess. The role of assessing risk was given to private rating agencies, which were paid to grade these instruments according to their level of risk and monitor them regularly for changes in risk profile.

Fourth, the ability of the banking system to "produce" credit assets or financial products meant that the ultimate limit to credit was the state of liquidity in the system and the willingness of those with access to that liquidity to buy these assets off the banks. Within a structure of this kind periods of easy money and low interest rates increased the pressure to create credit assets and proliferate risk.

Fifth, financial liberalization increased the number of layers in an increasingly universalized financial system, with the extent of regulation varying across the layers. Where regulation was light, as in the case of investment banks, hedge funds and private equity firms, financial companies could borrow huge amounts based on a small amount of own capital and undertake leveraged investments to create complex products that were often traded over the counter rather than through exchanges.

Finally, while the many layers of the financial structure were seen as independent and were differentially regulated depending on how and from whom they obtained their capital (such as small depositors, pension funds or high net worth individuals), they were in the final analysis integrated in ways that were not always transparent. Banks that sold credit assets to investment banks and claimed to have transferred the risk, lent to or invested in these investment banks in order to earn higher returns from their less regulated activities. Investment banks that sold derivatives to hedge funds, served as prime brokers for these funds and therefore provided them credit. Credit risk transfer neither meant that the risk disappeared nor that some segments were absolved from exposure to such risk.

That this complex structure which delivered extremely high profits to the financial sector was prone to failure has been clear for some time. For example, the number of bank failures in the United States increased after the 1980s. During 1955-1981, failures of US banks averaged 5.3 per year, excluding banks kept from going under by official open-bank assistance. On the other hand, during 1982-1990, failures averaged 131.4 per year, or 25 times as many as 1955-1981. During the four years ending 1990, failures averaged 187.3 per year (Kareken, 1992). The most spectacular set of failures, was that associated with the Savings and Loan crisis, which was precipitated by financial behavior induced by liberalization. Finally, the collapse of Long Term Capital Management pointed to the dangers of leveraged speculation. Each time a mini-crisis occurred, there were calls for a reversal of liberalization and increased regulation. But financial interests that had become extremely powerful and had come to influence the US Treasury managed to stave off criticism, stall any reversal and even ensure further liberalization. The view that had come to dominate the debate was that the financial sector had become too complex to be regulated from outside; what was needed was self-regulation.

Underlying the current crisis were two consequences of the developments outlined above. First, the "originate-and-distribute" model migrated out of the banking system to other segments of the financial sector. Second, this was facilitated by the fact that in more ways than one this resulting diversification and proliferation of finance, was leveraged by the liberalized banking system. Because of this complex chain, institutions at every level assumed that they were not carrying risk or were insured against it. However, risk does not go away, but resides somewhere in the system. And given financial integration, each firm was exposed to many markets and most firms were exposed to each other as lenders, investors or borrowers. Any failure would have a domino effect that would damage different firms to different extents.

It was for this reason, we now know, that while the problems began with defaults on sub-prime loans, the crisis soon afflicted the core of the financial structure: the banking sector. As in 1933, the danger of systemic failure if banks were allowed to close left the state with no choice but to step in.

The Response to the Crisis

In the event, after much dithering, governments in the developed industrial countries bought new equity in private banks to recapitalize them, effectively nationalizing a large part of the private banking system. This occurs even when analysts and policy makers are still debating whether nationalization is the best "option" when dealing with the banking crisis. Many warn that the inability to accept a reality that has gone ahead of the debate on policy has in turn slowed what appears to be an inevitable process of nationalization and may be adding to the costs of the crisis (Roubini, 2009).

The perceived inevitability of the process under way has meant that it is not just "socialists" who have read the writing on the wall. Even staunch free market advocates like former Federal Reserve Chairman Alan Greenspan, who made the case for regulatory forbearance and oversaw a regime of easy money that fuelled the speculative bubble (which he declared was just "froth") that preceded this crisis, now see nationalization as inevitable. In an interview to the *Financial Times* (van Duyn, 2009), Greenspan, identified by the newspaper "as the high priest of *laissez-faire* capitalism", said: "It may be necessary to temporarily nationalize some banks in order to facilitate a swift and orderly restructuring. I understand that once in a hundred years this is what you do."

This ideological leap has come at the end of a long transition during which the understanding of the nature of the problem afflicting the banks in these countries has been through many changes. Starting with the perception that their problem was one of inadequate liquidity, assessments moved on to focus initially on the effect that the fear of counterparty risk was having on intra-bank and intra-corporate lending and trading, and then on the effect that depreciated or toxic assets which could not be valued was having on bank solvency.

How Large are the Losses?

Estimates of the losses banks have sustained and the volume of bad assets they carry on their balance sheets vary. In its update to the *Global Financial Stability Report* for 2008 (International Monetary Fund, 2009), issued on 28 January 2009, the IMF had estimated the losses incurred by US and European banks from bad assets that originated in the US at US$2.2 trillion. Barely two months earlier, it had placed the figure at US$1.4 trillion. Loss estimates seem to be galloping and we are still counting.

Projections of likely total losses are even larger. On 21 January 2009, Nouriel Roubini and Elisa Parisi-Capone had projected, in their *RGE Monitor*, that global loan losses and write downs on US originated securitizations would total US$1.6 trillion on US$12.37 trillion in un-securitized loans (Agence France-Presse, 2009). About US$1.1 trillion of this is estimated to be incurred by US banks and brokerages. Another two trillion dollars will have to be written off because of a fall in the value of financial holdings currently estimated at US$10.84 trillion. US banks and brokers possibly carry losses of US$600 billion to US$700 billion out of this amount. As a result, the total losses of the financial system were estimated at US$3.6 trillion, half of which were borne by US firms. If these assessments by Roubini and Capone are correct, the losses would overwhelm the US financial system, which, according to them, had a capitalization of US$1.3 trillion dollars in commercial banks and US$110 billion in investment banks as of the third quarter of 2008.

par or more, it would amount to blowing taxpayers' money to save badly behaved bank managers, since the assets were likely to be worth a fraction what they were actually bought for. On the other hand, if some scheme such as a reverse auction (or one in which sellers bid down prices to entice the buyer to acquire their assets) is used to acquire the bad assets, then the sale prices of these assets would be extremely low and the so-called good banks would incur huge losses which they would have to write down leading to insolvency (Elliott, 2009b). The only way out it appeared was if these banks just wrote down their assets and were saved from bankruptcy by the government through recapitalization or the injection of capital into them. Additional capital injection seemed unavoidable, but since such capital would only come from the government it raised the specter of nationalization.

Injecting capital need not, however, imply nationalization, if for example it takes the form of loans to banks or investments in preferred stock with no voting rights or limited voting rights. In the US, for example, the US$387 billion first phase of the US$700 billion Troubled Assets Relief Program (TARP) involved capital injections in various forms through a multitude of schemes (Office of the Special Inspector General for the Troubled Assets Relief Program [SIGTARP], 2009). Principal among these for the bank rescue effort were the Capital Purchase Program (CPP), the Targeted Investment Program (TIP) and the Asset Guarantee Program (AGP). More than 300 banks participated in the first in which capital was infused through purchases of "senior preferred stock" and acquisition of warrants that gave the government the right but not the obligation to buy common stock at a pre-specified price. As a senior preferred stock holder, the government is paid a fixed percentage return (before common stock holders are paid dividends) of 5 percent for the first five years and 9 percent thereafter, but does not have normal voting rights.[1] Firms can buy back the stock at prices at which they sold them after three years. In return for buying preferred stock, the government would be issued warrants.[2] In the case of the TIP and AGP too, which were directed specifically at Citigroup and Bank of America, preferred stock, warrants and loans were the means of financing and not the purchase of common equity (Table 11.1).

Tangible Common Equity

These forms of financing ensured that banks could be supported by the government without actual take over through common equity purchase. However, it soon became clear that the adequacy of these forms of financing depends on the volume of losses and write offs and the resulting capital

It needs noting that the equity base of most banks is relatively small even when they follow Basel norms with regard to capital adequacy. Banks can use a variety of assets to ensure such adequacy and the required volume of regulatory capital can be reduced by accumulating assets with high ratings (which we now know are not adequate indicators of risk). This results in the available regulatory capital being small relative to the risky asset-backed securities held by the banks, which, in turn, could lead to insolvency.

The IMF estimates that global banks that have already obtained much support including capital from governments would need further new capital infusions of around half a trillion to stay solvent. With that much and perhaps more capital going in, the case for public ownership of banking would be strong in some countries. By late January 2009, Bloomberg estimates, banks had written down US$792 billion in losses and raised US$826 billion in capital, of which US$380 billion came from governments (quoted in International Monetary Fund, 2009: 2). Across the world, write-downs and capital raised as of 15 December 2008 have been estimated at US$993 billion and US$918 billion respectively, with the figures for US and Europe as of mid-December being US$548 billion and US$678 billion and US$292 billion and US$318 billion respectively (World Economic Forum, 2009 and Figure 11.1). The high level of capital

Figure 11.1　Worldwide bank write-downs and credit losses versus capital raised till December 15, 2008 (US$ billion)

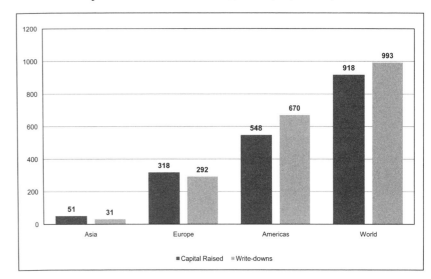

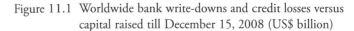

Source: World Economic Forum 2009, Figure 15.

raised in Europe relative to losses written down may be because of the faster moves by governments in the UK and Europe, especially the UK, Ireland and Iceland, to shore up bank balance sheets.

Interconnectedness

The infusion of capital and the government's presence in the banking sector is expected to increase because the recognition of losses tends to be gradual. The difficulty with bad derivative assets is that they have to be valued on mark-to-market principles. Since these assets are not all being traded, valuation is difficult and there is a lag in the recognition of the losses suffered through holding such assets. In the US, the process of price discovery began a long time back when in August 2007, Bear Stearns declared that investments in one of its hedge funds set up to invest in mortgage backed securities had lost all its value and those in a second such fund were valued at nine cents for every dollar of original investment. Despite that early discovery, even by the beginning of 2009, loss estimates were still rising.

The Bear Sterns experience made clear that once losses are discovered even in an investment bank, the implications are systemic. Bear Stearns was a highly leveraged institution. In November 2007 it had US$11.1 billion in tangible equity capital, which supported investments in US$395 billion of assets, reflecting a leverage ratio of more than 35 to one (Boyd, 2008). And its assets were reportedly less liquid than those of many of its competitors. Thus, it was not just that the assets held by the investment bank were bad, but that there were many other institutions, including banks, that were exposed to bad assets through their relationship with Stearns. Yet, they were slow in recognizing their potential losses. It is for this reason that the US government chose to "save" Bear Stearns by initially offering it an unlimited loan facility delivered through Wall Street Bank J.P. Morgan Chase, and then getting the latter to acquire the firm. As many recognized then, Bear Stearns was too "interconnected" to be allowed to fail at a time when financial markets were extremely fragile.

However, this lesson had not been learnt in full. When in September 2008, troubled Lehman Brothers Holdings Inc., the fourth largest invest-ment bank on Wall Street came to the table with requests for support, it was refused the same. This refusal of the state to take over the responsibility of managing failing firms was supposed to send out a strong message. Not only was Lehman forced to file for bankruptcy, but a giant like Merrill Lynch that had also notched up large losses due to sub-prime related exposures decided that it should sort matters out before there were no suitors interested

in salvaging it as well. In a surprise move, Bank of America spoken to as a potential buyer of Lehman was persuaded to Lynch instead, bringing down two of the major independ banks on Wall Street.

This was, however, only part of the problem that behind. The other major issue was the impact its bankrupt on its creditors. Citigroup and Bank of New York Mellon w to have an exposure to the institution that was placed a US$155 billion. A clutch of Japanese banks, led by Aozor owed an amount in excess of a billion. There were Europea had significant exposure. And all of these were already faced balance sheets (Financial Times Reporters, 2008). Soon trou banking markets with a spurt of bank failures seeming inevita indications of this problem had emerged at least a year-and-a what was surprising was that the full import of the problem not recognized. As noted earlier, the perception was that the pro by these institutions—inadequate liquidity in the market and mark down asset values because of the temporary problem crea sub-prime crisis—could be easily addressed.

The Road to Capital Infusion

In what followed, central banks pumped huge amounts of liquidit system and reduced interest rates. In the US, the Federal Reserv to hold the worthless paper that the banks had accumulated and them credit at low interest rates in return. But the problem woul away. By then, every institution suspected that every other institu insolvent and did not want to risk lending. The money was there, b would not flow through the pipe without damaging consequences financial system and for the real economy.

It was at this point that it was realized that what needed to be d to clear out the bad assets with the banks. Among the smart ideas thou for the purpose was the notion of splitting the system into "good" and banks. If a set of bad banks could be set up with public money, anc banks acquired the bad assets of the banks, the balance sheets of the it was argued, will be repaired. The bad banks themselves can serve a reconstruction corporations that might be able to sell off a part of thei assets as the good banks get about their business and the economy rev

This idea missed the whole point, because it did not take accou the price at which the bad assets were to be acquired. If they were acqu

Table 11.1 First phase TARP commitments by program as of January 23, 2009
(US$ billion)

Program	Amount	Form
Capital Purchase Programme (CPP)	194.2	Senior Preferred Stock and Warrants of Common Stock
Systemically Significant Failing Institutions (SSFI): AIG	40	Senior Preferred Stock
Targeted Investment Program (TIP): Citigroup and Bank of America	40	Senior Preferred Stock and Warrants of Common Stock
Asset Guarantee (AGP): Citigroup and Bank of America	5	Insurance against Preferred Stock Premium or Guarantees or Non-Recourse Loans against Assets
Automotive Industry Financing Program (AIFP)	20.8	Investment and Senior Preferred Membership Interest

Source: SIGTARP (2009: Table ES.1, p. 6).

infusion required. If these are large, for example, preferred stock is not good enough. Such stock or even loans are senior in the capital structure and are not the immediate means of covering losses, because holders of those kinds of financial assets need to be compensated first when losses force liquidation of some assets. Only holders of common equity immediately absorb losses when incurred and need to be provided for. So, it is the common equity base that gets eroded first and it is when capital of this kind is reasonably adequate that solvency is guaranteed. In the final analysis, solvency depends on tangible common equity (TCE) which not only excludes intangible assets (such as goodwill) from the measure of assets, but also preferred stock, including shares issued to the US Treasury.

The TCE ratio measures the ratio of tangible common equity to total tangible assets, and depending on circumstances relating to the balance sheets of banks and their bottom lines, the required level of the TCE ratio for solvency could be high. Estimates of required TCE ratios, therefore, vary, but analysts hold that banks with tangible common equity below 3 percent of assets should consider raising more capital (Shen, 2009). Not surprisingly, as banks and insurance companies such as AIG report larger and larger losses and write downs, the need to shore up their TCE ratios has increased. Further, since debt requires paying interest and preferred stock requires payment of fixed dividends, while dividends on equity are variable and only need to be paid out of profits, the presence of a large volume of debt and preferred stock affects the liquidity of the banks, whereas the presence of common equity does not.

An interventionist government can, of course, seek to buffer systemic effects by forcing creditors and preferred stock holders to bear the losses of firms they have financed. The difficulty is that if the government decides to enforce conversion of loans provided by private lenders into common equity, these lenders would lose the protection afforded to a holder of senior capital. Further, if large amounts of new common equity is issued in return for debt, there is a danger that the value of that equity could quickly fall below the price at which loans are converted to equity, transferring the losses from the banks concerned to the lenders and creating ripple effects that can have systemic implications for the financial sector as a whole. Those possibilities are real because bank bonds amount to a quarter of US investment-grade corporate bonds (Wolf, 2009). It is for this reason that many, like Alan Greenspan, suggested that nationalization that protects creditors or holders of senior debt is the answer to the problem of widespread bank insolvency. Though debt-equity swaps are common means of dealing with bankruptcies, they may not be the best route to take in the current circumstances. Nationalization recommends itself because it prevents the spread of fear and uncertainty among creditors to or investors in the liabilities of banks, such as insurance and pension funds.

As a result, there is increasing pressure in the case of a number of financial institutions to convert preferred stock acquired by the government (and not the private sector) into common equity. Conversion of that kind is bound to increase the share of common equity held by the government in the banks. The moment that exceeds 51 percent this amounts to nationalization. Even when the share of government equity is lower than 51 percent, it can be large enough to give government significant influence or even control over the banks concerned. With the material basis for influencing or even determining bank decisions and behavior, the government cannot absolve itself of the responsibility of ensuring that banks provide credit to facilitate a recovery, that such credit is not concentrated in the hands of a few sectors and sections, and that bank managers behave in ways that are socially acceptable. The pressure to oversee and regulate the payment of salaries, bonuses, retrenchment benefits and pensions to managers in service or asked to quit for overseeing failure in the nationalized banks is only the more discussed set of responsibilities that the government cannot avoid.

What is of significance is that this responsibility now holds in a wide segment of the banking system. The US Treasury is putting 19 banks, with assets of more than US$100 billion, through a stress-testing program, aimed at assessing the losses they are likely to sustain under alternative scenarios regarding the projected fall in GDP in the second and third quarters of 2009. This would be the basis on which the question of whether and, if so, how much of additional capital these banks would require would be answered. Initially, this capital is to be provided through the issue of convertible preferred securities to the Treasury, to be replaced with capital raised from private sources in the form of common equity. If that does not happen within a specified period (currently six months), these securities will be converted into equity on an "as-needed basis".

Many see this as an attempt to postpone the decision to issue common equity to the government in the hope that nationalization can be averted. If conversion occurs, such nationalization is inevitable given the scale of the government's holding of preferred equity and the volume of losses that banks are estimated to be carrying. Thus, in the case of Citigroup, by mid-February the government held US$52 billion worth of preferred shares, which was five times the firm's market value as of 20 February (Son, 2009). Bank of America, which had received US$45 billion in TARP funds in exchange for preferred shares and warrants, would be 66 percent owned by the government if its entire stake were converted to common equity. The figure would be 69 percent in the case of Regions Financial Corp. in Birmingham, Alabama, which had received US$3.5 billion from the US. And, it would be a huge 83 percent at Fifth Third Bancorp, which had received US$3.4 billion from TARP.

Conversion of the government's preferred stock, loans and warrants to common equity would create a socialized banking system particularly because the banks involved include the big ones. In the US for example, the four biggest commercial banks—JPMorgan Chase, Citigroup, Bank of America and Wells Fargo—hold 64 percent of the assets of all US commercial banks. According to reports, in January 2009, Bank of America, the largest US bank in terms of assets, had tangible common equity that stood at 2.83 percent of tangible assets, Citigroup had a lower 1.5 percent ratio, and JPMorgan Chase & Co., had tangible common equity equal to 3.8 percent of tangible assets (Shen, 2009).

Skepticism that the threat of insolvency in banking can be solved with the help of private capital also arises because of the sizes of these institutions. It was partly that problem that encouraged governments outside the US to accept back-door nationalization in the case of institutions that are too big to fail. Though the financial crisis originated in the US, nationalization occurred first in Iceland (were the need was immediate), Ireland and the UK, where banking majors Royal Bank of Scotland and Lloyds Group are now under dominant public control, and others are expected to follow.[3]

Alternatives to Nationalization

Yet, resistance to nationalization in the US continues. A number of arguments have been made against nationalization (Blinder, 2009). The two most powerful ones are that since the problem of valuation of assets would not go away with nationalization, the amount of tax-payers' money that may have to be pumped could prove enormous and indefensible. The other is that there are more than 8,300 banks in the US, and once the nationalization process starts, it would be impossible to draw the line to limit the process. This again would amount to skimming the taxpayer far too much.

To deal with this dilemma of the immediate need to nationalize, but also of perceived constraints to and ideological objections to doing so, there are two options that are being recommended. The first is to use regulatory devices to ensure that bank managers, shareholders and creditors adopt policies that can restore the viability of and confidence in the banking system. The government as regulator has enough measures at hand to ensure that stakeholders behave in a fashion that suits the system. This could include getting creditors and private holders of preferred stock to convert to common equity.

The second route being recommended is that of temporary nationalization.[4] Take over the ailing banks by buying into common equity, it is argued, but only till such time as their health is restored and they can be privatized so that the government's investments using tax payers' money is largely, if not fully, recouped. The expectation that investments can be recouped may be belied for long, leading either to losses for the tax payer or a continuation of nationalized banking.

However, the Swedish experience during the banking crisis of the early 1990s is often quoted as an example of what can be done. A combination of a real estate bubble financed with credit and an interest rate shock resulted in 1991 in large losses at Första Sparbanken, Sweden's largest savings bank. Other banks, including Nordbanken, the country's third-largest commercial bank, also began reporting big losses. As a first step to resolve the problem, the Swedish government, which owned a significant proportion of common stock in these banks chose to buy into new shares and buy out the private shareholders at the equity issue price. The government also provided a blanket guarantee of all bank loans in the Swedish banking system. Moreover, the Swedish central bank provided liquidity by depositing large foreign currency reserves in troubled banks, and by allowing banks to borrow freely the Swedish currency. All this having been done, the banks were split into good and bad banks, where the bad banks which took over doubtful assets functioned like asset reconstruction corporations that were financed with loans from the parent banks and equity from the government. The task of these entities was to liquidate, in an orderly fashion, the troubled assets so as to maximize recovery. Once the crisis was resolved, the good bank was auctioned off to recoup tax payers' money and restore private ownership (Eckbo, 2009; Viotti, 2000). This form of restructuring is an option if the crisis is largely restricted to a segment of the banking sector. However, as Blinder (2009) notes: "The Swedes had a relatively simple task. They never had to deal with institutions of the size and complexity of our (the US') banking behemoths." Moreover, if the government was so successful in resolving the crisis, what prevents it from retaining bank control to prevent such crises in the future. Unless it is shown that public ownership has costs which far outweigh its ability to pre-empt crisis, privatization cannot be logically justified.

Further, as noted at the beginning of this paper there is a more serious issue to contend with. The almost inexorable tendency to public ownership of banking in the US can be traced to sources deeper than just a crisis due to mismanagement. It rests in the fact that even under capitalism, the core of the banking system must be publicly owned, since regulation required to ensure its stability reduces relative profits and discriminates against private owners of banks. This is why a system regulated by Glass-Steagall and all it represented, that served the US well during the Golden Age of high growth, had to give way to deregulation. But as we know now, such deregulation seems to inevitably lead back to nationalization. So capitalism appears to need a publicly owned banking system for its proper functioning. That is a factor that must be confronted and resolved if the current move to nationalization is to be just "temporary", as Greenspan wants it to be.

The Other Case for Public Banking

There is one obvious lesson from the current crisis. Despite the proclaimed sophistication of the current Anglo-Saxon model of the financial sector, its transparency, its accounting standards and its financial innovations that ostensibly reduce risk, it leads to failure with systemic implications. This is not surprising since the creation of the current financial structure was predicated on dismantling a regulatory structure expressly designed to deal with fragility.

The implications for developing countries are clear. They should stall and reverse the movement to private from public ownership or opt for public ownership if banking is fully private. This would serve a larger purpose. The regulatory framework that Glass-Steagall represented was created to deal with fragility. But intervention to shape financial structures is needed for another reason, viz. to use the financial sector as an instrumentality for broad-based and equitable growth. This is particularly required in late industrializing developing countries faced with international inequality and handicapped by an inadequately developed capitalist class.

Further, Glass-Steagall may not be a full solution today, and there could be contexts where a degree of financial integration could play a role. In particular, countries which want to use the financial structure as an instrument to further broad-based growth may need to opt for universal banks that follow unconventional lending strategies, when compared with the typical commercial bank. Many years ago, Gerschenkron had pointed to the role which certain institutional adjustments in the financial sector played in the success of late-industrializers like France and Germany. Basing his arguments on the roles played by Crédit Mobilier of the brothers Pereire in France and the "universal banks" in Germany, Gerschenkron (1962) argued that the creation of "financial organizations designed to build thousands of miles of railroads, drill mines, erect factories, pierce canals, construct ports and modernize cities" was hugely transformative. Financial firms based on the old wealth were typically in the nature of rentier capitalists and limited themselves to flotation of government loans and foreign exchange transactions. The new firms were "devoted to railroadization and industrialization of the country" and, in the process, influenced the behavior of old wealth as well.

As Gerschenkron (1962: 13) argued: "The difference between banks of the credit-mobilier type and commercial banks of the time (England) was absolute. Between the English bank essentially designed to serve as a source of short-term capital and a bank designed to finance the long-run investment needs of the economy there was a complete gulf. The German banks, which may be taken as a paragon of the type of the universal bank, successfully combined the basic idea of the credit mobilier with the short-term activities of commercial banks"

The banks, according to Gerschenkron, substituted for the absence of a number of elements crucial to industrialization: "In Germany, the various incompetencies of the individual entrepreneurs were offset by the device of splitting the entrepreneurial function: the German investment banks—a powerful invention, comparable in economic effect to that of the steam engine—were in their capital-supplying functions a substitute for the insufficiency of the previously created wealth willingly placed at the disposal of entrepreneurs. But they were also a substitute for entrepreneurial deficiencies. From their central vantage points of control, the banks participated actively in shaping the major—and sometimes even not so major—decisions of the individual enterprises. It was they who often mapped out a firm's paths of growth, conceived far-sighted plans, decided on major technological and locational innovations, and arranged for mergers and capital increases" (Gerschenkron, 1968: 137).

Thus, setting up Chinese Walls separating various segments of the financial sector may not be the best option. Nor could investment banks and hedge funds be abolished. What could however be done is to monitor investment banks and hedge funds and subject them to regulation, while seeking an institutional solution that would protect the core of the financial structure: the banking system. Fortunately, the current bail-out has provided the basis for such a transformation by opting for state ownership and influence over decision making.

A Role for Public Ownership

Can this be an important step in shaping an alternative regulatory structure in developing countries, in particular? Public ownership of banks could serve a number of overarching objectives:

➤ It ensures the information flow and access needed to pre-empt fragility by substantially reducing any incompatibility in incentives driving bank managers, on the one hand, and bank supervisors and regulators, on the other. This is a much better insurance against bank failure than efforts to circumscribe its areas of operation, which can be circumvented.

➤ By subordinating the profit motive to social objectives, it allows the system to exploit the potential for cross subsidization and to direct credit, despite higher costs, to targeted sectors and disadvantaged sections of society at different interest rates. This permits the fashioning of a system of inclusive finance that can substantially reduce financial exclusion.

➤ By giving the state influence over the process of financial intermediation, it allows the government to use the banking industry as a lever to advance the development effort. In particular, it allows for the mobilization of technical and scientific talent to deliver both credit and technical support to agriculture and the small-scale industrial sector.

This multifaceted role for state-controlled banking allows policies aimed at preventing fragility and avoiding failure to be combined with policies aimed at achieving broad-based and inclusive development. Directed credit at differential interest rates can lead economic activity in chosen sectors, regions and segments of the population. It amounts to building a financial structure in anticipation of real sector activities, particularly in underdeveloped and under-banked regions of a country.

The importance of public ownership to ensure financial inclusion cannot be overstressed. Central to a framework of inclusive finance are policies aimed at pre-empting bank credit for selected sectors like agriculture and small-scale industry. Pre-emption can take the form of specifying that a certain proportion of lending should be directed at these sectors. In addition, through mechanisms such as the provision of refinance facilities, banks can be offered incentives to realize their targets. Directed credit programs should also be accompanied by a regime of differential interest rates that ensure demand for credit from targeted sectors by cheapening the cost of credit. Such policies have been and are still used in developed countries as well.

Credit pre-emption, aimed at directing debt-financed expenditures to specific sectors, can also be directly exploited by the state. In many instances, besides a cash reserve ratio, the central bank requires a part of the deposits of the banking system to be held in specified securities, including government securities. This ensures that banks are forced to make a definite volume of investment in debt issued by government agencies. Such debt can be used to finance expenditures warranted by the overall development strategy of the government, including its poverty alleviation component. Beyond a point, however, these roles have to be dissociated from traditional commercial banks and located in specialized institutions.

Inclusive finance of this kind inevitably involves the spread of formal financial systems to areas where client densities are low and transaction costs are high. Further, to ensure sustainable credit up-take by disadvantaged groups, interest rates charged may have to diverge from market rates. This regime of differential or discriminatory interest rates may require policies of cross-subsidization and even government support to ensure the viability of chosen financial intermediaries. Intervention of this kind presumes a substantial degree of "social control" over commercial banks and development banking institutions.

It implies that "social banking" involves a departure from conventional indicators of financial performance such as costs and profitability and requires the creation of regulatory systems that ensure that the "special status" of these institutions is not misused. In sum, "inclusive finance" as a regime is defined as much by the financial structure in place as by policies such as directed credit and differential interest rates. To ensure compliance with financial inclusion guidelines, governments can use and have used public ownership of a significant section of the banking/financial system to ensure the realization of developmental and distributional objectives. This was recognized by governments in many countries in Europe, where banking development in the early post-World War II period took account of the vital differences between banking and other industries. Recognizing the role the banking industry could play, many countries with predominantly capitalist economic structures thought it fit either to nationalize their banks or to subject them to rigorous surveillance and social control. France, Italy and Sweden are typical examples in this respect. Overall, even as late as the 1970s, the state owned as much as 40 percent of the assets of the largest commercial and development banks in the industrialized countries (United Nations, 2005).

Conclusion

Thus, contemporary developments and historical experience illustrate the positive effects that public ownership can have in varying contexts, and offer it as a key element of a new model for global banking. But this is not to say that this one advance can resolve this crisis, guard against future ones and make finance developmental and inclusive. New governance structures to make public ownership work may be necessary. And the crisis offers other lessons for the kind of regulation we need to shape. What the crisis teaches us is that public ownership of banking is a necessary, even if not sufficient condition for stable, broad-based and inclusive growth.

Notes

1. The kind of preferred stock is a type of "hybrid" security, combining some of the risks and potential increased returns of equity but also some of the safety features of debt such as regular interest payments.
2. SIGTARP (2009: 38) gives the following example of how the warrants system works: "On 23 October 2008, Treasury purchased US$10 billion in Morgan Stanley preferred stock, and, as an incentive, received 65,245,759 warrants at a strike price of US$22.99. As of 23 January 2009, Morgan Stanley's stock

price was $18.71, which means that the warrants are 'out of the money'." To be "in the money", Morgan Stanley's stock price would have had to gain more than US$4.28.

3. However, even here the willingness to declare the process as nationalization is still lacking. The attempt in Europe is to create an "autonomous", but state-funded body between the government and the banks to create the impression of distance. The UK has the UK Financial Investments Ltd, Germany the SoFFin, and Belgium has transferred banking stakes to a pre-existing Federal Holding Company. This may blur the image of state control, but does not dilute such control.

4. There are other absurd proposals being floated. One is a public-private partnership in which private sector investors would be persuaded with federal incentives to join a venture to buy toxic assets from the banks. The federal incentives could include a guaranteed the floor value of the assets or subsidized financing. If so, the scheme would amount to creating a "bad bank" by providing government guarantees for toxic asset sales at pre-specified minimum prices and financing the bank with interest subsidies and loans from tax payers' money (Elliott, 2009a).

References

Agence France-Presse (2009). Global banking losses to hit 3.6 trillion dlrs: Roubini. 22 January. http://www.google.com/hostednews/afp/article/ALeqM5jAmJ_Prl0zODFJrmvFdmOb-X5W8A (accessed 8 March).

Blinder, Alan S. (2009). Nationalize? Hey, Not so fast. *New York Times*, 8 March.

Boyd, Roddy (2008). The last days of Bear Stearns. Fortune/CNNMoney.com. 31 March. http://money.cnn.com/2008/03/28/magazines/fortune/boyd_bear.fortune/ (accessed 20 December 2008).

Eckbo, B. Espen (2009). Scandinavia: Failed banks, state control and a rapid recovery. *Financial Times*, 22 January.

Elliott, Douglas J. (2009a). *Guaranteeing Toxic Assets: Choosing among the Options*. Brookings Institution, Washington, DC.

Elliott, Douglas J. (2009b). *The Administration's New Financial Rescue Plan*. Brookings Institution, Washington, DC.

Financial Times Reporters (2008). Lehman Brothers files for bankruptcy. *Financial Times*, 15 September.

Gerschenkron, Alexander (1962). *Economic Backwardness in Historical Perspective: A Book of Essays*. The Belknap Press of Harvard University Press, Cambridge, MA.

Gerschenkron, Alexander (1968). *Continuity in History and Other Essays*. The Belknap Press of Harvard University Press, Cambridge, MA.

Gup, Benton E., and John R. Walter (1991). Profitable large banks: The key to their success. In Donald Chew (ed.). *New Developments in Commercial Banking*. Blackwell, Cambridge, MA: 37-42.

International Monetary Fund (2009). Global Financial Stability Report: Market Update. GFSR Market Update. 28 January. http://www.imf.org/external/pubs/ft/fmu/eng/2009/01/index.htm (accessed February 20, 2009).

Kareken, John H. (1992). Regulation of commercial banking in the United States. In Peter Newman, Murray Millgate and John Eatwell (eds). *The New Palgrave Dictionary of Money and Finance*, Vol. 3. Macmillan, London: 315-319.

OECD (2000). *The Service Economy*. Organization for Economic Cooperation and Development, Paris.

Roubini, Nouriel (2009). Time to nationalize insolvent banks. February, Project Syndicate, New York. http://www.project-syndicate.org/commentary/roubini11 (accessed 10 March).

Sametz, A.W. (1992). Financial innovation and regulation in the United States. *Palgrave Dictionary of Finance*. The Macmillan Press, London: 71-75.

Shen, Linda (2009). Obama bank nationalization is focus of speculation (Update 3). Bloomberg.com. February 23. http://www.bloomberg.com/apps/news?pid=email_en&refer=home&sid=an.TP4kSHkuo (accessed March 8, 2009).

SIGTARP (2009). *Initial Report to the Congress: 6 February 2009*. Office of the Special Inspector General for the Troubled Asset Relief Program, Washington, DC.

Son, Hugh (2009). AIG may convert preferred shares to common. 23 February. http://www.bloomberg.com/apps/news?pid=email_en&refer=us&sid=aFvU7x_hoHYo (accessed 8 March 2009).

United Nations (2005). *World Economic and Social Survey 2005: Financing for Development*. United Nations Department of Economic and Social Affairs, New York.

van Duyn, Aline (2009). Thanks for the memories, but they don't tell the true story. *Financial Times*, 19 February.

Viotti, Staffan (2000). Dealing with banking crises — proposal for a new regulatory framework. *Economic Review*, 3.

Wolf, Martin (2009). To nationalize or not — that is the question. *Financial Times*, 3 March.

World Economic Forum (2009). *The Future of the Global System: A Near-Term Outlook and Long-Term Scenarios*. World Economic Forum, Geneva.

12

The Report of the Commission of Experts on Reform of the International Monetary and Financial System and Its Economic Rationale[1]

Jan Kregel

Background to the Commission

In the autumn of 2008, as the sub-prime mortgage crisis, that had begun a year earlier in the United States, turned into a global financial and economic crisis quickly spreading to other countries, the President of the United Nations General Assembly convened a panel of experts to discuss the crisis' implications for developing countries in an interactive dialogue with the General Assembly. As a result of this dialogue, he decided to appoint an independent Commission of Experts[2] on Reform of the International Monetary and Financial System, with the mandate to analyze the causes of the crisis, to assess its impacts on all countries and to suggest adequate responses to avoid its recurrence and to restore global economic stability.

In undertaking its work, the Commission sought to identify the broad institutional principles and policy options required for sustained global economic progress and stability, and to thereby ensure that the advantages of a closely interdependent world economy would be enjoyed by all countries, developed and less developed. It also sought to provide a range of credible and feasible proposals for reforming the international monetary and financial system, in the broad interest of the international community, and to identify and evaluate the merits and limitations of alternative reform proposals.

In response to this mandate, the Commission produced an initial set of Recommendations[3] that were considered at an Interactive Dialogue of the General Assembly in March 2009. Its subsequent, more extensive Preliminary Report served as an input to the preparatory process leading to the June 2009 Conference at the Highest Level on the World Financial and Economic Crisis and its Impact on Development, called for in the final outcome document of the Follow-up International Conference on Financing for Development to Review the Implementation of the Monterrey Consensus adopted at Doha on 2 December 2008.[4]

The Economic Background

The mandate of the Commission recalls the 1944 United Nations Conference on Monetary and Financial Affairs that gave rise to the Bretton Woods system. That Conference was convened to provide a response to the global financial crisis of the late 1920s and the subsequent Great Depression of the 1930s. It concentrated on the creation of an international monetary system that could provide exchange rate stability and prevent the beggar-thy-neighbor devaluations that had characterized the interwar period. It also sought a system that would not force policy makers to make deflationary adjustments in response to short-term balance of payment shocks, as had been the case under the old gold standard. Furthermore, it sought to design a system that would be free from cross-border hot money flows and addressed difficulties in achieving agreement over reparations and inter-allied war debts, which had contributed to the demise of the pre-war exchange rate system and distorted trade flows through their influence on exchange rates.

While the 1944 Conference was an intergovernmental meeting of government representatives drafting proposals for the formation of the international institutions, which have formed the architecture of the international monetary and financial system, the Commission is composed of independent experts seeking to provide answers and alternatives that could be used by other bodies dealing with reform issues at the intergovernmental level. The Commission aimed to deal with both recovery and reform policies, at both the national and international level, rather than focusing on the more limited scope of Bretton Woods.

The discussions of the Commission drew on two fundamental economic principles. The first is that in a world of extensive externalities, markets often generate sub-optimal outcomes if they are not constrained by the appropriate regulatory framework. Given the extent of interdependence in today's global economy, almost every policy decision has consequences beyond the national borders of the country that implements them. Since the crisis has not been contained in the developed economies' financial systems where it started, and has taken on global dimensions, the external impact of national policies must have as much importance as their domestic impact in individual countries. Consequently, a major priority for the international community must be to ensure that any measures proposed to help manage the crisis be assessed on two levels. They should achieve the desired domestic objectives and also complement and support domestic policies chosen in the other countries of the world.

This means that additional measures must be taken to ensure complementarity and coordination between those seeking crisis response measures and those seeking to build a more secure and stable international financial system. The Commission has tried to apply this principle at all levels of its analysis, from macroeconomic stimulus policies to microeconomic measures to improve regulation of financial systems and reform of the international financial system.

The second fundamental principle is that a satisfactory level of resource utilization at the global level depends on a sufficient level of aggregate demand in all the major economies. Fiscal policies need to be designed to meet the objectives of providing full and productive employment for domestic and global resources, rather than to provide a particular fiscal balance. If, because of a financial crisis, households and firms have to rebuild their asset positions by reducing consumption and increasing saving, the government will have to offset the resulting reduction in private demand by deficit spending. Otherwise, the decline in net demand would produce further declines in wealth and income, leading to a deflationary spiral similar to that during the Great Depression. In a globalized economy, it is important that the required size and impact of these measures be looked at on a globally integrated basis, rather than from the perspective of each individual national economy. This stresses the importance of identifying policy externalities in the design and assessment of government fiscal policies introduced to meet the crisis.

Causes of the Financial Meltdown in Developed Countries

It is now recognized that the loans made to sub-prime borrowers were, in many cases, fraudulent and, in almost all cases, unviable given the borrowers' income. Resolving the crisis thus requires an explanation of how and why the financial system in the US started to engage in these types of financial transactions.

In the 1980s, the United States started a process of liberalization and deregulation of financial institutions that had been subject to Glass-Steagall New Deal regulations that strictly limited the activities that they could engage in. Commercial banks were essentially limited to taking deposits and making short-term loans while investment banks engaged in capital market activities such as underwriting equity finance for firms and trading and acting as agents for these securities in secondary markets such as the stock exchange. As new financial institutions entered the market, they started to compete with existing institutions, and thus caused a decline in their income, and consequently, in their stability. Commercial banks and thrift institutions were especially vulnerable, and Congress decided that they could be made safer by allowing them more leeway to compete with these other institutions by removing restrictions on their activities.

At the same time, the ideological revolution in political and economic theory in favor of the efficiency of private activities led to a belief that the self-regulating nature of market competition would not only make regulation less important, but also eliminate distortions. This eventually led to a revision of US regulations that repealed the Glass-Steagall Act and introduced the Financial Modernization Act in 1999 that allowed financial institutions to operate in virtually any type of activity within a holding company structure. These moves were supported by the rapid introduction of financial innovations in risk management that suggested that they could replace regulation as the guarantee of stability of the financial system. These same policies encouraged the globalization of the financial system and through the proposals of institutions such as the Bank for International Settlements, the IMF, and the Financial Stability Forum, now the Financial Stability Board, pushed for opening up the financial systems in developing countries.

Globalization of Financial Markets and Propagation of the Crisis

The deliberations of the Commission were set in a fully multilateral framework. Since the current crisis has global dimensions and implications, the proposed solutions must also be global. The Commission's approach is also based on the recognition that one of the basic objectives of the original Bretton Woods system was to provide a mechanism of symmetric adjustment of international payments imbalances in such a way that the ability of any country to achieve full employment was not compromised.

The large international imbalances that characterize the current international system, and the use by many developed and developing countries of policies to support growth and development based on external demand, suggests that in the absence of unwarranted expansion in the financial sector, there would have been a structural deficiency of global demand. Resolving the financial crisis will thus be integrally linked to the need to provide adjustment to international imbalances that supports the level of aggregate global demand. Simply put, it is impossible for all countries to rely on external demand.

The Report also recognizes that asymmetry in the level of development of the major trading countries has contributed to the large international imbalances in international trade and finance. These imbalances have been the source of the excessive creation of debt to finance the level of demand required to provide growth for the global economy. In the US, which has been the major contributor to global demand through its large current account deficit, this has been achieved by providing consumers with the finance required to allow them to consume in excess of their incomes, the resulting indebtedness being covered by the bubble in housing prices that has allowed their debt to net wealth ratios to remain stable. In addition, low interest rates in the United States have meant that consumers could carry this debt burden without a large increase in the ratio of interest payments to income. On the other hand, the willingness of Western Europe and Japan to accept lower growth in order to maintain external surpluses and the willingness of Asian countries, in particular China, to increase their holdings of dollar assets to keep their exchange rates stable and demand for their exports growing, have been the counterparts to growing US household indebtedness.

With the rest of the world running an external credit balance and the US in a corresponding debt position, a debt crisis would eventually have broken out in US financial markets, particularly in the mortgage markets that were the engine of the increasing debt-financed US households' consumption. Since this debt position was the source of global demand, as soon as it started to reverse, there would be a global decline in demand and a global recession. As soon as house prices stabilized and started to decline, the financing to support global demand faltered as US households were unable to continue to finance their increasing levels of consumption.

The problem first surfaced in the weakest sector of the mortgage market, the sub-prime market, as households quickly started to default on their monthly payments. This would not have been particularly important except that with increasingly free and open international capital markets, financial institutions had globalized the financing of mortgage debt. Mortgages were previously considered to be idiosyncratic assets held on the balance sheets of local banks. Since each house and each borrower is different, direct knowledge of local conditions was required to evaluate the value of the asset being financed and the creditworthiness of the borrower seeking the financing, information that foreign lenders would find difficult and costly to acquire. However, by pooling a large number of diversified mortgages into a pool called a Residential Mortgage Backed

Security, a single composite asset that looked more like a fixed interest security was created. These "bonds" could then be packaged together to form a Collateralized Mortgage Obligation offering a range of individual securities resembling bonds, called tranches, each with a different risk profile from AAA to non-investment grade. This made it possible to sell them to institutional investors, but more importantly, it made it possible to sell them on a global basis since knowledge of the local conditions of the area in which the mortgages originated and the credit worthiness of the borrower was no longer considered important to the risk of the instrument.

The geographical diversification of the mortgages and the guarantees given to the particular tranche and its seniority in the repayment schedule of the CMO allowed investors to choose the risk profile consistent with their individual risk preferences; in addition to the belief that house prices in the US had never declined, there was the belief that regional real estate markets had never all declined at the same time.

These securities were sold primarily to investors throughout the developed world, and in particular to European banks, many of whom also started to offer similar types of securities on the basis of rising prices in their own real estate markets. Since many of these mortgages were written on the implicit assumption that if they could not be serviced out of household income, the underlying asset could be sold for a profit to pay off the mortgage, once house prices stopped rising, their value as well as the condition of the banks who had sold them (many of whom had decided to hold them as investments) became suspect. This was especially true of European countries, where regulations forbid the creation of such assets, but did not prevent banks from purchasing them. The result was widespread uncertainty over the viability of all banks, and the difficulties soon created a massive liquidity crisis as no bank was willing to lend to any other bank that might be insolvent as a result of the decline in the value of the mortgage securities it was holding on its balance sheet. This problem was exacerbated by the fact that many banks were holding these securities on a leveraged basis, that is they had borrowed to buy them, and as the value of the securities fell, the lenders called for additional security in the form of margin deposits that the banks were unable to raise due to the liquidity freeze.

Thus, what started as a problem in the repayment of sub-prime mortgages in the US soon became a crisis of the entire financial system on a global scale. The sustained increase in house prices, accompanied by falling interest rates, has allowed many households to access consumer credit based on the appreciating value of their mortgage equity via mortgage refinancing.

This increasing credit had allowed US consumers to continue to increase consumption expenditures even though real incomes had been stagnant through the new millennium. However, when households found it difficult to meet interest payments and suffered losses on the value of their houses, they had to cut back on expenditures, causing a decline in demand; many firms found that they could not meet their financial commitments and were unable to borrow from the banks because of the liquidity crisis. The financial market crisis thus quickly spread from the mortgage market to the lack of financing of the real productive sector as firms had no choice but to cut costs through firing workers, which cut incomes and demand even further, creating a downward spiral. This decline in demand was eventually transmitted to the developing world, as emerging market developing countries experienced capital outflows, and then to the real sector in developing countries as their exports declined.

Reforming the Financial System

Against this background, the Commission Report proposes far reaching financial market reforms in both developed and developing countries, since the former have been the cause of the crisis and often behind the liberalizing trend in developing countries. At the same time some developing countries, such as India, that have not followed these reforms have been largely exempt from the impact of the crisis. Thus, there is something to be learned from the policies of these countries as well. In addition, there is a need for systemic reform of the international financial system itself in order to provide coordination of policies across countries in a globally integrated financial and trading system.

How Should Reform be Decided?

Although the procedure followed by the United Nations in creating the Bretton Woods system provides a good example of how the reform process might proceed, current conditions and objectives are different from those of the 1940s. Forty-four countries, including 28 currently deemed as developing, were represented in the Bretton Woods negotiations. This is not true of the currently preferred approach of using the Group of 20 countries created after the Asian crisis. In a globalized trade and financial system, full representation of developing countries is a prerequisite for success in reforming the system since, as seen above from the discussion of the imbalances, they are an integral part of the operations and difficulties facing the system. Thus, the Report concludes that neither the G-7/8 nor the G-20 can provide the appropriate forum even with the inclusion of the so-called BRICs (Brazil, Russia, India and China). Only the G-192—referring to all the member countries of the United Nations—can provide credible representation to determine the process of reform. This does not mean that the actual technical work required needs to take place with 192 Member States' representatives, but simply that the work must be directed on the basis of democratic determination, accountable representation, and delegation of responsibility for the reform process. The appropriate representative group might be 8, 20, 33 or whatever number. The important point is that all countries should have a say in the process that determines representation and procedure.

Where to Start?

The Report seeks to identify and prioritize measures to be taken in response to the crisis based on the causes outlined above. This analysis suggests a number of solutions, but in choosing between them, it is important that they meet two conditions. They must be both immediate and, at the same time, contribute to systemic reform. Further they must clearly break with the previous system. The short-term measures should provide the building blocks for the new international financial system, and the new system has to support the response to the crisis.

The first priority is to reverse the current decline in real incomes and output through deficit financed government stimulus packages. These plans have to be "efficient" in supporting demand in the sense of providing the largest impact per dollar spent, but they must also be efficient in the sense of contributing the building blocks of the creation of a reformed international system. They also have to be globally coordinated to increase the impact per dollar of expenditure by increasing the value of the income multiplier. If only one country introduces a stimulus package, there will be leakage through increased imports that would reduce the multiplier. If all countries expand, the value of the multiplier for each country will be higher than if expansion is undertaken on a haphazard basis with some countries free riding.

It is also necessary to ensure that the programs do not create financial protectionism with support only being given to domestic financial institutions or firms. In general, larger stimulus policies should be made by countries with external surpluses—such as China, Japan, and the EU—to ensure that the stimulus does not further aggravate international imbalances.

In addition, since the crisis is global, and the solution has to be global, it is crucial that developing countries participate with their own stimulus plans. However, for many developing countries, this will require additional financing for their domestic stimulus plans. This is because it is more than likely that official funding sources, and international financial institutions, may impose restrictive fiscal conditions that would defeat the intention of the stimulus plans. Alternatively, countries may try to build up protective liquidity cushions in the form of foreign reserves. Thus, any coordinated stimulus that allows meaningful participation by developing countries will require new sources of finance to facilitate the participation of developing countries. A major conclusion of the Report is thus that developing countries will require new sources of short-term counter cyclical finance if they are to participate in the global stimulus and that this financing will be a direct determinant of the efficiency of the individual stimulus plans of all countries.

It is also important that the external financing for the developing countries should not increase or create new unsustainable debt burdens for developing countries for this would also defeat the intention of the global package to support incomes and increase stability. The Report thus proposes that developed countries use one percent of their own domestic stimulus plans for direct expenditure support in developing countries, additional to existing ODA commitments. This would provide additional stimulus without increasing external debt. In addition, where possible, financing should be supplied on a grant or concessional basis.

The Commission was concerned, in particular, that short-term stimulus spending should not compete with longer-term structural development programs. The Report thus suggests that the international community consider the creation and interim funding of a special facility to provide support for those countries acting decisively in response to the crisis and who have introduced systems to protect their populations from the impact of the crisis on their standard of living. An international commitment to provide permanent financial support for developing countries to respond to the crisis could produce the additional benefit of creating built-in anti-cyclical expenditures that could act as automatic stabilizers while at the same time providing long-term social support.

New Finance Facility for Developing Country Stimulus Plans

In light of the causes and impact of the crisis, the Commission recommends the creation of a new Credit facility to provide funding for stimulus packages in developing countries. This could be created, either as a new stand-alone entity, or as an independent unit within an existing international financial institution such as the World Bank. In either case, in order to move as rapidly as possible, the Report proposes the use of existing personnel for administration of the facility. However, if it is created, the facility should have a new, and more representative governance structure that would provide a pattern for the introduction of voice and representation reform in the existing IFIs—as called for in the Monterrey Consensus and reiterated in the 2008 Doha Declaration. This would respond to the efficiency criterion of serving both short-term and longer-term needs at the same time. The Facility could be funded by direct grants from developed countries, or by the creation of new sources of global liquidity.

With regard to the utilization of the funds, there are different (complementary) options. First, there is an urgent need for balance-of-payments and budget financing, to increase developing countries' capacities for anti-cyclical fiscal expenditures. These could be in key investments, where some emerging markets have a particular interest, such as developing agriculture in Africa and their capacity to export, thus contributing to food security in other regions such as in Asian and Arab countries. Another possibility is to use those funds to help developing countries finance guarantees for trade credit or for the debt of their corporations, forestalling the risk of a run on these corporations. Funds could be organized on a regional basis.

Reforming Global Regulation to Enhance Global Economic Stability

While there are many competing theories about the cause of the crisis, there is little dispute that it originated in the financial sector of the developed economies, in particular in the mortgage market in the United States. Undoubtedly the economic philosophy of market fundamentalism that had inspired recent institutional and regulatory changes was a major contributory factor. It is therefore not surprising that the Commission Report dedicates nearly twice as much space to the subject of financial regulation than to any other of its proposals. This is because discussion of the reform and regulation of the financial system has to be approached from a number of different dimensions.

First, there is the need to distinguish the formulation of national regulations from the coordination of such regulations at the global level, requiring a reform of the international financial regulatory system. While many financial institutions operate across national borders and thus across national regulatory regimes, there is, as yet, no global entity charged with the regulation of such institutions. In addition, most financial regulation applies to the safety and stability of individual financial institutions, but is seldom approached from the point of view of the impact of regulation on the operation of the system as a whole. But this is precisely where the greatest problems occurred. Thus, the necessity of systemic reforms, as the whole is greater than the sum of its parts.

Any international regulation of specific individual financial institutions has an impact on the stability of national financial systems; just as the impact of regulatory systems of different individual countries has an impact on the stability of the global system. One implication of market fundamentalism has been that such distinctions were considered unnecessary since the individual institutions looking after their own best interests in conditions of market competition would provide the most efficient form of counterparty regulation.

The Report provides extensive criticism of an inherent contradiction in this view relating to the distribution and transparency of market information. If the market is to be perfectly efficient in evaluating risks, then information must be fully available to all participants; but since information is costly to collect and assess, there will be an incentive for those who obtain it to keep it private. The market pursuit of information will thus be unable to produce perfect information. Full information would only prevail if it were freely available and distributed as a public good. Thus, there are substantial externalities associated with full information, and it is well established that the market is highly inefficient in dealing with these externalities. This is a *prima facie* case for market failure, linked to traditional arguments concerning externalities, and leads to the necessity for government intervention in the form of market regulations.

While the Commission Report recognizes that different countries, at different stages of development, will find different regulatory structures more effective in meeting their particular needs, it recommends an overarching regulatory structure in the form of a Global Financial Authority, while recognizing that such an institution is not likely to be instituted quickly. Nonetheless the Report encourages all countries to make progress toward cooperation and communication in the formulation of regulatory and supervisory policies applied uniformly across countries. This does not necessarily mean uniformity of policies, but simply more global supervision of financial institutions that operate cross border.

In terms of national regulations, the Report relies on two basic principles. The first is that whatever specific regulations are adopted must apply to all financial institutions and financial instruments for if regulation is not comprehensive, it will soon be undermined by regulatory arbitrage, with risk channeled to those areas with the lightest regulation. Second, in order to ensure comprehensive coverage, regulation must be active, continuous and, above all, dynamic to ensure that it covers any and all new instruments and areas of activity that develop over time.

Many of the difficulties in the current crisis were the result of regulations failing to keep up with the speed of financial innovations in terms of products and operating procedures. It is for this reason that the Commission has recommended that foreign financial institutions should be subject to the regulations of the country in which they operate and should be fully capitalized in the host country, rather than being subject to home country regulations which would allow them to bypass local regulations. This concern is also at the basis of the recommendation that developing countries in particular should apply active capital account management in the form of prudential management of foreign borrowing.

The Report notes that credit rating agencies are supposed to play a key role in financial markets by reducing information asymmetries between issuers and investors. Yet, the risk assessments of rating agencies have been highly pro-cyclical and played a role in exacerbating the present crisis. The Report thus calls for greater transparency in the way that rating agencies discuss and present their analyses, clarifying assumptions made and the sensitivity of the results to these assumptions. They should be required to provide information concerning their overall past performance, and/or an independent government agency should provide such information, which would enhance "positive" competition among rating agencies.

The Commission considered the uniformity of application of regulation to be particularly important in the area of derivative markets, an area which has been singled out as being at the centre of much of the instability in both national and international markets. While the Report does not take a position on the utility of any particular type of instrument, it does apply the principle of uniformity of regulation by recommending that all such contracts be traded on regulated exchanges with appropriate margins applied by the clearing agency. It is the bilateral over-the-counter trading environment rather than the instruments themselves that is considered to have been deficient.

The Commission did not take a position on an expanded role for capital adequacy requirements in the evolution of the crisis. However, it did note that existing regulations dealing with capital adequacy were highly pro-cyclical and recommended countercyclical provisioning requirements, using the maturity of funding as means for evaluating capital assets.

The Report also recommends a template for national regulatory structures based on two apex institutions: a New Central Bank (NCB) focusing on macroeconomic issues, and a Financial Regulatory Authority (FRA), focusing on micro-issues. The two institutions should be closely coordinated with each other so that the NCB would be aware of the macroeconomic consequences of actions taken by the FRA. This is especially important since micro-prudential regulations have macroeconomic consequences. The FRA would comprise several sub-commissions: a Securities and Exchange Commission, an Insurance Commission, a Financial Products Safety Commission, an Accounting Oversight Commission, and a Financial Systems Stability Commission (which, *inter alia*, would look at the inter-linkages among financial institutions and the vulnerability of the failure of one to that of others). It would have cross-cutting committees to ensure that similar functions performed by different institutions are treated similarly.

The Financial Systems Stability Commission could impose high margin requirements or large down payments for products sold to retail customers if it felt that there is growing excess leverage in the economy or in the market. The Accounting Oversight Commission would ensure that the information provided by firms is not misleading and represents the best estimate of the overall state of the firm, including its vulnerability. It might, over time, develop a broader set of metrics that may be of use to investors and other regulators. It would seek to prohibit off-balance sheet exposures, but recognize that financial institutions have been creative, both in their accounting and in devising ways of circumventing regulations and accounting standards, and be given broad discretion to impose additional reporting requirements and to employ conservative methodologies in the valuation of risk.

New International Reserve Currency

The funds for the new facility could be mobilized by means of another of the major structural proposals of the Report: a New International Reserve Currency. The unwinding of the global imbalances which played an important role in this crisis can only be addressed if there is a better way of dealing with international economic risks facing countries than the current practice of accumulating international foreign exchange reserves in US dollars. The magnitude of this crisis and the inadequacy of international responses may motivate further accumulations, worsening the deflationary bias in the global system and impairing prospects for a robust recovery.

The difficulties associated with using a national currency as the international reserve currency are known as the Triffin Paradox. A reformed system could be based on an expanded role for the Special Drawing Rights (SDRs), with regular or cyclically adjusted emissions calibrated to the size of reserve accumulations. In the existing dollar-based international system the need to accumulate international reserves leads to a reduction in global demand and aggravation of the global imbalances. Keynes's proposals for international currency reform were based on the need to eliminate the negative impact on global demand of asymmetric adjustment to international imbalances that had characterized the gold standard system. However, it was also clear that a simple substitution of the unit of international accounting for international reserves would not resolve the asymmetry problem. Eliminating global imbalances would require coordinated action, either by multilateral deliberation and coordination or by rule. Keynes' Clearing Union proposals contained simple rules of adjustment. A successful reform will also require a decision on the rules of adjustment for international imbalances if it is to be successful.

International Institutional Innovations

Global Economic Coordination Council

In the present context, deliberation and coordination seem more promising than an agreement on rules of adjustment and for this reason, the Report proposes a Global Economic Coordination Council (GECC) to provide a democratically representative alternative to the G-20. This would include UN system chief executives and Heads of Government to coordinate international adjustment of imbalances. The Council would be at a level equivalent with the General Assembly and the Security Council. Representation would be based on a constituency system, and designed to ensure that all regions and all major economies are represented. Important global institutions, such as the World Bank, IMF, WTO, ILO and members of the UN Secretariat dealing with economic and social issues, would provide supporting information and participate in the Council. This would be a democratically representative alternative to the G-20. It should meet to assess developments and provide leadership on economic, social and environmental issues. Its goal should be to promote development, as well as secure consistency and coherence in the policy goals of the major international organizations. It should also support consensus building among governments on efficient and effective solutions on issues of global economic governance. The Council could also promote the accountability of all international economic organizations, identify gaps that need to be filled to ensure the efficient operation of the global economic and financial system, and help set the agenda for global economic and financial reforms.

International Expert Panel

As an intermediate step to the creation of the Council, an International Expert Panel, patterned after the current Intergovernmental Panel on Climate Change, could be created to provide independent advice on international policy coordination. There should also be an appropriate mechanism within the United Nations system for institutionally independent analysis on questions of global economic policy, including its social and environmental dimensions. The Panel would offer advice to the General Assembly and ECOSOC, as well as to relevant international organizations, to enhance their capacity for sound decision-making in these areas, to identify gaps and deficiencies in the global economic architecture, and to assess progress and problems in the functioning of the global economic and social system. It would also help foster a constructive dialogue in a regular venue for fruitful exchanges among policy makers, the academic world and key international organizations. The Panel should be composed of well-respected experts, academics, civil society advocates and other independent analysts from all over the world. It should follow, analyze and assess long-term trends, key developments and major dynamics for global change affecting all people around the globe, identify problems in the global economic and financial architecture, and provide options for coherent international action and recommendations for political decision-making processes.

New Policy Surveillance Mechanism

The Report notes the need for an independent and even-handed macro-economic surveillance mechanism. Existing surveillance of policies by the IMF has often failed to apply its mandate to sustain growth and employment while emphasizing price stability. The GECC and the International Panel of Experts could play an important role in monitoring the adequacy of surveillance and whether these deficiencies have been adequately addressed.

Monitoring and Restructuring Developing Country Debt

As already noted, the Commission was concerned that the full participation of developing economies in the global stimulus effort should not create additional debt burdens or compete with funding for existing national development strategies. Indeed, one of the difficulties facing developing country participation in the global response to the crisis is their existing indebtedness and its treatment by the international financial institutions and international lenders. The Report thus proposes a reconsideration of the way these institutions view debt sustainability to widen its purview to include cyclical as well as longer-term implications.

In this regard, the Commission calls on the United Nations to strengthen the advisory role of the UN Conference on Trade and Development (UNCTAD), and for the establishment of a Foreign Debt Commission that would help developing countries to better monitor their debt positions and help them avoid unsustainable positions, thus reducing the need for debt restructuring. The aim would also be to reinforce national mechanisms to control capital inflows and outflows to ensure debt sustainability as well as to prevent financial crisis arising from rapid capital reversals. It would provide advice on ways to enhance external debt management and crisis prevention and resolution, as well as help debt-distressed countries return to debt sustainability.

Given the way in which financial globalization, and in particular securitization, have changed the channels of lending and the representation of lenders in debt resolution, the Report also proposes an International Debt Restructuring Court, similar to national bankruptcy courts. This court should be independent, rather than organized under the auspices of the IMF, considering its now discarded proposal for a Sovereign Debt Restructuring Mechanism (SDRM). This court would promote agreed international principles, differentiate among distinct debt categories, and may also determine debts that could be considered "odious". If national courts were required to recognize the legitimacy of the international court this would greatly facilitate the exit of countries from unsustainable positions. It would also replace the International Centre for Settlement of Investment Disputes (ICSID) currently operating within the World Bank Group.

Intergovernmental Tax Cooperation

In addition to recognizing the importance of a multilateral framework for the treatment of debt, the Commission noted distortions that have been created for developing countries from differences in fiscal regimes. The Report thus calls for an International Tax Compact to strengthen the voice and participation of developing countries in ongoing processes of coordination of national tax systems. To this end it recommends the upgrading of the existing Committee of Experts on International Cooperation in Tax matters to intergovernmental status and urges all countries to adopt voluntary exchanges of information as the most efficient way to ensure that developing countries are not the victims of tax arbitrage and evasion.

The Role of the Report in the Reform Process

As already mentioned, the aim of the Report was not to provide a blueprint for the reform and re-regulation of the international financial system, but rather to raise questions to be answered if such a reform is to be attempted and to provide analysis of the various possible policy responses to those questions. The choices of the policies to be adopted must be left to the appropriately constituted democratically representative forum, as was the case with the decisions at Bretton Woods. It thus provides a guide or a roadmap for discussion and decision. The preliminary version of the Report has already served that role as a background document to the United Nations Conference on the World Financial and Economic Crisis held in June 2009. The final version was made available in September in time for the opening of the 64th session of the General Assembly and for those Member States involved in the G-20 process, as well as for further debate during the *ad hoc* open-ended working group called upon to report by the end of the 64th General Assembly.

Notes

1. The Final Report of the Commission of Experts of the President of the UN General Assembly on Reform of the International Monetary and Financial System is available at http://www.un.org/ga/econcrisissummit/docs/FinalReport_CoE.pdf. It is divided into six chapters and includes a Foreword by the President of the General Assembly. Chapter I provides an introduction, Chapter II deals with Macroeconomic Issues and Perspectives, Chapter III with Reforming Global Regulation to Enhance Global Economic Stability, Chapter IV with International Institutions, Chapter V with International Financial Innovations, and Chapter VI offers Concluding Comments.

2. The members of the Commission are Joseph Stiglitz (USA) (Chair), Andrei Bougrov (Russia), Yousef Boutros-Ghali (Egypt), Jean-Paul Fitoussi (France), Charles A.E. Goodhart (UK), Robert Johnson (USA), Jomo Kwame Sundaram (United Nations Secretariat), Benno Ndulu (Tanzania), José Antonio Ocampo (Colombia), Pedro Páez (Ecuador), Avinash Persaud

(Barbados), Yaga Venugopal Reddy (India), Rubens Ricupero (Brazil), Eisuke Sakakibara (Japan), Chukwuma Soludo (Nigeria), Heidemarie Wieczorek-Zeul (Germany), Yu Yongding (China), Zeti Akhtar Aziz (Malaysia) and Jan Kregel (USA) (Rapporteur).

3. Available at http://www.un.org/ga/president/63/interactive/worldfinancialcrisis.shtml.

4. See UN Resolution A/RES/63/239.

13

Special Drawing Rights and the Reform of the Global Reserve System

José Antonio Ocampo*

The debate surrounding the international monetary system has heated up in recent years through three different channels. Prior to the current crisis, attention was focused on the large global imbalances that the world economy had accumulated, as well as on the rationale for the massive accumulation of foreign exchange reserves by developing countries, which were part of that process. When the crisis erupted, attention shifted to the generation of international liquidity and countercyclical macroeconomic policies. The revitalization of the International Monetary Fund was an essential part of this process. This led to the decision of the Group of 20 (G20) at its meeting in London in April 2009 to inject resources into the Fund on a large scale, including a special emission of Special Drawing Rights (SDRs) equivalent to US$250 billion, which in turn revitalized this dormant mechanism of international monetary cooperation.

The third channel, the focus of this chapter, is the reform of the global monetary system as such and, in particular, of the global reserve system. The proposal by the Governor of The People's Bank of China (Zhou, 2009) correctly placed this issue on the agenda (Helleiner, 2009). Obviously, the biggest concern for the Chinese is the large potential losses to them, as the major holders of US dollar assets, of a disorderly depreciation of the dollar caused, in part, by the expansionary fiscal and monetary policies underway to combat the worst global financial and economic crisis since the Great Depression. Simultaneously with the Chinese call to rethink global monetary arrangements, the Commission of Experts convened by the President of the UN General Assembly on Reforms of the International

Monetary and Financial System (the Stiglitz Commission) also made a call for deep reforms of the global reserve system (United Nations, 2009b).

Both sets of ideas were taken up at the UN Conference on the World Financial and Economic Crisis and Its Impacts on Development, held in New York on 24-26 June 2009. In particular, paragraph 36 of the Outcome Document of the Conference states: "We acknowledge the calls by many States for further study of the feasibility and advisability of a more efficient reserve system, including the possible function of SDRs in any such system and the complementary roles that could be played by various regional arrangements" (United Nations, 2009a).

This chapter argues that a better global reserve system can and should be based on a SDR-based IMF together with a network of regional reserve funds. The next section analyses problems that the current system faces. This leads to closer analysis of the proposed reforms. The last section briefly discusses some complementary reforms.

Problems of the Current System

Three Fundamental Flaws of the System

Since the collapse in the early 1970s of the "dollar-gold exchange standard" established at Bretton Woods, the global monetary system has been primarily based on the use of fiduciary US dollars as means of payment and assets denominated in dollars as the major form of foreign exchange reserves. Although other characterizations are possible, this system can be best termed a "fiduciary dollar standard". Since other national and regional currencies (the euro, in particular) compete with the dollar for this international role, the system can also be described—but only secondarily—as one in which alternative fiduciary currencies from a few powerful economies compete with one another as reserve assets and international means of payment. Flexible exchange rates among competing world currencies is another feature of the system.

The financial globalization that began following the collapse of the original Bretton Woods arrangement generated another feature that is more the result of the functioning of the global *financial* system, but has profound implications for the monetary system, especially the fact that developing countries are subject to strong pro-cyclical swings in financing, which generate significant macroeconomic risks (Prasad *et al.*, 2003; Ocampo, Kregel and Griffith-Jones, 2007: Ch. 1). What this implies is that the integration of developing countries into global financial markets involves integration into a market segmented by risk categories, in which high-risk borrowers are subject to strong pro-cyclical swings (Frenkel, 2008). This combined with the additional risks associated with the pro-cyclical nature of international trade, on which developing countries have increasingly relied. Some pro-cyclical features of international trade patterns, particularly commodity price fluctuations, were old, but accentuated in recent years by the "financialization" of commodity futures markets (UNCTAD, 2009: Ch. 3). In the absence of a global lender of last resort, the risks generated by pro-cyclical finance and trade have generated a defensive or precautionary demand for foreign exchange reserves by developing countries—a mechanism that has come to be called "self-insurance", or better still, "self-protection"—which has also contributed to the global imbalances (Aizenman and Lee, 2007; Carvalho, 2009; Ocampo, 2007/8, 2009; United Nations, 2009b).

As this chapter will argue, the current global reserve system is both unstable and inequitable. Like all preceding systems, it lacks mechanisms to mutually offset the balance of payments' surpluses and deficits of different economies (i.e., global imbalances) without adversely affecting world economic activity. Although most of these macroeconomic effects are contractionary, particularly during crises, the fiduciary dollar standard can also generate expansionary effects during global business upswings. Following conventional terminology, I will refer to these effects as the global "deflationary" and "inflationary" biases of the system, although their actual effects may be on world economic activity—that is, on the intensity of the world business cycle—rather than on prices.

More specifically, the system faces three fundamental flaws (Ocampo, 2009). First, it suffers from the deflationary bias characteristic of any system in which the burden of macroeconomic adjustment falls on deficit countries. As this was emphasized by Keynes in the debates that preceded the creation of the Bretton Woods institutions (BWIs), it can be called the *anti-Keynesian or deflationary bias*. The second relates to the instabilities associated with the use of a *national* currency as an *international* currency. As this was emphasized by Robert Triffin in the debates of the 1960s, it came to be called the *Triffin dilemma*.

The nature of this problem was significantly transformed, however, by the transition from the dollar-gold exchange standard to the fiduciary dollar standard. Since the accumulation of international reserves by developing countries basically involves foreign exchange reserves, the system forces a net transfer of resources from those countries to the major economies issuing the global reserve currencies. This third flaw of the system can therefore be called the *inequity bias* which—as pointed out by the Zedillo Commission, created as part of the preparations for the 2002 Monterrey Conference on Financing for Development—is a form of "reverse aid" (United Nations, 2001).

Furthermore, the inequities of the system have increased with the huge accumulation of foreign exchange reserves in the developing world over the past two decades as a result of the need for self-protection generated by highly pro-cyclical capital flows to developing countries *and* the lack of adequate "collective insurance" to manage balance of payments crises. However, although such reserve accumulation may be a rational response of each developing country to the problems posed by the global system, it generates "fallacy of composition" effects that contribute to global imbalances, and thus to the potential instability of the system (Ocampo, 2007/08). This interaction between the second and third flaws of the system can be called the *inequity-instability link*. As the three flaws follow a historical sequence, it is therefore relevant to discuss them in terms of the historical debates on the design of the international monetary system.

The anti-Keynesian bias

As already noted, the first of these problems was highlighted by Keynes during the debates that surrounded the creation of the BWIs, particularly the IMF (see a fascinating account of these debates in Skidelsky, 2000, Part Two). The fundamental problem is that the current system, as indeed all international monetary systems that have preceded it, places the burden of macroeconomic adjustment on countries running balance of payments deficits. These countries have to adjust, either because they lack adequate external financing, or because they view as undesirable the associated increase of their debt ratios or, more generally, their net liability position *vis-à-vis* the rest of the world. Surplus countries may also face pressures to adjust, particularly those associated with the domestic inflationary effects that balance of payments surpluses generate. But the *external* pressures to adjust that they face are weaker or, indeed, non-existent. This asymmetric burden of adjustment, in turn, generates a global deflationary bias. This bias is particularly strong during global crises when the lack of adequate financing forces deficit countries to adjust.

Since Keynes' (1942-43) proposal to create a more symmetric system by establishing an International Clearing Union was not accepted, the Bretton Woods system was born with this inherent flaw. But even a system in which all deficit countries can automatically finance their deficits may still face a deflationary bias in so far as the macroeconomic policy authorities respond asymmetrically to the build up of a net external liability compared to a net external asset position.

The debates surrounding the creation of the BWIs were, of course, overburdened by the expectation that the Second World War would leave the US with a *structural* balance of payments surplus (using the terminology Latin American structuralists later made popular)—i.e., a surplus that, within reasonable bounds, cannot simply be corrected by exchange rate adjustments—whereas Great Britain and Western Europe in general would be left with structural deficits. This made the US quite reluctant to adopt a system in which it would have to provide virtually unlimited financing to Europe. The US offered instead a very imperfect substitute, the "scarce currency clause", which has never been used. More important was the acceptance by the US of capital controls as an essential feature of post-war arrangements.

The feared structural surpluses and deficits did indeed materialize in the form of what came to be called the "dollar shortage", with the solution coming in the form of the US providing financing to Western Europe through the Marshall Plan and a regional arrangement, the European Payments Union, both of which paved the way for the eventual restoration of *current account* convertibility, which was more or less complete by 1958 when the European Economic Community was born. The broad-based adoption by European countries of *capital account* convertibility would only come much later, and was only completed in 1990, soon to be followed by a set of major European balance of payments crises.

The Triffin Dilemma

As Kregel (2009) has recently emphasized, the anti-Keynesian bias implies that the most fundamental problem of any international monetary arrangement is the operation of the adjustment mechanism in the face of global imbalances, rather than the specific asset that serves as the international currency. Nonetheless, the role of the dollar at the centre of the system generated problems, which were debated in the 1960s. Robert Triffin (1961, 1968) emphasized the essential issue: an *international* reserve system based on a *national* currency is inherently unstable. Given the importance that the Triffin dilemma has assumed in recent discussions, including its specific mention in the Chinese critique of the current system, it is worth quoting the original formulation at length:

> [...] reactions of the outer countries [tend to generate] generalized waves of confidence or diffidence in the future convertibility and stability of the dollar. This makes the position of the center country

highly precarious in the long run. It can, in the early phases of the popularity of its currency as a reserve instrument, finance much larger and more persistent deficits than it would be able to incur otherwise. If, however, the center country uses its leeway in this manner, the time is bound to come when other countries will shift from dollar hoarding to dollar dishoarding [...].

On the other hand, if the United States restores full balance in its external transactions, it will cease to feed a world reserve pool [...].

In either case, the use of a national currency as a prime feeder of reserve assets for the rest of the world is bound to introduce a highly erratic and unpredictable factor both in the much vaunted mechanism of balance-of-payments adjustment and in the actual pace of growth—or contraction—of the world reserve pool (Triffin, 1968: pp. 87-88).

A major issue at the time, of course, was the possibility that other countries could transform their dollar reserves into gold. The attempt to collectively manage the erosion of the gold backing for the dollar through the "gold pool" ultimately proved to be futile (Eichengreen, 2007). This eventually led to abandonment of dollar-gold convertibility in the early 1970s. The discussions of the 1960s therefore focused on ways to create, in a more orderly (or less "capricious", to use the preferred term at that time) manner, an adequate supply of world liquidity free from the inherent instability generated by the Triffin dilemma. Although different alternatives were suggested, the solution was the creation of a global fiduciary asset—SDRs—which was expected to become the main global reserve asset over time (see an account of this history in Solomon, 1977, chs. 4-8).

As a digression, it should be pointed out that an interesting alternative proposed in the 1960s was to design a commodity-based reserve system (Hart, Kaldor and Tinbergen, 1964). This idea, which goes back to Keynes' *Treatise on Money*, had interesting countercyclical features: world liquidity would automatically increase during global business downswings, which tended to depress commodity prices, and automatically decreased during business upswings, when commodity prices boomed. Equally interesting, this countercyclical effect would benefit developing countries, which were largely producers of raw materials and thus most adversely affected by the pro-cyclical pattern of commodity prices.

The transition to the fiduciary dollar standard did not eliminate the Triffin dilemma, but changed its features. The US was now able to run "much larger and more persistent deficits than it would be able to incur otherwise", without facing the constraint of dollar-gold convertibility, as flexible exchange rates would take care of adjusting the supply and demand for dollars. To the extent that the US does not regard the actual or likely weakening of its currency as a problem to be corrected, as has been typical in recent decades, this has made US monetary policy even more independent than during the era of the dollar-gold exchange standard. It has also implied that, contrary to Keynes' views, the reduced constraints on US balance of payments' deficits imply that the fiduciary dollar standard could actually generate an inflationary, rather than a deflationary bias.

The deterioration in the current account since the mid-1970s and the eventual transformation of the US investment position into a net liability position from the second half of the 1980s, are both the result of the greater freedom that the US has to run balance of payments deficits and the inflationary bias that the system generates, at least during business cycle upswings. In this regard, it must be recalled that the US generally ran current account surpluses when the dollar-gold exchange standard prevailed, and dollar liquidity provision to the rest of the world was made through the capital account. The counterpart was, of course, the building of a large US investment position abroad. In contrast, under the fiduciary dollar standard that followed, the US current account deficits became the rule rather than the exception.

As Figure 13.1 indicates, the joint evolution of the US current account deficit and the real exchange rate of the major reserve currency have been reflected in three dominant patterns over the past three and

Figure 13.1 US current account balance and real exchange rate

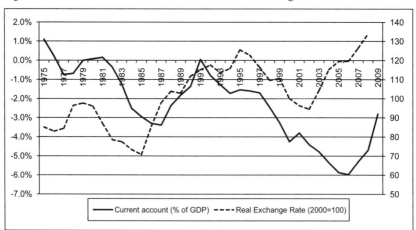

Source: IMF, *International Financial Statistics*. The real exchange rate is depicted here to show an increase when there is a real depreciation (the opposite convention to that used by the IMF). It is calculated as the inverse of the real exchange rate estimated by the Fund.

a half decades: (1) a long-term deterioration in the current account; (2) increasingly intense cycles of both the current account and the real dollar exchange rate; and (3) although exchange rate fluctuations have played an important role in determination of the US current account, major corrections of US deficits have been associated with US slowdowns or recessions which, in turn, had major contractionary effects on the world economy. The correction of the US deficit in 2008 and 2009 is part of the latter pattern.

During the three and a half decades that the fiduciary dollar standard has been in place, the Triffin dilemma has displayed somewhat different characteristics from those in the past, when it was originally formulated. In short, it has shown an inflationary bias during upswings in the business cycle, particularly the most recent ones, and has generated unprecedented—and, indeed, increasing—volatility in both the US current account and the real dollar exchange rate. As a result, the dollar has increasingly lost what, in fact, is the essence of a good international reserve asset: a stable value. A major implication of the strong fluctuations in the US deficit is, of course, that the generation of global liquidity has become even more "erratic" or "capricious" than under the original Bretton Woods system.

It should be emphasized that the length and intensity of the most recent—and longest—cycle of the US current account has determinants that go beyond the US economy. In particular, although the appreciation of the dollar in the second half of the 1990s helps explain the renewed deterioration in the current account, the magnitude of this deterioration is undoubtedly, associated with the role of the US as the "consumer of last resort" during the major crisis in emerging markets that started in East Asia in 1997. In this context, the 2001 US recession only had minor effects on its current account. Furthermore, the deterioration of this deficit up to 2006, despite the gradual, but strong depreciation of the dollar that started in 2003, can only be explained by the fallacy of composition effects of self-protection in the developing world (see the next section).[1]

The length and intensity of this long phase of the US current account deficit that transformed its net investment position into a net liability position—another unprecedented condition of the country at the centre of the global reserve system—has, for many years, generated fears that official and private agents may be unwilling to continue to accumulate dollar assets (Summers, 2004; Williamson, 2004). As we will see below, the recent crisis generated some paradoxes in this regard, but the risk to the global reserve system of a reduced demand for dollar assets is of renewed concern. The views expressed by the Chinese central bank governor in March 2009 are an indication that this risk will continue to be at the centre of concerns regarding the sustainability of the current global reserve system.

From the point of view of the US, its position at the centre of the current global reserve system has had both positive and negative implications. On the positive side, the most important advantage is that it does not face the constraint of dollar-gold convertibility, and thus enjoys greater monetary independence. The system also generates a demand for US Treasury bonds, which helps to finance the US fiscal deficits. As the US has, by now, accumulated important net liabilities with the rest of the world, another interesting advantage is that dollar depreciation generates a positive wealth (real balance) effect, as such a change increases the value of foreign assets owned by US residents, while their liabilities remain unchanged. This also implies, however, that depreciation of the US dollar has a weaker effect in correcting its current account deficit, as the wealth and relative price effects of such depreciation run in opposite directions (United Nations, 2005: ch. I). On the negative side, the fact that US current account deficits are necessary to provide a *net* supply of dollar assets to the rest of the world implies that it does not entirely capture the benefits of its expansionary monetary and fiscal policies (Stiglitz, 2006: ch. 9).

Growing Inequities of the System and the Inequity-Instability Link

The transfer of resources from developing countries to the US that the system requires—its inequity bias—was built into its initial post-war design. However, they remained limited as long as developing countries' foreign exchange reserves were not sizable. As Figure 13.2 indicates, the level of these reserves were not unlike those held by industrial countries up to the 1980s—about 3 percent of GDP; China had reserves equivalent to 6 percent of GDP at the end of that decade.

In contrast, over the past two decades, such reserves boomed and started to diverge from those of industrial countries, with China the most aggressive. By 2007, it had accumulated non-gold reserves equivalent to 46.7 percent of its GDP. The boom in reserve accumulation was equally impressive in the rest of the developing world and in all regions (Table 13.1). By 2007, middle income countries, excluding China, and low income countries held foreign exchange reserves equivalent to 20.6 percent and 16.2 percent of GDP respectively.

The major waves of foreign exchange reserve accumulation clearly followed the two major financial crises experienced by the developing

Figure 13.2 Reserves minus gold as % of GDP
(left hand scale, except China)

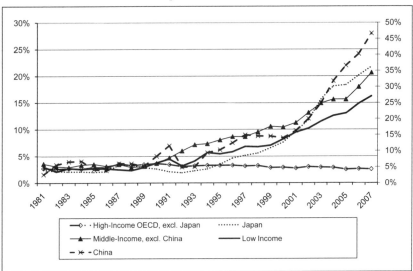

world—the mainly Latin American debt crisis of the 1980s and the broad-based crisis of emerging market countries that started in East Asia in 1997. In this sense, they can be seen as a response by developing countries to the risks generated by increased openness—trade opening, domestic financial liberalization, and capital account liberalization. However, although reserve accumulation started after the Latin American crisis of the 1980s, the Asian crisis was the most important turning point. It revealed, in particular, the lack of appropriate global institutions to manage emerging and developing country crises, and the particular deficiencies associated with the only form of "collective insurance" available: highly conditional IMF lending. As a result of this trend, the annual additional demand for reserves by developing countries, excluding China, shot up from US$299 billion (an average of US$43 billion per year) in 1991-1997 to US$1,593 billion (US$319 billion per year) in 2003-2007; the accumulation of reserves by China has been equally impressive in the recent period (see Table 13.1).

The recent pattern of reserve accumulation differs, of course, across countries and regions (see, among others, Akyüz, 2008; Carvalho, 2009; Yu, 2007). The largest group of countries continued to run current account deficits during the 2003-2007 global boom; for them, the only source of reserve accumulation was net capital flows. The second group, which includes China and several major mineral exporting countries, ran joint current

Table 13.1 Foreign exchange reserves of middle- and low-income countries

	Non-gold reserves, % of GDP				Reserve increase, billion dollars		
	1990	1997	2002	2007	1991-97	1998-02	2003-07
Middle income	4.1%	9.7%	14.9%	27.0%	398.7	318.7	2,742.2
China	8.3%	15.0%	20.0%	46.7%	113.2	148.4	1,239.2
Excluding China	3.7%	8.6%	13.1%	20.6%	285.5	170.3	1,503.1
Low income	3.8%	6.8%	10.2%	16.2%	13.7	18.3	89.7
Europe and Central Asia	…	6.6%	13.1%	24.3%	…	64.3	631.5
East Asia and Pacific	…	13.9%	20.5%	41.3%	…	196.3	1,417.9
Excluding China	…	12.2%	21.6%	26.0%	0.0	48.0	178.7
South Asia	0.9%	5.6%	12.3%	16.4%	26.9	50.2	109.1
Middle East and North Africa	7.9%	14.7%	20.2%	33.4%	34.0	30.8	150.4
Latin America and Caribbean	4.2%	8.1%	9.0%	12.6%	121.7	-11.4	277.5
Sub-Saharan Africa	4.4%	8.1%	9.8%	16.2%	15.6	6.8	101.2

Source: World Bank, World Development Indicators, based on information from IMF.

account and capital account surpluses. The third are basically oil exporters with strong current account surpluses that are net exporters of capital.

There are three competing explanations for this increase in the demand for reserves by developing countries. The first, which I view as the most compelling, is that reserve accumulation is the result of "self-protection" in a broad sense which, as I will argue below, can also be seen as a countercyclical motive. This interpretation receives its most important support from the fact that the major waves of reserve accumulation have followed the two most important financial crises in the developing world.

A second explanation is provided by the "Second Bretton Woods" literature (see Dooley, Folkerts-Landau and Garber, 2003). According to this school of thought, the basic explanation for reserve accumulation is "mercantilism", particularly by East Asian countries' undervaluation of their exchange rates as part of their export-led strategies. A reinforcing factor may be the lack of appropriate mechanisms for exchange rate coordination in export-led economies, which generates incentives to keep exchange rates competitive—a point made some time ago by Sakakibara (2003) in calling for increasing macroeconomic policy coordination in East Asia. One implication of this view is that, for these countries, the benefits of stable, but weak exchange rates exceed the costs of reserve accumulation. An implication at the global level is that, for the same reason, these countries are willing to continue financing the US current account deficit.

The idea that competitive exchange rates and strong current account balances tend to accelerate economic growth in developing countries has, of course, a respectable tradition in the development literature (see, for example, Rodrik, 2007; Frenkel and Taylor, 2007; Prasad *et al.*, 2008; Frenkel and Rapetti, 2009). However, this interpretation misses one important empirical fact: that reserve accumulation in the developing world is closely associated with fluctuations in capital flows—i.e., that it tends to smooth out the pro-cyclical capital flows that affect developing countries (Ocampo, 2007/08, 2009). Indeed, one basic explanation provided in the literature for the strong association between a strong current account and economic growth is that it reduces dependence on volatile capital flows.

A third explanation for reserve accumulation is the "financial stability" motive (Obstfeld, Shambaugh and Taylor, 2008). The basic argument is that international reserves are necessary for financially open economies to counter the incentives to eventually transform money balances into foreign exchange (i.e., capital flight). However, the fact that reserve fluctuations are closely associated with capital account cycles means that it is difficult to distinguish this from self-protection.

The self-protection motive can be understood in a broad sense as the attempt by developing countries to manage the strong pro-cyclical shocks they face in a globalized economy. These shocks originate in the pro-cyclical patterns of the capital flows to these countries, but also in the pro-cyclical patterns of commodity prices and the volume of international trade. In this sense, the demand for reserves is the result of application of a broad "precautionary" principle learned from financial crises. In particular, experience indicates that allowing the real exchange rate to appreciate and the current account to deteriorate sharply during foreign exchange booms almost inevitably leads to a balance of payments crisis—and very commonly to both balance of payments and domestic financial crises— once the temporary condition of foreign exchange availability comes to an end. It makes sense, therefore, to respond to cyclical swings in export revenues by accumulating foreign exchange during booms to be used during subsequent crises.

In so far as cyclical shocks from the capital or trade accounts tend to generate pro-cyclical macroeconomic policy responses (Kaminsky *et al.*, 2004; Stiglitz *et al.*, 2006; Ocampo and Vos, 2008: ch. IV), active foreign exchange management can be seen as an attempt to increase the room for maneuver of countercyclical macroeconomic policies (Ocampo, 2008; Ocampo *et al.*, 2009: ch. 7). *In this sense, the self-protection motive can be renamed "countercyclical".* It is also important to emphasize that generally, the "intermediate" policy target is the exchange rate. So, smoothing out the effects of external shocks on the exchange rate is, in a sense, the essential feature of self-protection or countercyclical foreign exchange management.

Interestingly, in the case of capital account fluctuations, the self-protection motive goes beyond the Guidotti-Greenspan rule, according to which countries should keep foreign exchange reserves at least equivalent to short-term external liabilities. Indeed, to the extent that capital account fluctuations involve *medium-term* cycles (Ocampo *et al.*, 2007, ch. I; Ocampo, 2008), the demand for precautionary international reserves should be proportional to *total* external liabilities, with the proportion larger for economies that have liberalized their capital accounts more.

Foreign exchange reserve accumulation is obviously costly, both because foreign exchange reserves have low yields and there are costs associated with sterilizing its domestic monetary effects (Rodrik, 2006). Some alternative strategies should be considered. Saving exceptional export receipts and associated fiscal revenues from natural resource-intensive activities, have long been accepted as good practice, and are equivalent to reserve accumulation. In contrast, exchange rate flexibility to increase the room for manoeuvre of countercyclical monetary policy, a favorite instrument of orthodox inflation targeting, is *not* a good alternative, as it merely transfers the pro-cyclicality of foreign exchange availability to the exchange rate and is likely to reproduce the risks that self-protection is trying to avoid—the generation of unsustainable current account deficits during booms.

In this regard, one paradox of macroeconomic policy management that characterizes developing countries in recent decades is that exchange rate flexibility has been generally complemented by active interventions in foreign exchange markets and a rising demand for reserves. This has made flexible, but highly interventionist exchange rate regimes quite common in the developing world. This is not so much a reflection of "fear of floating", but rather, a recognition that, as much as fixed exchange rates, clean floats generate pro-cyclical effects on the economy, albeit of a different nature (Ocampo, 2008).

In this sense, and when the source is pro-cyclical capital flows, a better strategy is to regulate capital flows. In particular, to the extent that controls on inflows are able to reduce the magnitude of reserve accumulation, they reduce the cost of foreign exchange management. In fact, the need to accumulate reserves when capital inflows are excessive, destroys the rationale for capital inflows in the first place, which is to transfer resources to the recipient country. It also undermines the other rationale for capital account liberalization—to diversify risks—as countries feel they need larger foreign exchange reserves to protect themselves against capital account reversals.

Obviously, as already pointed out, the choice of self-protection is associated with the fact that the globalized economy we live in lacks adequate collective insurance. Furthermore, available IMF crisis lending is deemed unacceptable by many countries due to the conditionalities typically attached. In the past, these have included adoption of pro-cyclical macroeconomic policies during crises—which self-protection seeks to avoid (United Nations, 2009b). In this sense, the self-protection or countercyclical motive behind the high demand for foreign exchange reserves by developing countries is associated with both pro-cyclical capital account and trade shocks *and* the perception of inadequate mechanisms at the global level to provide liquidity to developing countries during balance of payments crises.

What matters, from the point of view of the global reserve system, is recognition that self-protection or countercyclical foreign exchange management—while understandable from the point of view of the individual country—generates fallacy of composition effects that tend to worsen global imbalances and generate a global deflationary bias. Indeed, if a large group of developing countries follows this route, they generate a current account surplus and an additional demand for "safe assets" that can be used as reserves. They will then have contractionary effects on the world economy unless matched by current account deficits and the supply of such assets by industrial countries. As indicated earlier, during the 2003-2007 global boom, both were supplied by the US, but in an unsustainable way, as the current crisis and renewed fears of loss of value of dollar denominated assets have underscored. This is the essence of the *inequity-instability link*.

Therefore, self-protection is not only costly for individual countries, but also a source of global instability. However, the problem cannot be solved simply by asking developing countries to appreciate their currencies and to generate current account deficits as this has proven to be a risky combination in the past—as revealed again during the current crisis by the collapse of several Central and Eastern European economies that pursued this strategy. We must start by addressing the reason for the desire for self-protection, namely the strongly pro-cyclical capital and trade flows and the inadequacy of collective insurance for balance of payments crises—in short, by reforming the global reserve system.

Reforming the System

Alternative Reform Routes

The proponents of the Second Bretton Woods hypothesis have recently argued that the current crisis was not accompanied by a run on the dollar, but rather, by its appreciation (Dooley, Folkerts-Landau and Garber, 2009). However, we should not presume that the current global monetary system is therefore stable. The strengthening of the dollar after the financial meltdown of September 2008 was the result of two factors. The first was the demand for dollars to finance withdrawals from non-banking financial institutions in the US—an important part of the strong de-leveraging process unleashed by the crisis. The second reason was the "flight to safety" in the context of a limited supply of alternative "safe assets". In particular, the absence of a unified European bond market and the perception by many agents that the euro is backed by a heterogeneous group of countries of unequal strength has meant that the assets of only a few European countries are considered comparable with those of the US as "safe assets", but their supply has been more limited. However, with the gradual return to normalcy, downward pressures on the dollar returned in the second quarter of 2009. The yen has also strengthened due to the reversal of the Japanese "carry trade"—a phenomenon similar to the demand for dollars generated by de-leveraging.

An effect of the crisis with longer-term implications is the reduction of global imbalances. As during previous US recessions, the US current account deficit has been narrowing (Figure 13.1). With the reduction of commodity prices, the surpluses of several commodity exporting countries were significantly eroded or even disappeared. The collapse of world trade has had similar effects on the surpluses of some major manufacturing exporters, including Japan, some other East Asian countries and, more recently, even China. Nonetheless, although the reduction of global imbalances reduces the risks of collapse of the current reserve system, new risks have been generated by the massive expansion of the US Federal Reserve balance sheet and the large US federal fiscal deficits, which are projected to increase the US public sector debt to levels not experienced since the Second World War. Thus, the global system is certainly not free from a dollar crisis.

One way the system could naturally evolve is, of course, by becoming a fully multi-currency reserve system—a feature which, as has been pointed out, is already present, but remains a secondary feature of the current world monetary system. The advantage of a multi-reserve currency arrangement is that it would provide all—but especially developing countries—the benefit of diversifying their foreign exchange reserve assets. However, none of the other deficiencies of the system would be addressed. In particular, it would continue to be inequitable, as the benefits from reserve currency status would still be captured by industrial countries (though a few developing countries, particularly China, would be able to benefit from reserve diversification by other countries). But this reform would not eliminate the deflationary or anti-Keynesian bias of the system, nor would it reduce developing countries' need for reserves for self-protection.

The exchange rate flexibility among major currencies is, paradoxically, both an advantage and a potential cost of a multicurrency system. The benefit would be derived from the absence of the major problem the two previous systems faced—namely, the eventual un-sustainability of fixed rate parities. This was, indeed, a major problem that led to the collapse of both bimetallism in the nineteenth century and the original Bretton Woods arrangement based on a fixed gold-dollar parity. However, while substitution among currencies facilitates diversification, it can lead to exchange rate volatility among the major reserve currencies. This may generate the call for fixed parities among the major currencies, which would probably be unsustainable in a world of free capital movements—and would eliminate the flexibility of the system, which is precisely one of its virtues. Furthermore, all individual reserve currencies would still lack the basic advantage that a global reserve system should have—a stable value. Given their high demand for foreign exchange reserves, developing countries would suffer disproportionately from the instability of reserve currencies' exchange rates.

The alternative reform route would be to design an architecture based on a truly global reserve asset, which could also have broader uses in the global monetary system. Although some such voices are being heard again, returning to gold, which Keynes called the "barbarous relic", would be a non-starter. In particular, such a restoration of the role of gold would be inconsistent with the "embedded liberalism" of earlier post-war arrangements—i.e., that the commitment to free markets is tempered by a broader commitment to social welfare and full employment (Eichengreen, 1996). The opposite approach would, of course, be to return to Keynes' proposal for an International Clearing Union or a similar solution (see, for example, D'Arista, 1999).

However, the most viable option is to pursue the transition launched in the 1960s with the creation of SDRs, fulfilling the objective then included in the IMF Articles of Agreement of "making the special drawing right the principle reserve asset in the international monetary system" (Article VIII, Section 7 and Article XXII). As Triffin (1968) envisioned, this would complete the transition apparent since the nineteenth century of putting *fiduciary* currencies (or fiat money) at the centre of modern monetary systems.[2]

This reform should certainly meet the objectives outlined by the Chinese central bank governor: "an international reserve currency should first be anchored to a stable benchmark and issued according to a clear set of rules, therefore to ensure orderly supply; second, its supply should be flexible enough to allow timely adjustment according to the changing demand; third, such adjustments should be disconnected from economic conditions and sovereign interests of any single country" (Zhou, 2009). But, in addition to providing a more orderly international monetary system rid of the Triffin dilemma, which is what these objectives imply, desirable reform should also correct, at least partially, two other problems of the system—namely, the lack of pressure on surplus countries to adjust, and the specific asymmetries that developing countries face due to pro-cyclical capital flows and the absence of adequate collective insurance.

SDR-based Global Reserve System

The nature of the expectations of SDRs that a reformed system must meet would be different today from what they were when this instrument of international monetary cooperation was created.[3] The issue of inadequate provision of international liquidity at the centre of early post-war debates, and also surrounding early discussion of SDRs, is not important now, except in extraordinary conjunctures. If anything, the fiduciary dollar standard has actually exhibited an inflationary bias for long periods of time. However, this underscores the fact that the world still needs a less "erratic and unpredictable" system for providing global reserves (to use Triffin's characterization), as the call by the Chinese central bank governor—for a system that ensures an "orderly supply" of the international reserve currency—indicates. However, other problems also receiving attention in the 1960s continue to be significant or even more important today, particularly the need for a more symmetric system, access to liquidity for developing countries and associated equity issues.

The initial allocations of SDRs in 1970-1972 were equivalent to 9.5 percent of the world's non-gold reserves (Williamson, 2009). But despite the new allocation made in 1979-81, which brought accumulated allocations to SDR21.4 billion (slightly over US$33 billion at early August 2009 exchange rates), the total now accounts for an insignificant 0.5 percent of world non-gold reserves today. The special one-time allocation approved by the IMF Board of Governors in 1997 for SDR21.4 billion, meant to equalize the benefits to new (those that joined after the previous SDR allocations) with old Fund members, will now be finally made effective, thanks to its approval by the United States Congress in June 2009. Following the call made by the G-20 in April 2009, a new allocation equivalent to US$250 billion was approved by the IMF Executive Board in July 2009. These two allocations will bring the stock of SDRs to approximately 5 percent of global non-dollar reserves, still a very modest amount.

In recent years, proposals for SDR allocations have reflected two different approaches. The first is issuing SDRs in a countercyclical way, thus avoiding issuance (or even destroying those previously made) during boom periods, when they could feed into world inflationary pressures, and concentrating them in periods of world financial stress, when they would have countercyclical effects (United Nations, 1999; Camdessus, 2000; Ocampo, 2002; Akyüz, 2005; Ffrench-Davis, 2007). The second approach proposes regular allocations of SDRs reflecting additional world demand for reserves (Stiglitz, 2006: ch. 9). Considering the increase in reserves over the past two decades, the Stiglitz Commission's proposed allocations would be equivalent to US$150 to US$300 billion a year[4]—also the magnitude of SDRs to be issued in the long term with a countercyclical approach.

The most desirable reform involves moving to a fully SDR-based IMF with a clear countercyclical purpose. This would involve countercyclical *allocations* of SDRs, which would generate "unconditional" liquidity, together with countercyclical IMF *financing*, made entirely in SDRs, to provide "conditional" liquidity to countries facing balance of payments' crises. The best alternative to fulfill this second objective is the mechanism first proposed by Polak (1979; 2005: chs. 7-8) three decades ago—IMF lending during crises, which would actually involve creating new SDRs (in a way similar to how lending by central banks creates domestic money, a mechanism heavily used during the current crisis), but such SDRs would be automatically destroyed once such loans are paid for. There would, of course, be limits on the magnitude of such lending, both overall and for individual countries' borrowing.[5] The combination of these two reforms should, of course, considerably increase the size of the IMF, which has lagged significantly behind that of the world economy since the 1970s, particularly in relation to capital flows (IMF, 2009), and therefore, the provision of collective insurance.

One alternative to combining the allocations of SDRs with the lending capacity of the Fund is to treat those SDRs not used by countries to which they are allocated as deposits in (or lending to) the IMF that can be used by the institution to lend to countries in need. This would also solve the recurrent problem of making more resources available to the IMF during crises. Note, in this regard, that the traditional solution, and that approved by the G-20 in April 2009, has been to allow the IMF to borrow from member states under different modalities. But this mechanism is problematic, as it gives excessive power to the countries providing the financing (Kenen, 2001). Although it would be necessary to use it again during the current crisis, it is sub-optimal relative to quota increases, and both are, in turn, sub-optimal relative to a fully SDR-based IMF along the lines outlined above.[6] One advantage of such a system is that it would eliminate the need for the IMF to manage a multiplicity of currencies, only a small fraction of which (30 percent according to Polak's estimates) can be used for IMF lending.

This solution would also make clear what "backing" for SDRs involves. Strictly speaking, as with national currencies, the essential issue is not backing, but the willingness of parties to unconditionally accept fiat money when paid by another party. Backing would be provided by lending and investments made with SDR deposits. During booms, the normal instrument would be bonds from member countries that have a high level of liquidity and can be redeemed in convertible currencies. The agreed mix of such bond purchases could also be the basis of the SDR basket. During crises, of course, part of such bond holdings would be redeemed to generate funds to lend to countries facing balance of payments' crises. Both aspects would mimic the way central banks operate.

These proposals must be complemented by reforms in four other areas. First, the debate on distribution of IMF quota allocations should continue as, despite recent improvement, they do not reflect the realities of the world economy today. Of course, in a fully SDR-based IMF, "quotas" would have entirely different implications to what they have today. In particular, they would not involve actual contribution of resources to the institution, but would still determine the shares of countries in SDR allocations, their borrowing limits and, together with assigned basic votes, their voting power.

Secondly, mechanisms would have to be established to improve adjustments to the global imbalances. Increasing macroeconomic policy coordination would provide part of the solution—although institutionally based in the IMF, rather than through *ad hoc* arrangements (read G7/8 or G20). In this regard, the multilateral surveillance of global imbalances launched by the Fund in 2006 was an interesting step in that direction, but it lacked binding commitments by the parties and an accountability mechanism.[7] On top of that, adjustment pressures on deficits vs. surplus countries must be more symmetric to reduce the deflationary or anti-Keynesian bias. Part of the solution would be to adopt at least one part of Keynes' original plan for a post-war arrangement: the creation of generous overdraft (or in the terminology of the Fund, drawing) facilities that can be used *unconditionally* by *all* IMF members up to a certain limit and for a pre-established time period. Another part would involve penalizing countries with large surpluses and/or excessive reserves, relative to the size or their economies, by suspending their right to receive SDR allocations. Of course, the definition of excessive reserves would have to take into account the exceptional demand by developing countries for reserves.

Thirdly, and crucially, from the point of view of developing countries, the solution adopted must reduce the special asymmetries that these countries face, reflected in the huge disparities in demand for reserves by developing vs. developed economies, which are at the centre of both the inequities of the current reserve system and the inequity-instability links (Ocampo, 2009). This could be done through a mix of two types of reforms: (i) asymmetric issues of SDRs, giving larger allocations to countries with the highest demand for reserves (i.e., mainly developing countries); and (ii) creation of a "development link" in SDR allocations, as proposed by the Group of Experts convened by UNCTAD in the 1960s (UNCTAD, 1965); one possible mechanism would be allowing the IMF to buy bonds from multilateral development banks with the SDRs not utilized by member states, which would then finance developing countries' demands for long-term financial resources.[8]

Finally, it would be essential that IMF credit lines, their conditionalities and the current stigma associated with borrowing from this institution be overcome, so that countries would actually prefer collective insurance over self-protection.[9] Positive steps in this direction were taken by the IMF in March 2009 with the creation of the Flexible Credit Line for crisis prevention purposes, doubling other credit lines, and eliminating the ties between structural conditionalities and loan disbursements. One basic deficiency of the new line, however, is that it unduly divides developing countries into two categories, those with supposedly good policies and those with ostensibly bad policies, which is not only an unclear, if not arbitrary division, but also increases the risks for countries not classified in the first category, as Dervis (2008) pointed out in relation to its predecessor, the Short-term Credit Line. It also effectively transformed the IMF into a sort of credit rating agency.

Reforms could either limit the use of SDRs as a reserve asset (as it is now) or allow its broader use, as proposed in the past by Kenen (1983), Polak (2005, Part II) and, more recently, by Zhou (2009), among others. In the short-term, however, it may be useful to concentrate on reforming the global reserve system, rather than the broader monetary system. In the short term, this would imply that although the role of the dollar as the major *reserve* asset would be eroded, it would still keep its role as the major international *means of payment*, also creating demands for associated services of the US financial system (Cooper, 1987, ch. 7).

As pointed out recently by Bergsten (2007), and as envisioned in the debates of the late 1970s, it would be useful to create a substitution account, which would allow countries to transform their dollar reserves into SDR-based assets issued by the Fund, to provide stability to the current system. The June 2009 IMF decision to issue SDR-denominated bonds to some emerging economies could be considered a step in that direction. Although part of the potential costs for the IMF of such an account could be financed with its gold reserves and even by the new SDR allocations, it would be difficult, however, to adopt such mechanisms without the US assuming at least part of the associated risks—a problem that blocked the adoption of this mechanism three decades ago.

The current environment could actually be a good time to introduce these reforms. First, the inflationary risks associated with SDR issues are minimal. Second, the United States would continue to enjoy full policy freedom to pursue the expansionary fiscal and monetary policies it has embarked on, without having to take into account the implications for the stability of the current reserve system. It would also free the US from the need to generate current account deficits to provide world liquidity, which has adverse aggregate demand effects for its economy. And it would continue to enjoy, in any case, the benefits of the use of the dollar as the dominant means of payment in the world.

Complementary Role of Regional Monetary Arrangements

Regional monetary arrangements should be considered part of the broader reform of the international monetary system. Indeed, as I have argued before (Ocampo, 2002), the IMF of the future should be conceived as the apex of a network of regional reserve funds—that is, a system closer in design to the European Central Bank or the Federal Reserve System rather than the unique global institution it currently is. By providing complementary forms of collective insurance and forums for macroeconomic policy dialogue among regional partners, regional arrangements would help increase the stability of the global monetary system. Such arrangements would also give stronger voice and ownership to smaller countries, and are more likely to respond to their specific demands. This principle is already applied today in multilateral development financing, as the World Bank is complemented by regional development banks and, in some parts of the world, by sub-regional and inter-regional banks (Ocampo, 2006).

In the monetary arena, regional agreements can take different forms: payments agreements, swap arrangements among central banks, reserve pools and common central banks. In the developing world, they include a few regional central banks in West Africa and the Eastern Caribbean, several regional payments agreements (e.g., among members of the Latin American Integration Association), the Latin American Reserve Fund (essentially an Andean arrangement with Costa Rica and Uruguay as well) and the 2000 Chiang Mai Initiative among the ASEAN countries, China, Korea and Japan. The latter is, obviously, the largest of all. Although it was conceived initially as a network of bilateral swap arrangements, it has been committed since 2005 to full multilateralization, and agreed in May 2009 to complete this process, expand its resources to US$120 billion and finish the design of its surveillance mechanism. If it evolves into a structured reserve fund, this arrangement could actually issue its own currency which, even if used only as an international currency, would be attractive for many central banks outside East Asia.

The major criticism of these arrangements is that they are ineffective in protecting against systemic events due to likely contagion effects among its members. However, as the experience of the Latin American Reserve Fund indicates, even in a narrowly defined region, contagion does not eliminate the fact that demands for liquidity by members have different intensities and variable lags, making a reserve fund viable and desirable. This also reflects the fact that correlation among some relevant macroeconomic variables (foreign exchange reserves, terms of trade) is not necessarily very high, even if such a fund expands to include other major Latin American countries, whereas correlations in other variables (capital flows, in particular) is high, but not close to unity. Furthermore, lending at the onset of a crisis can actually serve as a preventive mechanism that reduces contagion, and thus, as a powerful mechanism of collective insurance. In narrower terms, reserve pooling is useful if the variability of the reserve pool is lower than that of each of the members' foreign exchange reserves (Machinea and Titelman, 2007; Ocampo and Titelman, 2009).

Regional monetary arrangements should thus be actively promoted by the international community. In this regard, a major incentive to their formation would be a provision that SDR allocations would be proportional, not only to IMF quotas, but also to reserves that developing countries have placed in common reserve funds—thus making pooled reserves equivalent to IMF quotas for this purpose (United Nations, 1999; Ocampo, 2002). They can also be the building blocks for broader reforms. The Stiglitz Commission has suggested that the new global monetary system could be built bottom up through a series of agreements among regional arrangements (United Nations, 2009b: ch. V).

Complementary Reforms

The design of a SDR-based IMF, together with the promotion of a network of regional reserve arrangements, would go a long way to correct the basic problems of the fiduciary dollar standard under which the world monetary system has operated since the early 1990s. In principle, correcting the Triffin dilemma seems technically easier, whereas reducing the deflationary or anti-Keynesian bias and the inequities of the system *vis-à-vis* developing countries is harder. Any reform of the system is, in any case, politically difficult and would take time. But it is an effort worth making, as the risks that the current system faces are far from insignificant.

Obviously, the reform of the global reserve system is only part of the needed reform of the global financial architecture. Two complementary reforms have been hinted at in other parts of this chapter, and should be underscored in this final section.

The first is the need to place the IMF at the centre of world macroeconomic policy management. This role includes strengthening the surveillance of major economies and acting as a forum for macroeconomic policy coordination. It is essential, in this regard, to overcome the traditional reliance on *ad hoc* mechanisms for the latter purpose—the G5, then the G7, and now, the G20. This is the only inclusive way to provide a clear institutional structure for such coordination and to ensure developing countries of voice in associated processes. Indeed, the current crisis provides the opportunity to put the IMF back at the centre of global macroeconomic policymaking, as its original design envisioned, and not only as a mechanism to finance emerging markets and other developing countries' balance of payments needs, the major role it has played since the mid-1970s.

The second is to rethink the positive role that capital account regulations can play in a reformed global financial system. Despite financial liberalization over the past few decades, such regulations are still allowed under the IMF's Articles of Agreement. In particular, well-designed regulations can reduce the risks that developing countries face (in a world in which finance is strongly pro-cyclical), expand the room for maneuver of countercyclical macroeconomic policies and reduce the costs of self-protection. Such regulations could include reserve requirements on cross-border flows, minimum stay periods, and prohibitions on lending in foreign currencies to economic agents who do not have revenues in those currencies. The Fund should be encouraged, not only to tolerate, but to actually advise countries on what regulations to impose in particular circumstances. Indeed, it is hard to understand why the focus on the global regulatory structure that should emerge from the crisis, particularly *macro*-prudential regulations, has neglected this issue, by concentrating exclusively on national prudential regulations (regional in the case of the European Union), leaving aside the risks associated with cross-border flows.

Notes

*   The views expressed in this chapter have been enriched by debates in the Commission of Experts of the President of the UN General Assembly on Reforms of the International Monetary and Financial System, of which the author is a member. My views on these issues have been enriched by multiple discussions, particularly with Stephany Griffith-Jones, Jan Kregel, Jomo K.S., Rakesh Mohan, Thomas Palley, Joseph E. Stiglitz, Lance Taylor, Eduardo Wiesner and John Williamson. This chapter draws, in part, from a previous and a parallel paper by the author (Ocampo, 2007/08; 2009). Support from the Ford Foundation is gratefully acknowledged.

1.   Barbosa-Filho *et al.* (2008) have analyzed the domestic dynamics of this process, which has been dominated by pro-cyclical household (and, more generally, private) borrowing, partly mitigated by countercyclical government borrowing—in sharp contrast to the traditional story of the "twin" external and fiscal deficits.

2.   The reform could also be implemented by creating a new institution (a Global Reserve Bank) or a new institutional framework on the basis of regional arrangements. See, in this regard, United Nations (2009b: ch. V).

3.   See good summaries of the debates of the 1960s in Solomon (1977) and Triffin (1968). An interesting contrast between the role of SDRs then and now is provided by Clark and Polak (2004) and Williamson (2009).

4.   The first figure is equivalent to the increase of world reserves in 1998-2002, whereas the second is less than 40 percent of the much larger increase during 2003-2007. For this reason, the Commission suggests that even US$300 billion might be insufficient.

5.   These proposals would eliminate the traditional division between what are called the General Resource and the SDR Accounts. See Polak (2005, part II).

6.   In turn, the current quota system could be improved by making contributions exclusively in the currencies of the member countries, thus eliminating the obligation by developing countries to make a fourth of their contribution in SDRs or hard currencies. This would make quotas equivalent to a generalized swap arrangement among central banks.

7.   The discussions of the early 1970s could be illustrative in this regard. The US backed at the time a "reserve indicator" system, under which each IMF member would have been assigned a target level of reserves and forced to adjust to keep reserves around that target (see Williamson, 2009).

8.   A third alternative would be to use the SDRs allocated to developed countries to finance additional aid for the poorest countries and the provision of global public goods (Stiglitz, 2006: ch. 9; Ffrench-Davis, 2007). This proposal has many virtues, but poses the problem that such transfers are fiscal in character, and may thus require the approval of national parliaments in every case.

9.   This point has been emphasized by the Stiglitz Commission (United Nations, 2009b), which has also suggested the creation of alternative credit facilities.

References

Aizenman, Joshua, and Jaewoo Lee (2007). International reserves: Mercantilist vs. precautionary view, theory and evidence. *Open Economies Review*, 18 (2), April: 191-214.

Akyüz, Yılmaz (2005). Reforming the IMF: Back to the drawing board. Global Economy Series No. 7, Third World Network, Penang.

Akyüz, Yılmaz (2008). Current global financial turmoil and Asian developing countries. Global Economy Series No. 11, Third World Network, Penang.

Barbosa-Filho, Nelson H., Codrina Rada, Lance Taylor and Luca Zamparelli (2008). Cycles and trends in US net borrowing flows. *Journal of Post-Keynesian Economics*, 30 (4), Summer.

Bergsten, Fred (2007). How to solve the problem of the dollar. *Financial Times*, 10 December.

Camdessus, Michel (2000). An agenda for the IMF at the start of the 21st century. Remarks at the Council on Foreign Relations, February, New York.

Carvalho, Fernando Cardim de (2009). The accumulation of international reserves as a defensive strategy: Reasons and limitations of self "insurance". In Stephany Griffith-Jones, José Antonio Ocampo and Joseph E. Stiglitz (eds). *Time for a Visible Hand: Lessons from the 2008 World Financial Crisis*. Oxford University Press, New York.

Clark, Peter B., and Jacques J. Polak (2004). International liquidity and the role of the SDR in the international monetary system. *IMF Staff Papers*, 51 (1): 49-71. Reproduced in Polak (2005: ch. 9).

Cooper, Richard (1987). *The International Monetary System: Essays in World Economics*. MIT Press, Cambridge, MA.

D'Arista, Jane (1999). Reforming the privatized international monetary and financial architecture. *Financial Markets and Society*, November.

Dervis, Kemal (2008). Fairness for emerging markets. *Washington Post*, 3 November.

Dooley, Michael P., David Folkerts-Landau and Peter Garber (2003). An essay on the revived Bretton Woods system. NBER Working Paper No. 9971, September, National Bureau of Economic Research, Cambridge, MA.

Dooley, Michael P., David Folkerts-Landau and Peter Garber (2009). Bretton Woods II still defines the international monetary system. NBER Working Paper No. 14731, February, National Bureau of Economic Research, Cambridge, MA.

Eichengreen, Barry (1996). *Globalizing Capital: A History of the International Monetary System*. Princeton University Press, Princeton.

Eichengreen, Barry (2007). *Global Imbalances and the Lessons of Bretton Woods*. MIT Press, Cambridge, MA.

Ffrench-Davis, Ricardo (2007). SDRs for a globalization with development. Presented at the meeting of Technical Group of the Initiative for Action against Hunger and Poverty, January, Santiago.

Frenkel, Roberto (2008). From the boom in capital inflows to financial traps. In José Antonio Ocampo and Joseph E. Stiglitz (eds). *Capital Market Liberalization and Development.* Oxford University Press, New York.

Frenkel, Roberto, and Lance Taylor (2007). Real exchange rate, monetary policies and employment. In José Antonio Ocampo, Jomo K.S. and Sarbuland Khan (eds). *Policy Matters: Economic and Social Policies to Sustain Equitable Development.* Orient Longman, Zed Books and Third World Network, Hyderabad, London and Penang, chapter 11.

Frenkel, Roberto, and Martin Rapetti (2009). Economic development and the international financial system. In Stephany Griffith-Jones, José Antonio Ocampo and Joseph E. Stiglitz (eds). *Time for a Visible Hand: Lessons from the 2008 World Financial Crisis.* Oxford University Press, New York.

Hart, A.G., Nicholas Kaldor and Jan Tinbergen (1964). The case for an international commodity reserve currency. UNCTAD, Geneva. Reproduced in Nicholas Kaldor, *Essays on Economic Policy II: Vol. IV of Collected Economic Essays.* Holmes and Meier, New York, 1980, ch. 18.

Helleiner, Eric (2009). The IMF and the SDR: What to make of China's proposals?. Processed, July, University of Waterloo, Waterloo, Canada,.

IMF (2009). Review of the adequacy of and options for supplementing Fund resources. 12 January, International Monetary Fund, Washington, DC.

Kaminsky, Graciela L., Carmen M. Reinhart and Carlos A. Végh (2004). When it rains, it pours: Procyclical capital flows and macroeconomic policies. NBER Working Paper No. 10780, September, National Bureau of Economic Research, Cambridge, MA.

Kenen, Peter B. (1983). Use of SDR to supplement or substitute for other means of finance. In George M. von Furstenberg (ed.). *International Money and Credit: The Policy Roles.* International Monetary Fund, Washington, DC, ch. 7.

Kenen, Peter B. (2001). *The International Financial Architecture: What's New? What's Missing?* Institute for International Economics, Washington, DC.

Keynes, John M. (1942-43). The Keynes plan. Reproduced in J. Keith Horsefield (ed.). *The International Monetary Fund 1945-1965: Twenty Years of International Monetary Cooperation. Vol. III: Documents.* International Monetary Fund, Washington, D.C., 1969, pp. 3-36.

Kregel, Jan (2009). Some simple observations on the reform of the international monetary system. Policy Note 8, The Levy Economics Institute of Bard College, Annandale-on-Hudson, NY.

Machinea, José Luis, and Daniel Titelman (2007). Less volatile growth? The role of regional financial institutions. *CEPAL Review,* 91, April.

Obstfeld, Maurice, Jay C. Shambaugh and Alan M. Taylor (2008). Financial stability, the trilemma, and international reserves. NBER Working Paper 14217, August, National Bureau of Economic Research, Cambridge, MA.

Ocampo, José Antonio (2002). Recasting the international financial agenda. In John Eatwell and Lance Taylor (eds). *International Capital Markets: Systems in Transition.* Oxford University Press, New York.

Ocampo, José Antonio (2006). Regional financial cooperation: Experiences and challenges. In José Antonio Ocampo (ed.). *Regional Financial Cooperation.* Brookings Institution and ECLAC, Washington, DC, chapter 1.

Ocampo, José Antonio (2007/08). The instability and inequities of the global reserve system. *International Journal of Political Economy*, 36 (4), Winter.

Ocampo, José Antonio (2008). A broad view of macroeconomic stability. In Narcis Serra and Joseph E. Stiglitz (eds). *The Washington Consensus Reconsidered: Towards a New Global Governance.* Oxford University Press, New York.

Ocampo, José Antonio (2009). Reforming the global reserve system. In Stephany Griffith-Jones, José Antonio Ocampo and Joseph E. Stiglitz (eds). *Time for a Visible Hand: Lessons from the 2008 World Financial Crisis.* Oxford University Press, New York.

Ocampo, José Antonio, Jan Kregel and Stephany Griffith-Jones (2007). *International Finance and Development.* Zed Books, London.

Ocampo, José Antonio, and Rob Vos (2008). *Uneven Economic Development.* Orient Longman, Zed Books and Third World Network, Hyderabad, London and Penang.

Ocampo, José Antonio, Codrina Rada and Lance Taylor (2009). *Developing Country Policy and Growth: A Structuralist Approach.* Columbia University Press, New York.

Ocampo, José Antonio, and Daniel Titelman (2009). Subregional financial cooperation: The South American experience. *Journal of Post-Keynesian Economics*, forthcoming.

Polak, Jacques J. (1979). Thoughts on an International Monetary Fund based fully on SDR. Pamphlet Series No. 28, International Monetary Fund, Washington, DC.

Polak, Jacques J. (2005). *Economic Theory and Financial Policy: Selected Essays of Jacques J. Polak 1994-2004.* Edited by James M. Boughton, M. E. Sharpe, Armonk, NY.

Prasad, Eswar S., Kenneth Rogoff, Shang-Jin Wei and M. Ayhan Rose (2003). Effects of financial globalization on developing countries: Some empirical evidence. Occasional Paper 220, International Monetary Fund, Washington, DC.

Prasad, Eswar S., Raghuram R. Rajan and Arvind Subramanian (2007). Foreign capital and economic growth. *Brooking Papers on Economic Activity*, No. 1, Brookings Institution, Washington, DC.

Rodrik, Dani (2006). The social costs of foreign exchange reserves. *International Economic Journal*, 20 (3), September.

Rodrik, Dani (2007). The exchange rate and economic growth: Theory and evidence. Processed, July. John F. Kennedy School of Government, Harvard University, Cambridge, MA.

Sakakibara, Eisuke (2003). Asian cooperation and the end of Pax Americana. In Jan Joost Teunissen and Mark Teunissen (eds). *Financial Stability and Growth in Emerging Economies.* FONDAD, The Hague.

Skidelsky, Robert (2000). John Maynard Keynes: Fighting for Freedom, 1937-1946. Penguin/Viking, New York.

Solomon, Robert (1977). *The International Monetary System, 1945-1976: An Insider's View*. Harper & Row, New York.

Stiglitz, Joseph E. (2006). *Making Globalization Work*. W.W. Norton, New York.

Stiglitz, Joseph E., José Antonio Ocampo, Shari Spiegel, Ricardo Ffrench-Davis and Deepak Nayyar (2006). *Stability with Growth: Macroeconomics, Liberalization, and Development*. Oxford University Press, New York.

Summers, Lawrence H. (2004). The U.S. current account deficit and the global economy. Per Jacobson Lecture, International Monetary Fund, Washington, DC.

Triffin, Robert (1961). *Gold and the Dollar Crisis*. Revised edition. Yale University Press, New Haven.

Triffin, Robert (1968). *Our International Monetary System: Yesterday, Today and Tomorrow*. Random House, New York.

UNCTAD (1965). *International Monetary Issues and the Developing Countries: Report of the Group of Experts*. United Nations Conference on Trade and Development, New York.

UNCTAD (2009). *The Global Economic Crisis: Systemic Failures and Multilateral Remedies*. United Nations Conference on Trade and Development, Geneva.

United Nations (1999). Towards a new international financial architecture: Report of the Task Force of the Executive Committee on Economic and Social Affairs of the United Nations. http://www.un.org/esa/coordination/ecesa/ecesa-1.pdf

United Nations (2001). *Report of the High-level Panel on Financing for Development* (Zedillo Report). United Nations, New York. www.un.org/reports/financing

United Nations (2005). *World Economic Situation and Prospects, 2005*. United Nations, New York.

United Nations (2009a). *Outcome Document of the Conference on the World Financial and Economic Crisis and Its Impacts on Development*. A/CONF.214/3, 22 June.

United Nations (2009b). *Report of the Commission of Experts convened of the President of the UN General Assembly on Reforms of the International Monetary and Financial System* (Stiglitz Commission). United Nations, New York.

Williamson, John (2004). The future of the global financial system. *Journal of Post-Keynesian Economics*, 26 (4), Summer.

Williamson, John (2009). Understanding Special Drawing Rights. Policy Brief, June, Peterson Institute for International Economics, Washington, DC.

Yu, Yongding (2007). Global imbalances and China. *The Australian Economic Review*, 40 (1).

Zhou Xiaochuan (2009). Reform the international monetary system. People's Bank of China, Beijing. http://www.pbc.gov.cn/english//detail.asp?col=6500&ID=178

Index

Permissions